"Rajeev Bhattacharya's book is a *tour de force* in its treatment of a variety of topics dealing with financial markets and the rigorous use of mathematical tools of analysis as well as Big Data to better understand how securities are priced and how markets behave. The book covers an impressive and important range of topics that includes market efficiency, options, market microstructure, and the use of high-frequency data, equities, and fixed income securities. It is unusual in that it delightfully (and in an almost quirky way) blends the philosophical foundations of concepts with mathematical rigor and simple illustrative examples to deepen the reader's understanding. A must read for graduate students in finance and economics, and others interested in a deep dive into these topics."

Anjan Thakor, *John E. Simon Professor of Finance, Director of the WFA Center for Finance and Accounting Research, Olin Business School, Washington University, St. Louis, U.S.*

"I am very pleased to see this book come to market. It will be a great resource for a graduate or advanced undergraduate course on Big Data in finance. I especially like the fact that sample code and data are accessible to the reader."

Tom Smith, *Professor, Department of Applied Finance, Macquarie Business School, Macquarie University, Australia*

"The unique signature of Dr. Bhattacharya's book is how it brings together economic thinking and financial data sciences, a tapestry woven around the core theme of market efficiency. What is efficiency anyway? Do we just think of markets as efficient or inefficient, or are there degrees of market efficiency? What data do we have to test it? How do we use it? Finally, what do we find? Dr. Bhattacharya offers ideas and answers aplenty, taking the reader through a fascinating ride with a 360-degree view of economics, data, and metrics in the stock, options, and fixed-income markets. Perhaps most remarkably, the book features original research with primary data. In real life, Dr. Bhattacharya enlightens and entertains – this book is no different a great addition to the bookshelf for practitioners, policymakers, and academics alike."

Nagpurnanand Prabhala, *Francis J. Carey, Jr. Professor of Finance, Carey Business School, Johns Hopkins University, U.S.*

"This book provides an excellent coverage of classical finance theory, application, and coding – something that is all too rare in today's market. The strength of this book is in tying theory and practice together. The sections discussing event studies and their application to intraday data are particularly impressive."

Daniel Taylor, *Arthur Andersen Professor of Finance and Accounting, Director, Wharton Forensic Analytics Lab, The Wharton School, University of Pennsylvania, U.S.*

"Rajeev is extremely precise (his daughter tells him that he is 'too precise, all the time') and extreme precision with facts and logic is a virtue, especially when accompanied by an immense mathematical sophistication. He is suspicious of claims of simplistic linearity in a hopelessly non-linear world and is always impatient with hubristic assertions of opinions as fact. He has a very scientific appreciation for nuance and is quite comfortable with the messiness and ambiguity of the real world on one hand and with the elegance and clarity of theory on the other. This is a powerful book blending theories of economics and econometrics to provide an excellent learning tool for generations of new researchers. A highly recommended text for a graduate or advanced undergraduate course on Big Data in finance enriched by examples of data and codes to analyze the data."

Mahendra Gupta, *Former Dean, Geraldine & Robert Virgil Professor of Accounting and Management, Olin Business School, Washington University, St. Louis, U.S.*

"If you are looking for a book that goes beyond the textbook understanding of Big Data and delves into the real-life applications of data analytics in finance, then look no further! In his book, Rajeev Bhattacharya brings together the art of data science with contemporary use-cases to tackle challenges and questions that practitioners in financial services face. This helps the reader not only understand how Big Data can be leveraged but also deepen their knowledge on relevant questions around the metrics, economics, particularities of financial data, and even the code that should be utilized."

Markos Zachariadis, *Chair in Financial Technology & Information Systems, Alliance Manchester Business School, Founding Director, Centre for Financial Technology Studies, University of Manchester, U.K.*

"In the era of digital transformation, the financial world faces a monumental challenge: harnessing the power of Big Data. Dive into the captivating world of finance and data analytics with this wide-ranging book, as it unveils the potential and implications of Big Data in finance."

Glenn MacDonald, *John M. Olin Distinguished Professor of Economics and Strategy, Olin Business School, Washington University, St. Louis, U.S.*

"This book represents a significant milestone in amalgamating theoretical understanding and practical implementations in the rapidly expanding domain of Big Data in finance. The author has conducted a thorough examination of an extensive dataset comprising a magnitude of observations in the order of tens of trillions. This rigorous analysis has yielded insights of considerable importance."

Sanjiv Sabherwal, *Eunice and James L. West Endowed Chair, Chair of the Department of Finance and Real Estate, College of Business, University of Texas, Arlington, U.S.*

"An intriguing, broad book on Big Data in finance, both from a theoretical and empirical perspective. The discussion of market efficiency at the security level is particularly valuable, since most other studies only focus on efficiency with respect to characteristics or events. Bhattacharya breaks new ground in considering distinctions between *ex-ante* and *ex-post* arbitrage risk."

Jeffrey Pontiff, *Professor and James F. Cleary '50, DBA H '93 Chair in Finance, Carroll School of Management, Boston College, U.S.*

"This is a must-have book for not only advanced undergraduate and graduate students but also for new generational researchers who are interested in Big Data in finance. The author provides a good balance between theory and practice as well as making the data and codes fully available for the readers. Highly recommended!"

Kien Tran, *Professor of Econometrics, University of Lethbridge, Canada*

"This book is a serious discussion of finance and data analytics addressing the challenge from the Big Data perspective and focused on market efficiency. The implications of Rajeev Bhattacharya's book for philosophers are at least twofold. First, its big picture contributes to the ongoing debate on the nature of science and scientific methods with an emphasis on the significance of the falsification criterion in science. Second, it dissects the concepts of known unknowns and unknown unknowns, overlapping some of the themes covered in a recent philosophy book, *Beyond Uncertainty: Reasoning with Unknown Possibilities*. I strongly recommend this book to decision-theoretic philosophers keen on exploring uncertainty and ambiguity further."

Prasanta Bandyopadhyay, *Professor of Philosophy, Montana State University, U.S.*

"This new book addresses an important topic on which there is much interest; the book proposes an innovative approach to the problem of not knowing what we don't know. In my view this issue is entangled with Gödel's incompleteness theorem and therefore it goes to the foundations of logic. I strongly recommend the topic and endorse the book to the reader."

Graciela Chichilnisky, *Professor of Economics and Statistics, Columbia University, U.S.*

"A compendium of conceptual deliberations in risk and uncertainty in finance, empirically confirmed with Big Data analysis. This book is an excellent resource for scholars and students of finance and Big Data analytics. Access to computing code can make harnessing the power of Big Data more accessible to the average user. I am heartened to see this book arrive. It will make a great text for courses emphasizing Big Data in finance, which has special relevance in the current age of supercomputing."

Vivek Pandey, *Professor of Finance, University of Texas, Tyler, U.S.*

"The availability of high-frequency and large datasets in finance is sparking a revolution of sorts in the way that industry practitioners quantify and manage risk. Risk exposures can now be monitored in real-time and examined using a multitude of sophisticated models and techniques. Indeed, the skills needed to analyze and interpret big data are in demand and will only continue to garner more importance as data-driven decisions become the norm for governments, policymakers, and businesses. This book is a goldmine for anyone who wants to learn not only about contemporary methods to quantify uncertainty and risk, but also the theory that underpins them. The applications presented in the book are extremely valuable as they illustrate practical examples of employing these methods in finance."

Hamid Yahyaei, *Specialized Lecturer in Applied Finance, Macquarie University, Australia*

"As I went through the chapters, the words that came to mind were: informative, intelligent, disciplined, scientific, amusing, and practical. The book makes an honest effort to marry theory with empirics, to follow Immanuel Kant's view that 'theory without practice is empty, practice without theory is blind.' Interspersed with interesting and apt quotes and anecdotes, the chapters in the book present key theoretical tools for statistical inference and econometric analysis and then apply them to questions related to financial market efficiency. I found these practical applications especially relevant for today's financial markets influenced by fast-moving news. The Big Data analyses of intraday bond and stock market data are fascinating. The book will be a key reference for students, researchers, and practitioners."

Dilip Ratha, *Founder, Ratha Global, U.S.*

"This book is long overdue in the market. It is a total refresh of where the financial scholarship is in the field and a very welcome addition to the existing literature. It is highly relevant to professionals and to the academic community."

Joseph Bial, *Partner, Paul, Weiss, Rifkind, Wharton & Garrison LLP, U.S.*

"Rajeev Bhattacharya, Ph.D., has produced what will likely be looked upon as the seminal piece on tying the very best among thought leaders in finance to some of the most cutting-edge subjects within the art and science of finance itself. Its contemporary application of modern principles to the wide range of issues within brings new light to the trajectory of where our field is headed. Future scholars would be well served to give this treatise a good read."

Robert MacLaverty, *Managing Director, SEDA Finance, U.S.*

"I have had the pleasure of working with Dr. Bhattacharya as an expert consultant. He has a wonderful way of discussing complex academic theories in a manner that non-academics and juries can understand. This book is no different, parsing complex theories with logical, matter-of-fact analysis of the impact of data on pricing and decision making."

Robert Thompson, *Partner, Bryan Cave Leighton Paisner (BCLP), U.S.*

ADVANCED ANALYTICS IN FINANCIAL MARKETS

Big Data analytics has emerged as a powerful tool, transforming the global financial market by enabling more informed decision-making, enhancing predictive capabilities, and improving risk management. By leveraging vast amounts of data, advanced analytics can provide real-time insights into market trends, forecast potential downturns, and identify investment opportunities. This innovative book is one of the first advanced textbooks to address the rapidly evolving field of Big Data in finance.

Drawing on the author's extensive research, consulting, and teaching experience, it applies advanced theoretical and empirical methods to massive high-frequency databases to explore important areas of finance, including market efficiency, equities, fixed income securities, options, and market microstructure. This book begins with an introduction to risk and uncertainty before exploring applications of advanced analytics to daily data, as well as applications to Big Data with intraday data. It concludes with suggestions for future work. Sample raw databases, SAS software code, and intermediate and output data files are made available to help readers to work with real data and perform their own analyses.

Advanced Analytics in Financial Markets is the ideal textbook for advanced undergraduate and graduate courses in finance, Big Data, and advanced analytics, as well as a reference book for scholars and practitioners.

Rajeev R. Bhattacharya, Ph.D., is a finance professor at Macquarie University and the president of Washington Finance and Economics, with over 30 years of research, consulting, and teaching experience in finance and Big Data. He lives with his wife and daughter in a suburb of Washington, DC.

Routledge Advanced Texts in Economics and Finance

40. Contemporary Issues in Quantitative Finance
Ahmet Can Inci

41. Behavioral Economics, Fourth Edition
Behavioral Economics, Fourth Edition

42. Efficiency and Productivity Analysis
Using Copulas in Stochastic Frontier Models
Artem Prokhorov

43. Real Estate Economics
A Point-to-Point Handbook
Nicholas G. Pirounakis

44. Applied Spatial Statistics and Econometrics, Second Edition
Data Analysis in R
Edited by Katarzyna Kopczewska

45. Advanced Analytics in Financial Markets
Rajeev R. Bhattacharya

For more information about this series, please visit: www.routledge.com/Routledge-Advanced-Texts-in-Economics-and-Finance/book-series/SE0757

ADVANCED ANALYTICS IN FINANCIAL MARKETS

Rajeev R. Bhattacharya

Routledge
Taylor & Francis Group
LONDON AND NEW YORK

Designed cover image: Galeanu Mihai / Getty Images

First published 2027
by Routledge
4 Park Square, Milton Park, Abingdon, Oxon OX14 4RN

and by Routledge
605 Third Avenue, New York, NY 10158

Routledge is an imprint of the Taylor & Francis Group, an informa business

British Library Cataloguing-in-Publication Data:
A catalogue record for this book is available from the British Library

ISBN: 978-1-041-00168-3 (hbk)
ISBN: 978-1-041-00167-6 (pbk)
ISBN: 978-1-003-60848-6 (ebk)

DOI: 10.4324/9781003608486

Typeset in Times New Roman
by codeMantra

Access the Support Material: www.routledge.com/9781041001676

Dedication to the goddesses in my family:

To my daughter, Meghna, whose unbridled intellectual curiosity and fierce independence enabled this book;

To my wife, Kamalini, whose phenomenal strength allows me to be the goofball that I am; and

To my dearly departed mother, Minati, whose indomitable dignity and ferocious protectiveness caused her children and grandchildren to be good human beings.

CONTENTS

FOREWORD

In a sense, Rajeev and I began our academic careers together. In 1988, as a freshly-minted Ph.D., I joined the Department of Economics at the University of Rochester as an Assistant Professor, the same year that Rajeev commenced his Ph.D. studies there. He was a student in the very first course I taught, a Ph.D. course in mathematical economics and later in my advanced doctoral course on game theory. I was self-aware enough to realize that I was an argumentative person, but in Rajeev, I rapidly realized that I had more than met my match. Over the several years we both spent at Rochester, I got to know Rajeev well, personally and professionally, through those arguments that covered not just our common professional areas of economics, mathematics, and game theory but also our interests in bridge, cricket, politics, and many other fields.

Our paths diverged after Rochester. I moved to New York to the Stern School of Business and shifted my academic focus to work in finance, including, in particular, risk-management and derivative securities. Rajeev moved to Australia to the University of New South Wales and later worked as a management consultant with the Boston Consulting Group. We lost contact for almost two decades. When we reconnected, I was delighted to find that his area of professional work too had shifted to finance, including with the Berkeley Research Group and now as President of Washington Finance and Economics. He has also served on the faculty of Georgetown University, Washington University in St. Louis, and the University of Maryland, where he has taught courses on Big Data in finance, capital markets, and derivatives. The current book is an outcome of his thinking deeply, and in a very independent manner, on those subjects.

That independence of thought comes through in the very beginning of the book, where Rajeev contrasts risk and uncertainty as the difference between "known unknowns" (a situation in which, like the toss of a coin, one knows the entire universe of possible outcomes, even if not which particular outcome has occurred) versus "unknown unknowns" (where even the entire universe of possible outcomes is not known). The former situation is, of course, amenable to modeling via standard mathematical tools; the latter is captured through the notions of generalized events (the complement of a generalized event may not itself be a generalized event), generalized probabilities (which are such that the generalized probability – *GenProb* – of the known universe could be less than one), and generalized random variables. Known unknowns and unknown unknowns are reconciled through the result that the expectation of a random variable conditioned upon the known universe equals the expectation of a generalized random variable that is reconciled with the random variable over the known universe; this result enables the empirical work in this book. While "truth" in this world is absolute, individuals, because of imperfect information, may perceive the truth differently.

The rest of the book then develops the implications of this view of the world for general scientific discourse and, in particular, for financial analysis. In the second part of the book, Rajeev develops a number of results of subsequent importance including quantifying the *ex post* ***GenProb*** of a hypothesis; and an alternative way to think about and model significance of observed relationships compared to the usual statistical significance used in academic studies.

The third and fourth parts of the book then move to applications in finance, the main subject matter of the book, but the analysis of which requires the technical machinery developed earlier. The third part uses daily data to study market efficiency and event studies in the context of equities and options. The fourth and last part of the book then uses intraday data to analyze event studies and the efficiency of markets for equities and fixed income securities, especially how efficiency is affected by factors such as short sales costs & constraints, transactions costs and constraints, dispersions of investor valuations, and the COVID-19 lockdowns.

It is impossible to even skim through this book and not learn something new. It certainly gave me considerable food for thought; and it will do so for every curious reader, whether student, academic or practitioner. *Buon Appetito!*

Raghu Sundaram
Senior Vice-Chancellor and Head of Global Strategy,
Dean Emeritus, Stern School of Business,
Edward I. Altman Professor of Credit and Debt Markets,
Professor of Finance,
New York University

PREFACE

Big Data in finance is arguably the most important recent development in the democratization of economic opportunity. Improvements in computation and methods in econometrics and machine learning have enabled us to generate insights into markets and economies and have enormous promise for future learners. This book, based on two decades of teaching, research and consulting on the applications of Big Data to finance, is meant to guide learners in using data and appropriate frameworks of uncertainty and information to understand financial markets and make decisions in various situations involving uncertainty. Providing detailed calculations, nuanced reasoning into the analyses of the data presented, raw databases for continued research and applications/examples of how empirical methods and Big Data are used (and can be used) in financial markets, the business world in general, and even government policy, this comprehensive text will develop future professionals who can use Big Data for prediction and effective decision making under uncertainty. Examples of questions that this book will assist the reader in answering include (a) Was the Global Financial Crisis a structural change? (b) Is a stock that is easier or cheaper to short more accurately priced? (c) How different are bonds or options from stocks in terms of risk? (d) How can an investor make extraordinary returns? (e) What are the impacts of events such as a merger or acquisition? (f) What are the fundamental differences between different market systems, such as those in the U.S., Australia, Sweden, China, and India? and (g) How can a society use financial policies to achieve its socioeconomic objectives?

Market efficiency is a very important concept and is well recognized for its importance in guiding many market activities. In particular, if the market for an asset is efficient, the market price of the asset equals its true economic value, which implies that investors can rely upon market prices for value – "reliance" on price for value is an important component of class certification in securities class actions, please see Bhattacharya et al. (2023) for details – and do not have to spend expensive time and resources (which are essentially only available to institutional investors) to further investigate the value of an asset. In other words, if the market for an asset is not efficient, the market price of the asset is misleading in terms of an investor's decisions. Efficient capital markets, therefore, provide substantial social benefits and are a *sine qua non* for the democratization of markets and the protection of investors, and constitute a critical mission of regulatory bodies such as the U.S. Securities and Exchange Commission (SEC) and the U.S. Financial Industry Regulatory Authority (FINRA). The second part of this book (Chapters 3–5) and the third part (Chapters 6–8) differ on the use of daily data versus high-frequency millisecond-level intraday data.

Data serve as the foundation of learning

As the legendary scientist W. Edwards Deming is famously supposed to have said, "In God we trust, everyone else must bring data." Analyzing Big Data is not a scalable version of the programming that is done for smaller datasets, particularly in the context of finance. The definition of "Big Data" has two schools of thought. The economist's perspective was probably best articulated by Scott Bauguess, then deputy chief economist at the U.S. Securities and Exchange Commission, in 2016: "data that take more time to process than ... took to create" (Bauguess, 2016), please also see Goldstein et al. (2025, 2021) – we use about 25 TB of data for this book – whereas the computer scientist's vision is more about techniques. Samples of raw databases, intermediate and final datasets, and software code are available to all students and instructors so that they may continue their analyses and develop future projects.

Structure of the book

This book is structured into three parts, covering theoretical foundations (uncertainty versus risk, scientific method) and practical applications using large datasets. Part 1 details the scientific method. Parts 2 and 3 apply these measurements to determine efficiency. The second part (Chapters 3–5) and the third part (Chapters 6–8) differ on the use of daily data versus high-frequency millisecond-level intraday data.

Part 1

In Chapter 1, we discuss the difference between risk and probability (***Prob***) in the world of known unknowns versus uncertainty and generalized probability

(***GenProb***) in the world of unknown unknowns, the impact of information upon them, and the reconciliation between ***Prob*** and ***GenProb***.

The world of finance is full of unknown unknowns, such as (a) self-regulatory bodies such as the U.S. self-appointed Financial Industry Regulatory Authority (FINRA), (b) federal regulators (the "alphabet soup") such as the Securities and Exchange Commission (SEC), Commodity Futures Trading Commission (CFTC), and Consumer Financial Protection Bureau (CFPB), (c) international organizations such as the World Bank (WB), International Monetary Fund (IMF), Financial Stability Board (FSB), and Bank for International Settlements (BIS), (d) state regulators, (e) central banks such as the U.S. Federal Reserve Board (Fed), European Central Bank (ECB), Reserve Bank of Australia (RBA), Reserve Bank of India (RBI), (f) financial engineering by investment banks, hedge funds, and other financial players, (g) technological developments such as financial technology (FinTech), artificial intelligence (AI), and machine learning (ML), (h) transformations of attitude to risk by investors and proprietary traders, and (i) pandemics, regime and visa changes, and wars. It is, therefore, essential that we use the methods of uncertainty, generalized events, and generalized probability that we have developed in this book for any serious work in finance. In Chapter 2, we discuss the rigorous distinction between public information and market information, and the scientific method versus faith. We develop the methodology of replacing each variable, except for each classification or time variable, by the cumulative Gaussian *Prob* of its *Z-Score* (*x*) = (*x minus Mean* (*x*))/(*Standard Deviation* (*x*)). As a result, impacts are rendered comparable, allowing a systematic and objective definition of actual significance, which is different from statistical significance. Also, "almost any parameter can be found to be significantly different from zero if the sample size is large enough," (Kennedy, 2003), in other words, pretty much everything is statistically significant when one is working with massive datasets, as we are in the third part of this book. We also detail the total impact of an exogenous variable, the oft-misunderstood notion of systemic (versus idiosyncratic), and finally, the pervasive problems in Big Data work, including endogeneity and simultaneity, and the cutting-edge empirical methods of dealing with them.

Part 2

The second part provides the first set of applications of the theory and empirics of this book to independent, systematic, and objective Big Data work in finance, using daily data to study arbitrage risk, objective measures of market efficiency, and options.

Chapter 3 provides a general methodology to measure the arbitrage risk, which is a negative proxy for the market efficiency, of a stock for any relevant period, to calculate the arbitrage risk of each U.S. exchange-listed common stock for every calendar year from 1988 to 2010. A series of simple reduced form regressions is analyzed to find that market efficiency is significantly affected by turnover (negatively), the number of market makers for Nasdaq stocks (negatively), and serial correlation in the Capital Asset Pricing Model of the stock (positively).

In Chapter 4, for every U.S.-listed security for every year between 2001 and 2017, four different event studies calculate four separate objective measures of the market efficiency for that security for that year. These studies provide an objective characterization of that security's market for that year to determine whether it is sufficiently efficient or not. These methodologies are applied to Petrobras's American Depositary Receipt (ADR), traded as PBR on the New York Stock Exchange, 2001–2017, and conclude that the Petrobras Court reached the incorrect conclusion when it certified a 2010–2015 class period because the market for PBR was sufficiently efficient in 2010, 2011, and 2014, but not sufficiently efficient in 2012, 2013, and 2015. These methodologies are also applied to the valuation of each U.S.-listed firm in 2001–2017. Three examples are as follows: (a) the market for GS (Goldman Sachs Group, Inc., common equity) was sufficiently efficient in each year in 2001–2017, and consequently market prices represented value for Goldman Sachs over 2001–2017; (b) the market for MSFT (Microsoft Corporation, common equity) was sufficiently efficient in 2001 and 2003–2017 and therefore market prices represented value for Microsoft Corporation in 2001–2017 except for 2002; and (c) the market for AAME (Atlantic American Corporation, common equity) was not sufficiently efficient in any year in 2001–2017, and therefore market prices did not represent value for Atlantic American Corporation in 2001–2017.

In Chapter 5, five separate measures of deviation from Put-Call Parity of options on a stock without splits or dividends are used as separate negative measures of the efficiency of the market ecosystem consisting of the underlying stock, derivatives, and risk-free securities. Three-Stage Least Squares (3SLS) are used to estimate this structural system, separately for Nasdaq and non-Nasdaq U.S. stocks, over 1996–2015, finding, contrary to much previous theoretical and empirical work, that the impact of short sales costs & constraints on market efficiency is not significantly negative and that the impact of trading volume on market efficiency is not significantly positive.

Part 3

The third part provides the second set of applications of the theory and empirics of this book to independent, systematic, and objective Big Data work in finance, using millisecond-level high-frequency intraday data for event studies and market efficiency work for equities and fixed income securities.

In Chapter 6, using high-frequency millisecond-level intraday data from TAQ, TRACE, I/B/E/S, and Capital IQ, using daily data from CRSP, Compustat, CRSP-Compustat Merged Database, and FRED, for all publicly traded U.S. stocks for January 2014–September 2021, the evidence is that idiosyncratic reactions are systemically all out of the system within two hours after a potentially material event. A dataset of systematic, independent, and objective characterizations of each TICKER-year, TICKER-halfyear, TICKER-quarter, and TICKER-month, as statistically and actually significant efficient, statistically and actually significant inefficient, or otherwise, is available from the authorand finds that capital markets during the first two-three months of the COVID-19 lockdown were statistically and actually significantly less efficient.

In Chapter 7, six systematic and ordinal direct measures of market efficiency of equities are developed based on controlled contrasts between absolute idiosyncratic returns in relevant halfhours versus absolute idiosyncratic returns in control halfhours. Applying an eight-equation structural model with market efficiency as a function of exogenous factors and endogenous market activities, and each endogenous market activity as a function of exogenous factors and all other endogenous activities, using high-frequency millisecond-level intraday data on all U.S. public companies over January 2014–September 2021, we find that market efficiency did not improve with time.

Chapter 8 studies the impact of time and characteristics of the issuing firm on market efficiency of fixed income (FI) securities. We study two different metrics, depending on how a potential material event is determined, with three different announcement windows for each, based on event studies, with high-frequency millisecond-level intraday fixed income and equity data on all publicly traded U.S. companies over January 2014–September 2021, as separate objective and systematic measures of the efficiency of the market for an FI security. An eight-equation structural model with market efficiency of an FI security as a function of exogenous factors and endogenous market activities, and each endogenous market activity as a function of the exogenous factors and all other endogenous market activities, applying Three Stage Least Squares and Errors in Variables to estimate the structural system, using panel-based instrumentation strategies, finds that market efficiency of FI securities has not improved with time, that investor valuation dispersion and short sales costs & constraints of equity of issuing firm have significant negative associations with market efficiency of FI securities, and that transaction costs & constraints of equity of issuing firm has an ambiguous association with market efficiency of FI securities.

Chapter 9 summarizes the book's objectives, methods, and conclusions, and provides detailed suggestions for future research.

Who is this book for?

This book can be used to teach a number of advanced undergraduate and graduate courses on Big Data in Finance, Data Analysis, and Advanced Analytics. We have posted three example syllabi for standalone courses that are taught using this book as a textbook. These courses differ in the level of applications of the provided raw databases, intermediate and final datasets, and SAS software: Syllabus 1 focuses only on the empirical results, without requiring students to do any computer programming; Syllabus 2 focuses on writing code to derive the results of this book, and Syllabus 3 focuses on writing SAS code to empirically answer many important questions in finance and business.

Syllabus 1

Financial Markets and Institutions is intended for advanced undergraduate or graduate students. It discusses the basic objectives of financial institutions and markets, details the industry structure and regulatory environment, and analyzes the decision variables on which management should concentrate to achieve its objectives.

Syllabus 2

Big Data in Finance is intended for advanced undergraduate or graduate students, involving building expertise in computer coding in SAS and its applications to financial markets; however, everything is introduced from first principles. The course applies advanced analytical techniques that are used to analyze Big Data to study important topics in finance detailed in this book, such as market efficiency, event studies, equities, fixed income securities, and options.

Syllabus 3

Applications of Advanced Analytics in Finance is intended for advanced undergraduate or graduate students. This course teaches students to use SAS for storage, processing, and advanced analytics in finance, in order to rigorously answer questions of interest to students, such as the difference between bonds or options from stocks in terms of risk, the steps to take for an investor to make extraordinary returns, or the impacts of events such as a merger or acquisition.

Instructor support

Samples of syllabi and raw databases, intermediate and final datasets, and software code are available to all students and instructors so that they may continue their analyses and develop future projects.

Philosophical underpinnings

The most important takeaway from this book is the supremacy of truth, and as is detailed in Chapter 1, we mere mortals with limited abilities and imperfect and asymmetric information can perceive the actual and objective truth imperfectly and differently, but there is no such thing as "your truth" or "my truth," or an "alternative truth," for the truth is absolute. Similarly, the notion of "truth" is meaningless to a litigator; all that matters to a litigator is what a litigator can convince a "fact finder" or "trier of fact" (typically, a judge or a jury) to be the truth. Also, truth is not determined by majority or even by consensus; for instance, U.S. Supreme Court Justice Oliver Wendell Holmes's dissent in *Abrams v. United States* (1919) that "the best test of truth is the power of the thought to get itself accepted in the competition of the market" is contrary to the scientific method. See, for example, the "Paradox of the Chinese Emperor's Nose," as explained by Professor Richard Feynman, Nobel Prize in Physics, 1965: "Nobody was permitted to see the Emperor of China, and the question was, 'What is the length of the Emperor of China's nose?' To find out, you go all over the country asking people what they think the length of the Emperor of China's nose is, and you ... [combine them] ... And that would be very 'accurate' because you [combined the information from] so many people. But it's no way to find anything out; when you have a very wide range of people who contribute without looking carefully at it, you don't improve your knowledge of the situation by [combining]." This is exactly the fallacy underlying the Wikipedia approach of content being written and edited by a large number of people who might not know much about the relevant topic or might not put in any effort in acquiring any information about the relevant topic. When the book *Hundert Autoren gegen Einstein* (a hundred authors against Einstein) was published, Professor Albert Einstein, Nobel Prize in Physics, 1921, is supposed to have responded that "If I were wrong, then one would have been enough."

Our framework is different from but compatible with "relativism" in general and "epistemic relativism" in particular, and is also consistent with the Jaina framework of "*Anekāntavāda*" (not-one sidedness). The *Muṇḍaka Upaniṣad* says, "*satyameva jayate*" (the truth alone triumphs). A scholar's only objective is disinterested pursuit of the absolute truth – an "impassioned argument" is disqualifying in scholarly work (see the description, for instance, of Spears and Geruso (2025) in Ip (2025)) – as opposed to an activist for whom the narrative, cause, or ideology is more important than the truth – activists such as Mohandas Gandhi or Nelson Mandela never pretended to be unbiased, whereas some activists just do not seem to understand the contradictions between the truth and a narrative (however well-intentioned) – see, for example, Hossam Shabat's March 24, 2025, post on X, "I risked everything to report the truth ... I did all this because I believe in the Palestinian cause" (Shabat, 2025) is internally inconsistent.

We discuss in Chapter 1 that knowing the entire universe of possible outcomes, even if not knowing what particular outcome has occurred, is a situation of known unknowns, and is the domain of risk, whereas not knowing the entire universe of possible outcomes is a situation of unknown unknowns and is the domain of uncertainty; the notion of unknown unknowns was popularized by U.S. secretary of defense Donald Rumsfeld in 2002, and was articulated, potentially for the first time in 1955, by Joseph Luft and Harrington Ingham. If one knows the event A, i.e., if A is known, then does one know *not-A*, the unknown? In such a case, if one does know the unknown, the *not-A*, then one is in the domain of the known unknown, that of risk and probability, but if one does not know the unknown, the *not-A*, then one is in the domain of the unknown unknown, that of uncertainty and generalized probability. Without the detailed mathematical modeling of unknown unknowns (uncertainty and generalized probability) done in Chapter 1, versus the standard known unknowns (risk and probability), one cannot even begin to understand unknown unknown events such as the COVID-19 Pandemic of —2020–2021 or the Global Financial Crisis of —2007–2009. As pointed out in Section 1.4 on the philosophical underpinnings of our mathematical modeling, which also describes the famous ancient Hindu, Buddhist, and Jaina story of the elephant and six blind individuals, each blind individual's information about the elephant is such that (s)he could not have possibly known the entire universe of outcomes, so the standard formulation of events and probability (***Prob***) (as described in Section 1.2) does not apply at all, whereas the developments in this book of uncertainty, generalized events, uncertainty algebras, and generalized probability (***GenProb***) (as detailed in Section 1.3) do apply. Probability (or generalized probability) can be objective, empirically objective, or subjective, a function of the relevant information risk (or uncertainty) algebra. This book provides a measure theoretic generalization of standard ***Prob*** theory under risk to a theory of ***GenProb*** under uncertainty and the reconciliation between the two. This book shows that the ***GenProb*** measure over the known universe is conceptually and computationally very different from a reconciled ***Prob*** measure conditioned upon the known universe, but given a random variable and a generalized random variable that are reconciled over a known universe, the expectation of the random variable conditioned upon the variable belonging to the known universe equals the expectation of the generalized random variable – *this result makes possible all the empirical work in this book, especially the distinction between traditional econometrics and statistics on one hand versus artificial intelligence and machine learning on the other (please see the examples detailed in Section 2.6)*. A rigorous distinction between public information and market information, which is critical to understanding finance, is detailed in this book.

As detailed in Chapter 1, the methodology of scientific analysis is "behind the veil," i.e., the methodology cannot depend on the results or desired results or a "preapproved narrative." Examples of non-scientific methods include "data mining," described as "the process of using computers and automation to search large sets of data for patterns and trends" (Rutgers (2025)), which effectively becomes trawling through data to find support for predicted results or desired results, and "*p*-hacking," which "occurs when researchers select or collect data or statistical analyses until nonsignificant results become significant ... *p*-hacking is widespread throughout science" – please see the strong criticisms in, for instance, Head et al. (2015). Immanuel Kant is supposed to have said that "theory without practice is empty, practice without theory is blind," and that "experience without theory is blind, but theory without experience is mere intellectual play," the scientific method, therefore, demands a marriage of theory and empirics, where the empirics is based on the theory and the theory is refined based on the empirics; the scientific method demands that every single hypothesis be tested by actual empirical work. Fields that are unable to follow these principles lack scientific rigor and have no place in a university or a modern society, beyond fiction or theology, of course, where actual facts are irrelevant. For instance, "this is how we do it here" as a dispositive answer to any question is entirely anti-intellectual. "Science is the belief in the ignorance of experts," Richard Feynman, Nobel Prize in Physics, 1965, in Feynman (2011) – obviously, this does not mean that expertise is not important; it just means that as far as the scientific method is concerned, reputation is irrelevant and definitely not dispositive, only facts and logic matter.

Consider a hypothesis that one is trying to test and evidence that one is trying to use. The scientific method, that the *ex post* ***GenProb*** of a hypothesis equals the value ratio of evidence times the *ex ante* ***GenProb*** of the hypothesis, where the value ratio of evidence for the hypothesis is how much the ***GenProb*** of the evidence increased as a result of the hypothesis, is detailed in Chapter 1. This, of course, has substantial implications in all fields of empirical work, especially in finance, pharmaceuticals, and litigation. Updating ***GenProb*** on the basis of new information is scientific — the only arbiters of "final" are God, and the Supreme Court, I suppose — and since the criterion of falsifiability is essential to a scientific theory, that faith consists of a degenerate prior, ***GenProb*** $\in \{0,1\}$ — whereas the scientific method requires a non-degenerate prior, ***GenProb*** $\notin \{0,1\}$. Science goes much beyond slogans such as "march for science" or "follow the science" that are "full of sound and fury [and good intentions], signifying nothing." In this book, the terms "degenerate" and "non-degenerate" are used purely in their mathematical senses, ***GenProb*** $\in \{0,1\}$ and ***GenProb*** $\notin \{0,1\}$ respectively, as detailed in Chapter 1, and do not have any moral implications. One has the right to one's faith, one's degenerate prior, but one has to acknowledge that one's degenerate prior has no implications for someone else, and also, the search for truth has to acknowledge someone else's right to their faith; for instance, describing the Mormon faith as "absurd" is indeed absurd, whereas the most one can say is that one has a different degenerate prior than the other. For instance, the assertion that Jesus Christ was the son of God, or that the Quran was revealed by God to Prophet Muhammad, or that the Jewish people were given the whole land of Israel by God, is each an article of faith, a degenerate prior that a person has the right to believe in but is not empirically testable, and therefore, is not binding on anyone else. Indeed, I find that faith can be beautiful; for instance, our daughter was born on Saraswati Puja, the day of worship of the Hindu goddess of knowledge, hence her middle name, *Vidya* (knowledge or wisdom), or the power of prayer, even if it is "all in the mind," when a loved one is ill. But it is *my* faith, *my* degenerate prior that I have the right to but which cannot be empirically testable, so it is not the slightest bit binding upon anyone else. As Galileo Galilei plaintively said when forced to recant his finding that the earth moves around the sun, "and yet it moves." "Flat earthers" are those who insist that their degenerate prior should be everyone's degenerate prior, and it would not be an exaggeration to say that civilization begins when one realizes that people who disagree do not necessarily have horns. "The theologian H. Richard Niebuhr (younger brother of Reinhold) explained the [monomania] fallacy thus: 'There is no greater barrier to understanding than the assumption that the standpoint which we happen to occupy is a universal [or the only correct] one.' It is an error embedded in human nature," Morrow (2016). For example, the great Dharmic faiths of Hinduism, Buddhism, Jainism, and Sikhism insist on tolerating and accepting faiths even when one does not agree, and even when one does not understand, because one degenerate prior, being non-testable, is just as legitimate or illegitimate as any other degenerate prior; a statement along the lines of "that's not how it works" is absurd.

Finally, "it is the extreme of anti-intellectualism to assert, in effect, that 'I don't get it [and/or I am unable to explain it to my parents], so it must be wrong' " (Bhattacharya, 2019), and as the late legendary biochemist (and popular science author) Professor Isaac Asimov famously put it, "There is a cult of ignorance ... and there always has been. The strain of anti-intellectualism has been a constant thread winding its way through our political and cultural life, nurtured by the false notion that democracy means that 'my ignorance is just as good as your knowledge' " (Asimov, 1980). We would like you to also consider this anecdote, showing how the scientific method works, about the late Professor Daniel Kahneman, Nobel Prize in Economics, 2002: "He was ... relentlessly self-critical. I once showed him a letter I'd gotten from a reader telling me — correctly but rudely — that I was wrong about something. 'Do you have any idea how lucky you are to have thousands of people who can tell you you're wrong?' Danny said. ... Most people hate changing their mind; he liked nothing better, when the evidence justified it," Zweig (2024).

To summarize, it is profoundly important for all of us to recognize the importance of, and indeed, scrupulously and consistently practice, the scientific method. I hope that all readers of this book will understand that the criticisms in this book, even when strident, are all intended in good faith and as honest descriptions of the stringent requirements of the scientific method, especially when applied to Big Data in finance.

References

Asimov, I., 1980, "A Cult of Ignorance," *Newsweek*, January 21, 1980.

Bauguess, S., 2016, "Has Big Data Made Us Lazy?" *U.S. Securities and Exchange Commission*, October 21, 2016 (https://www.sec.gov/newsroom/speeches-statements/bauguess-american-accounting-association-102116).

Bhattacharya, R., 2019, "Nash Bargaining Solution and Its Generalizations in Intellectual Property Litigation," *Journal of International Business & Law*, XIX(1), 50–60.

Bhattacharya, R., Bial, J., and Evans, A., 2023, "It is Imperative to Perform Event Studies Only With High-Frequency Intraday Data for Securities Litigations and Valuations," *Journal of International Business & Law*, 23(1), 1–28.

Feynman, R., 2011, *Feynman on Scientific Method*, Seabala (https://youtu.be/EYPapE-3FRw).

Goldstein, I., Spatt, C., and Ye, M., 2021, "Big Data in Finance," *Review of Financial Studies*, 34(7), 3213–3225.

Goldstein, I., Spatt, C., and Ye, M., 2025, "The Next Chapter of Big Data in Finance," *Review of Financial Studies*, 38(3), 605–622.

Head, M., Holman, L., Lanfear, R., Kahn, A., and Jennions, M., 2015, "The Extent and Consequences of P-Hacking in Science," *PLoS Biol*, 13(3), 1–15.

Ip, G., 2025, "The Depopulation Bomb," *Wall Street Journal*, July 27, 2025.

Kennedy, P., 2003, *A Guide to Econometrics*, Cambridge, MA: MIT Press.

Morrow, L., 2016, "The Hedgehogs of Critical Race Theory," *Wall Street Journal*, July 19, 2016.

Rutgers University, 2025, "Learn Coding and more Online," *Rutgers* University (https://bootcamp.rutgers.edu/blog/what-is-data-mining/).

Shabat, H., 2025, "This is Hossam's team, and we are sharing his final message," *@HossamShabatj (https://x.com/HossamShabat),* March 24, 2025.

Spears, D., and Geruso, M., 2025, *After the Spike: Population, Progress, and the Case for People*, New York, NY: Simon & Schuster.

Zweig, J., 2024, "The Psychologist Who Turned the Investing World on Its Head," *Wall Street Journal*, March 29, 2024.

ABOUT THE AUTHOR

Rajeev R. Bhattacharya, Ph.D., has three decades of experience in research, teaching, consulting, and management in the fields of finance, economics, and Big Data. He is a finance professor at Macquarie University in Sydney and has served on the full-time faculty of the University of Maryland, Washington University in St. Louis, Georgetown University, and the University of New South Wales; he teaches financial economics, derivatives, and advanced analytics.

Rajeev's original research, teaching, and consulting are at the frontiers of quantitative methods in finance. His recent publications on diligence and objectivity of analyst forecasts and event studies using millisecond-level high-frequency data have proven particularly influential. He has written on the impact of COVID-19 and of self-regulation on capital markets, and has published highly regarded books and articles in leading journals on stocks, bonds, options, and other topics.

He is the president of Washington Finance and Economics and has worked in senior capacities at leading consulting firms such as the Berkeley Research Group. Rajeev has a Ph.D. in economics from the University of Rochester. He lives with his wife and daughter in a suburb of Washington, DC.

ACKNOWLEDGMENTS

I am especially grateful to Tom Smith, Mahendra Gupta, Glenn MacDonald, Raghu Sundaram, Ryan Cooper, Michael McDonald, Joseph Bial, Jeffrey Pontiff, Simon Wheatley, and Wenli Zhao. I am very grateful to the outstanding team at Routledge, Aimée Crickmore, Michelle Gallagher, Chloe Herbert, and Karthik Orukaimani, whose kind but thoughtful and honest suggestions have transformed this book significantly for the better.

I thank Deborah Abbott, Tim Adler, Reena Aggarwal, Alta Ahmad, Kaisar Ahmad, M. Zafar Anis, Zahid Bajwa, Ray Ball, Prasanta Bandyopadhyay, Henk Berkman, Pat Brown, Philip Brown, Ajay Chakrabarti, Alicia Chakrabarti, Anil Chakrabarti, Saurav Chakrabarti, Srabanti Chakrabarti, Ahi Chakraborty, Margrit Chakraborty, Shibasheesh Chakraborty, Jivas Chakravarthy, Aloka Chakravarty, Dipto Chakravarty, Robert Chang, Manojit Chatterjee, Nilanjana Chatterjee, Sourav Chatterjee, Malay Chattopadhyay, Ila Chaturvedi Sarkar, Martijn Cremers, Pierre Cremieux, Glenn Davis, Ted Davis, Timothy Devinney, Peter Dodd, Nancy Dunham, Wayne Dunham, Mark Erwin, Philip Evans, Mark Flood, Jed Frees, Eric Frye, Mriganka Ganguly, Sumita Ganguly, Simon Grant, John Greenberg, Anirban Gupta, Barton Hamilton, Gautam Hazarika, David Hirshleifer, Denada Ibrushi, Siamak Jawadi, Gergana Jostova, Deeksha Karki, Murray Kemp, Bill Kennedy, Shervin Khodabandeh, Ron King, Stephen King, Claudia Koch, Robert Korajczyk, Pete Kyle, Paige LaRose, Bob Larner, Loc Le, John Lee, Julie Lee, Andi Li, Tom Loncar, Ahmed Mahmud, Marcie Mao, David Marcus, Leslie Marx, Marcia Mayer, Lionel McKenzie, Yasir Mehboob, Shubha Mehrotra, Todd Milbourn, Robert Minchin, Romel Mostafa, Gautam Mukherjee, Vikram Nanda, Nandu Nayar, David Nelson, Rebecca Nelson, Namhoang Nguyen,

Jackson Nickerson, Stephen O'Brien, Lee Ohanian, Tava Olsen, Elizabeth Ooi, Prasad Padmanabhan, Dipen Patel, Alex Philipov, Nripesh Podder, Tultul Podder, Nagpurnanand Prabhala, Chaya Ray, Madhab Ray, Mark Ready, Maureen Regan, Adhiraj Roy, Amitava Roy, Sanjiv Sabherwal, Samuel Salario, Nandini Samanta, Anthony Saunders, Gary Schmirer, Sunando Sengupta, Hersh Shefrin, Lei Shi, Sath Shukla, Debajyoti Sinha, Erik Sirri, Pablo Slutzky, Saul Solomon, Tayfun Sonmez, Bin Srinidhi, Deokumar Srivastava, Walter Tappe, David Teece, Anjan Thakor, Riya Thebaud, Robert Thompson, William Thomson, Kien Tran, Sanjay Unni, Juthika Chakraborty Wise, Hamid Yahyaei, Yossi Yassour, and Todd Zenger (in alphabetical order), and seminar participants at Australian National University, University of Auckland, Macquarie University, University of Maryland at College Park, St. Mary's University, University of Texas at Arlington, University of Texas at Dallas, University of Texas at Rio Grande Valley, University of Warsaw, University of Western Australia, and the U.S. Securities and Exchange Commission.

Last, but definitely not the least, I thank my thousands of graduate and undergraduate students at the University of New South Wales, Washington University in St. Louis, Georgetown University, University of Maryland at College Park, Johns Hopkins University, and George Mason University, especially Michael Abeshouse, Michael Abramson, Sarthak Aggarwal, Abir Agrawal, Sebastian Aguirre Espinoza, Parth Ahluwalia, Shveta Arora, Bruce Bachenheimer, Rachel Balven, Shreya Bansal, Ricky Berger, Lisa Biancani, Blaise Blitz, George Bogdanovic, Matthew Bonaguidi, Rahul Bhargava, Lucas Boardman, Kyle Brinker, Bruce Buchanan, Marco Calamandrei, Melissa Cameron, Kimberly Renner Campbell, CJ Campeau, Justin Carbaugh, Darren Challis, Ashish Chaturvedi, Ingrid Chen, Wee-Lin Chen, Xiaomeng Chen, Yuanyi Chen, Joo Chung, Jonathan Cohen, Boyd Coleman, RJ Crotser, Debasish Das, Duarte de Carvalho, Sancia De Jersey, Jacopo De Maio, Amelia De Paola, Hailey Desiderio, Justin di Lollo, Dan Dieso, Sachin Dixit, Chi Doan, Colin Dowling, Avery Edwards, Kent Fatzinger, Lionel Faucher, Chris Fernandes, Aneesha Fernandez, Cidell Fletcher, Runlin Fu, Suvir Garkel, Michael Gassmann, Nick Gavino Vera, Rohan Gill, Jason Goldstein, Andy Gomez, Tracey Grennan, Martin Groen, Zhizhou Gu, Aaron Guo, Rundan Guan, Changtong Han, Margaret Hansen, Jameel Haralson, Spencer Herzog, Tanjulan Holloway, Adam Hostetter, Jeremy Huelsman, Kate Hyun, Yi Ji, Francisco Jimenez Palomo, Venkatesh Kannan, Christina Kearns, Sharon Kenny, David Kestenbaum, Khushboo Khandelwal, Juliana Kim, Garin Kirkpatrick, Carla Kleinhappel Mateus, Ainitieken Kuerxiati, Katerina Ladygo, Adam Lavallee, Bridget Lavelle, sMatt Ledyard, Junhao Li, Nathan Li, Michael Lindsay, Kenneth Ling, Yanxi Liu, Yunhan Liu, Eric Ljungqvist, David Logan, Mikey Lowell, Abdulrahman Lubbad, Jaden Luy, Chase Lynch, Shohua Ma, Will Magrath, Adam Mandel, Marlon Marquez Martinez, Brendan Mason, Jonathan McCluskey, Richard McKenna, Matt McMahon, Abby Meland, Sheikh Mia, Fabricio Miguez,

Ryan Milonovich, Sindhu Muppala, Pip Murphy, Throshni Naidoo, Prashob Nair, Elizabeth Nalunga, Venkatesh Narayanan, Minh Nguyen, Mavis Ni, Javier Nieto, Gabriel Nunez, Bart Onkenhout, Lisa Orthwein, Tiffany Pai, Jodie Parlett, Timothy Petterson, James Picariello, Nico Prioli, Kieran Redmond, Joshua Renalds, Alex Rozett, Kyle Ryan, Else Saucedo, Mark Schwager, Kelly Scott, Stanley Seat, Vanita Sehgal, Victoria Shakespeare, Patrick Shan, Yunshu Shao, Deana Sheremeta, Yi Shi, Tanveer Singh, Alessandra Sirabella, Daniela Sirabella, Kartick Sivaram, Adam Smith, Kebang Song, Justin Soto, Khalid Soudi, Michael Steiner, Connor Sullivan, Sidharth Sunder, Soji Swaraj, Hogan Tong, Saskia Vischer, Ryan Vogel, Lauren Waggoner, Aarya Walvekar, Lauren Wieringa, Jennifer Mulholland Wilson, Ashley Winograd, Jiakang Wu, Marcus Wuttke, Xing Xia, Anthony Zdrojewski, Yifan Zhang, and Yiwen Zhang (in alphabetical order), for suffering through previous versions of this book, and for their encouragement and their respectful (although thankfully, never reverential) and honest feedback.

PART I

The Scientific Method

1
THEORY

1.1 Introduction

Knowing the entire universe of possible outcomes, even if not knowing what particular outcome has occurred, is a situation of known unknowns, and is the domain of risk, whereas not knowing the entire universe of possible outcomes is a situation of unknown unknowns, and is the domain of uncertainty; we will be using this terminology throughout this book. This distinction between known unknowns and unknown unknowns was popularized by U.S. Secretary of Defense Donald Rumsfeld in 2002, and this dichotomy was articulated, potentially for the first time in 1955, by Joseph Luft and Harrington Ingham; this framework is different from but consistent with the formulations of Sarasvathy, Simon and Lave (1998), Ellsberg (1961), Luce (1959), Savage (1954), Arrow (1951), and Knight (1921), in reverse chronological order. If we know the event A, the known, then do we know *not-A*, the unknown? In such a case, if we do know the unknown, the *not-A*, then we are in the domain of the known unknown, that of risk and probability, but if we do not know the unknown, the *not-A*, then we are in the domain of the unknown unknowns, that of uncertainty and generalized probability. Without the detailed mathematical modeling of unknown unknowns (uncertainty and generalized probability) done in this chapter versus the standard known unknowns (risk and probability), one cannot even begin to understand unknown unknowns such as the COVID-19 pandemic of 2020-2023 or the Global Financial Crisis of 2007-2009. As we detail in the Preface, the world of finance is full of unknown unknowns, such as the actions of (a) self-regulatory bodies such as the U.S. Financial Industry Regulatory Authority (FINRA), (b) federal regulators (the "alphabet soup") such as the Securities and Exchange Commission

DOI: 10.4324/9781003608486-2

(SEC), Commodity Futures Trading Commission (CFTC), and Consumer Financial Protection Bureau (CFPB), (c) international organizations such as the World Bank (WB), International Monetary Fund (IMF), Financial Stability Board (FSB), and Bank for International Settlements (BIS), (d) state regulators, (e) central banks such as the U.S. Federal Reserve Board (Fed), European Central Bank (ECB), Reserve Bank of Australia (RBA), Reserve Bank of India (RBI), financial engineering by (f) investment banks, (g) hedge funds, and (h) other financial players, technological developments such as (i) financial technology (FinTech), (j) artificial intelligence (AI), and machine learning (ML), transformations of attitude to risk by (k) investors and (l) proprietary traders, and finally, (m) *force majeure* events such as pandemics, regime and visa changes, and wars. It is, therefore, essential that we use the methods of uncertainty, generalized events, and generalized probability that we have developed in this book for any serious work in finance. As we point out in Section 1.4 on the philosophical underpinnings of our mathematical modeling, which also describes the famous ancient Hindu, Buddhist, and Jaina story of the elephant and six blind individuals, each blind individual's information about the elephant is such that (s)he could not have possibly known the entire universe of outcomes, so the standard formulation of events and probability (as described below in Section 1.2) does not apply at all, whereas our developments of uncertainty, generalized events, uncertainty algebras, and generalized probability (as detailed below in Section 1.3) do apply.

We provide in this chapter a measure-theoretic generalization of standard probability theory under risk to a theory of generalized probability under uncertainty, and we provide the reconciliation between the two. We show that the generalized probability measure over the known universe is conceptually and computationally different from even a reconciled probability measure conditioned upon the known universe, but given a random variable and a generalized random variable that are reconciled over a known universe, the expectation of the random variable conditioned upon the variable belonging to the known universe equals the expectation of the generalized random variable — this result makes possible all the empirical work in this book and, in conjunction with the details later in this chapter, enables the reconciliation between traditional econometrics and statistics on one hand and artificial intelligence and machine learning on the other.

1.2 Risk

In this section, we provide the measure-theoretic development of the popular notion of risk and probability — the "frequentist" interpretation of probability is that of relative frequency in the long run — please see Hájek (2023), Neyman (1977), von Mises (1928), Fisher (1922), and Venn (1866). It is often misattributed to Professor Albert Einstein, Nobel Prize in Physics, 2021, that "insanity is doing the same thing over and over again and expecting a different result," whereas the same thing over and over again with potentially different results is actually the province of probability, as we discuss in this section, and of generalized probability, as we discuss in Section 1.3.

In Section 1.3, we detail why the notions of risk and probability (and known unknowns) are not widely applicable and that, therefore, should be replaced with the more general notions of uncertainty and generalized probability (and unknown unknowns).

1.2.1 Events and Risk Algebra

Definition 1.1 *Consider a universe $\mathcal{F}$ of possible outcomes. Knowing what the entire universe $\mathcal{F}$ of possible outcomes is, even if not knowing what particular outcome $f \in \mathcal{F}$ has occurred, is a situation of* ***known unknowns****, and is the domain of* ***risk****. Consider a collection $\mathbb{W}$ of subsets of the universe $\mathcal{F}$ of all possible outcomes, where each such member of $\mathbb{W}$ is called an* ***event*** *in $\mathbb{W}$. The collection $\mathbb{W}$ of possible events is called a* ***risk algebra*** *if $\mathbb{W}$ contains the universe of all possible outcomes and contains complements and unions of component sets,*

1. *The universe is an event:*

$$\mathcal{F} \in \mathbb{W} \tag{1.1}$$

2. *If a set is an event, so is the complement of the set:*

$$A \in \mathbb{W} \Longrightarrow A^{\mathsf{C}} = \{f \in \mathcal{F} : f \notin A\} \in \mathbb{W} \tag{1.2}$$

3. *The union of a sequence of events is also an event:*

$$A_1, A_2, \ldots \in \mathbb{W} \Longrightarrow \bigcup_{i=1,2,\ldots} A_i \in \mathbb{W} \tag{1.3}$$

1.2.2 Interpretation of a Risk Algebra

A risk algebra $\mathbb{W}_{it}$ is simply a collection of events, and to say that $\mathbb{W}_{it}$ represents information of i at time t means that, at time t, i knows which event in $\mathbb{W}_{it}$ has occurred. That risk algebra $\mathbb{W}_{it}$ represents the information available to individual/public/organization i at time t means the following:

1. If $A \in \mathbb{W}_{it}$, then given any outcome $f \in \mathcal{F}$, i knows at time t whether $f \in A$ or $f \notin A$; in other words, if $A \in \mathbb{W}_{it}$ then i's information can distinguish between the event A and the event not-A
2. If $A \notin \mathbb{W}_{it}$, then given any outcome $f \in \mathcal{F}$, i does not know at time t whether $f \in A$ or $f \notin A$

1.2.2.1 Lack of Information about the Known Unknown

Consider a risk algebra that consists only of the universe of possible outcomes $\mathcal{F}$ and its complement, the null set $\emptyset$:

$$\mathbb{W}_{it} = \{\mathcal{F}, \emptyset\} \tag{1.4}$$

then at time t, i only knows whether the universe of possible outcomes has occurred and therefore, whether, the empty set has occurred; in other words, $\mathbb{W}_{it} = \{\mathcal{F}, \emptyset\}$ represents entire lack of information, and is the smallest possible risk algebra on the universe $\mathcal{F}$ of possible outcomes.

1.2.2.2 Full Information

Consider a risk algebra that consists of every single subset of the universe $\mathcal{F}$ of possible outcomes, i.e.,

$$\mathbb{W}_{it} = 2^{\mathcal{F}} \tag{1.5}$$

then at time t, i knows exactly which outcome has occurred; in other words, $\mathbb{W}_{it}$ represents full information, and is the largest possible risk algebra on $\mathcal{F}$.

1.2.2.3 Comparison of Information

If

$$\mathbb{K}_{it} \subseteq \mathbb{J}_{it} \tag{1.6}$$

then

$$A \in \mathbb{K}_{it} \Longrightarrow A \in \mathbb{J}_{it} \tag{1.7}$$

then, consider the information of i at time t represented by risk algebra $\mathbb{K}_{it}$. For $A \in \mathbb{K}_{it}$, i knows if outcome $f \in A$, and therefore, i knows if outcome $f \in A \in \mathbb{J}_{it}$, and therefore, information represented by $\mathbb{J}_{it}$ is at least as rich as the information represented by $\mathbb{K}_{it}$.

Example 1.1 *Consider the following: I pick a number from 1 to 3, Outcomes are Ipick1, Ipick2, and Ipick3, and therefore,*

$$\textit{Universe of outcomes} = \{Ipick1, Ipick2, Ipick3\}$$

Events are subsets of the entire set of outcomes, and therefore,

Universe of events

$$= \left\{ \begin{array}{c} \emptyset, \\ \{Ipick1\}, \{Ipick2\}, \{Ipick3\}, \\ \{Ipick1, Ipick2\}, \{Ipick1, Ipick3\}, \{Ipick2, Ipick3\}, \\ \{Ipick1, Ipick2, Ipick3\} \end{array} \right\} \quad (1.8)$$

Events satisfy some properties: complements and unions and intersections are also events. Knowing an event means knowing that an event has occurred — we use "event time" versus chronological time. Consider the information scenario that you don't know what number I have picked, but you know that I have picked an even number. The set of events corresponding to your information about my number choice

$$= \left\{ \begin{array}{c} \emptyset, \\ \{Ipick2\}, \\ \{Ipick1, Ipick3\}, \\ \{Ipick1, Ipick2, Ipick3\} \end{array} \right\} \quad (1.9)$$

Consider the information scenario that you don't have any information about what number I have picked. The set of events corresponding to your information about my number choice

$$= \left\{ \begin{array}{c} \emptyset, \\ \{Ipick1, Ipick2, Ipick3\} \end{array} \right\} \quad (1.10)$$

Consider the information scenario that you know which number I have picked. The set of events corresponding to your information about my number choice

$$= \left\{ \begin{array}{c} \emptyset, \\ \{Ipick1\}, \{Ipick2\}, \{Ipick3\}, \\ \{Ipick1, Ipick2\}, \{Ipick1, Ipick3\}, \{Ipick2, Ipick3\}, \\ \{Ipick1, Ipick2, Ipick3\} \end{array} \right\} \quad (1.11)$$

1.2.2.4 Conditional Probability

Definition 1.2 *Consider events A, B such that $\boldsymbol{Prob}(B) > 0$ then conditional probability of event A, conditional on event B, is*

$$\boldsymbol{Prob}(A \mid B) = \frac{\boldsymbol{Prob}(A \cap B)}{\boldsymbol{Prob}(B)} \quad (1.12)$$

We will certify later how conditional probabilities can be defined even when the event B that the conditional probability is conditioned upon is such that $\boldsymbol{Prob}(B) = 0$.

Theorem 1.1 *For A, B events such that*

$$\textbf{\textit{Prob}}\,(A) \neq 0 \tag{1.13}$$

then

$$\textbf{\textit{Prob}}\,(A \mid B) = \frac{\textbf{\textit{Prob}}\,(B \mid A)}{\textbf{\textit{Prob}}(B)}\textbf{\textit{Prob}}\,(A) = \frac{\textbf{\textit{Prob}}\,(A)}{\textbf{\textit{Prob}}(B)}\textbf{\textit{Prob}}\,(B \mid A) \tag{1.14}$$

See, for instance, its coverage even in the non-academic literature such as Chivers (2021).

Corollary 1.1 *Let $\mathfrak{G}\,(B)$ be the risk algebra generated by event B, which consists of B, its complement, and all unions, and intersections of members of $\mathfrak{G}\,(B)$. Then, the conditional probability above is a special case of*

$$\textbf{\textit{Prob}}\,(A \mid \mathfrak{G}\,(B)) \tag{1.15}$$

for $B \in \mathfrak{G}\,(B)$.

We will discuss later how conditional probabilities can be defined when the conditioning event B is such that $\textbf{\textit{Prob}}(B) = 0$.

Example 1.2 *You are playing a card game, and you have two cards. You know what your two cards are, but your opponent does not. The universe of possible outcomes is known to you and your opponent, and the different risk algebras represent the different information scenarios relevant to you and your opponent.*

Example 1.3 *You can see a number up to one decimal place in accuracy.*

1.2.3 Random Variable

A random variable is a function from the universe of all possible outcomes to a (possibly multidimensional) Euclidean space.

Notation 1.1 *Let $\mathbb{R}$ denote the set of all real numbers, the* **Euclidean space** *of dimension 1. Let*

$$\mathbb{R}^T = \{(x_1, x_2, \ldots x_T) : x_t \in \mathbb{R}, \textit{for all } t = 1, \ldots, T\} \tag{1.16}$$

the cross product of T real lines, denote the collection of T-sized combinations of real numbers, the **Euclidean space** *of dimension T.*

Notation 1.2 *A* **cuboid** *of dimension T is denoted, for $a, b \in \mathbb{R}^T, b_t \geq a_t, t = 1, \ldots, T$,*

$$[a, b] = \left\{(x_1, \ldots, x_T) \in \mathbb{R}^T : b_t \geq x_t \geq a_t, t = 1, \ldots, T\right\} \tag{1.17}$$

Notation 1.3 *Let $\mathbb{B}^T$ denote the collection of* ***Borel sets*** *of dimension T, which are all the cuboids and unions and intersections of cuboids in the T-dimensional Euclidean space $\mathbb{R}^T$.*

Definition 1.3 *The set of* ***Borel sets*** *on an Euclidean space $\mathbb{R}^T$ is the risk algebra generated by all cuboids in the Euclidean space $\mathbb{R}^T$:*

$$\mathbb{B}^T = \mathcal{B}\left(\mathbb{R}^T\right) = \mathfrak{G}\left(\left\{[a,b] : a,b \in \mathbb{R}^T, b_t \geq a_t, t = 1, ..., T\right\}\right) \tag{1.18}$$

In other words, $\mathbb{B}^T$ is the collection of Borel sets of dimension T, which are all the cuboids and unions and intersections of cuboids in the T-dimensional Euclidean space $\mathbb{R}^T$.

Definition 1.4 *Consider an Euclidean space $\mathbb{R}^T$, and consider probability* ***Prob*** *on algebra $\mathbb{W}$. A variable*

$$X^T : \mathcal{F} \longrightarrow \mathbb{R}^T \tag{1.19}$$

is a ***random variable****, and is* ***measurable*** *with respect to risk algebra $\mathbb{W}$, or is* ***$\mathbb{W}$-measurable****, if the inverse image of a Borel set is an event in $\mathbb{W}$:*

$$\left\{f : X^T(f) \in B\right\} \in \mathbb{W}, \forall B \in \mathbb{B}^T \tag{1.20}$$

and, therefore,

$$\boldsymbol{Prob}\left(X^T \in B\right) = \boldsymbol{Prob}\left(\left\{f : X^T(f) \in B\right\}\right), \forall B \in \mathbb{B}^T \tag{1.21}$$

In other words, a random variable X is $\mathbb{W}$-measurable if the risk algebra $\mathbb{W}$ is rich enough to determine X. Obviously,

$$\boldsymbol{Prob}\left(X^T \in B\right) = \int_B \mathbf{d}\boldsymbol{Prob}\left(x^T\right), \forall B \in \mathbb{B}^T \tag{1.22}$$

and

$$\boldsymbol{Prob}\left(X^T \in \mathbb{R}^T\right) = \int_{\mathbb{R}^T} \mathbf{d}\boldsymbol{Prob}\left(x^T\right) = 1 \tag{1.23}$$

Definition 1.5 *The* ***cumulative probability CumulProb****$_{X^T}$ of random variable X^T is*

$$\begin{aligned} \boldsymbol{CumulProb}_{X^T}(x_1, x_2, ..., x_T) &= \boldsymbol{Prob}(X_1 \leq x_1, X_2 \leq x_2, ..., X_T \leq x_T) \\ &= \int_{-\infty}^{x_1} \int_{-\infty}^{x_2} \cdots \int_{-\infty}^{x_T} \mathbf{d}\boldsymbol{Prob}\left(X^T = (x_1, x_2, ..., x_T)\right) \end{aligned} \tag{1.24}$$

Definition 1.6 *A random variable X is* ***discrete*** *if there is a countable Borel set support (X) that is a support for its probability; i.e., if its probability is determined by a* ***probability mass function***

$$ProbMass_{X^T} : \mathbb{R}^T \longrightarrow \mathbb{R} \tag{1.25}$$

such that

$$\textbf{\textit{Prob}}\left(X^T \in B\right) = \sum_{x \in B \cap \textbf{\textit{support}}(X)} ProbMass_{X^T}(x), \forall B \in \mathbb{B}^T \tag{1.26}$$

and

$$\begin{aligned}\textbf{\textit{Prob}}\left(X^T \in \mathbb{R}^T\right) &= \sum_{x \in \textbf{\textit{support}}(X)} ProbMass_{X^T}(x) \\ &= 1\end{aligned} \tag{1.27}$$

Example 1.4 *Any random variable whose probability is determined by a* ***probability mass function*** *is continuous; examples include binomial and Poisson.*

Definition 1.7 *The* ***Lebesgue measure*** *on an Euclidean space $\mathbb{R}^T$ is such that a measure of a cuboid in $\mathbb{R}^T$ is the volume of the cuboid:*

$$\lambda([a, b]) = \prod_{t=1}^{T} (b_t - a_t), a, b \in \mathbb{R}^T, b_t \geq a_t \tag{1.28}$$

Definition 1.8 *A random variable is* ***absolutely continuous with respect to the Lebesgue measure*** *λ — or simply* ***continuous*** *— if the probability of the random variable taking values in a set of Lebesgue measure zero is also zero:*

$$\lambda(B) = 0 \Longrightarrow \textbf{\textit{Prob}}\left(X^T \in B\right) = 0, \forall B \in \mathcal{B}\left(\mathbb{R}^T\right) \tag{1.29}$$

i.e., for such a random variable, there exists a probability density function

$$ProbDensity : \mathbb{R}^T \longrightarrow \mathbb{R} \tag{1.30}$$

such that

$$\textbf{\textit{Prob}}\left(X^T \in B\right) = \int_B \textbf{\textit{ProbDensity}}(x)\,\mathbf{d}x, \forall B \in \mathcal{B}\left(\mathbb{R}^T\right) \tag{1.31}$$

and, therefore,

$$\begin{aligned}&ProbDensity_{(X_1, X_2, \ldots X_T)}((x_1, x_2, \ldots, x_T)) \\ &= \frac{\partial}{\partial x_1}\frac{\partial}{\partial x_2}\cdots\frac{\partial}{\partial x_T}\textbf{\textit{CumulProb}}_{(X_1, X_2, \ldots X_T)}((x_1, x_2, \ldots, x_T)) \\ &= \frac{\partial}{\partial x_1}\frac{\partial}{\partial x_2}\cdots\frac{\partial}{\partial x_T}\textbf{\textit{Prob}}(X_1 \leq x_1, X_2 \leq x_2, \ldots, X_T \leq x_T)\end{aligned} \tag{1.32}$$

and

$$\begin{aligned} ProbDensity_{X_n}(x_n) &= \frac{\partial}{\partial x_n}\textbf{\textit{CumulProb}}_{X_n}(x_n) \\ &= \frac{\partial}{\partial x_n}\textbf{\textit{Prob}}(X_n \le x_n) \end{aligned} \tag{1.33}$$

and

$$\begin{aligned} \textbf{\textit{Prob}}\left(X \in \mathbb{R}^T\right) &= \int_{\mathbb{R}^T} ProbDensity(x)\, \mathbf{d}x \\ &= 1 \end{aligned} \tag{1.34}$$

Example 1.5 *Any random variable whose probability is determined by a* ***probability density function*** *is continuous; examples include Gaussian (Normal), lognormal, exponential, or uniform.*

Example 1.6 *Density of Gaussian (Normal) distribution*

$$X \sim N\left(\mu, \sigma^2\right) \Longleftrightarrow f(x) = \frac{1}{\sigma\sqrt{2\pi}} e^{-\frac{(x-\mu)^2}{2\sigma^2}} \tag{1.35}$$

$\boldsymbol{E}(x) = \mu$ *and* $Var(X) = \sigma^2$ *suffice to describe the entire distribution. Its mean = median = mode and the distribution is symmetric.* ***With a large number of observations, any distribution converges to Normal ("Central Limit Theorem")*** *— please see Billingsley (2012).*

$$\textbf{\textit{Prob}}[a \le X \le b] = \int_a^b \frac{1}{\sigma\sqrt{2\pi}} e^{-\frac{(y-\mu)^2}{2\sigma^2}} \mathbf{d}y \tag{1.36}$$

$$\textbf{\textit{CumulProb}}_X(x) = \textbf{\textit{Prob}}[X \le x] \tag{1.37}$$

$$= \int_{-\infty}^x \frac{1}{\sigma\sqrt{2\pi}} e^{-\frac{(y-\mu)^2}{2\sigma^2}} \mathbf{d}y \tag{1.38}$$

$$\textbf{\textit{Prob}}[a \le X \le b] = \textbf{\textit{CumulProb}}_X(b) - \textbf{\textit{CumulProb}}_X(a) \tag{1.39}$$

$$\textbf{\textit{Prob}}[\mu - \sigma \le X \le \mu + \sigma] = 0.6827 \tag{1.40}$$

$$\textbf{\textit{Prob}}[\mu - 2\sigma \le X \le \mu + 2\sigma] = 0.9545 \tag{1.41}$$

$$\textbf{\textit{Prob}}[\mu - 3\sigma \le X \le \mu + 3\sigma] = 0.9973 \tag{1.42}$$

Distribution of two Normal variables can be characterized by just the means, variances, and covariance

$$X_1 \sim N\left(\mu_1, \sigma_1^2\right), X_2 \sim N\left(\mu_2, \sigma_2^2\right), Cov\left(X_1, X_2\right) = \lambda \tag{1.43}$$

with covariance matrix

$$Cov\left(X\right) = \begin{pmatrix} \sigma_1^2 & \lambda \\ \lambda & \sigma_2^2 \end{pmatrix} \tag{1.44}$$

i.e.,

$$\left(X_1, X_2\right) \sim N\left(\left(\mu_1, \mu_2\right), \begin{pmatrix} \sigma_1^2 & \lambda \\ \lambda & \sigma_2^2 \end{pmatrix}\right) \tag{1.45}$$

The distribution of multiple Normal variables can be characterized by just the means, variances, and covariance(s)

$$X_k \sim N\left(\mu_k, \sigma_k^2\right), \forall k, Cov\left(X\right) = \Sigma \tag{1.46}$$

i.e.,

$$X \sim N\left(\mu, \Sigma\right) \tag{1.47}$$

where

$$X = \left(X_1, ..., X_n\right)', \mu = \left(\mu_1, ..., \mu_n\right)' \tag{1.48}$$

and covariance matrix

$$\Sigma = \begin{pmatrix} \sigma_1^2 & \dots & \sigma_{1n} \\ \vdots & \ddots & \vdots \\ \sigma_{n1} & \dots & \sigma_n^2 \end{pmatrix} \tag{1.49}$$

is symmetric and positive semi-definite. A linear combination of Normal variables is also Normal

$$X_1 \sim N\left(\mu_1, \sigma_1^2\right), X_2 \sim N\left(\mu_2, \sigma_2^2\right), Cov\left(X_1, X_2\right) = \lambda \tag{1.50}$$

$$\begin{aligned} \Longrightarrow \quad & \alpha_0 + \alpha_1 X_1 + \alpha_2 X_2 \\ \sim \quad & N\left(\alpha_0 + \alpha_1\mu_1 + \alpha_2\mu_2, \alpha_1^2\sigma_1^2 + \alpha_2^2\sigma_2^2 + 2\alpha_1\alpha_2\lambda\right) \end{aligned} \tag{1.51}$$

More generally,

$$X \sim N\left(\mu, \Sigma\right) \tag{1.52}$$

$$\Longrightarrow \alpha_0 + \alpha' X \sim N(\alpha_0 + \alpha' \mu, \alpha \Sigma \alpha') \tag{1.53}$$

where

$$\alpha_0 \text{ and } \alpha \text{ are conforming matrices} \tag{1.54}$$

Note that α_0 is simply a translation and therefore, does not affect the covariance matrix.

Example 1.7 *Standard Normal*

$$X \sim N\left(\mu, \sigma^2\right) \Longleftrightarrow Z = \frac{X - \mu}{\sigma} \sim N(0, 1) = SN \tag{1.55}$$

Example 1.8 *Lognormal distribution*

$$Y \sim \boldsymbol{LN}\left(\mu, \sigma^2\right) \Longleftrightarrow \ln Y \sim N\left(\mu, \sigma^2\right) \tag{1.56}$$

1.2.4 Expectation of a Random Variable

The expectation of a random variable is a generalization of the notion of a weighted average.

Definition 1.9 ***Expectation*** *of a random variable X on $\mathbb{R}^T$ exists if*

$$\int_{\mathbb{R}} |x_n| \, \mathbf{d}\boldsymbol{Prob}\left(X_n = x_n\right) \text{ exists for each } n \tag{1.57}$$

and is equal to

$$\boldsymbol{E}\left(X_n\right) = \int_{\mathbb{R}} x_n \mathbf{d}\boldsymbol{Prob}\left(X_n = x_n\right) \text{ for each } n \tag{1.58}$$

Definition 1.10 *Expectation of a discrete random variable X on $\mathbb{R}^T$ exists if*

$$\sum_{x_n} |x_n| \, \boldsymbol{Prob}\left(X_n = x_n\right) \text{ exists for each } n \tag{1.59}$$

and is equal to

$$\boldsymbol{E}\left(X_n\right) = \sum_{x_n} x_n \boldsymbol{Prob}\left(X_n = x_n\right) \text{ for each } n \tag{1.60}$$

Example 1.9 *If X follows Binomial with parameters n, a natural number greater than 1, and $p \in [0, 1]$, then*

$$\boldsymbol{Prob}\left(X = x\right) = \binom{n}{x} p^x \left(1 - p\right)^{n - x}, x = 0, 1, \ldots, n \tag{1.61}$$

and

$$\boldsymbol{E}\left(X\right) = np \tag{1.62}$$

Example 1.10 *If X follows Poisson with parameter $\lambda > 0$, then*

$$\boldsymbol{Prob}\left(X = x\right) = \frac{\lambda^{x}\exp\left(-\lambda\right)}{x!}, x = 0, 1, ..., \tag{1.63}$$

and

$$\boldsymbol{E}\left(X\right) = \lambda \tag{1.64}$$

Definition 1.11 *Expectation of a continuous random variable X on $\mathbb{R}^{T}$ exists if*

$$\int_{\mathbb{R}} |x_n| \, ProbDensity_{X_n}\left(x_n\right) \mathbf{d}x \text{ exists for each } n \tag{1.65}$$

and is equal to

$$\boldsymbol{E}\left(X_n\right) = \int_{\mathbb{R}} x_n \boldsymbol{ProbDensity}_{X_n}\left(x_n\right) \mathbf{d}x \text{ for each } n \tag{1.66}$$

Example 1.11 *If X follows the exponential distribution with parameter $\lambda > 0$, then*

$$ProbDensity\left(x\right) = \left\{ \begin{array}{lll} \lambda\exp\left(-\lambda x\right) & if & x \geq 0 \\ 0 & otherwise & \end{array} \right\} \tag{1.67}$$

and

$$\boldsymbol{E}\left(X\right) = \frac{1}{\lambda} \tag{1.68}$$

Exercise 1.1

If you have never missed a flight, are you irrational?

If a lawyer has never lost a case, is she not picking the difficult cases?

Will a top hospital have high mortality?

1.2.5 Bayes Theorem

This mathematical result is typically attributed to the English polymath Thomas Bayes, and is thus, often referred to as Bayes' Theorem or Bayes' Theorem, or for simplicity, Bayes Theorem. It is arguably the most important result in mathematics; see, for instance, its coverage even in the non-academic literature such as Chivers (2021).

Theorem 1.2 ***(Bayes Theorem)*** *For $A, B \in \mathbb{G}$ events such that*

$$\boldsymbol{Prob}\left(A\right) \neq 0, \boldsymbol{Prob}\left(B\right) \neq 0 \tag{1.69}$$

then

$$\begin{aligned}\textbf{\textit{Prob}}\,(A \mid B) &= \frac{\textbf{\textit{Prob}}\,(B \mid A)}{\textbf{\textit{Prob}}(B)}\textbf{\textit{Prob}}\,(A) \\ &= \frac{\textbf{\textit{Prob}}\,(A)}{\textbf{\textit{Prob}}(B)}\textbf{\textit{Prob}}\,(B \mid A)\end{aligned} \tag{1.70}$$

Lemma 1.1 *Unconditional probability is the expectation of the conditional probabilities,*

$$\begin{aligned}\textbf{\textit{Prob}}\,(B) &= \textbf{\textit{E}}_Z\,(\textbf{\textit{Prob}}\,(B \mid Z)) \\ &= \int_z \textbf{\textit{Prob}}\,(B \mid z)\,\mathbf{d}\textbf{\textit{Prob}}\,(z)\end{aligned} \tag{1.71}$$

$$\begin{aligned}\textbf{\textit{Prob}}\left(B \mid z \in \widetilde{Z}\right) &= \textbf{\textit{E}}_{Z|z\in\widetilde{Z}}\,(\textbf{\textit{Prob}}\,(B \mid Z)) \\ &= \int_{z\in\widetilde{Z}} \textbf{\textit{Prob}}\,(B \mid z)\,\mathbf{d}\textbf{\textit{Prob}}_{Z|z\in\widetilde{Z}}\,(z)\end{aligned} \tag{1.72}$$

Example 1.12 ***Probability of a person being actually HIV-positive if her/his test result says she/he is.*** *Let us denote the event that a person is actually HIV-positive by pos and the event that the person is actually HIV-negative by neg. Let us denote the event that a person's test is positive by POS and the event that the person tests negative by NEG. Let us say that we have available to us an accurate test — its* sensitivity *(probability of true positive) is 90% — i.e.,*

$$\textbf{\textit{Prob}}\,(POS \mid pos) = 0.9 \tag{1.73}$$

which means that the probability of a false negative is

$$\textbf{\textit{Prob}}\,(NEG \mid pos) = 1 - 0.9 = 0.1 \tag{1.74}$$

Let's say that the specificity (probability of true negative) is 99%

$$\textbf{\textit{Prob}}\,(NEG \mid neg) = 0.99 \tag{1.75}$$

And, therefore, the probability of a false positive is

$$\textbf{\textit{Prob}}\,(POS \mid neg) = 1 - 0.99 = 0.01 \tag{1.76}$$

As of February 2025, approximately 1.2 million people in the U.S. were HIV-positive (https://www.hiv.gov/hiv-basics/overview/data-and-trends/statistics) and as of September 2025, the U.S. population was approximately 342.4 million (https://www.census.gov/popclock/), and therefore, the prevalence probability *is approximately*

$$\textbf{\textit{Prob}}\,(pos) \approx \left(\frac{1.2\ million}{342.4\ million}\right) \approx 0.0035 \tag{1.77}$$

and thus,

$$\textbf{\textit{Prob}}\,(neg) = 1 - 0.0035 = 0.9965 \tag{1.78}$$

But what is the critical question? You get to observe the result of the test, and what you want to know is the probability of the patient's being actually HIV-positive if the patient tests HIV-positive; i.e., you need to know the value of

$$\textbf{\textit{Prob}}\,(pos \mid POS) \tag{1.79}$$

i.e., you need to have the probabilities flipped. Now,

$$\begin{aligned}\textbf{\textit{Prob}}\,(POS) &= \textbf{\textit{Prob}}\,(POS \cap pos) + \textbf{\textit{Prob}}\,(POS \cap neg)\\ &= \textbf{\textit{Prob}}\,(POS \mid pos)\,\textbf{\textit{Prob}}\,(pos)\\ &\quad + \textbf{\textit{Prob}}\,(POS \mid neg)\,\textbf{\textit{Prob}}\,(neg)\\ &= (0.9)\,(0.0035) + (0.01)\,(0.9965) \approx 0.0131\end{aligned} \tag{1.80}$$

and

$$\textbf{\textit{Prob}}\,(NEG) = 1 - \textbf{\textit{Prob}}\,(POS) \approx 1 - 0.0131 \approx 0.9869 \tag{1.81}$$

and, therefore,

$$\begin{aligned}\textbf{\textit{Prob}}\,(pos \mid POS) &= \frac{\textbf{\textit{Prob}}\,(pos \cap POS)}{\textbf{\textit{Prob}}\,(POS)}\\ &= \frac{\textbf{\textit{Prob}}\,(POS \mid pos)\,\textbf{\textit{Prob}}\,(pos)}{\textbf{\textit{Prob}}\,(POS)}\\ &= \frac{(0.9)\,(0.0035)}{(0.9)\,(0.0035) + (0.01)\,(0.9965)}\\ &= \frac{(0.9)\,(0.0035)}{0.0131} \approx 0.6862\end{aligned} \tag{1.82}$$

$$\begin{aligned}\textbf{\textit{Prob}}\,(neg \mid POS) &= 1 - \textbf{\textit{Prob}}\,(pos \mid POS)\\ &\approx 0.3138\end{aligned} \tag{1.83}$$

That is, if a person tests HIV-positive, we have that at almost a third of the time, even such an accurate test will yield the wrong conclusion. Continuing,

$$\begin{aligned}\textbf{\textit{Prob}}\,(pos \mid POS) &= \frac{\textbf{\textit{Prob}}\,(POS \mid pos)\,\textbf{\textit{Prob}}\,(pos)}{\left(\begin{array}{c}\textbf{\textit{Prob}}\,(POS \mid pos)\,\textbf{\textit{Prob}}\,(pos)\\ +\textbf{\textit{Prob}}\,(POS \mid neg)\,(1-\textbf{\textit{Prob}}\,(pos))\end{array}\right)}\\ &= \frac{\textbf{\textit{Prob}}\,(POS \mid pos)\,\textbf{\textit{Prob}}\,(pos)}{\left(\begin{array}{c}\textbf{\textit{Prob}}\,(POS \mid pos)\,\textbf{\textit{Prob}}\,(pos)\\ +(1-\textbf{\textit{Prob}}\,(NEG \mid neg))\,(1-\textbf{\textit{Prob}}\,(pos))\end{array}\right)}\end{aligned} \tag{1.84}$$

which yields, by dividing the numerator and denominator above by

$$\textbf{\textit{Prob}}\,(POS \mid pos)\,\textbf{\textit{Prob}}\,(pos) \tag{1.85}$$

that

$$\textbf{\textit{Prob}}\,(pos \mid POS) = \frac{1}{1+\frac{(1-Specificity)}{Sensitivity}\left(\frac{1}{Prevalence}-1\right)} \tag{1.86}$$

which is increasing in specificity, sensitivity, and prevalence. And

$$\textbf{\textit{Prob}}\,(pos \mid POS) \gtreqless \frac{1}{2} \tag{1.87}$$

i.e., a positive test indicates that the patient is actually HIV-positive if and only if

$$Prevalence \gtreqless \frac{1-Sensitivity}{1-Sensitivity+Specificity} \tag{1.88}$$

1.2.6 Value Ratio of Evidence

If we are trying to test hypothesis $A \in \mathbb{W}$, and if we have evidence $B \in \mathbb{W}$, we can compute the **Value Ratio of Evidence** $B \in \mathbb{W}$ **for Hypothesis** A to determine if the value of the evidence $B \in \mathbb{W}$ in favor of hypothesis $A \in \mathbb{W}$, against hypothesis $A \in \mathbb{W}$, or neutral with respect to hypothesis $A \in \mathbb{W}$. We have shown some simple examples in this section, and there are many such examples in finance that we will discuss later in the context of market efficiency, and also in other fields, such as litigation, pharmaceuticals, and medicine.

Definition 1.12 *Consider hypothesis $A \in \mathbb{W}$ and evidence $B \in \mathbb{W}$ such that* $\textbf{\textit{Prob}}(B) > 0$. *Then,* $\textbf{\textit{Prob}}\,(A)$ *is the ex ante probability of hypothesis A,* $\textbf{\textit{Prob}}\,(A \mid B)$ *is the ex post probability of hypothesis A given evidence B, and the* ***Value Ratio of Evidence*** $B \in \mathbb{W}$ ***for Hypothesis*** *A is*

$$\textbf{\textit{Value Ratio of Evidence}}\,(B; A) = \frac{\textbf{\textit{Prob}}\,(B \mid A)}{\textbf{\textit{Prob}}(B)} \tag{1.89}$$

and therefore, Bayes Theorem can be restated as

$$\begin{aligned} &\boldsymbol{ExPost\ Prob}\,(A;B) \\ &= (\boldsymbol{Value\ Ratio\ of\ Evidence}\,(B;A))\,(\boldsymbol{ExAnte\ Prob}\,(A)) \end{aligned} \tag{1.90}$$

Corollary 1.2

- *If value ratio of evidence B for hypothesis A is greater than* **1**, *it means that evidence B is in favor of hypothesis A.*
- *If value ratio of evidence B for hypothesis A is less than* **1**, *it means that evidence B is against hypothesis A.*
- *If value ratio of evidence B for hypothesis A equals* **1**, *it means that evidence B is neutral with respect to hypothesis A.*
- *Higher the value ratio of evidence B for hypothesis A, the stronger the value of evidence B in favor of hypothesis A.*

Corollary 1.3 *If evidence* $B \in \mathbb{W}$ *is a realization of a random variable absolutely continuous with respect to the Lebesgue measure on* $\mathbb{R}^T$*, i.e., if*

$$\boldsymbol{Prob}\,(B = b) = 0, \forall b \in \mathbb{R}^T \tag{1.91}$$

then Bayes Theorem can be restated as follows:

$$\begin{aligned} \boldsymbol{Prob}\,(A \mid b) &= \frac{ProbDensity_{B|A}\,(b \mid A)}{\boldsymbol{ProbDensity}_B\,(b)} \boldsymbol{Prob}\,(A) \\ &= \frac{ProbDensity_{B|A}\,(b \mid A)}{\int_a ProbDensity_{B|A}\,(b \mid A = a)\,\mathbf{d}\boldsymbol{Prob}\,(a)} \boldsymbol{Prob}\,(A) \\ &= \boldsymbol{Value\ Ratio\ of\ Evidence}\,(b;A)\,\boldsymbol{Prob}\,(A) \end{aligned} \tag{1.92}$$

where Value Ratio of Evidence $B = b$ *for Hypothesis A is*

$$\boldsymbol{Value\ Ratio\ of\ Evidence}\,(b;A) = \frac{ProbDensity_{B|A}\,(b \mid A)}{\int_a ProbDensity_{B|A}\,(b \mid A = a)\,\mathbf{d}\boldsymbol{Prob}\,(a)} \tag{1.93}$$

Corollary 1.4 *If hypothesis* $A \in \mathbb{W}$ *is a realization of a random variable absolutely continuous with respect to the Lebesgue measure on* $\mathbb{R}^S$ *— i.e., if*

$$\boldsymbol{Prob}\,(A = a) = 0, \forall a \in \mathbb{R}^S$$

then,

$$\begin{aligned} ProbDensity_{A|B}\,(a \mid B) &= \frac{\boldsymbol{Prob}\,(B \mid a)}{\boldsymbol{Prob}(B)} ProbDensity_A\,(a) \\ &= \boldsymbol{Value\ Ratio\ of\ Evidence}\,(B;a)\,\boldsymbol{ProbDensity}_A\,(a) \end{aligned} \tag{1.94}$$

where Value Ratio of Evidence B for Hypothesis $A = a$ is

$$\begin{aligned}\textbf{\textit{Value Ratio of Evidence}}\,(B;a) &= \frac{\textbf{\textit{Prob}}\,(B \mid a)}{\textbf{\textit{Prob}}(B)} \\ &= \frac{\int_B \mathbf{d}\textbf{\textit{Prob}}\,(b \mid a)}{\int_B \mathbf{d}\textbf{\textit{Prob}}\,(b)}\end{aligned} \tag{1.95}$$

Corollary 1.5 *If hypothesis $A \in \mathbb{W}$ and evidence $B \in \mathbb{W}$ are realizations of random variables absolutely continuous with respect to the Lebesgue measure on $\mathbb{R}^S$ and $\mathbb{R}^T$ — i.e., if*

$$\textbf{\textit{Prob}}\,(A = a) = 0, \forall a \in \mathbb{R}^S$$

and

$$\textbf{\textit{Prob}}\,(B = b) = 0, \forall b \in \mathbb{R}^T$$

then,

$$\begin{aligned}\textit{ProbDensity}_{A|B}\,(a \mid b) &= \frac{\textit{ProbDensity}_{B|A}\,(b \mid a)}{\textbf{\textit{ProbDensity}}_B\,(b)}\textit{ProbDensity}_A\,(a) \\ &= \textbf{\textit{Value Ratio of Evidence}}\,(b;a)\,\textbf{\textit{ProbDensity}}_A\,(a)\end{aligned} \tag{1.96}$$

where Value Ratio of Evidence $B = b$ for Hypothesis $A = a$ is

$$\begin{aligned}&\textbf{\textit{Value Ratio of Evidence}}\,(b;a) \\ = &\frac{\textit{ProbDensity}_{B|A}\,(b \mid a)}{\textit{ProbDensity}_B\,(b)}\end{aligned} \tag{1.97}$$

Example 1.13 *Consider stock price,*

$$S_t \sim \textbf{\textit{LN}}\,(0, 1) \tag{1.98}$$

i.e., stock return,

$$\ln S_t \sim N\,(0, 1) \tag{1.99}$$

hypothesis,

$$A = \{S_t : \ln S_t > 0\} \tag{1.100}$$

and evidence,

$$B = \{S_t : \ln S_t > 10\%\} \tag{1.101}$$

then,

$$\begin{aligned}\textbf{\textit{Prob}}\,(B \mid A) &= \frac{\textbf{\textit{Prob}}\,(B \cap A)}{\textbf{\textit{Prob}}\,(A)}\ \textit{if}\ \textbf{\textit{Prob}}\,(A) > 0 \\ &= \frac{\textbf{\textit{Prob}}\,(B)}{\textbf{\textit{Prob}}\,(A)},\ \textit{since}\ B \subset A \\ &= \frac{\textbf{\textit{Prob}}\,\{S_t : \ln S_t > 0.1\}}{\textbf{\textit{Prob}}\,\{S_t : \ln S_t > 0\}} \\ &= \frac{1 - \textbf{\textit{Prob}}\,\{S_t : \ln S_t \leq 0.1\}}{1 - \textbf{\textit{Prob}}\,\{S_t : \ln S_t \leq 0\}} \\ &= \frac{1 - \textbf{\textit{CumulProb}}\,\{S_t : \ln S_t \leq 0.1\}}{1 - \textbf{\textit{CumulProb}}\,\{S_t : \ln S_t \leq 0\}}\end{aligned} \tag{1.102}$$

from Excel,

$$\begin{aligned}\textbf{\textit{CumulProb}}\,\{S_t : \ln S_t \leq 0.1\} &= \textit{NORMDIST}(0.1, 0, 1, \textit{TRUE}) \\ &= 0.539827837\end{aligned} \tag{1.103}$$

and therefore,

$$\textbf{\textit{Prob}}\,(B \mid A) = \frac{1 - 0.539827837}{0.5} = 0.92034$$

and, thus,

$$\begin{aligned}\textbf{\textit{Prob}}\,(B) &= \textbf{\textit{Prob}}\,\{S_t : \ln S_t > 0.1\} \\ &= 1 - 0.539827837,\ \textit{from above} \\ &= 0.46017\end{aligned} \tag{1.104}$$

and therefore,

$$\begin{aligned}\textbf{\textit{Value Ratio of Evidence}}\,(B; A) &= \frac{\textbf{\textit{Prob}}\,(B \mid A)}{\textbf{\textit{Prob}}(B)} \\ &= \frac{0.92034}{0.46017} = 2.0\end{aligned} \tag{1.105}$$

and therefore, Bayes Theorem can be restated as,

$$\textbf{\textit{ExPost Prob}}\,(A; B) = 2.0 \times \textbf{\textit{ExAnte Prob}}\,(A) \tag{1.106}$$

i.e., evidence,

$$B = \{S_t : \ln S_t > 10\%\} \tag{1.107}$$

is in favor of hypothesis,

$$A = \{S_t : \ln S_t > 0\} \tag{1.108}$$

Example 1.14 *Consider stock price,*

$$S_t \sim \boldsymbol{LN}(0,1) \tag{1.109}$$

i.e., stock return,

$$\ln S_t \sim N(0,1) \tag{1.110}$$

hypothesis,

$$A = \{S_t : \ln S_t > 0\} \tag{1.111}$$

and evidence,

$$B = \{S_t : -10\% < \ln S_t < 10\%\} \tag{1.112}$$

then,

$$\begin{aligned}
\boldsymbol{Prob}(B \mid A) &= \frac{\boldsymbol{Prob}(B \cap A)}{\boldsymbol{Prob}(A)} \; \textit{if}\, \boldsymbol{Prob}(A) > 0 \\
&= \frac{\boldsymbol{Prob}\{S_t : 0 < \ln S_t < 0.1\}}{\boldsymbol{Prob}\{S_t : \ln S_t > 0\}} \\
&= \frac{\boldsymbol{Prob}\{S_t : \ln S_t \le 0.1\} - \boldsymbol{Prob}\{S_t : \ln S_t \le 0\}}{1 - \boldsymbol{Prob}\{S_t : \ln S_t \le 0\}} \\
&= \frac{\boldsymbol{CumulProb}\{S_t : \ln S_t \le 0.1\} - \boldsymbol{CumulProb}\{S_t : \ln S_t \le 0\}}{1 - \boldsymbol{CumulProb}\{S_t : \ln S_t \le 0\}}
\end{aligned} \tag{1.113}$$

From Excel, we have,

$$\begin{aligned}
\boldsymbol{CumulProb}\{S_t : \ln S_t \le 0.1\} &= \textit{NORMDIST}(0.1, 0, 1, \textit{TRUE}) \\
&= 0.539827837
\end{aligned} \tag{1.114}$$

and of course,

$$\boldsymbol{CumulProb}\{S_t : \ln S_t \le 0\} = 0.5$$

and thus,

$$\boldsymbol{Prob}(B \mid A) = \frac{0.539827837 - 0.5}{0.5} = 0.079655675 \tag{1.115}$$

and, therefore,

$$\begin{aligned}
\boldsymbol{Prob}(B) &= \boldsymbol{Prob}\{S_t : -0.1 < \ln S_t < 0.1\} \\
&= \boldsymbol{CumulProb}\{S_t : \ln S_t \le 0.1\} \\
&\quad - \boldsymbol{CumulProb}\{S_t : \ln S_t \le -0.1\} \\
&= 0.539827837 - 0.460172163, \textit{from Excel}
\end{aligned} \tag{1.116}$$

for details,

$$\begin{aligned}\textbf{\textit{CumulProb}}\,\{S_t : \ln S_t \leq 0.1\} &= NORMDIST(0.1, 0, 1, TRUE)\\ \textbf{\textit{CumulProb}}\,\{S_t : \ln S_t \leq -0.1\} &= NORMDIST(-0.1, 0, 1, TRUE)\\ &= 0.079656\end{aligned}$$

and therefore,

$$\begin{aligned}\textbf{\textit{Value Ratio of Evidence}}\,(B; A) &= \frac{\textbf{\textit{Prob}}\,(B \mid A)}{\textbf{\textit{Prob}}(B)}\\ &= \frac{0.079656}{0.079656} = 1.0\end{aligned} \tag{1.117}$$

and therefore, Bayes Theorem can be restated as,

$$\textbf{\textit{ExPost Prob}}\,(A; B) = 1.0 \times \textbf{\textit{ExAnte Prob}}\,(A) \tag{1.118}$$

i.e., evidence,

$$B = \{S_t : -10\% < \ln S_t < 10\%\} \tag{1.119}$$

is neutral with respect to hypothesis,

$$A = \{S_t : \ln S_t > 0\} \tag{1.120}$$

Example 1.15 *Consider stock price,*

$$S_t \sim \textbf{\textit{LN}}\,(0, 1) \tag{1.121}$$

i.e., stock return,

$$\ln S_t \sim N\,(0, 1) \tag{1.122}$$

and hypothesis,

$$A = \{S_t : \ln S_t > 0\} \tag{1.123}$$

and evidence,

$$B = \{S_t : \ln S_t < -10\%\} \tag{1.124}$$

then,

$$\textbf{\textit{Prob}}\,(B \mid A) = \frac{\textbf{\textit{Prob}}\,(B \cap A)}{\textbf{\textit{Prob}}\,(A)} = \frac{\textbf{\textit{Prob}}\,(\emptyset)}{\textbf{\textit{Prob}}\,(A)},\ \textit{if}\ \textbf{\textit{Prob}}\,(A) > 0 \tag{1.125}$$

$$= 0$$

and,

$$\begin{aligned}\textbf{\textit{Prob}}\,(B) &= \textbf{\textit{Prob}}\,\{S_t : \ln S_t < -0.1\}\\ &= \textbf{\textit{CumulProb}}\,\{S_t : \ln S_t \leq -0.1\}\\ &= 0.460172163, \textit{ from Excel}\end{aligned} \tag{1.126}$$

and therefore,

$$\begin{aligned}\textbf{\textit{Value Ratio of Evidence}}\,(B; A) &= \frac{\textbf{\textit{Prob}}\,(B \mid A)}{\textbf{\textit{Prob}}(B)}\\ &= \frac{0}{0.460172163} = 0.0\end{aligned} \tag{1.127}$$

and therefore, Bayes Theorem can be restated as,

$$\textbf{\textit{ExPost Prob}}\,(A; B) = 0.0 \times \textbf{\textit{ExAnte Prob}}\,(A) \tag{1.128}$$

i.e., evidence,

$$B = \{S_t : \ln S_t < -10\%\} \tag{1.129}$$

is dispositively against hypothesis,

$$A = \{S_t : \ln S_t > 0\} \tag{1.130}$$

Example 1.16 *"Racial profiling" is a much debated policy in much of the developed world (see, for instance, Ryan et al. (2025)). In this example, we do not opine on the legal or moral justifications of a racial profiling policy for immigration enforcement in the U.S. (see, for example, Bravin and Timms (2025)), but simply apply the actual data to compute the value ratio of racial profiling in the context of unauthorized immigrants in the U.S. from Mexico, Central America, and South America. Consider hypothesis,*

$$A = \{\textit{U.S. resident is an unauthorized immigrant}\} \tag{1.131}$$

and evidence,

$$B - \{\textit{U.S. resident is from Mexico, Central America, or South America}\} \tag{1.132}$$

According to the U.S. Census Bureau (Barrett, 2023), the total population of the U.S. in 2023 was 334.9 *million, of whom, according to Pew Research (Passel and Krogstad, 2025),* 14 *million were unauthorized immigrants. Therefore,*

$$\textbf{\textit{Prob}}\,(A) = \frac{14.0 \textit{ million}}{334.9 \textit{ million}} \approx 4.2\% \tag{1.133}$$

As above, total population of the U.S. in 2023 was 334.9 *million (Barrett, 2023), of whom, according to Pew Research (Passel and Krogstad, 2025),* 9.2 *million were unauthorized immigrants from Mexico, Central America, and South America. Therefore,*

$$\textbf{\textit{Prob}}\,(B \cap A) = \frac{9.2\ \textit{million}}{334.9\ \textit{million}} \approx 2.7\% \tag{1.134}$$

where,

$$\begin{aligned} & B \cap A \\ & = \left\{ \begin{array}{c} \textit{U.S. resident is an unauthorized immigrant} \\ \textit{AND} \\ \textit{U.S. resident is from Mexico, Central America, or South America} \end{array} \right\} \end{aligned} \tag{1.135}$$

and therefore,

$$\begin{aligned} \textbf{\textit{Prob}}\,(B \mid A) &= \frac{\textbf{\textit{Prob}}\,(B \cap A)}{\textbf{\textit{Prob}}\,(A)} \\ &= \frac{2.7\%}{4.2\%} \approx 65.7\% \end{aligned} \tag{1.136}$$

and, according to USA Facts (2025), the proportion of the U.S. population that is from Mexico, Central America, or South America in 2022 was

$$\textbf{\textit{Prob}}\,(B) \approx 19.1\% \tag{1.137}$$

and therefore,

$$\begin{aligned} \textbf{\textit{Value Ratio of Evidence}}\,(B; A) &= \frac{\textbf{\textit{Prob}}\,(B \mid A)}{\textbf{\textit{Prob}}(B)} \\ &= \frac{65.7\%}{19.1\%} \approx 3.44 \end{aligned} \tag{1.138}$$

and therefore, Bayes Theorem can be restated as,

$$\textbf{\textit{ExPost Prob}}\,(A; B) = 3.44 \times \textbf{\textit{ExAnte Prob}}\,(A) \tag{1.139}$$

i.e., evidence,

$$B = \{\textit{U.S. resident is from Mexico, Central America, or South America}\} \tag{1.140}$$

strongly supports hypothesis,

$$A = \{\textit{U.S. resident is an unauthorized immigrant}\} \tag{1.141}$$

Example 1.17 *Applying what we learned in Example 1.16, let's now look at the corresponding calculations for unauthorized immigrants in the U.S. from India. As in Example 1.16, we do not opine in this example about the legal or moral justifications of a racial profiling policy for immigration enforcement in the U.S. (see, for example, Bravin and Timms (2025)), but empirically compute the value ratio of racial profiling in the context of unauthorized immigrants in the U.S. from India. Consider hypothesis,*

$$A = \{\textit{U.S. resident is an unauthorized immigrant}\} \tag{1.142}$$

and evidence,

$$B = \{\textit{U.S. resident is from India}\} \tag{1.143}$$

As above, according to the U.S. Census Bureau (Barrett, 2023), total population of the U.S. in 2023 was 334.9 *million, of whom, according to Pew Research (Passel and Krogstad, 2025),* 14 *million were unauthorized immigrants. Therefore,*

$$\textbf{\textit{Prob}}\,(A) = \frac{14.0\ \textit{million}}{334.9\ \textit{million}} \approx 4.2\% \tag{1.144}$$

Total population of the U.S. in 2023 was, as above, 334.9 *million (Barrett, 2023), of whom, according to Pew Research (Passel and Krogstad, 2025),* 675,000 *were unauthorized immigrants from India. Therefore,*

$$\textbf{\textit{Prob}}\,(B \cap A) = \frac{675,000}{334.9\ \textit{million}} \approx 0.2\% \tag{1.145}$$

where,

$$\begin{aligned} & B \cap A \\ & = \left\{ \begin{array}{c} \textit{U.S. resident is an unauthorized immigrant} \\ \textit{AND} \\ \textit{U.S. resident is from India} \end{array} \right\} \end{aligned} \tag{1.146}$$

and therefore,

$$\begin{aligned} \textbf{\textit{Prob}}\,(B \mid A) &= \frac{\textbf{\textit{Prob}}\,(B \cap A)}{\textbf{\textit{Prob}}\,(A)} \\ &= \frac{0.2\%}{4.2\%} \approx 4.8\% \end{aligned} \tag{1.147}$$

and, according to Pew Research (Im, 2025), the proportion of the U.S. population in 2023 that was from India,

$$\textbf{\textit{Prob}}\,(B) = \frac{5.2\ \textit{million}}{334.9\ \textit{million}} \approx 1.5\% \tag{1.148}$$

and therefore,

$$\begin{aligned}\textbf{\textit{Value Ratio of Evidence}}\,(B;A) &= \frac{\textbf{\textit{Prob}}\,(B\mid A)}{\textbf{\textit{Prob}}(B)} \\ &\approx \frac{4.8\%}{1.5\%} \approx 3.20\end{aligned} \tag{1.149}$$

and therefore, Bayes Theorem can be restated as,

$$\textbf{\textit{ExPost Prob}}\,(A;B) = 3.20 \times \textbf{\textit{ExAnte Prob}}\,(A) \tag{1.150}$$

i.e., evidence,

$$B = \{\textit{U.S. resident is from India}\} \tag{1.151}$$

supports hypothesis,

$$A = \{\textit{U.S. resident is an unauthorized immigrant}\} \tag{1.152}$$

1.2.7 Degenerate Prior Probability

If

$$\textbf{\textit{Prob}}\,(A) = 0 \tag{1.153}$$

then

$$\begin{aligned}\textbf{\textit{Prob}}\,(A\mid B) &= \frac{\textbf{\textit{Prob}}\,(A\cap B)}{\textbf{\textit{Prob}}\,(B)} \\ &\le \frac{\textbf{\textit{Prob}}\,(A)}{\textbf{\textit{Prob}}\,(B)} = 0\end{aligned} \tag{1.154}$$

If

$$\textbf{\textit{Prob}}\,(A) = \mathbf{1} \tag{1.155}$$

then, since

$$\textbf{\textit{Prob}}\,(\mathcal{F}\setminus A) = 0 \tag{1.156}$$

and

$$\begin{aligned}&\textbf{\textit{Prob}}\,(((\mathcal{F}\setminus A)\cap B)\cap B) \\ \le\ &\textbf{\textit{Prob}}\,(((\mathcal{F}\setminus A)\cap B)) = 0\end{aligned} \tag{1.157}$$

one has

$$\begin{aligned}\boldsymbol{Prob}(A \mid B) &= \frac{\boldsymbol{Prob}(A \cap B)}{\boldsymbol{Prob}(B)} \\ &= \frac{\boldsymbol{Prob}(A \cap B)}{\boldsymbol{Prob}((A \cap B) \cup ((\mathcal{F} \setminus A) \cap B))} \\ &= \frac{\boldsymbol{Prob}(A \cap B)}{\boldsymbol{Prob}(A \cap B) + \boldsymbol{Prob}((\mathcal{F} \setminus A) \cap B)} \\ &= \mathbf{1}\end{aligned} \tag{1.158}$$

1.2.8 Conditional Expectation

Conditional expectation, given a particular risk algebra, is used to model the impact of information corresponding to that risk algebra.

Definition 1.13 ***Conditional expectation*** *of a random variable X, given risk algebra* $\mathbb{I}$*, exists if*

$$\int_{\mathbb{R}^T} |x| \, \mathbf{d}\boldsymbol{Prob}(x \mid \mathbb{I}) \text{ exists} \tag{1.159}$$

and

$$\boldsymbol{E}(X \mid \mathbb{I}) = \frac{\int_{\mathbb{R}^T} x\mathbf{d}\boldsymbol{Prob}(x \mid \mathbb{I})}{\int_{\mathbb{R}^T} \mathbf{d}\boldsymbol{Prob}(x \mid \mathbb{I})} \tag{1.160}$$

Definition 1.14 *One can also provide a more primitive and equivalent definition of conditional expectation of X, given risk algebra* $\mathbb{I}$,

$$\boldsymbol{E}(X \mid \mathbb{I}) \tag{1.161}$$

is an $\mathbb{I}$*-measurable random variable such that*

$$\int_G \mathbf{d}\boldsymbol{Prob}(x \mid \mathbb{I}) > 0, \forall G \in \mathbb{I} \tag{1.162}$$

$$\int_G \boldsymbol{E}(X \mid \mathbb{I}) \, \mathbf{d}\boldsymbol{Prob}(x) = \frac{\int_G x\mathbf{d}\boldsymbol{Prob}(x)}{\int_G \mathbf{d}\boldsymbol{Prob}(x \mid \mathbb{I})}, \forall G \in \mathbb{I} \tag{1.163}$$

Lemma 1.2 *Consider a risk algebra that consists only of the entire universe* $\mathcal{F}$*, then at time t, i only knows, trivially, if the universe has occurred; in other words,* $\mathbb{G}_{it}^{Naïve} = \mathcal{F}$ *represents complete lack of information, and is the smallest possible risk algebra on* $\mathcal{F}$*. Then, conditional expectation, given total lack of information, equals unconditional expectation*

$$\boldsymbol{E}(X \mid \mathcal{F}) = \boldsymbol{E}(X) \tag{1.164}$$

Consider a risk algebra that consists of every single subset of the universe, i.e.,

$$\mathbb{G}_{it}^{Full} = 2^{\mathcal{F}} \tag{1.165}$$

then at time t, i knows exactly which outcome has occurred; in other words, $\mathbb{G}_{it}^{Full}$ *represents full information, and conditional expectation, given full information is*

$$\boldsymbol{E}\left(X \mid \mathbb{G}_{it}^{Full}\right) \tag{1.166}$$

In general, therefore, conditioning on different risk algebras allows one to measure reality with respect to different information scenarios.

Lemma 1.3 *For event A, consider the* ***indicator random variable***

$$\mathbf{1}_A(\omega) = \left\{ \begin{array}{lll} 1 & \textit{if} & \omega \in A \\ 0 & \textit{otherwise} & \end{array} \right\} \tag{1.167}$$

then the unconditional expectation of the indicator random variable is the relevant unconditional probability

$$\boldsymbol{E}(\mathbf{1}_A) = \boldsymbol{Prob}(A) \tag{1.168}$$

and the conditional expectation of the indicator random variable is the relevant conditional probability

$$\boldsymbol{E}(\mathbf{1}_A \mid \mathbb{I}) = \boldsymbol{Prob}(A \mid \mathbb{I}) \tag{1.169}$$

where $\mathbb{I}$ *is the risk algebra generated by the indicator random variable* $\mathbf{1}_A$.

Summary 1.1 *The above result also provides us with a characterization of conditional probability even when the event conditioned upon has zero probability.*

1.3 Uncertainty

This entire section generalizes the material we have discussed in Section 1.2. Knowing the entire universe of possible outcomes, even if not knowing what particular outcome has occurred, is a situation of known unknowns, and is the domain of risk, discussed in Section 1.2, whereas not knowing the entire universe of possible outcomes is a situation of unknown unknowns and is the domain of uncertainty; the notion of unknown unknowns was popularized by U.S. Secretary of Defense Donald Rumsfeld in 2002 and was articulated, potentially for the first time in 1955, by Joseph Luft and Harrington Ingham. Secretary Rumsfeld further stated that "reports that say that something hasn't happened are always interesting to me, because as we know, there are known knowns; there are things we know we know. We also know there are known unknowns; that is to say we know there are some things we do not know. But there are also unknown unknowns — the ones we don't know we don't know," Rumsfeld (2002). As Neil deGrasse Tyson famously said, "you can't be a scientist if you're uncomfortable with ignorance," Tyson (2013).

If one knows the event A, i.e., if A is known, then does one know *not-A*, the unknown? In such a case, if one does know the unknown, the *not-A*, then one is in the domain of the known unknown, that of risk and probability, but if one does not know the unknown, the *not-A*, then one is in the domain of the unknown unknown, that of uncertainty and generalized probability. Without the detailed mathematical modeling of unknown unknowns (uncertainty and generalized probability) done in this section, versus the standard known unknowns (risk and probability) done in Section 1.2, one cannot even begin to understand unknown unknown events such as the COVID-19 Pandemic of 2020-2022, or the Global Financial Crisis of 2007-2010.

Definition 1.15 *Consider a universe $\mathcal{F}$ of possible outcomes. Not knowing what the entire universe $\mathcal{F}$ of possible outcomes consists of is a situation of* ***unknown unknowns****, and is the domain of* ***uncertainty****. Consider a collection $\mathbb{G}$ of sets, where each member of $\mathbb{G}$ is called a* ***generalized event*** *in $\mathbb{G}$. The collection $\mathbb{G}$ of generalized events is called an* ***uncertainty algebra*** *if*

1.

$$\bigcup_{A\in\mathbb{A}} A \in \mathbb{G} \text{ for any collection } \mathbb{A} \subseteq \mathbb{G} \tag{1.170}$$

2.

$$\bigcap_{A\in\mathbb{A}} A \in \mathbb{G} \text{ for any collection } \mathbb{A} \subseteq \mathbb{G} \tag{1.171}$$

3.

$$\begin{aligned} \mathbf{Span}\left(\mathbb{G}\right) \setminus A &\in \mathbb{G}, \forall A \in \mathbb{G}, \\ \textit{where } \mathbf{Span}\left(\mathbb{A}\right) &= \bigcup_{A\in\mathbb{A}} A \text{ for any collection } \mathbb{A} \subseteq \mathbb{G} \end{aligned} \tag{1.172}$$

Often, a distinction is made between an algebra and a sigma-algebra in that the former requires that the union of a finite number of sets in an algebra also belongs to it, whereas the latter requires this for a countably infinite number of sets as well. This distinction is not important for the purposes of this book, so we will restrict attention to the latter and, for simplicity, refer to it as an algebra.

The following are integral to the fundamental differences between uncertainty that is modeled through generalized events and risk that is modeled through events.

Let, as above, $\mathcal{F}$ be the set of all possible outcomes, let $\mathbb{W}$ be the set of all events, and let $\mathbb{G}$ be the set of all generalized events. Then, $\mathcal{F}$ is an event but not necessarily a generalized event, i.e., $\mathcal{F} \in \mathbb{W}$ but it is **not** necessary that $\mathcal{F} \in \mathbb{G}$. Also, if A is an event, then so is its complement — in other words, $A \in \mathbb{G} \Longrightarrow A^{\mathsf{C}} = \{f \in \mathcal{F} : f \notin A\} \in \mathbb{W}$. But if A is a generalized event, then it is not necessary that so be its complement — in other words, $A \in \mathbb{G} \nRightarrow A^{\mathsf{C}} = \{f \in \mathcal{F} : f \notin A\} \in \mathbb{G}$ — in the world of uncertainty, therefore, if we know that something occurred, it is not necessary for us to know the entire set of possible outcomes that did not occur, but we do know the possible outcomes within the known universe that did not occur; see Definition 1.16 below. The span of a risk algebra is the entire set of outcomes, i.e., $\mathbb{W}$ is a risk algebra $\Longrightarrow Span(\mathbb{W}) = \mathcal{F}$; but the span of an uncertainty algebra need not be the entire set of outcomes, i.e., $\mathbb{G}$ is an uncertainty algebra $\nRightarrow Span(\mathbb{G}) = \mathcal{F}$. We will explicitly detail in Definitions 1.16 and 1.21 below this possible difference between the known universe $Span(\mathbb{G})$ and the entire universe $\mathcal{F}$ in the context of uncertainty, under which, the universe of all possible outcomes $\mathcal{F}$ need not be known; in other words, it is not necessary for the universe of all possible outcomes to be a generalized event.

Definition 1.16 *The set of known unknowns, the **known universe**, is*

$$\mathbf{Span}\,(\mathbb{G}) = \bigcup_{A \in \mathbb{G}} A \subseteq \mathcal{F} \tag{1.173}$$

Everything else

$$\mathcal{F} \setminus \mathbf{Span}\,(\mathbb{G}) \tag{1.174}$$

is unknown unknown.

Definition 1.17 *The uncertainty algebra **generated** by a class $\mathbb{A}$ of subsets of the universe $\mathcal{F}$ is the smallest uncertainty algebra containing all sets in $\mathbb{A}$:*

$$\mathfrak{G}\,(\mathbb{A}) = \bigcap \{\mathbb{F} \textit{ uncertainty algebra on } \mathcal{F} : \mathbb{A} \subseteq \mathbb{F}\} \tag{1.175}$$

If $\mathbb{A}$ is an uncertainty algebra, then the uncertainty algebra generated by the class of subsets is the same class of subsets: $\mathfrak{G}\,(\mathbb{A}) = \mathbb{A}$.

Definition 1.18 *A collection of generalized events $\mathbb{H} \subseteq \mathbb{G}$ is an **information partition** of $\mathbb{G}$ if*

1.

$$A \in \mathbb{H}, B \in \mathbb{H} \Longrightarrow A \cap B = \emptyset \tag{1.176}$$

2.

$$\bigcup_{A_x \in \mathbb{H}} A_x = \bigcup_{F \in \mathbb{G}} F \tag{1.177}$$

Corollary 1.6 *Whenever a set belongs to an information partition $\mathbb{H}$, a strict superset does not:*

$$A \in \mathbb{H}, A \subseteq B \in \mathbb{H} \Longrightarrow A = B \tag{1.178}$$

Definition 1.19 *Consider information partitions $\mathbb{I}$ and $\mathbb{J}$ of uncertainty algebra $\mathbb{G}$. Then $\mathbb{I}$ is a **reduction** of $\mathbb{J}$*

$$\mathbb{I} \preceq \mathbb{J} \tag{1.179}$$

if

$$I \in \mathbb{I} \Longrightarrow I \subseteq J, \textit{for some } J \in \mathbb{J} \tag{1.180}$$

Definition 1.20 *An information partition is **irreducible** if no further reduction of an information partition is possible; i.e., $\mathbb{I}$ is an **irreducible partition** of $\mathbb{G}$ if $\mathbb{J}$ is a reduction of $\mathbb{I}$ implies that $\mathbb{J} = \mathbb{I}$:*

$$\mathbb{J} \preceq \mathbb{I} \Longrightarrow \mathbb{J} = \mathbb{I} \tag{1.181}$$

1.3.1 Interpretation of an Uncertainty Algebra

An uncertainty algebra $\mathbb{G}_{it}$ is simply a collection of generalized events, and to say that $\mathbb{G}_{it}$ represents information of i at time t means that, at time t, i knows which generalized event in $\mathbb{G}_{it}$ has occurred. That uncertainty algebra $\mathbb{G}_{it}$ represents the information available to individual/public/organization i at time t means the following:

1. If $A \in \mathbb{G}_{it}$, then given any outcome $f \in \mathcal{F}$, i knows at time t that $f \in A$
2. If $A \notin \mathbb{G}_{it}$, then given any outcome $f \in \mathcal{F}$, i does not know at time t whether $f \in A$

1.3.1.1 Lack of Information about the Known Unknown

Consider an uncertainty algebra that consists only of the known universe

$$\mathbb{G}_{it} = \{\textbf{Span}\,(\mathbb{G})\} \tag{1.182}$$

then at time t, i only knows that the universe of possible outcomes has occurred; in other words, $\mathbb{G}_{it} = Span(\mathbb{G})$ represents lack of information about the known unknown, and is the smallest possible uncertainty algebra on the known universe $Span(\mathbb{G})$.

1.3.1.2 Full Information about the Known Unknown

Consider an uncertainty algebra that consists of every single subset of the known universe $Span(\mathbb{G})$, i.e.,

$$\mathbb{G}_{it} = 2^{\mathbf{Span}(\mathbb{G})} \tag{1.183}$$

then at time t, i knows exactly which outcome within the known universe $Span(\mathbb{G})$ has occurred; in other words, $\mathbb{G}_{it}$ represents full information within the known universe, and is the largest possible uncertainty algebra on $Span(\mathbb{G})$.

1.3.1.3 Comparison of Information about the Known Unknown

If

$$\mathbb{K}_{it} \subseteq \mathbb{J}_{it} \tag{1.184}$$

then

$$A \in \mathbb{K}_{it} \Longrightarrow A \in \mathbb{J}_{it} \tag{1.185}$$

then, consider the information of i at time t represented by uncertainty algebra $\mathbb{K}_{it}$. For $A \in \mathbb{K}_{it}$, i knows if outcome $f \in A$, and therefore, i knows if outcome $f \in A \in \mathbb{J}_{it}$, and therefore, information represented by $\mathbb{J}_{it}$ is at least as rich as the information represented by $\mathbb{K}_{it}$.

1.3.2 Generalized Probability

We now introduce the notion of generalized probability in the context of uncertainty.

Definition 1.21 *Uncertainty algebra $\mathbb{G}$ has a* ***generalized probability***

$$\boldsymbol{GenProb} : \mathbb{G} \longrightarrow [0,1] \tag{1.186}$$

if

1. *If the empty set is a generalized event, then the generalized probability that the outcome belongs to an empty set is zero:*

$$\emptyset \in \mathbb{G} \Longrightarrow \boldsymbol{GenProb}(\emptyset) = 0 \tag{1.187}$$

2. *The generalized probability that the outcome belongs to the union of a sequence of disjoint generalized events is equal to the sum of the generalized probabilities that the outcome belongs to each event:*

$$A_1, A_2, \ldots \in \mathbb{G} \text{ and } A_i \cap A_j = \emptyset, i \neq j \tag{1.188}$$

$$\Longrightarrow \boldsymbol{GenProb}\left(\bigcup_{i=1,2,\ldots} A_i\right) = \sum_{i=1,2,\ldots} \boldsymbol{GenProb}(A_i)$$

3. *The ℵ, **Aleph** or **Amithyā**, the **generalized probability of the entire known universe**, is between zero and one:*

$$\aleph = \boldsymbol{GenProb}\left(\mathbf{Span}\left(\mathbb{G}\right)\right) = \boldsymbol{GenProb}\left(\bigcup_{A \in \mathbb{G}} A\right) \in [0, 1] \tag{1.189}$$

which is the generalized probability of known unknowns.

The potential difference between $\aleph = \boldsymbol{GenProb}\left(\mathbf{Span}\left(\mathbb{G}\right)\right)$ and 1 is a fundamental contribution of this chapter.

Definition 1.22 *A generalized event $A \in \mathbb{G}$ is a **support** of generalized probability **GenProb** if*

$$\boldsymbol{GenProb}\left(A\right) = \aleph = \boldsymbol{GenProb}\left(\mathbf{Span}\left(\mathbb{G}\right)\right) \tag{1.190}$$

Definition 1.23 *Consider generalized events*

$$A, B \in \mathbb{I}_{it} \tag{1.191}$$

such that

$$\boldsymbol{GenProb}\left(B\right) > 0 \tag{1.192}$$

*then the **conditional generalized probability** of generalized event A, given the generalized event B, is*

$$\boldsymbol{GenProb}\left(A \mid B\right) = \frac{\boldsymbol{GenProb}\left(A \cap B\right)}{\boldsymbol{GenProb}(B)} \tag{1.193}$$

We will certify later how conditional probabilities can be defined when the event B such that $\boldsymbol{GenProb}(B) = 0$. In general, for generalized event A and uncertainty algebra $\mathbb{I}$, the conditional generalized probability of A, given information $\mathbb{I}$,

$$\boldsymbol{GenProb}\left(A \mid \mathbb{I}\right) \tag{1.194}$$

is an $\mathbb{I}$-measurable generalized random variable such that

$$\int_G \boldsymbol{GenProb}\left(A \mid \mathbb{I}\right) \mathbf{d}\boldsymbol{GenProb} = \boldsymbol{GenProb}\left(A \cap G\right), G \in \mathbb{I} \tag{1.195}$$

1.3.3 Independence of Generalized Events

Definition 1.24 *Generalized events A, B are independent with respect to generalized probability function **GenProb** if*

$$\boldsymbol{GenProb}\left(A \mid B\right) = \boldsymbol{GenProb}\left(A\right) \tag{1.196}$$

$$\mathbf{GenProb}\,(B \mid A) = \mathbf{GenProb}\,(B) \tag{1.197}$$

Lemma 1.4 *Generalized events A, B are independent with respect to generalized probability function **GenProb** if and only if*

$$\mathbf{GenProb}\,(A \cap B) = \mathbf{GenProb}\,(A)\,\mathbf{GenProb}\,(B) \tag{1.198}$$

1.3.4 Conditional Generalized Probability

Conditional generalized probability allows us to model information mathematically.

Definition 1.25 *Consider generalized events*

$$A, B \in \mathbb{I}_{it} \tag{1.199}$$

such that

$$\mathbf{GenProb}\,(B) > 0 \tag{1.200}$$

*then the **conditional generalized probability** of generalized event A, given the generalized event B, is*

$$\mathbf{GenProb}\,(A \mid B) = \frac{\mathbf{GenProb}\,(A \cap B)}{\mathbf{GenProb}(B)}$$

We will certify later how conditional probabilities can be defined when the event B such that $\mathbf{GenProb}(B) = 0$.

In general, for generalized event A and uncertainty algebra $\mathbb{I}$, the conditional generalized probability of A, given information $\mathbb{I}$,

$$\mathbf{GenProb}\,(A \mid \mathbb{I}) \tag{1.201}$$

is an $\mathbb{I}$-measurable generalized random variable such that

$$\int_G \mathbf{GenProb}\,(A \mid \mathbb{I})\, \mathbf{d}\mathbf{GenProb} = \mathbf{GenProb}\,(A \cap G)\,, G \in \mathbb{I} \tag{1.202}$$

1.3.5 Independence of Generalized Events

Definition 1.26 *Generalized events A, B are independent with respect to generalized probability function **GenProb** if*

$$\mathbf{GenProb}\,(A \mid B) = \mathbf{GenProb}\,(A) \tag{1.203}$$

$$\mathbf{GenProb}\,(B \mid A) = \mathbf{GenProb}\,(B) \tag{1.204}$$

Lemma 1.5 *Generalized events A, B are independent with respect to generalized probability function **GenProb** if and only if*

$$\textbf{\textit{GenProb}}\,(A \cap B) = \textbf{\textit{GenProb}}\,(A)\,\textbf{\textit{GenProb}}\,(B) \tag{1.205}$$

1.3.6 Generalized Random Variable

A generalized random variable is a function from the set of known unknowns to a (possibly multidimensional) Euclidean space.

Notation 1.4 *Let $\mathbb{R}$ denote the set of all real numbers, the **Euclidean space** of dimension* 1. *Let*

$$\mathbb{R}^T = \{(x_1, x_2, ...x_T) : x_t \in \mathbb{R}, \textit{for all } t = 1, ..., T\} \tag{1.206}$$

*the cross product of T real lines, denote the collection of T-sized combinations of real numbers, the **Euclidean space** of dimension T.*

Notation 1.5 *A **cuboid** of dimension T is denoted, for $a, b \in \mathbb{R}^T, b_t \geq a_t, t = 1, ..., T$,*

$$[a, b] = \left\{(x_1, ..., x_T) \in \mathbb{R}^T : b_t \geq x_t \geq a_t, t = 1, ..., T\right\} \tag{1.207}$$

Notation 1.6 *Let $\mathbb{B}^T$ denote the collection of **Borel sets** of dimension T, which are all the cuboids and unions and intersections of cuboids in the T-dimensional Euclidean space $\mathbb{R}^T$.*

Definition 1.27 *The set of **Borel sets** on an Euclidean space $\mathbb{R}^T$ is the uncertainty algebra generated by all cuboids in the Euclidean space $\mathbb{R}^T$:*

$$\mathbb{B}^T = \mathcal{B}\left(\mathbb{R}^T\right) = \mathfrak{G}\left(\left\{[a, b] : a, b \in \mathbb{R}^T, b_t \geq a_t, t = 1, ..., T\right\}\right) \tag{1.208}$$

In other words, $\mathbb{B}^T$ is the collection of Borel sets of dimension T, which are all the cuboids and unions and intersections of cuboids in the T-dimensional Euclidean space $\mathbb{R}^T$.

Definition 1.28 *Consider an Euclidean space $\mathbb{R}^T$, and consider generalized probability **GenProb** on generalized algebra $\mathbb{G}$. A variable*

$$X^T : \textbf{Span}\,(\mathbb{G}) \longrightarrow \mathbb{R}^T \tag{1.209}$$

*is a **generalized random variable**, and is **measurable** with respect to uncertainty algebra $\mathbb{G}$, or is $\mathbb{G}$**-measurable**, if the inverse image of a Borel set is a generalized event in $\mathbb{G}$:*

$$\left\{f : X^T(f) \in B\right\} \in \mathbb{G}, \forall B \in \mathbb{B}^T \tag{1.210}$$

and, therefore,

$$\textbf{\textit{GenProb}}\left(X^T \in B\right) = \textbf{\textit{GenProb}}\left(\left\{f : X^T(f) \in B\right\}\right), \forall B \in \mathbb{B}^T \tag{1.211}$$

In other words, a generalized random variable X is $\mathbb{G}$-measurable if the uncertainty algebra $\mathbb{G}$ is rich enough to determine X. Obviously,

$$\boldsymbol{GenProb}\left(X^T \in B\right) = \int_B \mathbf{d}\boldsymbol{GenProb}\left(x^T\right), \forall B \in \mathbb{B}^T \tag{1.212}$$

and

$$\begin{aligned} \boldsymbol{GenProb}\left(X^T \in \mathbb{R}^T\right) &= \int_{\mathbb{R}^T} \mathbf{d}\boldsymbol{GenProb}\left(x^T\right) \\ &= \boldsymbol{GenProb}\left(\mathbf{Span}\left(\mathbb{G}\right)\right) = \aleph \end{aligned} \tag{1.213}$$

Definition 1.29 *The* ***cumulative generalized probability*** $\boldsymbol{CumulGenProb}_{X^T}$ *of generalized random variable* X^T *is*

$$\begin{aligned} & \boldsymbol{CumulGenProb}_{X^T}\left(x_1, x_2, ..., x_T\right) \\ = \; & \boldsymbol{GenProb}\left(X_1 \leq x_1, X_2 \leq x_2, ..., X_T \leq x_T\right) \\ = \; & \int_{-\infty}^{x_1} \int_{-\infty}^{x_2} \cdots \int_{-\infty}^{x_T} \mathbf{d}\boldsymbol{GenProb}\left(X^T = \left(x_1, x_2, ..., x_T\right)\right) \end{aligned} \tag{1.214}$$

Definition 1.30 *A generalized random variable X is* ***discrete*** *if there is a countable Borel set support* (X) *that is a support for its generalized probability; i.e., if its generalized probability is determined by a* ***generalized probability mass function***

$$\boldsymbol{GenProbMass}_{X^T} : \mathbb{R}^T \longrightarrow \mathbb{R} \tag{1.215}$$

such that

$$\boldsymbol{GenProb}\left(X^T \in B\right) = \sum_{x \in B \cap \boldsymbol{support}(X)} \boldsymbol{GenProbMass}_{X^T}(x), \forall B \in \mathbb{B}^T \tag{1.216}$$

and

$$\begin{aligned} \boldsymbol{GenProb}\left(X^T \in \mathbb{R}^T\right) &= \sum_{x \in \boldsymbol{support}(X)} \boldsymbol{GenProbMass}_{X^T}(x) \\ &= \boldsymbol{GenProb}\left(\mathbf{Span}\left(\mathbb{G}\right)\right) = \aleph \end{aligned} \tag{1.217}$$

Definition 1.31 *The* ***Lebesgue measure*** *on an Euclidean space* $\mathbb{R}^T$ *is such that a measure of a cuboid in* $\mathbb{R}^T$ *is the volume of the cuboid:*

$$\lambda\left(\left[a, b\right]\right) = \prod_{t=1}^{T} \left(b_t - a_t\right), a, b \in \mathbb{R}^T, b_t \geq a_t \tag{1.218}$$

Definition 1.32 *A generalized random variable is* ***absolutely continuous with respect to the Lebesgue measure*** λ *— or simply* ***continuous*** *— if the generalized* *probability of the generalized random variable taking values in a set of Lebesgue measure zero is also zero:*

$$\lambda(B) = 0 \Longrightarrow \boldsymbol{GenProb}\left(X^T \in B\right) = 0, \forall B \in \mathcal{B}\left(\mathbb{R}^T\right) \tag{1.219}$$

For instance, any generalized random variable whose generalized probability is determined by a ***generalized probability density function****, such as normal, lognormal, exponential, or uniform, is continuous; i.e., for such a random variable, there exists a generalized probability density function*

$$\boldsymbol{GenProbDensity} : \mathbb{R}^T \longrightarrow \mathbb{R} \tag{1.220}$$

such that

$$\boldsymbol{GenProb}\left(X^T \in B\right) = \int_B \boldsymbol{GenProbDensity}(x)\, \mathbf{d}x, \forall B \in \mathcal{B}\left(\mathbb{R}^T\right) \tag{1.221}$$

and, therefore,

$$\begin{aligned} & \boldsymbol{GenProbDensity}_{(X_1,X_2,\ldots X_T)}\left((x_1,x_2,\ldots,x_T)\right) \\ = & \frac{\partial}{\partial x_1}\frac{\partial}{\partial x_2}\cdots\frac{\partial}{\partial x_T}\boldsymbol{CumulGenProb}_{(X_1,X_2,\ldots X_T)}\left((x_1,x_2,\ldots,x_T)\right) \\ = & \frac{\partial}{\partial x_1}\frac{\partial}{\partial x_2}\cdots\frac{\partial}{\partial x_T}\boldsymbol{GenProb}\left(X_1 \le x_1, X_2 \le x_2, \ldots, X_T \le x_T\right) \end{aligned} \tag{1.222}$$

and

$$\begin{aligned} \boldsymbol{GenProbDensity}_{X_n}(x_n) &= \frac{\partial}{\partial x_n}\boldsymbol{CumulGenProb}_{X_n}(x_n) \\ &= \frac{\partial}{\partial x_n}\boldsymbol{GenProb}\left(X_n \le x_n\right) \end{aligned} \tag{1.223}$$

and

$$\begin{aligned} \boldsymbol{GenProb}\left(X \in \mathbb{R}^T\right) &= \int_{\mathbb{R}^T} \boldsymbol{GenProbDensity}(x)\, \mathbf{d}x \\ &= \aleph = \boldsymbol{GenProb}\left(\mathbf{Span}\left(\mathbb{G}\right)\right) \end{aligned} \tag{1.224}$$

1.3.7 Expectation of a Generalized Random Variable

Expectation of a generalized random variable is a generalization of the notion of a weighted average.

Definition 1.33 ***Expectation*** *of a generalized random variable X on* $\mathbb{R}^T$ *exists if*

$$\aleph_n = \int_{\mathbb{R}} \mathbf{d}\boldsymbol{GenProb}\left(X_n = x_n\right) > 0 \text{ for each } n \tag{1.225}$$

and, if,

$$\int_{\mathbb{R}} |x_n| \,\mathbf{d}\boldsymbol{GenProb}\left(X_n = x_n\right) \text{ exists for each } n \tag{1.226}$$

and, is equal to

$$\boldsymbol{E}\left(X_n\right) = \frac{\int_{\mathbb{R}} x_n \mathbf{d}\boldsymbol{GenProb}\left(X_n = x_n\right)}{\aleph_n} \text{ for each } n \tag{1.227}$$

Definition 1.34 *Expectation of a discrete generalized random variable X on $\mathbb{R}^T$ exists if*

$$\aleph_n = \sum_{x_n} \boldsymbol{GenProb}\left(X_n = x_n\right) > 0 \text{ for each } n \tag{1.228}$$

$$\sum_{x_n} |x_n| \,\boldsymbol{GenProb}\left(X_n = x_n\right) \text{ exists for each } n \tag{1.229}$$

and is equal to

$$\boldsymbol{E}\left(X_n\right) = \frac{\sum_{x_n} \left(x_n\right) \boldsymbol{GenProb}\left(X_n = x_n\right)}{\aleph_n} \text{ for each } n \tag{1.230}$$

Definition 1.35 *Expectation of a continuous generalized random variable X on $\mathbb{R}^T$ exists if*

$$\aleph_n = \int_{\mathbb{R}} \boldsymbol{GenProbDensity}_{X_n}\left(x_n\right) \mathbf{d}x > 0 \text{ for each } n \tag{1.231}$$

$$\int_{\mathbb{R}} |x_n| \,\boldsymbol{GenProbDensity}_{X_n}\left(x_n\right) \mathbf{d}x \text{ exists for each } n \tag{1.232}$$

and is equal to

$$\boldsymbol{E}\left(X_n\right) = \frac{\int_{\mathbb{R}} \left(x_n\right) \boldsymbol{GenProbDensity}_{X_n}\left(x_n\right) \mathbf{d}x}{\aleph_n} \text{ for each } n \tag{1.233}$$

1.3.8 Bayes Theorem for Generalized Events

Theorem 1.3 ***(Bayes Theorem)*** *For $A, B \in \mathbb{G}$ generalized events such that*

$$\boldsymbol{GenProb}(A) \neq 0, \boldsymbol{GenProb}(B) \neq 0 \tag{1.234}$$

then

$$\begin{aligned} \boldsymbol{GenProb}(A \mid B) &= \frac{\boldsymbol{GenProb}(B \mid A)}{\boldsymbol{GenProb}(B)} \boldsymbol{GenProb}(A) \\ &= \frac{\boldsymbol{GenProb}(A)}{\boldsymbol{GenProb}(B)} \boldsymbol{GenProb}(B \mid A) \end{aligned} \tag{1.235}$$

1.3.9 *Value Ratio of Evidence*

If we are trying to test hypothesis $A \in \mathbb{W}$, and if we have evidence $B \in \mathbb{W}$, we can compute the **Value Ratio of Evidence** $B \in \mathbb{W}$ **for Hypothesis** A to determine if the value of the evidence $B \in \mathbb{W}$ in favor of hypothesis $A \in \mathbb{W}$, against hypothesis $A \in \mathbb{W}$, or neutral with respect to hypothesis $A \in \mathbb{W}$. In Section 1.2.6, we have shown some simple examples, and there are many such examples in finance that we will discuss later in the context of market efficiency, and also in other fields, such as litigation, pharmaceuticals, and medicine.

Definition 1.36 *Consider hypothesis $A \in \mathbb{G}$ and evidence $B \in \mathbb{G}$ such that **GenProb**$(B) > 0$. Then, **GenProb**(A) is the ex ante generalized probability of hypothesis A, **GenProb**$(A \mid B)$ is the ex post generalized probability of hypothesis A given evidence $B \in \mathbb{G}$, and the **Value Ratio of Evidence** B **for Hypothesis** A is*

$$\textbf{\textit{Value Ratio of Evidence}}\,(B; A) = \frac{\textbf{\textit{GenProb}}\,(B \mid A)}{\textbf{\textit{GenProb}}(B)} \tag{1.236}$$

and therefore, Bayes Theorem can be restated as

$$\begin{aligned} \textbf{\textit{ExPost GenProb}}\,(A; B) = & \,(\textbf{\textit{Value Ratio of Evidence}}\,(B; A)) \\ & (\textbf{\textit{ExAnte GenProb}}\,(A)) \end{aligned} \tag{1.237}$$

Corollary 1.7

- *If value ratio of evidence B for hypothesis A is greater than 1, it means that evidence B is in favor of hypothesis A.*
- *If value ratio of evidence B for hypothesis A is less than 1, it means that evidence B is against hypothesis A.*
- *If value ratio of evidence B for hypothesis A equals 1, it means that evidence B is neutral with respect to hypothesis A.*
- *Higher the value ratio of evidence B for hypothesis A, the stronger the value of evidence B in favor of hypothesis A.*

Corollary 1.8 *If evidence $B \in \mathbb{G}$ is a realization of a generalized random variable absolutely continuous with respect to the Lebesgue measure on $\mathbb{R}^T$, i.e.,*

$$\textbf{\textit{GenProb}}\,(B = b) = 0, \forall b \in \mathbb{R}^T \tag{1.238}$$

then Bayes Theorem can be restated as follows:

$$\begin{aligned} \textbf{\textit{GenProb}}\,(A \mid b) &= \frac{\textbf{\textit{GenProbDensity}}_{B|A}\,(b \mid A)}{\textbf{\textit{GenProbDensity}}_{B}\,(b)} \textbf{\textit{GenProb}}\,(A) \\ &= \frac{\textbf{\textit{GenProbDensity}}_{B|A}\,(b \mid A)}{\int_a \textbf{\textit{GenProbDensity}}_{B|A}\,(b \mid A = a)\, \mathbf{d}\textbf{\textit{GenProb}}\,(a)} \textbf{\textit{GenProb}}\,(A) \\ &= \textbf{\textit{Value Ratio of Evidence}}\,(b; A)\, \textbf{\textit{GenProb}}\,(A) \end{aligned} \tag{1.239}$$

where Value Ratio of Evidence B = b for Hypothesis A is

$$\textit{\textbf{Value Ratio of Evidence}}\,(b;A) = \frac{\textit{\textbf{GenProbDensity}}_{B|A}\,(b \mid A)}{\int_a \textit{\textbf{GenProbDensity}}_{B|A}\,(b \mid A=a)\,\mathbf{d}\textit{\textbf{GenProb}}\,(a)} \tag{1.240}$$

Corollary 1.9 *If hypothesis* $A \in \mathbb{G}$ *is a realization of a random variable absolutely continuous with respect to the Lebesgue measure on* $\mathbb{R}^S$ *— i.e.,* $\textit{\textbf{Prob}}\,(A=a) = 0, \forall a \in \mathbb{R}^S$ *— then,*

$$\begin{aligned}\textit{\textbf{GenProbDensity}}_{A|B}\,(a \mid B) &= \frac{\textit{\textbf{GenProb}}\,(B \mid a)}{\textit{\textbf{GenProb}}(B)}\textit{\textbf{GenProbDensity}}_A\,(a)\\ &= \textit{\textbf{Value Ratio of Evidence}}\,(B;a)\,\textit{\textbf{GenProbDensity}}_A\,(a)\end{aligned} \tag{1.241}$$

where Value Ratio of Evidence B for Hypothesis A = a is

$$\begin{aligned}\textit{\textbf{Value Ratio of Evidence}}\,(B;a) &= \frac{\textit{\textbf{GenProb}}\,(B \mid a)}{\textit{\textbf{GenProb}}(B)}\\ &= \frac{\int_B \mathbf{d}\textit{\textbf{GenProb}}\,(b \mid a)}{\int_B \mathbf{d}\textit{\textbf{GenProb}}\,(b)}\end{aligned} \tag{1.242}$$

Corollary 1.10 *If hypothesis* $A \in \mathbb{G}$ *and evidence* $B \in \mathbb{G}$ *are realizations of generalized random variables absolutely continuous with respect to the Lebesgue measure on* $\mathbb{R}^S$ *and* $\mathbb{R}^T$ *— i.e.,* $\textit{\textbf{GenProb}}\,(A=a) = 0, \forall a \in \mathbb{R}^S$ *and* $\textit{\textbf{GenProb}}\,(B=b) = 0, \forall b \in \mathbb{R}^T$*— then,*

$$\begin{aligned}\textit{\textbf{GenProbDensity}}_{A|B}\,(a \mid b) &= \frac{\textit{\textbf{GenProbDensity}}_{B|A}\,(b \mid a)}{\textit{\textbf{GenProbDensity}}_B\,(b)}\textit{\textbf{GenProbDensity}}_A\,(a)\\ &= \textit{\textbf{Value Ratio of Evidence}}\,(b;a)\,\textit{\textbf{GenProbDensity}}_A\,(a)\end{aligned} \tag{1.243}$$

where Value Ratio of Evidence B = b for Hypothesis A = a is

$$\textit{\textbf{Value Ratio of Evidence}}\,(b;a) = \frac{\textit{\textbf{GenProbDensity}}_{B|A}\,(b \mid a)}{\textit{\textbf{GenProbDensity}}_B\,(b)} \tag{1.244}$$

Example 1.18 *Consider stock price,*

$$S_t \mid \{S_t > 0\} \sim \boldsymbol{LN}(0,1) \tag{1.245}$$

$$\textit{such that } \aleph = \boldsymbol{GenProb}\,(S_t > 0) \in [0,1]$$

i.e., stock return,

$$\ln S_t \mid \{\ln S_t \in \mathbb{R}\} \sim N(0,1) \tag{1.246}$$

$$\textit{such that } \aleph = \boldsymbol{GenProb}\,\{\ln S_t \in \mathbb{R}\} \in [0,1]$$

$$\begin{aligned} \boldsymbol{CumulGenProb}_{S_t}(s_t) &= \boldsymbol{GenProb}\,(S_t \leq s_t) \\ &= \boldsymbol{GenProb}\,(\ln S_t \leq \ln s_t) \end{aligned}$$

$$\begin{aligned} \boldsymbol{CumulGenProb}_{S_t \mid \{S_t > 0\}}(s_t) &= \boldsymbol{GenProb}\,(S_t \leq s_t) \\ &= \boldsymbol{GenProb}\,(\ln S_t \leq \ln s_t) \end{aligned}$$

Consider hypothesis,

$$A = \{S_t : \ln S_t > 0\} \tag{1.247}$$

and evidence,

$$B = \{S_t : \ln S_t > 10\%\} \tag{1.248}$$

then,

$$\boldsymbol{GenProb}\,(B \mid A) = \frac{\boldsymbol{GenProb}\,(B \cap A)}{\boldsymbol{GenProb}\,(A)} \textit{ if } \boldsymbol{GenProb}\,(A) > 0 \tag{1.249}$$

$$= \frac{\boldsymbol{GenProb}\,(B)}{\boldsymbol{GenProb}\,(A)}, \textit{ since } B \subset A$$

$$= \frac{\boldsymbol{GenProb}\,\{S_t : \ln S_t > 0.1\}}{\boldsymbol{GenProb}\,\{S_t : \ln S_t > 0\}}$$

$$= \frac{\boldsymbol{GenProb}\,\{S_t : -\infty < \ln S_t < \infty\} - \boldsymbol{GenProb}\,\{S_t : -\infty < \ln S_t \leq 0.1\}}{\boldsymbol{GenProb}\,\{S_t : -\infty < \ln S_t < \infty\} - \boldsymbol{GenProb}\,\{S_t : \ln S_t \leq 0\}}$$

$$= \frac{(1 - \boldsymbol{Prob}\,\{S_t : \ln S_t \leq 0.1\})\,\boldsymbol{GenProb}\,(S_t > 0)}{(1 - \boldsymbol{Prob}\,\{S_t : \ln S_t \leq 0\})\,\boldsymbol{GenProb}\,(S_t > 0)}$$

$$if\,\aleph = \textbf{\textit{GenProb}}\,(S_t > 0) > 0$$

$$= \textbf{\textit{Prob}}\,(B \mid A)\;\; if\,\aleph = \textbf{\textit{GenProb}}\,(S_t > 0) > 0$$

since

$$\begin{aligned} \textbf{\textit{Prob}}\,(B \mid A) &= \frac{\textbf{\textit{Prob}}\,(B \cap A)}{\textbf{\textit{Prob}}\,(A)} \\ &= \frac{\textbf{\textit{Prob}}\,(B)}{\textbf{\textit{Prob}}\,(A)},\; since\; B \subset A \\ &= \frac{\textbf{\textit{Prob}}\,\{S_t : \ln S_t > 0.1\}}{\textbf{\textit{Prob}}\,\{S_t : \ln S_t > 0\}} \\ &= \frac{1 - \textbf{\textit{Prob}}\,\{S_t : \ln S_t \le 0.1\}}{1 - \textbf{\textit{Prob}}\,\{S_t : \ln S_t \le 0\}} \end{aligned} \tag{1.250}$$

In addition,

$$\begin{aligned} \textbf{\textit{GenProb}}\,(B) &= \textbf{\textit{GenProb}}\,\{S_t : \ln S_t > 0.1\} \\ &= \textbf{\textit{Prob}}\,(B)\,\textbf{\textit{GenProb}}\,(S_t > 0) \\ &= \aleph \textbf{\textit{Prob}}\,(B) \end{aligned} \tag{1.251}$$

and therefore,

$$\textbf{\textit{Value Ratio of Evidence}}\,(B; A)\;\; under\; \textbf{\textit{GenProb}} \tag{1.252}$$

$$= \frac{\textbf{\textit{GenProb}}\,(B \mid A)}{\textbf{\textit{GenProb}}(B)}$$

$$= \frac{\textbf{\textit{Prob}}\,(B \mid A)}{\aleph \textbf{\textit{Prob}}\,(B)}\;\; if\,\aleph = \textbf{\textit{GenProb}}\,(S_t > 0) > 0$$

since

$$\textbf{\textit{Value Ratio of Evidence}}\,(B; A)\;\; under\; \textbf{\textit{Prob}}\; is = \frac{\textbf{\textit{Prob}}\,(B \mid A)}{\textbf{\textit{Prob}}\,(B)}$$

and therefore,

$$\textbf{\textit{Value Ratio of Evidence}}\,(B; A)\;\; under\; \textbf{\textit{GenProb}} \tag{1.253}$$

$$= \frac{\textbf{\textit{Value Ratio of Evidence}}\,(B; A)\;\; under\; \textbf{\textit{Prob}}}{\textbf{\textit{GenProb}}\,(S_t > 0)}$$

$$if\,\textbf{\textit{GenProb}}\,(S_t > 0) > 0$$

and therefore,

$$\textbf{\textit{Value Ratio of Evidence}}\,(B; A)\;\; under\; \textbf{\textit{GenProb}} = \frac{2}{\aleph},\;\; if\,\aleph > 0 \tag{1.254}$$

and therefore, Bayes Theorem can be restated as,

$$\textbf{\textit{ExPost GenProb}}\,(A;B) = \frac{\mathbf{2}}{\aleph}\textbf{\textit{ExAnte GenProb}}\,(A) \tag{1.255}$$

$$\textit{if}\ \aleph > 0$$

and therefore, evidence,

$$B = \{S_t : \ln S_t > 10\%\} \tag{1.256}$$

is in favor of hypothesis,

$$A = \{S_t : \ln S_t > 0\} \tag{1.257}$$

if,

$$\textbf{\textit{Value Ratio of Evidence}}\,(B;A)\ \textit{under}\ \textbf{\textit{GenProb}} = \frac{2}{\aleph} > 1$$

i.e.,

$$\textit{if}\ \aleph > 0\ \textit{and since}\ \aleph < 2$$

1.3.10 Degenerate Prior Generalized Probability

If

$$\textbf{\textit{GenProb}}\,(A) = 0 \tag{1.258}$$

then

$$\begin{aligned} \textbf{\textit{GenProb}}\,(A \mid B) &= \frac{\textbf{\textit{GenProb}}\,(A \cap B)}{\textbf{\textit{GenProb}}\,(B)} \\ &\leq \frac{\textbf{\textit{GenProb}}\,(A)}{\textbf{\textit{GenProb}}\,(B)} = 0 \end{aligned} \tag{1.259}$$

If

$$\textbf{\textit{GenProb}}\,(A) = \aleph = \textbf{\textit{GenProb}}\,(\mathbf{Span}\,(\mathbb{G})) \tag{1.260}$$

then, since

$$\aleph = \textbf{\textit{GenProb}}\,(\mathbf{Span}\,(\mathbb{G})) = 0 \tag{1.261}$$

and

$$\begin{aligned} &\textbf{\textit{GenProb}}\,(((\mathbf{Span}\,(\mathbb{G}) \setminus A) \cap B) \cap B) \\ \leq\ &\textbf{\textit{GenProb}}\,(((\mathbf{Span}\,(\mathbb{G}) \setminus A) \cap B)) = 0 \end{aligned} \tag{1.262}$$

one has

$$\begin{aligned} \boldsymbol{GenProb}(A \mid B) &= \frac{\boldsymbol{GenProb}(A \cap B)}{\boldsymbol{GenProb}(B)} \\ &= \frac{\boldsymbol{GenProb}(A \cap B)}{\boldsymbol{GenProb}((A \cap B) \cup ((\mathbf{Span}(\mathbb{G}) \setminus A) \cap B))} \\ &= \frac{\boldsymbol{GenProb}(A \cap B)}{\boldsymbol{GenProb}(A \cap B) + \boldsymbol{GenProb}((\mathbf{Span}(\mathbb{G}) \setminus A) \cap B)} \\ &= \boldsymbol{GenProb}(\mathbf{Span}(\mathbb{G})) \end{aligned} \tag{1.263}$$

1.3.11 Conditional Expectation

Conditional expectation, given a particular uncertainty algebra, is used to model the impact of information.

Definition 1.37 ***Conditional expectation*** *of a generalized random variable X, given uncertainty algebra $\mathbb{I}$, exists if*

$$\int_{\mathbb{R}^T} \mathbf{d}\boldsymbol{GenProb}(x \mid \mathbb{I}) > 0 \tag{1.264}$$

and

$$\int_{\mathbb{R}^T} |x|\, \mathbf{d}\boldsymbol{GenProb}(x \mid \mathbb{I}) \;\; \textit{exists} \tag{1.265}$$

and

$$\boldsymbol{E}(X \mid \mathbb{I}) = \frac{\int_{\mathbb{R}^T} x\mathbf{d}\boldsymbol{GenProb}(x \mid \mathbb{I})}{\int_{\mathbb{R}^T} \mathbf{d}\boldsymbol{GenProb}(x \mid \mathbb{I})} \tag{1.266}$$

Lemma 1.6 *One can also provide a more primitive and equivalent definition of conditional expectation of X, given uncertainty algebra $\mathbb{I}$,*

$$\boldsymbol{E}(X \mid \mathbb{I}) \tag{1.267}$$

is an $\mathbb{I}$-measurable generalized random variable such that

$$\int_{G} \mathbf{d}\boldsymbol{GenProb}(x \mid \mathbb{I}) > 0, \forall G \in \mathbb{I} \tag{1.268}$$

$$\int_{G} \boldsymbol{E}(X \mid \mathbb{I})\, \mathbf{d}\boldsymbol{GenProb}(x) = \frac{\int_{G} x\mathbf{d}\boldsymbol{GenProb}(x)}{\int_{G} \mathbf{d}\boldsymbol{GenProb}(x \mid \mathbb{I})}, \forall G \in \mathbb{I} \tag{1.269}$$

Consider an uncertainty algebra that consists only of the known universe

$$\mathbb{G}_{it}^{Naïve} = \{\mathbf{Span}(\mathbb{G})\} \tag{1.270}$$

then at time t, i only knows if the known universe has occurred; in other words, $\mathbb{G}_{it}^{Naïve} = \{\mathbf{Span}(\mathbb{G})\}$ represents complete lack of information in the context of the known universe, and is the smallest possible uncertainty algebra on $\mathcal{F}$. Then, conditional expectation, given total lack of information, equals unconditional expectation

$$\boldsymbol{E}\left(X \mid \mathbb{G}_{it}^{Naïve}\right) = \boldsymbol{E}(X) \tag{1.271}$$

Consider an uncertainty algebra that consists of every single subset of the known universe of outcomes

$$\mathbb{G}_{it}^{Full} = 2^{\mathbf{Span}(\mathbb{G})} \tag{1.272}$$

then at time t, i knows exactly which outcome has occurred in the context of the known universe; in other words, $\mathbb{G}_{it}^{Full}$ represents full information in the context of the known universe, and conditional expectation, given full information in the context of the known universe

$$\boldsymbol{E}\left(X \mid \mathbb{G}_{it}^{Full}\right) \tag{1.273}$$

In general, therefore, conditioning on different uncertainty algebras allows one to measure reality with respect to different information scenarios.

Lemma 1.7 *If the generalized probability of the known universe*

$$\aleph = \boldsymbol{GenProb}(\mathbf{Span}(\mathbb{G})) > 0 \tag{1.274}$$

then unconditional generalized probability, normalized by the generalized probability of the known universe, is the expectation of the conditional generalized probabilities

$$\begin{aligned} \boldsymbol{E}_Z(\boldsymbol{GenProb}(B \mid Z)) &= \frac{\boldsymbol{GenProb}(B)}{\boldsymbol{GenProb}(\mathbf{Span}(\mathbb{G}))} \\ &= \frac{\int_z \boldsymbol{GenProb}(B \mid z)\,\mathbf{d}\boldsymbol{GenProb}(z)}{\boldsymbol{GenProb}(\mathbf{Span}(\mathbb{G}))} \end{aligned} \tag{1.275}$$

$$\begin{aligned} \boldsymbol{E}_{Z|z\in\widetilde{Z}}(\boldsymbol{GenProb}(B \mid Z)) &= \frac{\boldsymbol{GenProb}\left(B \mid z \in \widetilde{Z}\right)}{\boldsymbol{GenProb}(\mathbf{Span}(\mathbb{G}))} \\ &= \frac{\int_{z\in\widetilde{Z}} \boldsymbol{GenProb}(B \mid z)\,\mathbf{d}\boldsymbol{GenProb}_{Z|z\in\widetilde{Z}}(z)}{\boldsymbol{GenProb}(\mathbf{Span}(\mathbb{G}))} \\ &= \frac{\int_{z\in\widetilde{Z}} \boldsymbol{GenProb}(B \mid z)\,\mathbf{d}\boldsymbol{GenProb}_{Z|z\in\widetilde{Z}}(z)}{\aleph} \end{aligned} \tag{1.276}$$

Lemma 1.8 *For generalized event A, consider the* ***indicator random variable***

$$\mathbf{1}_A(\omega) = \left\{ \begin{array}{lll} 1 & \textit{if} & \omega \in A \\ 0 & \textit{otherwise} & \end{array} \right\} \tag{1.277}$$

then the unconditional expectation of the indicator random variable is the relevant unconditional generalized probability

$$\boldsymbol{E}(\mathbf{1}_A) = \boldsymbol{GenProb}(A) \tag{1.278}$$

and the conditional expectation of the indicator random variable is the relevant conditional generalized probability

$$\boldsymbol{E}(\mathbf{1}_A \mid \mathbb{I}) = \boldsymbol{GenProb}(A \mid \mathbb{I}) \tag{1.279}$$

where $\mathbb{I}$ *is the uncertainty algebra generated by the indicator random variable* $\mathbf{1}_A$.

Summary 1.2 *The above result also provides us with a characterization of conditional probability even when the event conditioned upon has zero probability.*

1.4 Philosophical Underpinnings

The *Ṛg Veda*, the most ancient text of Hinduism, says: *ekam sat viprāh vahudhā vadanti*, which translates to the truth is one, sages say differently, and in our mathematical modeling, it implies that there is no such thing as "your truth" or "my truth," or an "emotional truth," or an "alternative truth;" the truth is absolute, but we mere mortals, because of our different informational scenarios and limited reasoning capabilities, perceive and interpret the truth differently. This absolute truth was referred to, by Ādiguru Śankarācārya, in his development of *Advaita Vedānta*, as *brahma*, and to one's informational and reasoning imperfections as *māyā* (relativity) — "*brahma satya jagat mithyā*" (the truth is absolute, what one perceives contains measurement error, in the language of this book). Please see, for instance, Vivekananda (1955).

I saw a Facebook post a few years ago with a photograph purporting to show Mohandas Gandhi with the Fourteenth Dalai Lama (Tenzin Gyatso) as a grown man. When I pointed out that Gandhi died in 1948, when the Dalai Lama would have been twelve, that the Dalai Lama went to India for the first time in 1956, and that, therefore, the photograph could not be accurate, the poster replied "I don't care, this is *my* truth!" — "my truth" is not the truth, it is fiction, please see Galston (2024). "In [Hasan] Minhaj's approach to comedy, he leans heavily on his own experience as an Asian American and Muslim American, telling harrowing stories of law-enforcement entrapment and personal threats. For many of his fans, he has become an avatar for the power of representation in entertainment. But, after many weeks of trying, I had been unable to confirm some of the stories that he had told onstage. When we met on a recent afternoon, at a comedy club in the West Village, Minhaj acknowledged, for the first time, that many of the anecdotes he related in his Netflix specials were untrue. Still, he said that he stood by his work. 'Every story in my style is built around a seed of truth, he said. 'My comedy ... is seventy per cent emotional truth — this happened — and then thirty per cent hyperbole, exaggeration, fiction.' ... When it came to his stage shows, he told me, 'the emotional truth is first. The factual truth is secondary'" Malone (2023) — "emotional truth" is, again, not the truth, it is fiction. Similarly, the notion of "truth" is meaningless to a litigator; all that matters to a litigator is what a litigator can convince a "fact finder" or "trier of fact" (typically, a judge or a jury) to be the truth. Also, truth is not determined by majority or even by consensus, for instance, U.S. Supreme Court Justice Oliver Wendell Holmes's dissent in *Abrams v. United States* (1919) that "the best test of truth is the power of the thought to get itself accepted in the competition of the market" is entirely contrary to the scientific method. See, for example, the "Paradox of the Chinese Emperor's Nose," as explained by Professor Richard Feynman, Nobel Prize in Physics, 1965: "Nobody was permitted to see the Emperor of China, and the question was, 'What is the length of the Emperor of China's nose?' To find out, you go all over the country asking people what they think the length of the Emperor of China's nose is, and you ... [combine them] ... And that would be very 'accurate' because you [combined the information from] so many people. But it's no way to find anything out; when you have a very wide range of people who contribute without looking carefully at it, you don't improve your knowledge of the situation by [combining]" (Feynman (1985), in which, Professor Feynman provides strong critiques of "cargo cult science" and collective ignorance). This is exactly the fallacy underlying the Wikipedia approach of content being written and edited by a large number of people who might not know much about the relevant topic or might not put in much effort in acquiring any information about the relevant topic. When the book, *Hundert Autoren gegen Einstein* (a hundred authors against Einstein), was published (Israel et al., 1931), Professor Albert Einstein, Nobel Prize in physics, 1921, is supposed to have responded that "If I were wrong, then one would have been enough," see Hawking (1998).

As the late legendary U.S. Senator Daniel Patrick Moynihan (D., NY) insisted, "You are entitled to your opinion ... but you are not entitled to your own facts," and it is fundamentally unscientific when anything that contradicts, or is even inconsistent with, a preapproved or preferred narrative is labeled "misinformation" or "disinformation" or "violence against the truth."Also relevant are the tragic lies by Jason Arday, see Hennessey (2026).

The framework in this book is perfectly compatible with "Schrödinger's Cat" and the "Copenhagen Interpretation" in quantum mechanics — please see, for instance, Schrödinger (1935) and much more recently, Yu et al. (2025) — without needing to allow for the absurd notion of "superposition," that of the cat being simultaneously alive and dead, whereas our framework very reasonably models the cat being alive and the cat being dead as two mutually exclusive generalized events with generalized probabilities that depend on the uncertainty algebras that we are conditioning on. The "quantum" approach to probability — please see, for example, Bai et al. (2025) — is unnecessarily over-complicated for our purposes without providing any insights or applications. Also, the framework in this book is different from, although still compatible with, "relativism" in general and "epistemic relativism" in particular, and also consistent with the Jaina framework of "*Anekāntavāda*" (not-one sidedness) — please see Baghramian and Carter (2021). And finally, this framework can be understood as a celebration of "*satyameva jayate*" (the truth alone triumphs) in the *Muṇḍaka Upaniṣad* — please see Vivekananda (1955).

The following poem by the American poet John Godfrey Saxe is a funny take on the old Buddhist (narrated, for example, in *Tittha Sutta* and *Canki Sutta*), Jaina (told, for example, in *Syādvādamanjari*), and Hindu story of how six blind men engaging with an elephant had limited and different information and so perceived the elephant very differently. It would not be an exaggeration to say that civilization begins when one realizes that people who disagree do not necessarily have horns. "The theologian H. Richard Niebuhr (younger brother of Reinhold) explained the fallacy [of monomania] thus: 'There is no greater barrier to understanding than the assumption that the standpoint which we happen to occupy is a universal [or the only correct] one.' It is an error embedded in human nature." Morrow (2016). The point to note here is that each blind individual's information about the elephant is such that (s)he could not have possibly known the entire universe of outcomes, so the standard formulation of events, sigma-algebras, and probability (as described in Section 1.2) does not apply here at all, whereas the developments in this book of generalized events, uncertainty algebras, and generalized probability do apply.

"The Blind Men and the Elephant"
By John Godfrey Saxe
I.
It was six men of Indostan
To learning much inclined,
Who went to see the Elephant
(Though all of them were blind),
That each by observation
Might satisfy his mind.
II.
The First approached the Elephant,
And happening to fall
Against his broad and sturdy side,
At once began to bawl:

"God bless me! — but the Elephant
Is very like a wall!"
III.
The Second, feeling of the tusk,
Cried: "Ho! — what have we here
So very round and smooth and sharp?
To me 't is mighty clear
This wonder of an Elephant
Is very like a spear!"
IV.
The Third approached the animal,
And happening to take
The squirming trunk within his hands,
Thus boldly up and spake:
"I see," quoth he, "the Elephant
Is very like a snake!"
V.
The Fourth reached out his eager hand,
And felt about the knee.
"What most this wondrous beast is like
Is mighty plain," quoth he;
"'T is clear enough the Elephant
Is very like a tree!"
VI.
The Fifth, who chanced to touch the ear,
Said: "E'en the blindest man
Can tell what this resembles most;
Deny the fact who can,
This marvel of an Elephant
Is very like a fan!"
VII.
The Sixth no sooner had begun
About the beast to grope,
Than, seizing on the swinging tail
That fell within his scope,
"I see," quoth he, "the Elephant
Is very like a rope!"
VIII.
And so these men of Indostan
Disputed loud and long,
Each in his own opinion

Exceeding stiff and strong,
Though each was partly in the right,
And all were in the wrong!
MORAL.
So, oft in theologic wars
The disputants, I ween,
Rail on in utter ignorance
Of what each other mean,
And prate about an Elephant
Not one of them has seen!

1.5 Reconciliation between Risk and Uncertainty

It is important for us to understand the connection between uncertainty and corresponding risk, even though, as the following Example 1.19 demonstrates, they can represent quite different situations.

Example 1.19 *Consider the explosive allegations in a March 26, 2025, article in the Wall Street Journal that "soon after President Trump won the presidential election in November, British drugmaker GSK brought an unusual claim to federal prosecutors in Manhattan, according to people familiar with the matter. A senior GSK scientist, who formerly worked at rival Pfizer, had told GSK colleagues that Pfizer delayed announcing the success of its Covid vaccine in 2020 until after that year's election" (Dawsey, et al. (2025).*

Example 1.20 *As we discussed earlier, the COVID-19 Pandemic of 2020-22 was an unknown unknown for many (if not most), something that would not have been part of the span of the uncertainty algebra for most observers, and therefore, was a situation of uncertainty, whereas the different possible outcomes of the U.S. presidential election of 2020, as of the day before the election, were known unknowns, and therefore, could be modeled by risk.*

Lemma 1.9 *If the set of generalized events, an uncertainty algebra, $\mathbb{G}$, is a subset of the set of events, a risk algebra, $\mathbb{W}$, with probability measure **Prob**, then the conditional probability of an event, given the entire universe of known unknowns, equals the unconditional probability of the event*

$$\boldsymbol{Prob}\left(A \mid \mathrm{Span}\left(\mathbb{G}\right)\right) = \boldsymbol{Prob}\left(A\right), \forall A \in \mathbb{G} \tag{1.280}$$

Definition 1.38 *If the set of generalized events, an uncertainty algebra, $\mathbb{G}$, with generalized probability measure **GenProb**, is a subset of the set of events, a risk algebra, $\mathbb{W}$, with probability measure **Prob**, then the generalized probability measure **GenProb** and the probability measure **Prob** are **reconciled over** $\mathbb{G}$ if* *the conditional, given the universe of known unknowns* $\boldsymbol{Span}(\mathbb{G})$*, probability and generalized probability are equal,*

$$\boldsymbol{Prob}\left(A \mid \mathbf{Span}\left(\mathbb{G}\right)\right) = \boldsymbol{GenProb}\left(A \mid \mathbf{Span}\left(\mathbb{G}\right)\right) \tag{1.281}$$

$$\forall A \in \mathbb{G}$$

and similarly, a $\mathbb{W}$*-measurable random variable X and a* $\mathbb{G}$*-measurable generalized random variable Y are* ***reconciled*** *(Casella, G., & Berger, R., 2024)* ***over***$\mathbb{G}$ *if*

$$\boldsymbol{Prob}\left(X \in A \mid X \in \mathbf{Span}\left(\mathbb{G}\right)\right) = \boldsymbol{GenProb}\left(Y \in A \mid Y \in \mathbf{Span}\left(\mathbb{G}\right)\right) \tag{1.282}$$

$$\forall A \in \mathbb{G}$$

Example 1.21 *Consider stock price,*

$$S_t \mid \{S_t > 0\} \sim \boldsymbol{LN}(0,1)$$

$$\textit{such that } \aleph_n = \boldsymbol{GenProb}\left(S_t > 0\right) \in [0,1]$$

i.e., stock return,

$$\ln S_t \mid \{\ln S_t \in \mathbb{R}\} \sim N(0,1)$$

$$\textit{such that } \aleph_n = \boldsymbol{GenProb}\left(\ln S_t \in \mathbb{R}\right) \in [0,1]$$

then

$$ProbDensity_{\ln S_t \mid \{\ln S_t \in \mathbb{R}\}}\left(\ln s_t\right) = \exp\left(-\frac{(\ln s_t)^2}{2}\right), -\infty < \ln s_t < +\infty \tag{1.283}$$

and

$$\begin{aligned}
\boldsymbol{E}\left(\ln S_t \mid \{\ln S_t \in \mathbb{R}\}\right) &= \int_{-\infty}^{+\infty} \ln s_t \exp\left(-\frac{(\ln s_t)^2}{2}\right) \mathbf{d} \ln s_t \\
&= \int_{-\infty}^{0} \ln s_t \exp\left(-\frac{(\ln s_t)^2}{2}\right) \mathbf{d} \ln s_t \\
&\quad + \int_{0}^{+\infty} \ln s_t \exp\left(-\frac{(\ln s_t)^2}{2}\right) \mathbf{d} \ln s_t \\
&= -\int_{0}^{+\infty} \ln s_t \exp\left(-\frac{(\ln s_t)^2}{2}\right) \mathbf{d} \ln s_t \\
&\quad + \int_{0}^{+\infty} \ln s_t \exp\left(-\frac{(\ln s_t)^2}{2}\right) \mathbf{d} \ln s_t \\
&= -1 + 1 = 0
\end{aligned} \tag{1.284}$$

since

$$\begin{aligned}
\boldsymbol{E}\left(|\ln S_t| \mid \{\ln S_t \in \mathbb{R}\}\right) &= \int_0^{+\infty} |\ln s_t| \exp\left(-\frac{(\ln s_t)^2}{2}\right) \mathbf{d} \ln s_t \\
&= \int_{-\infty}^{0} (-\ln s_t) \exp\left(-\frac{(\ln s_t)^2}{2}\right) \mathbf{d} \ln s_t \\
&+ \int_0^{+\infty} \ln s_t \exp\left(-\frac{(\ln s_t)^2}{2}\right) \mathbf{d} \ln s_t \\
&= \int_0^{+\infty} x \ln s_t \exp\left(-\frac{(\ln s_t)^2}{2}\right) \mathbf{d} \ln s_t \\
&+ \int_0^{+\infty} \ln s_t \exp\left(-\frac{(\ln s_t)^2}{2}\right) \mathbf{d} \ln s_t \\
&= 1 + 1 = 2 < \infty
\end{aligned} \tag{1.285}$$

since

$$\int_0^{+\infty} \ln s_t \exp\left(-\frac{(\ln s_t)^2}{2}\right) \mathbf{d} \ln s_t = 1 \tag{1.286}$$

Consider $0 < a < b$*, then*

$$\begin{aligned}
\boldsymbol{Prob}\left(\ln S_t \in (a, b)\right) &= \int_a^b ProbDensity_{\ln S_t}(\ln s_t)\, \mathbf{d} \ln s_t \\
&= \int_a^b \exp\left(-\frac{(\ln s_t)^2}{2}\right) \mathbf{d} \ln s_t
\end{aligned} \tag{1.287}$$

Consider the conditional probability of $\ln S_t$ *given* $\ln S_t > 0$*, then*

$$\begin{aligned}
ProbDensity_{\ln S_t | \ln S_t > 0}(\ln s_t) &= \frac{ProbDensity_{\ln S_t}(\ln s_t)}{\boldsymbol{Prob}\left(\ln S_t > 0\right)} \\
&= \frac{\exp\left(-\frac{(\ln s_t)^2}{2}\right)}{\frac{1}{2}} \\
&= 2 \exp\left(-\frac{(\ln s_t)^2}{2}\right), 0 < \ln s_t < +\infty
\end{aligned} \tag{1.288}$$

$$ProbDensity_{\ln S_t|\ln S_t>0}(\ln s_t) = 0, -\infty < \ln s_t < 0 \tag{1.289}$$

and

$$\begin{aligned}
\boldsymbol{E}(\ln S_t \mid \ln S_t > 0) &= \int_0^{+\infty} \ln s_t \left(2\exp\left(-\frac{(\ln s_t)^2}{2}\right)\right) \mathbf{d}\ln s_t \\
&= 2\int_0^{+\infty} \ln s_t \exp\left(-\frac{(\ln s_t)^2}{2}\right) \mathbf{d}\ln s_t \\
&= 2
\end{aligned} \tag{1.290}$$

Consider $0 < a < b$*, then*

$$\begin{aligned}
\boldsymbol{Prob}(\ln S_t \in (a,b) \mid \ln S_t > 0) &= \int_a^b ProbDensity_{S_t|S_t>0}(x)\, \mathbf{d}\ln s_t \\
&= \int_a^b 2\exp\left(-\frac{(\ln s_t)^2}{2}\right) \mathbf{d}\ln s_t \\
&= 2\boldsymbol{Prob}(\ln S_t \in (a,b))
\end{aligned} \tag{1.291}$$

Now consider the generalized random variable Y that is reconciled with $\ln S_t$ *over* $\mathcal{B}_+$*, the Borel sets of the positive reals, then*

$$\boldsymbol{GenProbDensity}_Y(y) = \exp\left(-\frac{y^2}{2}\right), 0 < y < +\infty \tag{1.292}$$

but undefined elsewhere

and

$$\begin{aligned}
\boldsymbol{E}(Y) &= \frac{\int_0^{+\infty} y\exp\left(-\frac{y^2}{2}\right) \mathbf{d}y}{\boldsymbol{GenProb}(\mathbf{Span}(\mathcal{B}_+))}\mathbf{d}y \\
&= \frac{\int_0^{+\infty} y\exp\left(-\frac{y^2}{2}\right) \mathbf{d}y}{\frac{1}{2}} \\
&= 2\int_0^{+\infty} y\exp\left(-\frac{y^2}{2}\right) \mathbf{d}y \\
&= \boldsymbol{E}(\ln S_t \mid \ln S_t > 0)
\end{aligned} \tag{1.293}$$

Consider $0 < a < b$, *then*

$$\begin{aligned}
\textbf{\textit{GenProb}}\,(Y \in (a,b)) &= \int_a^b \textbf{\textit{GenProbDensity}}_Y\,(y)\,\mathbf{d}y \qquad (1.294)\\
&= \int_a^b \exp\left(-\frac{y^2}{2}\right)\mathbf{d}y\\
&= \textbf{\textit{Prob}}\,(\ln S_t \in (a,b))\\
&= \frac{1}{2}\textbf{\textit{Prob}}\,(\ln S_t \in (a,b) \mid \ln S_t > 0)
\end{aligned}$$

The following theorem shows that the generalized probability measure over its known universe is conceptually and computationally different from a reconciled probability measure conditioned upon the known universe, but given a random variable and a generalized random variable that are reconciled over a known universe, they are computationally linked in that the expectation of the random variable conditioned upon the variable belonging to the known universe equals the expectation of the generalized random variable.

Theorem 1.4 *If the set of generalized events* $\mathbb{G}$, *with generalized probability measure* ***GenProb****, is a subset of the set of events* $\mathbb{W}$ *such that*

$$\textbf{\textit{Prob}}\,(\mathbf{Span}\,(\mathbb{G})) > 0 \qquad (1.295)$$

with probability measure ***Prob****, and the generalized probability measure* ***GenProb*** *and the probability measure* ***Prob*** *are reconciled over* $\mathbb{G}$, *then*

1. *Probability and generalized probability of* $A \in \mathbb{G}$ *are equal for generalized probability measure* ***GenProb*** *and the probability measure* ***Prob*** *that are reconciled over* $\mathbb{G}$,

$$\frac{\textbf{\textit{Prob}}\,(A)}{\textbf{\textit{Prob}}\,(\textbf{\textit{Span}}\,(\mathbb{G}))} = \frac{\textbf{\textit{GenProb}}\,(A)}{\textbf{\textit{GenProb}}\,(\mathbf{Span}\,(\mathbb{G}))}, \forall A \in \mathbb{G} \qquad (1.296)$$

2. *If* Y *is a* $\mathbb{G}$*-measurable generalized random variable that is reconciled over* $\mathbb{G}$ *with a* $\mathbb{W}$*-measurable random variable* X*, then the expectations of* X *and* Y *are equal for generalized probability measure* ***GenProb*** *and the probability measure* ***Prob*** *that are reconciled over* $\mathbb{G}$,

$$\boldsymbol{E}\,(X \mid \mathbb{G}) = \boldsymbol{E}\,(Y) \qquad (1.297)$$

if the expectations exist.

3. *Value ratio of evidence* $B \in \mathbb{G}$ *for hypothesis* $A \in \mathbb{G}$ *under generalized probability measure* ***GenProb*** *equals the value ratio of evidence* $B \in \mathbb{G}$ *for*

hypothesis $A \in \mathbb{G}$ under the probability measure ***Prob*** *that is reconciled with* ***GenProb*** *over $\mathbb{G}$, divided by the* ***GenProb*** *of the known universe,*

$$\textbf{\textit{Value Ratio of Evidence}}\,(B;A)\ \textit{under}\ \textbf{\textit{GenProb}} = \frac{\textbf{\textit{Value Ratio of Evidence}}\,(B;A)\ \textit{under}\ \textbf{\textit{Prob}}}{\textbf{\textit{GenProb}}\,(\mathbf{Span}\,(\mathbb{G}))} \tag{1.298}$$

Corollary 1.11 *The above result makes possible all the empirical work in this book.*

As detailed in the Preface, the world of finance is full of unknown unknowns, such as (a) self-regulatory bodies such as the U.S. self-appointed and self-regulatory Financial Industry Regulatory Authority (FINRA), (b) federal regulators (the "alphabet soup") such as the Securities and Exchange Commission (SEC), Commodity Futures Trading Commission (CFTC), and Consumer Financial Protection Bureau (CFPB), (c) international organizations such as the World Bank (WB), International Monetary Fund (IMF), Financial Stability Board (FSB), and Bank for International Settlements (BIS), (d) state regulators, (e) central banks such as the U.S. Federal Reserve Board (Fed), European Central Bank (ECB), Reserve Bank of Australia (RBA), Reserve Bank of India (RBI), (f) financial engineering by investment banks, hedge funds, and other financial players, (g) technological developments such as FinTech, artificial intelligence, and machine learning, (h) transformations of attitude to risk by investors and proprietary traders, and (i) pandemics, regime and visa changes, and wars. It is, therefore, essential that we use the methods of uncertainty, generalized events, and generalized probability that we have developed in this book for any serious work in finance.

Definition 1.39 *Probability (or generalized probability) can be* ***purely objective*** *(for example, that the probability of a head on a fair coin is $1/2$),* ***empirically objective*** *(for example, based on data and specific weather models, the probability of snow tomorrow is 30%),* ***subjective*** *(for example, we think that the probability of Australia winning the cricket World Cup is 25%), or combinations of these.*

The above characterization is clearly a function of the relevant information risk (or uncertainty) algebra, and Pinker (2021), for instance, misunderstands the entire point of applications of probability (and generalized probability) outside of trivialities such as coin tosses by insisting that "all bets are off" outside of purely objective probabilities.

1.6 Intrinsic Uncertainty

With contributions from Nripesh Podder

For at least a millennium, many great minds, including John Maynard Keynes, Paul Samuelson, and Kenneth Arrow of more recent times, have engaged, at some time or other, in the pursuit of a solution to the St. Petersburg Paradox. This section is joint work with Nripesh Podder. Samuelson (1960) said "[o]ften to analyze a paradox is to dispel it. The St. Petersburg Paradox, in which Paul refuses to pay Peter the extraordinarily high price that ordinary calculation of mathematical expectation of money-gain computes for the privilege of Paul's receiving 2^i ducats if heads first appears at the i-th toss of a fair coin, made an important contribution to the history of philosophy and probability. It dramatized the fact that men feel that they value money at something different from their expected or arithmetic-mean values." See Peterson (2023) for a detailed history of the St. Petersburg Paradox and similar decision scenarios, and also Aumann (1977), Shapley (1977), and Ryan (1974). Menger (1967) generalizes it to show that if the utility function is unbounded, similar gambles can be constructed, but Arrow (1974) shows that an unbounded utility function violates continuity or completeness of expected utility theory and Aumann (1977) demonstrates that a bounded utility function fails "reasonable" requirements; see also Shapley (1977b). In other words, all previous attempts in the expected utility framework at dispelling the St. Petersburg Paradox have crucially relied upon strong and unreasonable risk aversion represented by, for instance, bounded utility functions. While the generalized expected utility framework has provided resolutions — see, for example, Machina (1982) — we propose a simple resolution of the St. Petersburg Paradox that works even under risk neutrality by suggesting a fundamental rethink of the expected utility framework through the identification of the uncertainty intrinsic to a situation.

1.6.1 Gender Proportion

We consider a couple which continues to reproduce until they have their first male child, at which point they stop. Assume that the probability that any pregnancy leading to a birth of a male child is equal to that of a female child; i.e., $\frac{1}{2}$. Let N be a discrete random variable representing the number of children in the family. Since the family will have only one male child in this model, the proportion of male children in the family is $\frac{1}{N}$. The random variable N, therefore, has the generalized probability distribution

$$\boldsymbol{GenProb}\left(N=n\right)=\left(\frac{1}{2}\right)^{n},n=1,2,... \tag{1.299}$$

Theorem 1.5 *Expected Proportion of Male Children*

$$\boldsymbol{E}\left(\frac{1}{N}\right)=\ln 2\approx 0.693>\frac{1}{2}=\frac{1}{\boldsymbol{E}\left(N\right)} \tag{1.300}$$

Proof. The expected number of children in a family $\boldsymbol{E}\left(N\right) = \sum_{n=1}^{\infty} n\left(\frac{1}{2}\right)^{n}$. Consider the well-known geometric series $f(x) = \sum_{n=0}^{\infty} x^n$ which converges to

$\frac{1}{1-x}$ for $|x| < 1$, and, therefore, $\sum_{n=1}^{\infty} nx^{n-1} = \frac{\mathbf{d}}{dx}f(x)$ converges to $\frac{1}{(1-x)^2}$ for $|x| < 1$, and, therefore, $\sum_{n=1}^{\infty} nx^n = x\sum_{n=1}^{\infty} nx^{n-1}$ converges to $= x\left(\frac{1}{(1-x)^2}\right)$ for $|x| < 1$, and, therefore, the expected number of children in a family $\boldsymbol{E}(N) = \sum_{n=1}^{\infty} n\left(\frac{1}{2}\right)^n = \left(\frac{1}{2}\right)\left(\frac{1}{\left(1-\left(\frac{1}{2}\right)\right)^2}\right) = 2$, and, therefore, $\frac{1}{E(N)} = \frac{1}{2}$. However, the expected proportion of male children $\boldsymbol{E}\left(\frac{1}{N}\right) = \sum_{n=1}^{\infty}\left(\frac{1}{n}\right)\left(\frac{1}{2}\right)^n$. Again consider the well-known geometric series $f(x) = \sum_{n=0}^{\infty}(x)^n$ which converges to $\frac{1}{1-x}$ for $|x| < 1$, and, therefore, $\int f(x)\,dx = \sum_{n=0}^{\infty}\frac{1}{n+1}x^{n+1} = \int\frac{1}{1-x}dx$converges to $-\ln(1-x)$ for $|x| < 1$, and, therefore, the expected proportion of male children $\boldsymbol{E}\left(\frac{1}{N}\right) = \sum_{n=1}^{\infty}\left(\frac{1}{n}\right)\left(\frac{1}{2}\right)^n = -\ln\left(1-\frac{1}{2}\right) = \ln 2 \approx 0.693 > \frac{1}{2}$.

Obviously, Jensen's Inequality holds, but when we want the average proportion of male children in a society which has this kind of preference, the question is which of the following is our variable of interest:

- The expected proportion of male children, which is $\boldsymbol{E}\left(\frac{1}{N}\right)$ — which also equals $p\,\mathbf{lim}\left(\frac{1}{N}\right)$ — which is almost 70%.
- The average number of male children divided by the average number of children, which is $\frac{1}{E(N)}$, which is equal to 50%.

We will answer this question in two essentially similar ways.

The first is to consider a society of m couples, each of which independently behaves in the way described above. Let N_i be the number of children of couple i. Then $N_1, ..., N_m$ are independent and identically distributed with common distribution the same as that of N referred to earlier. Then the total number of children in this society is $\sum_{i=1}^{m} N_i$, and the total number of male children is $\sum_{i=1}^{m} 1 = m$, and therefore, the proportion of male children in this m-couple society is $\frac{m}{\sum_{i=1}^{m} N_i}$, which, by the Strong Law of Large Numbers, converges, as $m \longrightarrow \infty$, to $\frac{1}{E(N)} = \frac{1}{2}$, even though the expected proportion for a couple $\boldsymbol{E}\left(\frac{1}{N}\right)$ (and $\boldsymbol{p}\mathbf{lim}\left(\frac{1}{N}\right)$) is about 70% — once again, obviously, Jensen's Inequality holds.

Let us now consider the second argument as to why under the same conditions there will be, on average, 50% male children in society. Assume that in that society a large number (say, 200 million) of married couples start having children. In the first round, we expect to see 100 million male and 100 million female children, making the proportion of male children 50%. The 100 million couples who have male children stop reproducing, and the 100 million couples with female children will now have a second child. What do we expect to see in the second round? Naturally, additional 50 million male and 50 million female children. Continuing with this logic, therefore, the cumulative number of male and female children will be the same. This argument is also grounded on the fact that in all large societies, approximately the same number of boys and girls are born every year.

The above arguments are to show that the random variable representing the intrinsic uncertainty here is the number of children in a family, N, and that the relevant male proportion is $\frac{1}{E(N)}$ and not $E\left(\frac{1}{N}\right)$ — i.e., given a function $g(N)$ of the intrinsic random variable N, the value of interest is $g(E(N))$ and *not* $E(g(N))$.

1.6.2 The St. Petersburg Paradox

One can easily see that in flipping a fair coin, the probability of getting the first heads in the t-th flip follows the same distribution as N. The random variable T represents the number of flips needed to get the first head. Since the payoff is 2^t if the first head occurs on the t-th flip, the expected payoff is $E\left(2^T\right)$.

Theorem 1.6

$$E\left(2^T\right) = \infty, \textit{ whereas } 2^{E(T)} = 4. \tag{1.301}$$

Proof. The expected payoff $E\left(2^T\right) = \sum_{t=1}^{\infty} 2^t \left(\frac{1}{2}\right)^t = \sum_{t=1}^{\infty} (1) = \infty$. On the other hand, the expected number of flips to obtain the first head $E(T) = \sum_{t=1}^{\infty} t\left(\frac{1}{2}\right)^t$. Once again, consider the well-known geometric series $f(x) = \sum_{n=0}^{\infty} x^n$, which converges to $\frac{1}{1-x}$ for $|x| < 1$, and, therefore, $\sum_{n=1}^{\infty} nx^{n-1} = \frac{\mathbf{d}}{dx}f(x)$ converges to $\frac{1}{(1-x)^2}$ for $|x| < 1$, and, therefore, $\sum_{n=1}^{\infty} nx^n = x\sum_{n=1}^{\infty} nx^{n-1} = x\left(\frac{1}{(1-x)^2}\right)$ converges for $|x| < 1$, and, therefore, the expected number of flips to obtain the first head, $E(T) = \sum_{t=1}^{\infty} t\left(\frac{1}{2}\right)^t = \left(\frac{1}{2}\right)\left(\frac{1}{\left(1-\left(\frac{1}{2}\right)\right)^2}\right) = 2$ and, $2^{E(T)} = 4$.

Like Samuelson (1960), many would think the odds offered in the game is infinity. However, let us just think that the mathematical expectation of a win in this game is a very large sum of money. It is called a paradox because no one is likely to bet even \$50, let alone a fortune, to play this game. Surely, there will be a lot of people for whom the disutility of losing \$50 will be more than compensated by the expected utility of being the richest person in the world. This has puzzled the world community for nearly 300 years and all previous attempts in the expected utility framework at dispelling the St. Petersburg Paradox have crucially relied upon strong risk aversion represented by, for instance, bounded utility functions. Menger (1967) generalizes the St. Petersburg Paradox to show that if the utility function is unbounded, similar gambles can be constructed; Arrow (1974) shows that unbounded utility function violates continuity or completeness of expected utility theory; and Aumann (1977) demonstrates that a bounded utility function fails "reasonable" requirements. Also see, for example, Machina (1982), for the generalized expected utility theory approach to the problem.

However, let us try to use arguments similar to the ones used in our first problem of determining male-female proportions. Suppose that the St. Petersburg game is to be played repeatedly a large number of times. What is the expected length of the game; i.e., what is the expected number of flips of the coin needed to obtain the first head? This is easily seen to be $\boldsymbol{E}(T) = 2$. In other words, if the St. Petersburg game were to be repeated infinitely, the average length would converge, almost surely, to 2. The question is: How much does one get on an average run? Since, on average, it takes two flips to get the first head, the fair value of the game should arguably be $2^{E(T)} = 2^2 = 4$, and that is the most a risk neutral person would be willing to pay to play the game. In other words, we are arguing that the *random variable corresponding to the intrinsic uncertainty* in the St. Petersburg problem is the length of the run T, and therefore, the summary value of interest is $2^{E(T)}$ and not $\boldsymbol{E}\left(2^T\right)$.

1.6.3 Intrinsic Uncertainty

Consider any situation involving uncertainty, where the random variable of interest (e.g., payoff) is X. Let there exist a random variable, say Y, which represents the uncertainty *intrinsic* to the situation, and let there exist a function g such that $X = g(Y)$. Our contention is that the relevant summary value is $g(E(Y))$, even though this may not be equal to the expectation $\boldsymbol{E}(g(Y))$ of the variable of interest.

The standard specifications of a probability space involve $(\Omega, \mathcal{F}, \mu)$, where Ω is the sample space, $\mathcal{F}$ is an algebra on Ω, and μ is a probability measure on $\mathcal{F}$. We propose that to describe an uncertainty situation, we need, in addition, to specify an *intrinsic uncertainty random variable* Y on $(\Omega, \mathcal{F}, \mu)$, where $\boldsymbol{E}(Y)$ exists and is finite such that, for any random variable of interest $X = g(Y)$, the *summary expectation value* is $g(\boldsymbol{E}(Y))$. In other words, to describe an uncertainty situation, one needs to specify a tuple $(\Omega, \mathcal{F}, \mu, Y)$ satisfying the above properties.

The above discussion is for when the individual is risk neutral, and the fundamental point of this part is that our resolution of the St. Petersburg Paradox works even when the individual is risk neutral. All previous attempts in the expected utility approach at dispelling the St. Petersburg Paradox have crucially relied upon strong risk aversion represented by, for instance, bounded utility functions, and while the generalized expected utility framework has provided resolutions, we propose a simple resolution of the St. Petersburg Paradox that works even under risk neutrality by suggesting a fundamental rethink of decision making under uncertainty through the identification of the uncertainty *intrinsic* to a situation.

1.6.4 Attitude to Uncertainty

We discuss the modifications necessary to our model to incorporate differing attitudes to risk. Let $u : \mathbb{R} \longrightarrow \mathbb{R}$ be the "utility function" representing the person's preferences over any pair of situations involving risk, and satisfying all the measurability properties that such a function needs to satisfy. Then, a complete specification of an uncertainty situation for such an individual would be $(\Omega, \mathcal{F}, \mu, Y, u)$, such that, for any random variable of interest $X = g(Y)$, where Y is the random variable representing the *intrinsic uncertainty*, the *summary expectation of utility* is $g(\boldsymbol{E}(u(Y)))$ — as opposed to $\boldsymbol{E}(u(g(Y))) = \boldsymbol{E}(u(X))$ in the expected utility framework — described by, for instance, von Neumann and Morgenstern (1944), Friedman and Savage (1948), Savage (1954), Arrow (1974), Pratt (1964), Grant and Polak (2013), and others — see the exhaustive summary in Grant and Van Zandt (2009) — i.e., given two lotteries $X_1 = g_1(Y)$ and $X_2 = g_2(Y)$, X_1 is weakly preferred to X_2 if and only if $g_1(\boldsymbol{E}(u(Y))) \geq g_2(\boldsymbol{E}(u(Y)))$. All the standard definitions such as *certainty equivalence* and *risk premium* can then be defined correspondingly for our model.

Our fundamental conclusion is that, given a particular situation, it is critical to identify the random variable representing the intrinsic uncertainty, in which case, one is able to dispel the St. Petersburg Paradox even under risk neutrality. In some problems, as in the two considered in this part, one can clearly identify the intrinsic uncertainty random variable using different arguments, but we have not been able to formalize these intuitions for general situations — i.e., we have not been able to formulate general principles of identification of the intrinsic random variable given any particular situation — our argument is that the intrinsic uncertainty is primitive to the description of an uncertainty situation, just in the same way that one needs to specify the topology when one discusses a continuity argument or to specify the algebra when describing a probability.

In this section, we have proposed a more realistic alternative to the expected utility paradigm; and this alternative approach would be complete if we could work out axioms to characterize the intrinsic uncertainty random variable. We urge you to pursue research on this issue.

1.7 Conclusions

In this chapter, we provided a measure-theoretic generalization of standard probability theory under risk to a theory of generalized probability under uncertainty, and we provided the reconciliation between the two — *this result makes possible all the empirical work in this book and enables the reconciliation between traditional econometrics and statistics on one hand versus artificial intelligence and machine learning on the other.* The next chapter details a rigorous distinction between public information and market information, which is critical to understanding finance, we replace each variable, except for each classification or time variable, by the standard cumulative Gaussian probability of its Z-score; this is a rigorization of the number of standard deviations approach to interpretation of coefficients; thus, we make the impacts systematic, objective, and comparable, thus allowing a systematic and objective characterization of actual significance, which is different from statistical significance.

References

Arrow, K., 1951, "Alternative Approaches to the Theory of Choice in Risk-taking Situations," *Econometrica*, 19, 417–426.

Arrow, K., 1974, *Essays in the Theory of Risk Bearing*, Amsterdam, The Netherlands: North Holland.

Aumann, R., 1977, "The St. Petersburg Paradox: A Discussion of Some Recent Comments," *Journal of Economic Theory*, 14(2), 443–445.

Baghramian, M., and Carter, J. A., 2021, "Relativism," In: Zalta, E., (Ed.), *Stanford Encyclopedia of Philosophy*, Stanford, CA: Stanford University. (https://plato.stanford.edu/archives/spr2025/entries/relativism/).

Bai, G., Buscemi, F., and Scarani, V., 2025, "Quantum Bayes' Rule and Petz Transpose Map from the Minimum Change Principle," *Physical Review Letters*, 135(9), 090203–090209.

Barrett, K., 2023, "U.S. Population Trends Return to Pre-Pandemic Norms as More States Gain Population," *U.S. Census Bureau*, December 19, 2023.

Billingsley, P., 2012, *Probability and Measure*, New York, NY: John Wiley & Sons.

Bravin, J., and Timms, M., 2025, "Supreme Court Lifts Limits on Immigration Raids in Los Angeles," *Wall Street Journal*, September 8, 2025.

Casella, G., and Berger, R., 2024, *Statistical Inference*, Pacific Grove, CA: Routledge Press.

Chivers, T., 2021, "The obscure maths theorem that governs the reliability of Covid testing," *The Guardian*, April 18, 2021.

Dawsey, J., Zuckerman, G., and Hopkins, J., 2025, "U.S. Prosecutors Probe Tip about Timing of Pfizer Vaccine," *Wall Street Journal*, March 26, 2025.

Ellsberg, D., 1961, "Risk, Ambiguity, and the Savage Axioms," *Quarterly Journal of Economics*, 75(4), 643–669.

Feynman, R., 1985, *Surely You're Joking, Mr. Feynman!: Adventures of a Curious Character*, New York, NY: W. W. Norton & Company.

Fisher, R. A., 1922, "On the Mathematical Foundations of Theoretical Statistics," *Philosophical Transactions of the Royal Society A*, 222, 309–368.

Friedman, M., and Savage, L. J., 1948, "Utility Analysis of Choices Involving Risk," *Journal of Political Economy*, 56(4), 279–304.

Galston, W., 2024, "Claudine Gay's 'My Truth' and the Truth," *Wall Street Journal*, January 9, 2024.

Grant, S., and Polak, B., 2013, "Mean-Dispersion Preferences and Constant Absolute Certainty Aversion," *Journal of Economic Theory*, 148(4), 1361–1398.

Grant, S., and Van Zandt, T., 2009, "Expected Utility," In: Anand, P., Puppe, C., and Pattanaik, P., (Eds.), *Handbook of Rational and Social Choice*, pp. 21–68, Oxford, UK: Oxford University Press.

Hájek, A., 2023, "Interpretations of Probability," In: Zalta, E. and Nodelman, U. (Eds.), *Stanford Encyclopedia of Philosophy*, Stanford, CA: Stanford University (https://plato.stanford.edu/entries/probability-interpret/).

Hawking, S., 1988, *A Brief History of Time*, New York, NY: Bantam Books.

Hennessey, M., 2026, "The Media Isn't Responsible for Jason Arday's Death," *Wall Street Journal*, August 20, 2026

Israel, H., Ruckhaber, E., and Weinmann, R., 1931, *Hundert Autoren gegen Einstein*, Leipzig, Germany: Voigtländer.

Knight, F., 1921, *Risk, Uncertainty and Profit*, Boston, MA: Houghton Mifflin.

Luce, R., 1959, *Individual Choice Behavior*, New York, NY: Wiley.

Machina, M., 1982, "'Expected Utility' Analysis without the Independence Axiom," *Econometrica*, 50(2), 277–323.

Malone, C., 2023, "Hasan Minhaj's 'Emotional Truths,'" *The New Yorker*, September 15, 2023.

Menger, K., 1967, "The Role of Uncertainty in Economics," In: Shubik, M. (Ed.), *Essays in Mathematical Economics in Honor of Oskar Morgenstern*, pp. 211–232, Princeton, NJ: Princeton University Press.

Morrow, L., 2016, "The Hedgehogs of Critical Race Theory," *Wall Street Journal*, July 19, 2016.

Neyman, J., 1977, "Frequentist Probability and Frequentist Statistics," *Synthese*, 36(1), 97–131.

Passel, J., and Krogstad, J. M., 2025, "U.S. Unauthorized Immigrant Population Reached a Record 14 Million in 2023," *Pew Research*, August 21, 2025.

Peterson, M., 2023, "The St. Petersburg Paradox," In: Zalta, E. and Nodelman, U., (Eds.), *Stanford Encyclopedia of Philosophy*, Stanford, CA: Stanford University.

Pinker, S., 2021, *Rationality: What It Is, Why It Seems Scarce, Why It Matters*, New York, NY: Penguin Books.

Pratt, J., 1964, "Risk Aversion in the Small and in the Large," *Econometrica*, 32(1/2), 122–136.

Rumsfeld, D., 2002, "Department of Defense News Briefing," *U.S. Department of Defense*, February 12, 2002.

Ryan, E., Detrow, S., Garsd, J., and Keatley, A., 2025, "The Supreme Court Clears the Way for ICE Agents to Treat Race as Grounds for Immigration Stops," *All Things Considered*, September 13, 2025.

Ryan, T., 1974, "The Use of Unbounded Utility Functions in Expected-Utility Maximization: Comment," *Quarterly Journal of Economics*, LXXXVIII, 133–135.

Samuelson, P., 1960, "The St. Petersburg Paradox as a Divergent Double Limit," *International Economic Review*, 1(1), 31–37.

Sarasvathy, S., Simon, H., and Lave, L., 1998, "Perceiving and Managing Business Risks: Differences between Entrepreneurs and Bankers," *Journal of Economic Behavior and Organization*, 33(2), 207–226.

Savage, L., 1954, *The Foundations of Statistics*, New York, NY: John Wiley & Sons.

Schrödinger, E., 1935, "Die gegenwärtige Situation in der Quantenmechanik," *Naturwissenschaften*, 23(48), 807–812.

Shapley, L., 1977, "Lotteries and Menus: A Comment on Unbounded Utilities," *Journal of Economic Theory*, 14(2), 446–453.

Tyson, N., 2013, *Space Chronicles*, New York, NY: W. W. Norton & Co., Inc.

USA Facts, 2025, "Our Changing Population: United States," *USA Facts*. https://usafacts.org/answers/is-the-population-growing-or-shrinking/country/united-states/

Venn, J., 1866, *The Logic of Chance: An Essay on the Foundations and Province of the Theory of Probability*, London: Macmillan.

Vivekananda, S., 1955, *Complete Works*, Mayavati, Uttarakhand, India: Advaita Ashrama.
von Mises, R., 1928, *Probability, Statistics, and Truth* (English trans. 1939/1957), New York, NY: Macmillan/Dover.
von Neumann, J., and Morgenstern, O., 1944, *Theory of Games and Economic Behavior*, Princeton, NJ: Princeton University Press.
Yu, X., Wilhelm, B., Holmes, D., Vaartjes, A., Schwienbacher, D., Nurizzo, M., Kringhøj, A., van Blankenstein, M., Jakob, A., Gupta, P., Hudson, F., Itoh, K., Murray, R., Blume-Kohout, R., Ladd, T., Anand, N., Dzurak, A., Sanders, B., Jamieson, D., and Morello, A., 2025, "Schrödinger Cat States of a Nuclear Spin Qudit in Silicon," *Nature Physics*, 21, 362–367.

2

EMPIRICS

2.1 Introduction

In the past chapter, we have discussed in detail the theoretical aspects of applying the scientific method to risk and uncertainty. In this chapter, we detail a rigorous distinction between public information and market information, which is critical to understanding finance — please see Bhattacharya and Gupta (2023) for an application of this methodology to diligence and objectivity of analyst forecasts. Later in this chapter, we replace each variable, except for each classification or time variable, by the standard cumulative Gaussian probability of its *Z*-score, this is a rigorization of the number of standard deviations approach to interpretation of coefficients — this also implicitly assumes Gaussian distributions — thus, we make the impacts comparable; this allows a systematic and objective characterization of actual significance, which is different from statistical significance. Therefore, all regression coefficients are systematic, objective, and comparable. For structural systems, the full association of two variables is measured by the total derivative, our method makes full associations comparable as well. We systematically define a full or partial association to be actually significantly positive (negative) at level λ if the relevant derivative is greater than λ (less than $-\lambda$). Finally, we discuss in detail the distinctions between traditional statistics and econometrics on one hand versus artificial intelligence and machine learning on the other, and we provide brief descriptions of advanced empirical methods, especially systemic versus idiosyncratic, positive and negative proxies, endogeneity, errors-in-variables, simultaneity, and instrumentation.

DOI: 10.4324/9781003608486-3

2.2 Public Information and Market Information

Market information is almost never observable to the public, and much of research in the field of finance is around attempting to infer market information from actual behavior. Consider the following example to motivate the concepts in this subsection: Walmart (NYSE: WMT), the *StudiedFirm*, provided, on April 4, 2023, an earnings per share (EPS) guidance for Q1-2024, Walmart (2023). Kate is an analyst with Goldman Sachs (NYSE: GS), she published an analyst report about WMT on April 5, 2023, please see TipRanks (2023); and so, Kate-Goldman is an *Analyst-AnalystFirm* covering WMT. If Jose were another analyst working with Goldman, then Jose-Goldman would be a separate *Analyst-AnalystFirm*, and if Kate were to leave Goldman and join JPMorgan Chase (NYSE: JPM), then Kate-JPM would be yet another *Analyst-AnalystFirm*. Please see Bhattacharya and Gupta (2023) on an application of this information structure to measure diligence, objectivity, quality, and accuracy by analysts and analyst firms.

Notation 2.1 *Index StudiedFirm by i, Analyst-AnalystFirm tuple by j, and time by t. Let the uncertainty algebra corresponding to information available to and processed by StudiedFirm i about itself at quarter t be* $\mathfrak{I}_{t,i}^{Firm,i}$. *Let the uncertainty algebra corresponding to information available to and processed by market participant l — for example, analysts, investors, and regulators — about StudiedFirm i at quarter t be* $\mathfrak{I}_{t,i}^{Participant,l}$. *Let the uncertainty algebra corresponding to information available to the market at quarter t about StudiedFirm i be* $\mathfrak{I}_{t,i}^{Market}$. *Let the uncertainty algebra corresponding to information available to the public at quarter t about StudiedFirm i be* $\mathfrak{I}_{t,i}^{Public}$, *available to everyone and everyone knows that everyone knows.*

- Star (*) denotes that the variable is unobservable to the public
- Left-arrow (←) denotes learning through research and analysis
- Right-arrow (→) denotes announcement to the public
- Left-right-arrow (↔) denotes both
- Hebrew letter denotes actual variables
- Roman letters denote variables observed or announced by the *StudiedFirm*
- Greek letters denote variables observed or announced by the *Analyst-AnalystFirm*

Assumption 2.1 *We also do **not** make any a priori assumptions about the richness of the information available to the Analyst-AnalystFirm compared to the richness of the information available to the StudiedFirm.*

Assumption 2.2 ***Basic competence*** *by market players requires that StudiedFirm's information about itself is at least as rich as public information.*

Assumption 2.3 *In addition, we make the relatively innocuous assumptions that there is* ***no memory loss****.*

Definition 2.1 *The uncertainty information algebra* ***generated*** *by a class* $\mathbb{A}$ *of subsets of the universe* $\mathcal{F}$ *is the smallest uncertainty algebra containing all sets in* $\mathbb{A}$*:*

$$\mathfrak{G}(\mathbb{A}) = \bigcap \{\mathbb{B} \text{ uncertainty algebra} : \mathbb{A} \subseteq \mathbb{B}\} \tag{2.1}$$

Lemma 2.1 *If* $\mathbb{A}$ *is an uncertainty information algebra, then the uncertainty algebra generated by the class of the subsets is the same class of subsets,* $\mathfrak{G}(\mathbb{A}) = \mathbb{A}$*.*

Definition 2.2 ***Market information*** *about StudiedFirm i at quarter t is the uncertainty algebra generated by the* ***union*** *of all the relevant asymmetric algebras of the StudiedFirm, and of all market participants:*

$$\mathfrak{I}_{t,i}^{Market} = \mathfrak{G}\left(\mathfrak{I}_{t,i}^{Firm,i} \bigcup_{l} \mathfrak{I}_{t,i}^{Participant,l}\right) \tag{2.2}$$

Definition 2.3 ***Public information*** *about StudiedFirm i at quarter t is the uncertainty algebra generated by the* ***intersection*** *of all the relevant asymmetric algebras of the StudiedFirm and of all market participants:*

$$\mathfrak{I}_{t,i}^{Public} = \mathfrak{G}\left(\mathfrak{I}_{t,i}^{Firm,i} \bigcap_{l} \mathfrak{I}_{t,i}^{Participant,l}\right) \tag{2.3}$$

Lemma 2.2 *Basic competence by market players requires that StudiedFirm's information about itself is at least as rich as public information (which is weakly poorer than market information; it follows from the definitions of public and market information above)*

$$\mathfrak{I}_{t,i}^{Public} \subseteq \mathfrak{I}_{t,i}^{Firm,i} \subseteq \mathfrak{I}_{t,i}^{Market}, \forall i, t \tag{2.4}$$

and that since an Analyst-AnalystFirm tuple is a market participant,

$$\mathfrak{I}_{t,i}^{Public} \subseteq \mathfrak{I}_{t,i}^{Analyst,j} \subseteq \mathfrak{I}_{t,i}^{Market}, \forall i, j, t \tag{2.5}$$

Please note that the above result does not require any assumptions and does not make any conclusions about the relative richness of the information available to the *StudiedFirm i* and to the *Analyst-AnalystFirm* tuple *j*.

Assumption 2.4 *In addition, we make the relatively innocuous assumptions that there is* ***no memory loss,***

$$\mathfrak{I}_{t,i}^{Public} \subseteq \mathfrak{I}_{t+1,i}^{Public}, \forall i, t \tag{2.6}$$

$$\mathfrak{I}_{t,i}^{Market} \subseteq \mathfrak{I}_{t+1,i}^{Market}, \forall i, t \tag{2.7}$$

$$\mathfrak{I}_{t,i}^{Firm,i} \subseteq \mathfrak{I}_{t+1,i}^{Firm,i}, \forall i, t \tag{2.8}$$

$$\mathfrak{I}_{t,i}^{Analyst,j} \subseteq \mathfrak{I}_{t+1,i}^{Analyst,j}, \forall i, j, t \tag{2.9}$$

The following, therefore, are the variables of interest regarding earnings (per share):

1. $\sqsupset_{it}^{*}$, the actual earnings (per share) of the *StudiedFirm i* in quarter *t*, it is not $\mathfrak{I}_{t,i}^{Public}$-measurable — i.e., it is not observable to the public (or the empiricist) at quarter *t* — and its measurability with respect to each of these different uncertainty information algebras $\mathfrak{I}_{t,i}^{Firm,i}$ and $\mathfrak{I}_{t,i}^{Analyst,j}$ determines the indices of diligence, objectivity, and quality in Bhattacharya and Gupta (2023).

2. $\overleftarrow{G_{it}^{*}} = E\left(\sqsupset_{it}^{*} \mid \mathfrak{I}_{t,i}^{Firm,i}\right)$, the *StudiedFirm i* learns $\overleftarrow{G_{it}^{*}}$ (the left-arrow ($\leftarrow$) denoting learning) as a result of its own research and analysis, and, as a result, $\overleftarrow{G_{it}^{*}}$ is $\mathfrak{I}_{t,i}^{Firm,i}$-measurable, but $\overleftarrow{G_{it}^{*}}$ is **not** $\mathfrak{I}_{t,i}^{Public}$- or $\mathfrak{I}_{t,i}^{Analyst,j}$-measurable — i.e., it is not observable to the public (or the empiricist) or the *Analyst-AnalystFirm* tuple *j* at quarter *t*.

3. $\overleftrightarrow{G_{it}}$, the guidance provided by *StudiedFirm i* at the beginning of quarter *t* about Y_{it}^{*}, and $\overleftrightarrow{G_{it}}$ (the left-right-arrow ($\leftrightarrow$) denoting learning and declaration) is $\mathfrak{I}_{t,i}^{Firm,i}$-, $\mathfrak{I}_{t,i}^{Public}$-, and $\mathfrak{I}_{t,i}^{Analyst,j}$-measurable — i.e., it is observable to the public (and the empiricist) at quarter *t*.

4. $\overleftarrow{\Phi_{ijt}^{*}} = E\left(\sqsupset_{it}^{*} \mid \mathfrak{I}_{t,i}^{Analyst,j}\right)$, the *Analyst-AnalystFirm* tuple *j* learns $\overleftarrow{\Phi_{ijt}^{*}}$ (the left-arrow ($\leftarrow$) denoting learning) as a result of its own research and analysis; as a result, $\overleftarrow{\Phi_{ijt}^{*}}$ is $\mathfrak{I}_{t,i}^{Analyst,j}$-measurable, but $\overleftarrow{\Phi_{ijt}^{*}}$ is **not** $\mathfrak{I}_{t,i}^{Public}$- or $\mathfrak{I}_{t,i}^{Firm,i}$-measurable — i.e., it is not observable to the public (or the empiricist) or the *StudiedFirm* at quarter *t*.

5. $\overleftrightarrow{\Phi_{ijt}}$, the forecast provided by *Analyst-AnalystFirm* tuple *j* about Y_{it}^{*}, and $\overleftrightarrow{\Phi_{ijt}}$ is $\mathfrak{I}_{t,i}^{Analyst,j}$-, $\mathfrak{I}_{t,i}^{Public}$-, and $\mathfrak{I}_{t,i}^{Firm,i}$-measurable — i.e., it is observable to the public (empiricist) at quarter *t*.

6. $\overleftrightarrow{Y_{it}}$, the announced earnings (per share) of the *StudiedFirm i* in quarter *t* provided at the beginning of quarter $(t+1)$, and $\overleftrightarrow{Y_{it}}$ is $\mathfrak{I}_{t+1,i}^{Firm,i}$-, $\mathfrak{I}_{t+1,i}^{Analyst,j}$-, and $\mathfrak{I}_{t+1,i}^{Public}$-measurable — i.e., it is observable to the public (empiricist) at quarter $(t+1)$.

TABLE 2.1 Variables of Interest Regarding Earnings Per Share

Information	**Quarter** t				**Quarter** $(t+1)$
Unknown			$\beth^*_{it}$		
StudiedFirm i	$\overleftarrow{G^*_{it}}$	$\overleftrightarrow{G_{it}}$		$\overleftrightarrow{\Phi_{ijt}}$	$\overleftrightarrow{Y_{it}}$
Analyst-AnalystFirm j		$\overleftrightarrow{G_{it}}$	$\overleftarrow{\Phi^*_{ijt}}$	$\overleftrightarrow{\Phi_{ijt}}$	$\overleftrightarrow{Y_{it}}$
Public/Empiricist		$\overleftrightarrow{G_{it}}$		$\overleftrightarrow{\Phi_{ijt}}$	$\overleftrightarrow{Y_{it}}$

The above modeling, therefore, implies the information categories listed in Table 2.1.

2.3 The Scientific Method Versus Faith

"If you toss a coin seven times, and all tosses come up heads, what is the chance of the eighth toss also turning up a head?" In this section, we show that information is powerful — please see, for instance, Akerlof (1970) on the importance of information — and that updating the generalized probability on the basis of new information is scientific — please see, for instance, Korb and Nicholson (2010) for applications of Bayesian updating to artificial intelligence — and, therefore, that the answer to the above question depends on the level of sureness about the prior probability that the coin is fair, and that the scientific method implies that the answer to the above question is greater than half. We then extend the analysis to the probability of gender-neutrality of birth on the basis of the observed number of female and male births in the U.S. and India; this provides the scientific measurements to inform the policy implications of alleged gender-selective abortions in India (and China). We point out that if the prior generalized probability (or, if appropriate, probability) is degenerate, i.e., if one is sure that the coin is fair or that birth is gender-neutral, then no amount of evidence can change the generalized probability (or, if appropriate, probability). In this book, the terms "degenerate" and "non-degenerate" are used purely in their mathematical senses, $\boldsymbol{GenProb} \in \{0,1\}$ (or, if appropriate, $Prob \in \{0,1\}$) and $\boldsymbol{GenProb} \notin \{0,1\}$ (or, if appropriate, $Prob \notin \{0,1\}$) respectively, as detailed in this chapter, without any moral connotations.

The criterion of falsifiability is essential to any scientific theory: A scientific theory must provide a set of facts, such that, if the set of facts were to eventuate, the theory would be falsified — please see, for instance, Popper (1959), and a discussion of closed epistemic systems in, for example, Luper (2020). We show that the existence of such falsifying facts would be rational if and only if the prior is non-degenerate; that the absence of such possible falsifying facts implies and is implied by the theory belonging in the realm of faith rather than science; that the requirement that a conclusion depend on evidence and therefore, change with additional evidence, is fundamental to the difference between science and faith; and that, therefore, a degenerate prior is entirely antithetical to the scientific method. "[F]aith ... is wholly independent of the epistemic concern that cares about evidential support. On this view, faith reveals its authenticity most clearly when it takes faith-propositions to be true contrary to the weight of the evidence" Bishop (2016). These statements paraphrase the famous "Render to Caesar the things that are Caesar's; and to God the things that are God's" (Romans 13:1) and "In God we trust, all others must bring data" (W. Edwards Deming) — skepticism is essential to the scientific method.

To summarize, a theory is scientific if and only if the prior is non-degenerate. Please see Popper (1959), and, in reverse chronological order, Bandyopadhyay et al. (2016), Taper and Lele (2011), Royall (1997), Edwards (1984), Skyrms (1984), and Kyburg (1983).

2.3.1 Tosses of a Coin

We first study the relatively simple experiment of tossing a coin.

Notation 2.2 *Let the a priori probability of the probability of head on one toss be denoted by* Ψ. *We denote the generalized event (or hypothesis) that a coin is* ***actually*** *fair by* **fair** *and the generalized event (or hypothesis) that a coin is* ***actually*** *unfair by* **unfair**. *We denote the generalized event (or hypothesis) that a coin results in a head by HEAD and the generalized event (or hypothesis) that a coin toss results in a tail by TAIL.*

Then,

$$Prob\,(HEAD \mid \Psi = \psi) = \psi \tag{2.10}$$

$$Prob\,(TAIL \mid \Psi = \psi) = 1 - \psi \tag{2.11}$$

and, therefore, the generalized probabilities in the case of n independent tosses,

$$Prob\left((HEAD)^n \mid \Psi = \psi\right) = (\psi)^n \tag{2.12}$$

$$Prob\left((TAIL)^n \mid \Psi = \psi\right) = (1 - \psi)^n \tag{2.13}$$

Notation 2.3 *Let the a priori probability that the coin is fair be given by*

$$Prob\left(\Psi = \frac{1}{2}; \alpha\right) = \alpha \tag{2.14}$$

2.3.1.1 Non-Degenerate Prior: $\alpha < 1$

In this book, the terms "degenerate" and "non-degenerate" are used purely in their mathematical senses — where ***GenProb*** $\in \{0, 1\}$ (or, if appropriate, *Prob* $\in \{0, 1\}$) and ***GenProb*** $\notin \{0, 1\}$ (or, if appropriate, *Prob* $\notin \{0, 1\}$) respectively — without any moral connotations.

Assumption 2.5 *Let the unfair generalized probabilities be uniformly distributed across* $(0, 1) \setminus \{\frac{1}{2}\}$ *with an a priori Bias Factor* β *as follows*

$$Prob\left(\Psi = \frac{m}{2k}; \alpha, \beta, k\right) = \frac{1 - \alpha - \beta}{2(k-1)}, m = 1, ..., k-1 \tag{2.15}$$

$$Prob\left(\Psi = \frac{m}{2k}; \alpha, \beta, k\right) = \frac{1 - \alpha + \beta}{2(k-1)}, m = k+1, ..., 2k-1 \tag{2.16}$$

Note that $\beta > 0$ implies that there is an *a priori* bias in favor of a higher probability of head and that $\beta < 0$ implies that there is an *a priori* bias in favor of a lower probability of head. First, one needs

$$\alpha + \sum_{m=1}^{k-1}\left(\frac{1 - \alpha - \beta}{2(k-1)}\right) + \sum_{m=k+1}^{2k-1}\left(\frac{1 - \alpha + \beta}{2(k-1)}\right) \equiv 1 \tag{2.17}$$

Second, one needs

$$\frac{1 - \alpha - \beta}{2(k-1)} \in [0, 1] \tag{2.18}$$

and

$$\frac{1 - \alpha + \beta}{2(k-1)} \in [0, 1] \tag{2.19}$$

which hold if and only if

$$-\min\{\alpha, 1 - \alpha\} \leq \beta \leq \min\{\alpha, 1 - \alpha\} \tag{2.20}$$

and

$$k \geq \max\left\{2, \frac{3 - \alpha + \beta}{2}, \frac{3 - \alpha - \beta}{2}\right\} \tag{2.21}$$

Please see Section 2.3.1.2 and note the serious discontinuities at $\alpha = 1$. Please refer to Section 2.3.3.3 for the equivalence of a non-degenerate prior with the scientific method. We arrive at the following result by applying Bayes Theorem (Theorem 1.3).

Theorem 2.1 *Let*

$$\alpha < 1 \tag{2.22}$$

$$-\min\{\alpha, 1-\alpha\} \leq \beta \leq \min\{\alpha, 1-\alpha\} \tag{2.23}$$

and

$$k \geq \max\left\{2, \frac{3-\alpha+\beta}{2}, \frac{3-\alpha-\beta}{2}\right\} \tag{2.24}$$

Then the probability of the coin being fair, conditional on n coin tosses resulting in n heads, is lower than the unconditional probability of the coin being fair,

$$\begin{aligned} Prob\left(\mathbf{fair} \mid (HEAD)^n ; \alpha, \beta, k\right) &= \left(\frac{1}{2}\right)^n \alpha \left(\frac{1}{4}\beta + \frac{1}{2}\right)^{-n} \\ & \quad (\in [0,1] \textit{ from conditions}) \\ &< Prob\left(\mathbf{fair}\right) \end{aligned} \tag{2.25}$$

and the probability of the coin being unfair, conditional on n coin tosses resulting in n heads, is higher than the unconditional probability of the coin being unfair,

$$\begin{aligned} Prob\left(\mathbf{unfair} \mid (HEAD)^n ; \alpha, \beta, k\right) &= 1 - \left(\frac{1}{2}\right)^n \alpha \left(\frac{1}{4}\beta + \frac{1}{2}\right)^{-n} \\ & \quad (\in [0,1] \textit{ from conditions}) \\ &> Prob\left(\mathbf{unfair}\right) \end{aligned} \tag{2.26}$$

For $m = 1, \ldots, k-1,$

the ex post probability of the probability of head being a number less than half, conditional on n coin tosses resulting in n heads, is lower than the corresponding ex ante probability,

$$\begin{aligned} Prob\left(\Psi = \frac{m}{2k} \mid (HEAD)^n ; \alpha, \beta, k\right) &= \left(\frac{m}{2k}\right)^n \frac{1-\alpha-\beta}{2(k-1)} \left(\frac{1}{4}\beta + \frac{1}{2}\right)^{-n} \\ & \quad (\in [0,1] \textit{ from conditions}) \\ &< Prob\left(\Psi = \frac{m}{2k}\right) \end{aligned}$$

and, taking the limits of both sides as $k, m \longrightarrow \infty, m < k,$

$$\begin{aligned} Prob\left(\Psi = \psi \mid (HEAD)^n ; \alpha, \beta\right) &\leq Prob\left(\Psi = \psi\right), \forall 0 \\ &\leq \psi < \frac{1}{2} \end{aligned} \tag{2.27}$$

therefore, the ex post probability of head on one toss being less than half, conditional on n coin tosses resulting in n heads, is (weakly) lower than the ex ante probability of head on one toss being less than half,

$$Prob\left(\Psi < \frac{1}{2} \mid (HEAD)^n ; \alpha, \beta\right) \leq Prob\left(\Psi < \frac{1}{2}\right) \tag{2.28}$$

And

$$For\ m = k + 1, \ldots, 2k - 1,$$

the ex post probability of the probability of head being a number greater than half, conditional on n coin tosses resulting in n heads, is higher than the corresponding ex ante probability,

$$\begin{aligned} Prob\left(\Psi = \frac{m}{2k} \mid (HEAD)^n ; \alpha, \beta, k\right) &= \left(\frac{m}{2k}\right)^n \frac{1 - \alpha + \beta}{2(k-1)} \left(\frac{1}{4}\beta + \frac{1}{2}\right)^{-n} \\ &\quad (\in [0, 1]\ from\ conditions) \\ &> Prob\left(\Psi = \frac{m}{2k}\right) \end{aligned}$$

and, taking the limits of both sides as $k, m \longrightarrow \infty, k < m < 2k$,

$$Prob\left(\Psi = \psi \mid (HEAD)^n ; \alpha, \beta\right) \geq Prob\left(\Psi = \psi\right), \forall \frac{1}{2} < \psi \leq 1$$

therefore, the ex post probability of head on one toss being greater than half, conditional on n coin tosses resulting in n heads, is (weakly) greater than the ex ante probability of head on one toss being greater than half,

$$Prob\left(\Psi > \frac{1}{2} \mid (HEAD)^n ; \alpha, \beta\right) \geq Prob\left(\Psi > \frac{1}{2}\right)$$

2.3.1.2 Degenerate Prior: $\alpha = 1$

This is the situation when it is fully sure that the coin is fair; i.e., no matter how much evidence is produced against the coin being unfair, that does not change the probability that the coin is fair; i.e.,

$$Prob\left(\Psi = \frac{1}{2}\right) = 1 \tag{2.29}$$

and therefore,

$$Prob\left(\Psi \neq \frac{1}{2}\right) = 0 \tag{2.30}$$

The following Theorem 2.2 is the very specific degenerate (in mathematical terms) and pathological (in statistical terms) situation many people think of when they assert that the chance of head on the next toss is exactly 50%, even after multiple successive tosses actually resulting in heads. Please see Section 2.3.3.3 for discussion on the equivalence of the scientific method and a non-degenerate prior.

Theorem 2.2 *If* $\alpha = 1$*, the probability of the coin being fair, conditional on n coin tosses resulting in n heads, is* 1*, and the probability of the coin being unfair, conditional on n coin tosses resulting in n heads, is* 0.

We started this section wanting to know what the probability of a head in the eighth toss was, after observing seven consecutive tosses eventuating in heads, and this depends on

$$Prob\left(\textbf{fair} \mid (HEAD)^7\right) \tag{2.31}$$

which, from Bayes Theorem,

$$= Prob\left((HEAD)^7 \mid \textbf{fair}\right) \frac{Prob\,(\textbf{fair})}{Prob\left((HEAD)^7\right)} \tag{2.32}$$

2.3.1.3 Non-Degenerate Prior: $\alpha < 1$

From the above computations, therefore,

$$Prob\left(\textbf{fair} \mid (HEAD)^7; \alpha, \beta, k\right) = \left(\frac{1}{2}\right)^7 \alpha \left(\frac{1}{4}\beta + \frac{1}{2}\right)^{-7} \quad (\in [0,1]\ \textit{from conditions}) \tag{2.33}$$

and

$$Prob\left(\textbf{unfair} \mid (HEAD)^7; \alpha, \beta, k\right) = 1 - \left(\tfrac{1}{2}\right)^7 \alpha \left(\tfrac{1}{4}\beta + \tfrac{1}{2}\right)^{-7} \quad (\in [0,1]\ \textit{from conditions}) \tag{2.34}$$

Figure 2.1 charts the *ex post* probability of the coin being fair, conditional on seven consecutive heads.

Please note that under the special case of the *a priori* Bias Factor being degenerate at $\beta = 0$, the conditional probability is the same as the unconditional probability.

Special Case: $\alpha = 0.99, \beta = 0.005$ Then, after observing seven successive tosses of a coin yielding seven heads, the *ex post* probability ($Prob$) of a head for

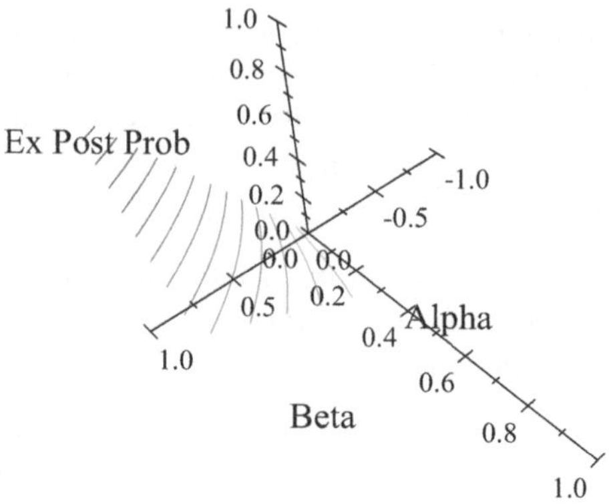

FIGURE 2.1 Ex Post *Prob* of coin being fair, conditional on seven consecutive heads, as function of α and β.

the eighth toss is as follows:

$$\begin{cases} = \frac{1}{2} & \text{with probability} \quad \begin{array}{l} = \left(\frac{1}{2}\right)^7 0.99 \left(\frac{1}{4}(0.005) + \frac{1}{2}\right)^{-7} \\ \approx 0.973 \end{array} \\ \neq \frac{1}{2} & \text{with probability} \quad \approx 1 - 0.973 = 0.027 \end{cases} \tag{2.35}$$

Special Case: $\alpha = 0.5, \beta = 0$ Then, after observing seven successive tosses of a coin yielding seven heads, the *ex post* probability (*Prob*) of a head for the eighth toss is as follows:

$$\begin{cases} = \frac{1}{2} & \text{with probability} \quad \begin{array}{l} = \left(\frac{1}{2}\right)^7 0.5 \left(\frac{1}{4}(0) + \frac{1}{2}\right)^{-7} \\ = 0.5 \end{array} \\ \neq \frac{1}{2} & \text{with probability} \quad = 1 - 0.5 = 0.5 \end{cases} \tag{2.36}$$

Special Case: $\alpha = 0.5, \beta = -0.1$ Then, after observing seven successive tosses of a coin yielding seven heads, the *ex post* probability (*Prob*) of a head for the eighth toss is as follows:

$$\begin{cases} = \frac{1}{2} & \text{with probability} \quad \begin{array}{l} = \left(\frac{1}{2}\right)^7 0.5 \left(\frac{1}{4}(-0.1) + \frac{1}{2}\right)^{-7} \\ \approx 0.716 \end{array} \\ \neq \frac{1}{2} & \text{with probability} \quad \approx 1 - 0.716 = 0.284 \end{cases} \tag{2.37}$$

Special Case: $\alpha = 0.99, \beta = 0.01$ Then, after observing seven successive tosses of a coin yielding seven heads, the *ex post* probability (*Prob*) of a head for the eighth toss is as follows:

$$\begin{cases} = \frac{1}{2} & \text{with probability} \quad \begin{aligned} &= \left(\tfrac{1}{2}\right)^7 0.99 \left(\tfrac{1}{4}(0.01) + \tfrac{1}{2}\right)^{-7} \\ &\approx 0.956 \end{aligned} \\ \neq \frac{1}{2} & \text{with probability} \quad \approx 1 - 0.956 = 0.044 \end{cases} \tag{2.38}$$

Special Case: $\alpha = 0.90, \beta = 0.05$ Then, after observing seven successive tosses of a coin yielding seven heads, the *ex post* probability $(Prob)$ of a head for the eighth toss is as follows:

$$\begin{cases} = \frac{1}{2} & \text{with probability} \quad \begin{aligned} &= \left(\tfrac{1}{2}\right)^7 0.99 \left(\tfrac{1}{4}(0.005) + \tfrac{1}{2}\right)^{-7} \\ &\approx 0.973 \end{aligned} \\ \neq \frac{1}{2} & \text{with probability} \quad \approx 1 - 0.973 = 0.027 \end{cases} \tag{2.39}$$

Special Case: $\alpha = 0.90, \beta = 0.1$ Then, after observing seven successive tosses of a coin yielding seven heads, the *ex post* probability $(Prob)$ of a head for the eighth toss is as follows:

$$\begin{cases} = \frac{1}{2} & \text{with probability} \quad \begin{aligned} &= \left(\tfrac{1}{2}\right)^7 0.90 \left(\tfrac{1}{4}(0.1) + \tfrac{1}{2}\right)^{-7} \\ &\approx 0.640 \end{aligned} \\ \neq \frac{1}{2} & \text{with probability} \quad \approx 1 - 0.640 = 0.360 \end{cases} \tag{2.40}$$

Special Case: $\alpha = 0.80, \beta = 0.1$ Then, after observing seven successive tosses of a coin yielding seven heads, the *ex post* probability $(Prob)$ of a head for the eighth toss is as follows:

$$\begin{cases} = \frac{1}{2} & \text{with probability} \quad \begin{aligned} &= \left(\tfrac{1}{2}\right)^7 0.80 \left(\tfrac{1}{4}(0.1) + \tfrac{1}{2}\right)^{-7} \\ &\approx 0.569 \end{aligned} \\ \neq \frac{1}{2} & \text{with probability} \quad \approx 1 - 0.569 = 0.431 \end{cases} \tag{2.41}$$

2.3.1.4 *Degenerate Prior:* $\alpha = 1$

Consider the extreme situation where it is fully sure that the coin is fair; i.e., no matter how much evidence is produced against the coin being fair, the probability does not change; i.e., $\alpha = 1$; then, after observing seven successive tosses of a coin yielding seven heads, the *ex post* probability $(Prob)$ of a head for the eighth toss is as follows:

$$Prob\left(\mathbf{fair} \mid (HEAD)^7\right) = 1 \tag{2.42}$$

and

$$Prob\left(\mathbf{unfair} \mid (HEAD)^7\right) = 0 \tag{2.43}$$

This is the situation many people think of when they assert that the chance of a head on the eighth toss is exactly 50%, even after seven successive tosses actually resulting in heads. The above results prove that the following assertion, in a 2020 BBC article, is naïve and does not hold under the slightest perturbation from the degenerate (in mathematical terms) and pathological (in statistical terms) $\alpha = 1$. "Many people believe the odds change so that the sequence must somehow even out [after a sequence of tails], increasing the chance of a heads on the subsequent goes ... imagine you are tossing a (fair) coin and you get the following sequence: Heads, Heads, Tails, Tails, Tails, Tails, Tails, Tails, Tails, Tails, Tails, Tails. What's the chance you will now get a heads? ... The chance of a heads is still 50% even if you've had 500 or 5,000 tails all in a row," Robson (2020). However, the truth, as we show in this theorem, is that for α even the slightest bit different from the degenerate (in mathematical terms) and pathological (in statistical terms) blind faith in complete sureness, the *ex post* chance of a head, after a sequence of tails, is actually **lower** than the *ex ante* chance of a head. This Robson (2020) article represents exactly the "culture of ignorance" and the "strain of anti-intellectualism" that Asimov (1980) strongly criticized and is the polar opposite of the following very telling anecdote about the late Professor Daniel Kahneman, Nobel Prize in Economics, 2002: "He was ... relentlessly self-critical. I once showed him a letter I'd gotten from a reader telling me — correctly but rudely — that I was wrong about something. 'Do you have any idea how lucky you are to have thousands of people who can tell you you're wrong?' Danny said. ... Most people hate changing their mind; he liked nothing better, when the evidence justified it," Zweig (2024). Skepticism is essential to the scientific method.

2.3.2 Gender Birth Numbers

We now apply our reasoning to the more interesting question about gender birth numbers.

Notation 2.4 *Let the a priori probability of the probability of female on one birth be denoted by* Γ. *We denote the generalized event (or hypothesis) that birth is* ***actually*** *gender-neutral by* **gender_neutral** *and the generalized event (or hypothesis) that birth is* ***actually*** *gender-biased by* **gender_biased**. *We denote the generalized event (or hypothesis) that a birth results in a female by FEMALE and the generalized event (or hypothesis) that a birth results in a male by MALE (please see Fisher (1930) for a scientific attempt to understand gender ratios).*

Lemma 2.3

$$Prob\,(FEMALE \mid \Gamma = \gamma) = \gamma \tag{2.44}$$

$$Prob\,(MALE \mid \Gamma = \gamma) = 1 - \gamma \tag{2.45}$$

and, therefore, the a priori unconditional generalized probabilities are

$$Prob\left((FEMALE)^n \mid \Gamma = \gamma\right) = (\gamma)^n \tag{2.46}$$

$$Prob\left((MALE)^n \mid \Gamma = \gamma\right) = (1 - \gamma)^n \tag{2.47}$$

$$Prob\left((FEMALE)^r\,(MALE)^{n-r} \mid \Gamma = \gamma\right) = \binom{n}{r}(\gamma)^r\,(1 - \gamma)^{n-r} \tag{2.48}$$

Notation 2.5 *Let the a priori probability that birth is gender-neutral be given by*

$$Prob\left(\Gamma = \frac{1}{2}; \theta\right) = \theta \tag{2.49}$$

We are interested in the probability of

$$\begin{aligned} & Prob\left(\textbf{gender\_neutral} \mid (FEMALE)^r\,(MALE)^{n-r}\right) \\ = \; & Prob\left((FEMALE)^r\,(MALE)^{n-r} \mid \textbf{gender\_neutral}\right) \\ & \times \frac{Prob\,(\textbf{gender\_neutral})}{Prob\left((FEMALE)^r\,(MALE)^{n-r}\right)} \end{aligned} \tag{2.50}$$

This provides the scientific measurements to inform the policy implications of gender-selective abortions in India and China.

2.3.2.1 Non-Degenerate Prior: $\theta < 1$

As mentioned above, the scientific method demands a non-degenerate prior.

Assumption 2.6 *Let the a priori gender-biased generalized probabilities be uniformly distributed across* $(0, 1) \setminus \{\frac{1}{2}\}$ *with an a priori Delta Factor of* δ *as follows*

$$Prob\,(\Gamma \in (a, b)\,; \theta, \delta) = (b - a)\,((1 - \theta) - \delta)\,, a < b < \frac{1}{2} \tag{2.51}$$

$$Prob\,(\Gamma \in (a, b)\,; \theta, \delta) = (b - a)\,((1 - \theta) + \delta)\,, \frac{1}{2} < a < b \tag{2.52}$$

Please see Section 2.3.2.2 and note the serious discontinuities at $\theta = 1$. Please refer to Section 2.3.3.3 for the equivalence of a non-degenerate prior with the scientific method. In other words, the gender-biased generalized probabilities have a density function

$$f(x) = \begin{cases} (1-\theta) - \delta, 0 < x < \frac{1}{2} \\ (1-\theta) + \delta, \frac{1}{2} < x < 1 \end{cases} \tag{2.53}$$

Therefore, for any measurable $A \subseteq [0, 1]$,

$$\begin{aligned} Prob\,(\Gamma \in A; \theta, \delta) \quad = \quad & \left(\int_{x \in A \cap \left(0, \frac{1}{2}\right)} ((1-\theta) - \delta)\, dx \right) \\ & + \left(\int_{x \in A \cap \left(\frac{1}{2}, 1\right)} ((1-\theta) + \delta)\, dx \right) \\ & + \mathbf{1}\left(x \in A \cap \left\{ \frac{1}{2} \right\} \right) \theta \end{aligned} \tag{2.54}$$

Note that $\delta > 0$ implies that there is an *a priori* bias in favor of a higher probability of female. First, one needs

$$\theta + \int_0^{\frac{1}{2}} ((1-\theta) - \delta)\, dz + \int_{\frac{1}{2}}^1 ((1-\theta) + \delta)\, dz \equiv 1 \tag{2.55}$$

Second, one needs

$$(1-\theta) - \delta \geq 0 \tag{2.56}$$

and

$$(1-\theta) + \delta \geq 0 \tag{2.57}$$

which hold if and only if

$$-\min\{\theta, 1-\theta\} \leq \delta \leq \min\{\theta, 1-\theta\} \tag{2.58}$$

We arrive at the following result by applying Bayes Theorem (Theorem 1.3).

Theorem 2.3 *Let*

$$0 < \theta < 1 \tag{2.59}$$

$$-\min\{\theta, 1-\theta\} \leq \delta \leq \min\{\theta, 1-\theta\} \tag{2.60}$$

The specific generalized probabilities of gender-neutrality of birth, conditional on n births resulting in r females, are as follows: For measurable $A \subseteq [0,1]$,

$$\begin{aligned} & Prob\left(\Gamma \in A \mid (FEMALE)^r (MALE)^{n-r}; \theta, \delta\right) \\ = & Prob\left((FEMALE)^r (MALE)^{n-r} \mid \Gamma \in A; \theta, \delta\right) \\ & \times \frac{Prob\,(\Gamma \in A; \theta, \delta)}{Prob\left((FEMALE)^r (MALE)^{n-r}; \theta, \delta\right)} \end{aligned} \tag{2.61}$$

where

$$\begin{aligned} \Pi\,(A;\theta,\delta) &= Prob\,(FEMALE; \theta, \delta \mid \Gamma \in A; \theta, \delta) \\ &= \frac{\int_{x \in A \cap \left(0, \frac{1}{2}\right)} ((1-\theta)-\delta)\, x dx}{\int_{x \in A \cap \left(0, \frac{1}{2}\right)} ((1-\theta)-\delta)\, dx} \\ &\quad + \frac{\int_{x \in A \cap \left(\frac{1}{2}, 1\right)} ((1-\theta)+\delta)\, x dx}{\int_{x \in A \cap \left(\frac{1}{2}, 1\right)} ((1-\theta)+\delta)\, dx} \\ &\quad + \mathbf{1}\left(x \in A \cap \left\{\frac{1}{2}\right\}\right)\frac{1}{2} \end{aligned} \tag{2.62}$$

$$\begin{aligned} Prob\,(\Gamma \in A; \theta, \delta) &= \left(\int_{x \in A \cap \left(0, \frac{1}{2}\right)} ((1-\theta)-\delta)\, dx\right) \\ &\quad + \left(\int_{x \in A \cap \left(\frac{1}{2}, 1\right)} ((1-\theta)+\delta)\, dx\right) \\ &\quad + \mathbf{1}\left(x \in A \cap \left\{\frac{1}{2}\right\}\right)\theta \end{aligned} \tag{2.63}$$

$$Prob\left((FEMALE)^r (MALE)^{n-r}; \theta, \delta\right) = \binom{n}{r}\left(\frac{1}{4}\delta + \frac{1}{2}\right)^r \left(\frac{1}{2} - \frac{1}{4}\delta\right)^{n-r} \tag{2.64}$$

$$(\in [0,1] \ \textit{from conditions})$$

Corollary 2.1 *The probability of n births resulting in all females, conditional on the a priori probability of gender-neutrality belonging to a measurable set A, is*

$$Prob\left((FEMALE)^n; \theta, \delta \mid \Gamma \in A; \theta, \delta\right) = (\Pi\,(A;\theta,\delta))^n \tag{2.65}$$

and the probability of n births resulting in r females and n − r males, conditional on the a priori probability of gender-neutrality belonging to a measurable set A, is

$$\begin{aligned} & Prob\left((FEMALE)^r (MALE)^{n-r} \mid \Gamma \in A; \theta, \delta\right) \\ = & \binom{n}{r} (\Pi\,(A;\theta,\delta))^r (1 - \Pi\,(A;\theta,\delta))^{n-r} \end{aligned} \tag{2.66}$$

Corollary 2.2 *In the special case of the a priori Delta Factor at degenerate $\delta = 0$, the probability of one birth resulting in a female, conditional on the a priori probability of gender-neutrality belonging to a measurable set $A \subseteq [0,1]$ is*

$$\begin{aligned} \Pi(A;\theta,0) &= Prob\,(FEMALE;\theta,0 \mid \Gamma \in A;\theta,0) \\ &= \frac{\int_{x \in A \setminus \{\frac{1}{2}\}} (1-\theta)\,x dx}{\int_{x \in A \setminus \{\frac{1}{2}\}} (1-\theta)\,dx} + \mathbf{1}\left(x \in A \cap \left\{\frac{1}{2}\right\}\right)\frac{1}{2} \\ &\quad (\in [0,1] \textit{ from conditions}) \end{aligned} \tag{2.67}$$

Corollary 2.3 *Under the special case that the a priori Delta Factor is degenerate at $\delta = 0$, the specific generalized probabilities of gender-neutrality of birth, conditional on n births resulting in r females, are as follows: For measurable $A \subseteq [0,1]$,*

$$\begin{aligned} & Prob\left(\Gamma \in A \mid (FEMALE)^r (MALE)^{n-r};\theta,0\right) \\ = \; & Prob\left((FEMALE)^r (MALE)^{n-r} \mid \Gamma \in A;\theta,0\right) \\ & \times \frac{Prob\,(\Gamma \in A;\theta,0)}{Prob\left((FEMALE)^r (MALE)^{n-r};\theta,0\right)} \end{aligned} \tag{2.68}$$

where

$$\begin{aligned} & Prob\left((FEMALE)^r (MALE)^{n-r} \mid \Gamma \in A;\theta,0\right) \\ = \; & \binom{n}{r} (\Pi(A;\theta,0))^r (1-\Pi(A;\theta,0))^{n-r} \end{aligned} \tag{2.69}$$

$$\begin{aligned} \Pi(A;\theta,0) &= \frac{\int_{x \in A \setminus \{\frac{1}{2}\}} (1-\theta)\,x dx}{\int_{x \in A \setminus \{\frac{1}{2}\}} (1-\theta)\,dx} \\ &\quad + \mathbf{1}\left(x \in A \cap \left\{\frac{1}{2}\right\}\right)\frac{1}{2} \end{aligned} \tag{2.70}$$

$$\begin{aligned} Prob\,(\Gamma \in A;\theta,0) &= \left(\int_{x \in A \setminus \{\frac{1}{2}\}} (1-\theta)\,dx\right) \\ &\quad + \mathbf{1}\left(x \in A \cap \left\{\frac{1}{2}\right\}\right)\theta \\ &\quad (\in [0,1] \textit{ from conditions}) \end{aligned} \tag{2.71}$$

$$Prob\left((FEMALE)^r (MALE)^{n-r};\theta,0\right) = \binom{n}{r}\left(\frac{1}{2}\right)^n \tag{2.72}$$

Corollary 2.4 *Under the special case that the a priori Delta Factor is degenerate at $\delta = 0$,*

1.

$$Prob\left(\textbf{gender\_neutral} \mid (FEMALE)^r\,(MALE)^{n-r};\theta,0\right) \tag{2.73}$$
$$= Prob\,(\textbf{gender\_neutral};\theta,0)$$

2.

$$Prob\left(\textbf{gender\_biased} \mid (FEMALE)^r\,(MALE)^{n-r};\theta,0\right) \tag{2.74}$$
$$= Prob\,(\textbf{gender\_biased};\theta,0)$$

If $\theta = 0.5$, $\delta = 0$, then the conditional probability of a female birth is as follows:

$$\begin{cases} = \frac{1}{2} & \text{with probability} & = \frac{2^n}{(2+0)^r(2-0)^{n-r}}0.5 = 0.5 \\ \neq \frac{1}{2} & \text{with probability} & = 1 - 0.5 = 0.5 \end{cases} \tag{2.75}$$

2.3.2.2 *Degenerate Prior: $\theta = 1$*

This is the situation when it is fully sure that birth is gender-neutral; i.e., no matter how much evidence is produced against birth being gender-neutral, that does not change the probability that birth is gender-neutral; i.e.,

$$Prob\left(\Gamma = \frac{1}{2}\right) = 1 \tag{2.76}$$

and therefore,

$$Prob\left(\Gamma \neq \frac{1}{2}\right) = 0 \tag{2.77}$$

Theorem 2.4 *If $\theta = 1$, the probability of birth being gender-neutral, conditional on n births resulting in r females, is 1, and the probability of birth being gender-biased, conditional on n births resulting in n female births, is 0; i.e.,*

$$Prob\left(\textbf{gender\_neutral} \mid (FEMALE)^r\,(MALE)^{n-r}\right) = 1 \tag{2.78}$$

and

$$Prob\left(\textbf{gender\_biased} \mid (FEMALE)^r\,(MALE)^{n-r}\right) = 0 \tag{2.79}$$

This is the situation many people think of when they assert that the probability of female on the next birth is exactly 50%, after **any** number of observed gender births. Please see Section 2.3.3.3 for a discussion of the equivalence of a non-degenerate prior with the scientific method.

2.3.3 Gender Birth Proportions

This subsection studies the most interesting question of gender birth proportions, which can speak to the impact of sex selection policies. Let, as before, the *a priori* probability that birth is gender-neutral be given by

$$Prob\left(\Gamma = \frac{1}{2}; \theta\right) = \theta \tag{2.80}$$

2.3.3.1 Non-Degenerate Prior: $\theta < 1$

Please see Section 2.3.3.2 and note the serious discontinuities at $\theta = 1$. Please refer to Section 2.3.3.3 for the equivalence of a non-degenerate prior with the scientific method. This provides the scientific measurements to inform the policy implications of gender-selective abortions in India and China.

Assumption 2.7 *Let the a priori gender-biased generalized probabilities be uniformly distributed across* $(0,1) \setminus \left\{\frac{1}{2}\right\}$ *with an a priori Delta Factor of* δ *as follows*

$$Prob\left(\Gamma \in (a,b); \theta, \delta\right) = (b-a)\left((1-\theta) - \delta\right), a < b < \frac{1}{2} \tag{2.81}$$

$$Prob\left(\Gamma \in (a,b); \theta, \delta\right) = (b-a)\left((1-\theta) + \delta\right), \frac{1}{2} < a < b \tag{2.82}$$

In other words, the gender-biased generalized probabilities have an unconditional density function

$$\begin{aligned} GenProbDensity_{\Gamma}(\gamma; \theta, \delta) &= \begin{cases} (1-\theta) - \delta, 0 < \gamma < \frac{1}{2} \\ (1-\theta) + \delta, \frac{1}{2} < \gamma < 1 \end{cases} \\ &= \mathbf{1}\left(0 < \gamma < \frac{1}{2}\right)\left((1-\theta) - \delta\right) \\ &\quad + \mathbf{1}\left(\frac{1}{2} < \gamma < 1\right)\left((1-\theta) + \delta\right) \end{aligned} \tag{2.83}$$

and, therefore,

$$
\begin{aligned}
Prob\,(\Gamma \in A;\theta,\delta) &= \int_{\gamma\in A} \mathbf{d}Prob_{\Gamma}(\gamma) && (2.84)\\
&= \mathbf{1}\left(\frac{1}{2}\in A\right)\theta \\
&\quad + \int_{\gamma\in A\setminus\{\frac{1}{2}\}} \boldsymbol{GenProbDensity}_{\Gamma}(\gamma;\theta,\delta)\,d\gamma \\
&= \mathbf{1}\left(\frac{1}{2}\in A\right)\theta \\
&\quad + \int_{\gamma\in A\setminus\{\frac{1}{2}\}} \left(\mathbf{1}\left(0<\gamma<\frac{1}{2}\right)((1-\theta)-\delta)\right)d\gamma \\
&\quad + \int_{\gamma\in A\setminus\{\frac{1}{2}\}} \left(\mathbf{1}\left(\frac{1}{2}<\gamma<1\right)((1-\theta)+\delta)\right)d\gamma
\end{aligned}
$$

As before,

$$\theta + \int_0^{\frac{1}{2}} ((1-\theta)-\delta)\,dz + \int_{\frac{1}{2}}^1 ((1-\theta)+\delta)\,dz \equiv 1 \tag{2.85}$$

And, we need

$$(1-\theta)-\delta \geq 0 \tag{2.86}$$

and

$$(1-\theta)+\delta \geq 0 \tag{2.87}$$

which hold if

$$-\min\{\theta,1-\theta\} \leq \delta \leq \min\{\theta,1-\theta\} \tag{2.88}$$

This result follows from the Weak Law of Large Numbers, please see Billingsley (2012). The Gaussian distribution is also known as the "Normal" distribution.

Theorem 2.5 *Let the observed proportion of female births be X. Then, for large n, the distribution of X, conditional on $\Gamma = \gamma$, is Gaussian with mean γ and variance $\frac{\gamma(1-\gamma)}{n}$.*

Corollary 2.5 *If the evidence B is a realization of a random variable absolutely continuous with respect to the Lebesgue measure on $\mathbb{R}^T$, i.e.,*

$$Prob\,(B=b) = 0, \forall b \in \mathbb{R}^T \tag{2.89}$$

then Bayes Theorem (Theorem 1.3).can be restated as follows:

$$
\begin{aligned}
& Prob\,(A \mid B = b) \\
= \; & \frac{GenProbDensity_{B|A}\,(b \mid A)}{GenProbDensity_{B}\,(b)} Prob\,(A) \\
= \; & \frac{GenProbDensity_{B|A}\,(b \mid A)}{\int_a GenProbDensity_{B|A}\,(b \mid A = a)\,\mathbf{d}Prob\,(a)} Prob\,(A)
\end{aligned}
\tag{2.90}
$$

In other words, Prob (A) *is the prior probability of hypothesis A, the* ***Value Ratio of Evidence*** $B = b$ *for the hypothesis A is*

$$
\begin{aligned}
& Value\ Ratio\ of\ Evidence\,(B = b; A) \\
= \; & \frac{GenProbDensity_{B|A}\,(b \mid A)}{GenProbDensity_{B}\,(b)}
\end{aligned}
\tag{2.91}
$$

and therefore, Bayes Theorem can be restated as (ex post probability of hypothesis A) equals (value ratio of evidence B for hypothesis A) times (ex ante probability of hypothesis A).

We arrive at the following results by applying Bayes Theorem (Theorem 1.3).

Theorem 2.6 *Let*

$$\theta < 1 \tag{2.92}$$

$$-\min\{\theta, 1-\theta\} \leq \delta \leq \min\{\theta, 1-\theta\} \tag{2.93}$$

The probability of gender-neutrality of birth, conditional on the observed gender proportion of births x and number of births n, is

$$
\frac{\theta \frac{1}{\sqrt{\frac{\left(\frac{1}{2}\right)\left(1-\left(\frac{1}{2}\right)\right)}{n}}\sqrt{2\pi}} \exp\left(-\frac{\left(x-\left(\frac{1}{2}\right)\right)^2}{2\frac{\left(\frac{1}{2}\right)\left(1-\left(\frac{1}{2}\right)\right)}{n}}\right)}{\left(\begin{array}{l}
\int_0^{\frac{1}{2}} \frac{(1-\theta)-\delta}{\sqrt{\frac{\gamma(1-\gamma)}{n}}\sqrt{2\pi}} \exp\left(-\frac{(x-\gamma)^2}{2\frac{\gamma(1-\gamma)}{n}}\right) d\gamma \\
+\frac{\theta}{\sqrt{\frac{\left(\frac{1}{2}\right)\left(1-\left(\frac{1}{2}\right)\right)}{n}}\sqrt{2\pi}} \exp\left(-\frac{\left(x-\left(\frac{1}{2}\right)\right)^2}{2\frac{\left(\frac{1}{2}\right)\left(1-\left(\frac{1}{2}\right)\right)}{n}}\right) \\
+\int_{\frac{1}{2}}^{1} \frac{(1-\theta)+\delta}{\sqrt{\frac{\gamma(1-\gamma)}{n}}\sqrt{2\pi}} \exp\left(-\frac{(x-\gamma)^2}{2\frac{\gamma(1-\gamma)}{n}}\right) d\gamma
\end{array}\right)}
\tag{2.94}
$$

The density function of the probability of gender-neutrality of birth, conditional on the observed gender proportion of births x and number of births n, is

for $\gamma \in \left(0, \frac{1}{2}\right)$

$$\frac{\frac{1}{\sqrt{\frac{\gamma(1-\gamma)}{n}}\sqrt{2\pi}}\exp\left(-\frac{(x-\gamma)^2}{2\frac{\gamma(1-\gamma)}{n}}\right)((1-\theta)-\delta)}{\left(\begin{array}{l}\int_0^{\frac{1}{2}}\frac{(1-\theta)-\delta}{\sqrt{\frac{\gamma(1-\gamma)}{n}}\sqrt{2\pi}}\exp\left(-\frac{(x-\gamma)^2}{2\frac{\gamma(1-\gamma)}{n}}\right)d\gamma\\ +\frac{\theta}{\sqrt{\frac{\left(\frac{1}{2}\right)\left(1-\left(\frac{1}{2}\right)\right)}{n}}\sqrt{2\pi}}\exp\left(-\frac{\left(x-\left(\frac{1}{2}\right)\right)^2}{2\frac{\left(\frac{1}{2}\right)\left(1-\left(\frac{1}{2}\right)\right)}{n}}\right)\\ +\int_{\frac{1}{2}}^{1}\frac{(1-\theta)+\delta}{\sqrt{\frac{\gamma(1-\gamma)}{n}}\sqrt{2\pi}}\exp\left(-\frac{(x-\gamma)^2}{2\frac{\gamma(1-\gamma)}{n}}\right)d\gamma\end{array}\right)} \tag{2.95}$$

and

for $\gamma \in \left(\frac{1}{2}, 1\right)$

$$\frac{\frac{1}{\sqrt{\frac{\gamma(1-\gamma)}{n}}\sqrt{2\pi}}\exp\left(-\frac{(x-\gamma)^2}{2\frac{\gamma(1-\gamma)}{n}}\right)((1-\theta)+\delta)}{\left(\begin{array}{l}\int_0^{\frac{1}{2}}\frac{(1-\theta)-\delta}{\sqrt{\frac{\gamma(1-\gamma)}{n}}\sqrt{2\pi}}\exp\left(-\frac{(x-\gamma)^2}{2\frac{\gamma(1-\gamma)}{n}}\right)d\gamma\\ +\frac{\theta}{\sqrt{\frac{\left(\frac{1}{2}\right)\left(1-\left(\frac{1}{2}\right)\right)}{n}}\sqrt{2\pi}}\exp\left(-\frac{\left(x-\left(\frac{1}{2}\right)\right)^2}{2\frac{\left(\frac{1}{2}\right)\left(1-\left(\frac{1}{2}\right)\right)}{n}}\right)\\ +\int_{\frac{1}{2}}^{1}\frac{(1-\theta)+\delta}{\sqrt{\frac{\gamma(1-\gamma)}{n}}\sqrt{2\pi}}\exp\left(-\frac{(x-\gamma)^2}{2\frac{\gamma(1-\gamma)}{n}}\right)d\gamma\end{array}\right)} \tag{2.96}$$

Theorem 2.7 *Let*

$$\theta < 1 \tag{2.97}$$

$$-\min\{\theta, 1-\theta\} \leq \delta \leq \min\{\theta, 1-\theta\} \tag{2.98}$$

Let there be T independent and identically distributed observations gender proportion of births $(x_1, x_2, ..., x_T)$ *and number of births* $(n_1, n_2, ...n_T)$*.Then, the probability of gender-neutrality of birth, conditional on the T observed gender proportion of births* $X^T = (x_1, x_2, ..., x_T)$ *and number of births* $N^T = (n_1, n_2, ..., n_T)$*,* *is*

$$\frac{\theta\prod_{t=1}^{T}\frac{1}{\sqrt{\frac{\left(\frac{1}{2}\right)\left(1-\left(\frac{1}{2}\right)\right)}{n_t}}\sqrt{2\pi}}\exp\left(-\frac{\left(x_t-\left(\frac{1}{2}\right)\right)^2}{2\frac{\left(\frac{1}{2}\right)\left(1-\left(\frac{1}{2}\right)\right)}{n_t}}\right)}{\prod_{t=1}^{T}\left(\begin{array}{c}\int_0^{\frac{1}{2}}\frac{(1-\theta)-\delta}{\sqrt{\frac{\gamma(1-\gamma)}{n_t}}\sqrt{2\pi}}\exp\left(-\frac{(x_t-\gamma)^2}{2\frac{\gamma(1-\gamma)}{n_t}}\right)d\gamma\\+\frac{\theta}{\sqrt{\frac{\left(\frac{1}{2}\right)\left(1-\left(\frac{1}{2}\right)\right)}{n_t}}\sqrt{2\pi}}\exp\left(-\frac{\left(x_t-\left(\frac{1}{2}\right)\right)^2}{2\frac{\left(\frac{1}{2}\right)\left(1-\left(\frac{1}{2}\right)\right)}{n_t}}\right)\\+\int_{\frac{1}{2}}^{1}\frac{(1-\theta)+\delta}{\sqrt{\frac{\gamma(1-\gamma)}{n_t}}\sqrt{2\pi}}\exp\left(-\frac{(x_t-\gamma)^2}{2\frac{\gamma(1-\gamma)}{n_t}}\right)d\gamma\end{array}\right)} \tag{2.99}$$

And the density function of the probability of gender-neutrality of birth, conditional on the observed gender proportion of births $X^T = (x_1, x_2, ..., x_T)$ and number of births $N^T = (n_1, n_2, ..., n_T)$, is

for $\gamma \in \left(0, \frac{1}{2}\right)$

$$\frac{((1-\theta)-\delta)\prod_{t=1}^{T}\frac{1}{\sqrt{\frac{\gamma(1-\gamma)}{n_t}}\sqrt{2\pi}}\exp\left(-\frac{(x_t-\gamma)^2}{2\frac{\gamma(1-\gamma)}{n_t}}\right)}{\prod_{t=1}^{T}\left(\begin{array}{c}\int_0^{\frac{1}{2}}\frac{(1-\theta)-\delta}{\sqrt{\frac{\gamma(1-\gamma)}{n_t}}\sqrt{2\pi}}\exp\left(-\frac{(x_t-\gamma)^2}{2\frac{\gamma(1-\gamma)}{n_t}}\right)d\gamma\\+\frac{\theta}{\sqrt{\frac{\left(\frac{1}{2}\right)\left(1-\left(\frac{1}{2}\right)\right)}{n_t}}\sqrt{2\pi}}\exp\left(-\frac{\left(x_t-\left(\frac{1}{2}\right)\right)^2}{2\frac{\left(\frac{1}{2}\right)\left(1-\left(\frac{1}{2}\right)\right)}{n_t}}\right)\\+\int_{\frac{1}{2}}^{1}\frac{(1-\theta)+\delta}{\sqrt{\frac{\gamma(1-\gamma)}{n_t}}\sqrt{2\pi}}\exp\left(-\frac{(x_t-\gamma)^2}{2\frac{\gamma(1-\gamma)}{n_t}}\right)d\gamma\end{array}\right)} \tag{2.100}$$

and

for $\gamma \in \left(\frac{1}{2}, 1\right)$

$$\frac{((1-\theta)+\delta)\prod_{t=1}^{T}\frac{1}{\sqrt{\frac{\gamma(1-\gamma)}{n_t}}\sqrt{2\pi}}\exp\left(-\frac{(x_t-\gamma)^2}{2\frac{\gamma(1-\gamma)}{n_t}}\right)}{\prod_{t=1}^{T}\left(\begin{array}{c}\int_0^{\frac{1}{2}}\frac{(1-\theta)-\delta}{\sqrt{\frac{\gamma(1-\gamma)}{n_t}}\sqrt{2\pi}}\exp\left(-\frac{(x_t-\gamma)^2}{2\frac{\gamma(1-\gamma)}{n_t}}\right)d\gamma\\+\frac{\theta}{\sqrt{\frac{\left(\frac{1}{2}\right)\left(1-\left(\frac{1}{2}\right)\right)}{n_t}}\sqrt{2\pi}}\exp\left(-\frac{\left(x_t-\left(\frac{1}{2}\right)\right)^2}{2\frac{\left(\frac{1}{2}\right)\left(1-\left(\frac{1}{2}\right)\right)}{n_t}}\right)\\+\int_{\frac{1}{2}}^{1}\frac{(1-\theta)+\delta}{\sqrt{\frac{\gamma(1-\gamma)}{n_t}}\sqrt{2\pi}}\exp\left(-\frac{(x_t-\gamma)^2}{2\frac{\gamma(1-\gamma)}{n_t}}\right)d\gamma\end{array}\right)} \tag{2.101}$$

Finally, we compute the conditional interval probability of gender-neutrality of birth, given the T observed gender proportion of births $X^T = (x_1, x_2, ..., x_T)$ and number of births $N^T = (n_1, n_2, ..., n_T)$.

Theorem 2.8 *Let*

$$\theta < 1 \tag{2.102}$$

$$-\min\{\theta, 1-\theta\} \leq \delta \leq \min\{\theta, 1-\theta\} \tag{2.103}$$

and

$$0 \leq \varepsilon \leq \frac{1}{2} \tag{2.104}$$

Let there be T independent and identically distributed observations gender proportion of births $(x_1, x_2, ..., x_T)$ *and number of births* $(n_1, n_2, ...n_T)$*. Then, the interval probability of gender-neutrality of birth, conditional on the T observed gender proportion of births* $(x_1, x_2, ..., x_T)$ *and number of births* $(n_1, n_2, ...n_T)$*, is*

$$Prob\left(\Gamma \in \left(\frac{1}{2} - \varepsilon, \frac{1}{2} + \varepsilon\right) \mid X^T; \theta, \delta, N^T\right) \tag{2.105}$$

is

$$\frac{\theta \prod_{t=1}^{T} \frac{1}{\sqrt{\frac{\left(\frac{1}{2}\right)\left(1-\left(\frac{1}{2}\right)\right)}{n_t}}\sqrt{2\pi}} \exp\left(-\frac{\left(x_t - \left(\frac{1}{2}\right)\right)^2}{2\frac{\left(\frac{1}{2}\right)\left(1-\left(\frac{1}{2}\right)\right)}{n_t}}\right)}{\prod_{t=1}^{T}\left(\begin{array}{c} \int_0^{\frac{1}{2}} \frac{(1-\theta)-\delta}{\sqrt{\frac{\gamma(1-\gamma)}{n_t}}\sqrt{2\pi}} \exp\left(-\frac{(x_t-\gamma)^2}{2\frac{\gamma(1-\gamma)}{n_t}}\right) d\gamma \\ + \frac{\theta}{\sqrt{\frac{\left(\frac{1}{2}\right)\left(1-\left(\frac{1}{2}\right)\right)}{n_t}}\sqrt{2\pi}} \exp\left(-\frac{\left(x_t - \left(\frac{1}{2}\right)\right)^2}{2\frac{\left(\frac{1}{2}\right)\left(1-\left(\frac{1}{2}\right)\right)}{n_t}}\right) \\ + \int_{\frac{1}{2}}^{1} \frac{(1-\theta)+\delta}{\sqrt{\frac{\gamma(1-\gamma)}{n_t}}\sqrt{2\pi}} \exp\left(-\frac{(x_t-\gamma)^2}{2\frac{\gamma(1-\gamma)}{n_t}}\right) d\gamma \end{array}\right)}$$
$$+ \int_{\frac{1}{2}-\varepsilon}^{\frac{1}{2}} \frac{((1-\theta)-\delta) \prod_{t=1}^{T} \frac{1}{\sqrt{\frac{\gamma(1-\gamma)}{n_t}}\sqrt{2\pi}} \exp\left(-\frac{(x_t-\gamma)^2}{2\frac{\gamma(1-\gamma)}{n_t}}\right)}{\prod_{t=1}^{T}\left(\begin{array}{c} \int_0^{\frac{1}{2}} \frac{(1-\theta)-\delta}{\sqrt{\frac{\gamma(1-\gamma)}{n_t}}\sqrt{2\pi}} \exp\left(-\frac{(x_t-\gamma)^2}{2\frac{\gamma(1-\gamma)}{n_t}}\right) d\gamma \\ + \frac{\theta}{\sqrt{\frac{\left(\frac{1}{2}\right)\left(1-\left(\frac{1}{2}\right)\right)}{n_t}}\sqrt{2\pi}} \exp\left(-\frac{\left(x_t - \left(\frac{1}{2}\right)\right)^2}{2\frac{\left(\frac{1}{2}\right)\left(1-\left(\frac{1}{2}\right)\right)}{n_t}}\right) \\ + \int_{\frac{1}{2}}^{1} \frac{(1-\theta)+\delta}{\sqrt{\frac{\gamma(1-\gamma)}{n_t}}\sqrt{2\pi}} \exp\left(-\frac{(x_t-\gamma)^2}{2\frac{\gamma(1-\gamma)}{n_t}}\right) d\gamma \end{array}\right)} d\gamma \tag{2.106}$$

$$+\int_{\frac{1}{2}}^{\frac{1}{2}+\varepsilon} \frac{((1-\theta)+\delta)\prod_{t=1}^{T}\frac{1}{\sqrt{\frac{\gamma(1-\gamma)}{n_t}}\sqrt{2\pi}}\exp\left(-\frac{(x_t-\gamma)^2}{2\frac{\gamma(1-\gamma)}{n_t}}\right)}{\prod_{t=1}^{T}\left(\begin{array}{c}\int_0^{\frac{1}{2}}\frac{(1-\theta)-\delta}{\sqrt{\frac{\gamma(1-\gamma)}{n_t}}\sqrt{2\pi}}\exp\left(-\frac{(x_t-\gamma)^2}{2\frac{\gamma(1-\gamma)}{n_t}}\right)d\gamma\\ +\frac{\theta}{\sqrt{\frac{\left(\frac{1}{2}\right)\left(1-\left(\frac{1}{2}\right)\right)}{n_t}}\sqrt{2\pi}}\exp\left(-\frac{\left(x_t-\left(\frac{1}{2}\right)\right)^2}{2\frac{\left(\frac{1}{2}\right)\left(1-\left(\frac{1}{2}\right)\right)}{n_t}}\right)\\ +\int_{\frac{1}{2}}^{1}\frac{(1-\theta)+\delta}{\sqrt{\frac{\gamma(1-\gamma)}{n_t}}\sqrt{2\pi}}\exp\left(-\frac{(x_t-\gamma)^2}{2\frac{\gamma(1-\gamma)}{n_t}}\right)d\gamma\end{array}\right)}d\gamma$$

2.3.3.1.1 Application to Observed Birth Proportions in the U.S. and India: Please see Section 2.3.3.2 and note the serious discontinuities at $\theta = 1$. Please see Section 2.3.3.3 for the equivalence between the scientific method and a non-degenerate prior. Table 2.2 provides the scientific measurements to inform the policy implications of alleged gender-selective abortions in India (and China).

2.3.3.2 *Degenerate Prior: $\theta = 1$*

The following result speaks to the pathological case of blind faith.

Theorem 2.9 *If $\theta = 1$, the conditional probability of birth being gender-neutral, given T observations of $(x_1, x_2, \ldots, x_T)$ female birth proportions, is 1, and the conditional probability of birth being gender-biased, given T observations of $(x_1, x_2, \ldots, x_T)$ female birth proportions, is 0.*

This is the situation many people think of when they assert that the chance of a female birth is exactly 50%, even after many repeated observations of gender proportions of births. In particular, note the serious discontinuities above at $\theta = 1$.

2.3.3.3 *Falsifiability and Non-Degenerate Prior*

The criterion of falsifiability is essential to a scientific theory: A scientific theory must provide a set of facts, such that, if they were to eventuate, would rationally falsify the theory — please see, for instance, Popper (1959), and a discussion of closed epistemic systems in, for example, Luper (2020).

TABLE 2.2 Observed Gender Proportions of Birth, 2017

Country	Total Number of Births	Female Proportion of Births
India	25,732,835	0.47037
U.S.	4,089,024	0.48852

Source: World Bank

In Sections 2.3.1.1 and 2.3.1.2 for coin tosses, Sections 2.3.2.1 and 2.3.2.2 for birth numbers, and Sections 2.3.3.1 and 2.3.3.2 for birth proportions, we have clearly demonstrated that if and only if the prior is non-degenerate can there exist a set of facts that can rationally falsify a theory; in other words, a theory is falsifiable if and only if the prior is non-degenerate; and thus, a theory is scientific if and only if the prior is non-degenerate.

"Faith ... is wholly independent of the epistemic concern that cares about evidential support. On this view, faith reveals its authenticity most clearly when it takes faith-propositions to be true contrary to the weight of the evidence" Bishop (2016). The requirement, therefore, that a conclusion depend on evidence and therefore, change with additional evidence, is fundamental to the difference between science and faith, and therefore, a degenerate prior implies and is implied by the theory belonging in the realm of faith, rather than science. A scientific theory must provide a set of facts, such that, if the set of facts were to eventuate, the theory would be falsified.

For example, is "anthropogenic climate change" a scientific theory? What falsifying events would negate the theory? And conversely, is "climate denial" a scientific theory? What falsifying events would negate this theory?

To take a recent example from the field of finance, Professor Kenneth Rogoff spoke recently about "belie[f] in Fed independence" (Timiraos, 2025). First, "belief in Fed independence" is nonsensical, so we have to presume that by that phrase, he meant to refer to the belief that Fed independence is beneficial. Second, the scientific method would demand that "Fed independence is beneficial" be a scientific theory, which can, thus, be tested or falsified by actual data, not a statement of "belief," which admits to no such falsifiability or testability. Third, as we have emphasized in Chapter 1, truth is objective and not determined by majority voting or consensus, so the fact that there were "18 signatories on a ... brief [that] was signed by every living former Fed chair ... as well as senior economic advisers to Republican and Democratic presidents" (even leaving aside the self-serving nature of such statements) is not dispositive proof, although under the reasonable assumption that the opinions of these eighteen signatories were informed, this brief does provide evidence in favor of the scientific hypothesis that Fed independence is beneficial (please see Section 1.3.9 for details on the value ratio of evidence). Fourth, that something as important as monetary policy should be determined by unelected and unaccountable bureaucrats who are appointed through opaque and convoluted processes for extraordinarily long terms is exactly the argument for a "benevolent dictator." Finally, and most to the point of this book, given all the uncertainties in the financial world over the last few decades, it seems somewhat presumptuous to assert that because something is supposed to have worked for a hundred years implies that Fed independence would be beneficial in the future as well — as an aside, the signatories to the brief referred to above claimed that "central-bank independence

... has helped make the United States' economy the strongest in the world," whereas in terms of monetary policy independence, the U.S. ranks 82nd-87th in the world (Jordan and Luther, 2020).

For another example, consider the recent controversy about pregnant women taking acetaminophen, "[i]n an extraordinary public announcement that contradicted widespread medical consensus ... President [Donald] Trump warned that acetaminophen is a potential cause of autism" (Loftus et al., 2025), the scientific method demands that neither widespread medical consensus nor President Trump's warning determines dispositively the truth or otherwise of the scientific theory that acetaminophen is a potential cause of autism, although, as in the previous example, under the reasonable assumption that the opinions of medical experts were informed, this "widespread medical consensus" does provide evidence against the scientific hypothesis that the taking of acetaminophen by pregnant mothers can cause autism in their children (please see Section 1.3.9 for details on the value ratio of evidence).

To summarize, "science is the belief in the ignorance of experts," Richard Feynman, Nobel Prize in Physics, 1965, in Feynman (2011) — obviously, this does not mean that expertise is not important; it just means that as far as the scientific method is concerned, reputation is irrelevant and definitely not dispositive; only facts and logic matter — please see, also the recent U.S. Supreme Court judgment on the "'Chevron deference,' which refers to the doctrine under which courts historically deferred to a federal agency's interpretation of an ambiguous statute that the agency administers," Legal Information Institute (2025).

2.4 Conversations with Data

When using a new dataset or reengaging with a dataset, it is incumbent upon us to get our hands dirty with the data, over and beyond how the databases are used to answer any particular questions or test any particular hypotheses. In particular, one needs to identify the fields and scope of the data; one needs to calculate summary statistics of and correlation coefficients among all variables — you need to "interrogate the data," and "have detailed conversations with the data," get "intimately familiar with the data," perform sanity checks, especially with the Z-scores of all variables, and do preliminary regressions to make sure that the data are being interpreted correctly and that their limitations are identified properly. Such expertise on the data can also open up new avenues of research, can answer new questions, and possibly most importantly, avoid unpleasant surprises in empirical work.

2.5 Statistical Versus Actual Significance

Broadly speaking, the definition of "Big Data" has two schools of thought. The economist's perspective was probably best articulated by Scott Bauguess, then deputy chief economist at the U.S. Securities and Exchange Commission (SEC), in 2016: "data that take more time to process than ... took to create" (Bauguess, 2016), please also see Goldstein et al. (2025, 2021) — we use about 25 TB of data for this book — whereas the computer scientist's vision is more about techniques.

Statistical significance is well understood; it is a measure of the precision of the estimate of the association of two variables; please see, for instance, McShane and Gal (2017). Also, "almost any parameter can be found to be significantly different from zero if the sample size is large enough," (Kennedy, 2003) and "with large sample sizes, parameters can be estimated very precisely ... which usually results in statistical significance," (Wooldridge, 2013) — in other words, pretty much everything is statistically significant when one is working with massive datasets, as we do in the third part of this book.

However, statistical significance does not imply that the association of two variables is actually meaningful, and here, we develop the methodology, when dealing with large numbers of observations, of replacing each variable x, except for each classification or time variable, by

$$\Phi\left(\textit{Z-Score}\left(x\right)\right) = \Phi\left(\frac{x - \textit{Mean}\left(x\right)}{\textit{StDev}\left(x\right)}\right) \sim \mathbb{U}\left[0,1\right] \tag{2.107}$$

where Φ is the cumulative probability function of a standard Gaussian random variable and $\mathbb{U}$ represents a uniform distribution. This transformation renders all our variables ordinal, comparable, and non-parametric, that do not depend on any sequential properties, and therefore, all our regression coefficients are systematic, objective, and comparable, as in a coefficient β on the regression of the regressand y on the regressor x means that a 1 *percent point* increase in the cumulative probability of x is associated with a β *percent point* increase in the cumulative probability of y. This is a rigorization of the number of standard deviations approach to interpretation of coefficients — "scale the usual coefficient estimates so that they measure the number of standard deviation changes in the dependent variable due to a standard deviation change in the explanatory variable," (Kennedy, 2003) — which also implicitly assumes Gaussian distributions.

Definition 2.4

$$\frac{\mathbf{d}F}{\mathbf{d}x} \tag{2.108}$$

is ***actually significant positive at level*** λ *if*

$$\frac{\mathbf{d}F}{\mathbf{d}x} > \lambda \tag{2.109}$$

and is ***actually significant negative at level*** λ *if*

$$\frac{\mathbf{d}F}{\mathbf{d}x} < -\lambda \tag{2.110}$$

Notation 2.6 *Actually significant positive (negative) association is indicated by light (dark) grey shading. Actual significance at level 1 is indicated by regular font, actual significance at level 5 by bold font, and actual significance at level 10 by bold and italic font.*

It is worth pointing out that $Percentile\,(x) \simeq RoundUp\,(100\Phi\,(Z\text{-}Score\,(x)))$ and, therefore, $\frac{\mathbf{d}F}{\mathbf{d}x} \geq 1$ implies that a move of x to one higher percentile causes F to move up (approximately) $Round\left(\frac{\mathbf{d}F}{\mathbf{d}x}\right)$ percentiles, $\frac{\mathbf{d}F}{\mathbf{d}x} \leq -1$ implies that a move of x to one higher percentile causes F to move down (approximately) $Round\left(\frac{\mathbf{d}F}{\mathbf{d}x}\right)$ percentiles, and $0 \leq \left|\frac{\mathbf{d}F}{\mathbf{d}x}\right| < 1$ implies that a move of x to one higher percentile causes F to stay in (approximately) the same percentile.

Similarly, $\frac{\mathbf{d}F}{\mathbf{d}\mathbf{1}_A}$ (or $\frac{\partial F}{\partial \mathbf{1}_A}$), where $\mathbf{1}_A$ is the indicator variable corresponding to set A, means that there is a $\frac{\mathbf{d}F}{\mathbf{d}\mathbf{1}_A}$ (or $\frac{\partial F}{\partial \mathbf{1}_A}$) higher cumulative probability of F for membership in A. Similarly, $\frac{\mathbf{d}F}{\mathbf{dt}}$ (or $\frac{\partial F}{\partial \mathbf{t}}$), where $\mathbf{t}$ is a time period, means that there is a $\frac{\mathbf{d}F}{\mathbf{dt}}$ (or $\frac{\partial F}{\partial \mathbf{t}}$) increase in cumulative probability of F from one time period to the next.

Using the same arguments as above, $Millenile\,(x) \simeq RoundUp\,(1{,}000\Phi\,(Z\text{-}Score\,(x)))$, $Decile\,(x) \simeq RoundUp\,(10\Phi\,(Z\text{-}Score\,(x)))$, $Quartile\,(x) \simeq RoundUp\,(4\Phi\,(Z\text{-}Score\,(x)))$, etc. Please see Aman et al. (2019) for a robust defense of "responsible science," that science needs to have integrity and relevance, and the appropriate level of actual significance obviously depends on the context and the judgment of the researcher.

2.6 Econometrics/Statistics Versus Artificial Intellligence/Machine Learning

The focus of traditional statistics and econometrics is the explanation of the real world, whereas the focus of machine learning (ML) and artificial intelligence (AI) is prediction. Consider the overarching model

$$Y = X\beta + \varepsilon \tag{2.111}$$

with

$$COV(X, \varepsilon) = 0 \tag{2.112}$$

We use the "Training Data"

$$Y^{Train} = X^{Train}\beta + \varepsilon^{Train} \tag{2.113}$$

to estimate the model, which provides the Ordinary Least Squares (OLS) estimates $\widehat{\beta}_{OLS}^{Training}$, which is unbiased and consistent under $COV\left(X^{Train}, \varepsilon^{Train}\right) = 0$,

$$\widehat{\beta}_{OLS}^{Train} = \left(X^{Train\prime}X^{Train}\right)^{-1} X^{Train\prime}Y^{Train} \tag{2.114}$$

As this book makes abundantly clear, OLS is often not the appropriate estimation method, so, in general, let's denote the best estimate of the parameter β, using the Training Data, by $\widehat{\beta}^{Train}$. We then apply these Training Data estimates to predict as follows, using the "Testing Data,"

$$\widehat{Y}^{Test} = X^{Test}\widehat{\beta}^{Train} \tag{2.115}$$

As explained below, all variables in this book are stripped of cardinality; therefore, every data point is an approximate percentile and hence, ordinal, and such comparability enables non-parametric work. Because our statements are modest and use ordinal variables and instrumental variables, applying the training model to make predictions about unknown unknowns makes perfect sense — for example, the results in this book are based on training data of the U.S., and one can apply these coefficients to make predictions about Australian or other data; see, for instance, Nagel (2021) and Athey and Imbens (2019). As repeatedly emphasized in Chapter 9,

- You should consider using AI/ML logic and apply the estimates from the training data of U.S. equities markets, as discussed in Chapter 6, to other equities markets, for instance, in Australia, New Zealand, and Sweden, which had substantially different responses to the COVID-19 pandemic.
- You should consider using AI/ML logic and apply the estimates from the training data of U.S. equities markets, as discussed in Chapter 7, to other major equities markets, for instance, in the UK and Japan.
- You should consider using AI/ML logic and apply the estimates from the training data of U.S. FI markets, as discussed in Chapter 8, to other major FI markets, for instance, in Germany and France.

It is very important to emphasize that there is nothing magical (good or bad) or terrifying about AI and ML. Only a pure theorist without any empirical expertise, such as the celebrity theoretical physicist Stephen Hawking, could come to the science fiction opinion (constrained not by facts but only by one's imagination — see Professor Fei-Fei Li's quote below — for instance, the USS Enterprise is imagined to travel faster than the speed of light in *Star Trek*) that future developments in AI, not wars or pandemics or famines, "could spell the end of the human race" — please see Cellan-Jones (2014) — whereas empirical work such as Stanford University's "One Hundred Year Study on Artificial Intelligence" (Stanford, 2021) have not found any evidence that AI/ML poses any "imminent threat" to humanity. "Debate over whether or not [artificial general intelligence] is realistic — and if so, a threat to humanity if its creators lose control — is one of the major controversies among scientists and developers in the field (AFP, 2025)." Brynjolfsson et al. (2025) "examines changes in the labor market for occupations exposed to generative artificial intelligence ... find[s] that since the widespread adoption of generative AI, early-career workers (ages 22–25) in the most AI-exposed occupations have experienced a 13 percent relative decline in employment even after controlling for firm-level shocks ... employment for workers in less exposed fields and more experienced workers in the same occupations has remained stable or continued to grow ... adjustments occur primarily through employment rather than compensation ... employment declines are concentrated in occupations where AI is more likely to automate, rather than augment, human labor." Ma (2025) reports that "pioneering computer scientist Geoffrey Hinton, whose work has earned him a Nobel Prize and the moniker 'godfather of AI,' said artificial intelligence will spark a surge in unemployment and profits," and Coacci (2025) claims that "61% of white collar workers think AI will replace their current role in 3 years — but they're too busy enjoying less stress to worry right now."

The fundamental empirical notion that the output is only as good as the input — colorfully referred to as "Garbage in, Garbage Out" (GIGO) — holds perfectly for artificial intelligence and machine learning as well; Gmail, for instance, regularly sends emails from my wife and daughter to my spam folder, and various voice-recognition systems are impossible with non-English or non-American accents; for example, Burnistoun (2011) is a hilarious BBC comedy skit about voice-recognition failures with Scottish accents.

"Efforts to build artificial intelligence (AI) that could solve all the world's problems at a stroke are 'nonsense,' leading researcher Michael Jordan [Pehong Chen Distinguished Professor in the Department of Electrical Engineering and Computer Science and the Department of Statistics at the University of California, Berkeley, and the inaugural 2022 World Laureates Association Prize Laureate in Computer Science or Mathematics — see WLA (2022) — who was found to be "the most influential computer scientist" in 2016 — see Bohannon (2016) — told scientists in Paris [on February 6, 2025] ahead of [the following] week's global AI summit. Jordan ... was taking aim at claims from industry figures like OpenAI chief Sam Altman or Anthropic's Dario Amodei that so-called artificial general intelligence (AGI) is only years away. AGI is the hoped-for holy grail of AI research that would surpass humans in all fields. 'This super AGI thing that can answer any question, it knows everything... this is nonsense,' machine learning and statistics expert Jordan said at an AI conference at France's prestigious Polytechnique engineering school. He criticized the fact that companies are spending 'billions and trillions' to achieve what he said was for now an illusory goal. Today's AI models can 'predict really, really well' thanks to their access to vast quantities of human-generated data, including from the internet, Jordan said. But AI 'can't know everything, because what's in my mind right now is the context of what I'm going to do next today. You cannot know that,' he added. 'And if it doesn't know that, it can't give me good advice.' Large language models (LLMs) that power AI chatbots like ChatGPT are like 'a lot of little experts' able to respond to highly specific questions but are 'not intelligent entities.' Jordan characterized today's developments in AI as 'a new engineering field emerging, like civil engineering' but working with 'human decisions and data and flows on networks.' That makes it suited to solving specific complex problems like improving transportation or healthcare, he suggested. 'This whole development of this wonderful engineering field is really being held back by this whole AI aspiration, building a super robot that takes over and helps you for all your tasks at home and all these other things,' Jordan said. 'I don't think there's ever been an era in human history where a new field of technology has arisen where there was so much hype and hysteria,' he added (AFP, 2025)."

"Fei-Fei Li [Sequoia Professor in the Computer Science Department at Stanford University, and a Founding Co-Director of Stanford's Human-Centered AI Institute] ... and startup founder sometimes known as 'the Godmother of AI,' has ... said policy must be based on 'science, not science fiction.' In other words, policymakers should focus on the current reality of AI, not on grandiose futuristic scenarios, 'whether utopia or apocalypse.' In particular, Li said that it's critical for policymakers to understand that chatbots and copilot programs 'are not forms of intelligence with intentions, free will or consciousness,' so they can avoid 'the distraction of far-fetched scenarios' and focus instead on 'vital challenges' (Ha, 2015)." The current popularity of engines such as ChatGPT has brought into focus "generative AI, sometimes called gen AI, ... artificial intelligence (AI) that can create original content such as text, images, video, audio or software code in response to a user's prompt or request" (Stryker and Scapicchio, 2025), but is not particularly relevant to the substantive content of this book.

There is an almost mystical relationship that is postulated between sparsity (where the number of "features" is higher than the number of observations), whereas in this book, as is the case in much of finance, we have access to very high levels and numbers of observations, so we do not worry in this book about this distinction that is mostly irrelevant for our purposes; in other words, we do not worry in this book about not having enough observations, and in particular, our definition of "Big Data" goes back to Bauguess (2016), as "data that take more time to process than ... took to create." Nagel (2021) makes the fundamental distinction between "supervised learning" (where the estimation of models on the basis of training data is evaluated on the training data) and "unsupervised learning" — this distinction is important but not particularly important to the theoretical and empirical work of this book. Hens (2022) writes in his review of Nagel (2021) that "from a finance point of view, Machine Learning is nothing more than advanced econometrics in which rigorous proofs on efficiency and unbiasedness of estimators are replaced by massive computations: 'coding instead of proving.' Fortunately, Nagel (2021) does not fall into this trap but shows step-by-step using mathematical

TABLE 2.3 Terminology in Machine Learning and Artificial Intelligence Versus Traditional Econometrics and Statistics

Machine Learning and Artificial Intelligence	Traditional Statistics and Econometrics
Training Learning,	Estimation
Learner Algorithm,	Model Estimator
Features,	Covariates
	Explanatory Variables
	Independent Variables
	Predictors
Target Label Output,	Dependent Variable
Example Instance	Data Point Observation

Source: Nagel (2021), Table 1.1.

formulas that Machine Learning has its roots in what we all know: regressions and principal component analyses. Nagel (2021) makes very useful distinctions. For example, it distinguishes supervised and non-supervised learning. In supervised learning one has target data, which the machine tries to predict so that it always gets feedback how well it has done — a simple example of this is rolling a window in which one performs a regression through time. In unsupervised learning one does not attempt to predict a target; instead one tries to find a compressed summary capturing the main features of the data. ... in principle Machine Learning can be used in finance to exploit the enormous data sets (firm characteristics, investor sentiment, etc.) that have become available in recent years." Table 2.3 draws together the purely terminological distinctions between machine learning and artificial intelligence on one hand versus traditional statistics and econometrics on the other.

2.7 Total Impact of an Exogenous Variable

In structural systems which are often necessary to model complex relationships, the full association of two variables is measured by the total derivative, which is calculated across equations from all the relevant partial derivatives; therefore, the normalization referred to in Section 2.5 also makes the total impacts systematic, objective, and comparable. Given a differentiable function

$$F(x_1, x_2, ..., x_m, y_1, ..., y_n) : \mathbb{R}^{m+n} \longrightarrow \mathbb{R}^l \tag{2.116}$$

where, $\forall j = 1, ..., n$,

$$y_j = y_j(x_1, x_2, ..., x_m) \tag{2.117}$$

are endogenous, and the exogenous variables

$$(x_1, x_2, \ldots, x_m) \tag{2.118}$$

are not perfectly correlated; i.e.,

$$\left[\frac{\mathbf{d}x_i}{\mathbf{d}x_k}\right]_{i,k=1}^{m} = \mathfrak{I}_m \text{ (} (m \times m) \text{ identity matrix)} \tag{2.119}$$

then, $\forall s = 1, \ldots, l$,

$$\begin{aligned}\frac{\mathbf{d}F_s(x_1, x_2, \ldots, x_m, y_1, \ldots, y_n)}{\mathbf{d}z} &= \frac{\partial F_s}{\partial x_1}\frac{\mathbf{d}x_1}{\mathbf{d}z} + \frac{\partial F_s}{\partial x_2}\frac{\mathbf{d}x_2}{\mathbf{d}z} + \cdots + \frac{\partial F_s}{\partial x_m}\frac{\mathbf{d}x_m}{\mathbf{d}z} \\ &+ \frac{\partial F_s}{\partial y_1}\frac{\mathbf{d}y_1}{\mathbf{d}z} + \frac{\partial F_s}{\partial y_2}\frac{\mathbf{d}y_2}{\mathbf{d}z} + \cdots + \frac{\partial F_s}{\partial y_n}\frac{\mathbf{d}y_n}{\mathbf{d}z}\end{aligned} \tag{2.120}$$

and thus, $\forall k = 1, \ldots, m, \forall s = 1, \ldots, l$,

$$\frac{\mathbf{d}F_s}{\mathbf{d}x_k} \text{ (total impact)} = \frac{\partial F_s}{\partial x_k} \text{ (direct impact)} + \sum_{j=1}^{n} \frac{\partial F_s}{\partial y_j}\frac{\mathbf{d}y_j}{\mathbf{d}x_k} \text{ (indirect impact)} \tag{2.121}$$

Consider a separative linear model such that $\forall s = 1, \ldots, l$,

$$F_s(x_1, x_2, \ldots, x_m, y_1, \ldots, y_n) = \zeta_s + \sum_{k=1}^{m} \alpha_{sr}x_r + \sum_{r=1}^{n} \gamma_{sr}y_r \tag{2.122}$$

such that $\forall j = 1, \ldots, n$,

$$y_j = \beta_{j0} + \sum_{k=1}^{m} \beta_{jk}x_i \tag{2.123}$$

are endogenous, and where the exogenous variables

$$(x_1, x_2, \ldots, x_m) \tag{2.124}$$

are not perfectly correlated; i.e.,

$$\left[\frac{\mathbf{d}x_i}{\mathbf{d}x_k}\right]_{i,k=1}^{m} = \mathfrak{I}_m \text{ (} (m \times m) \text{ identity matrix)} \tag{2.125}$$

then, if $\forall j = 1, \ldots, n, \forall k = 1, \ldots, m, \forall s = 1, \ldots, l$,

$$\alpha_{sr} = \frac{\partial F_s}{\partial x_k} \tag{2.126}$$

$$\gamma_{sj} = \frac{\partial F_s}{\partial y_j} \tag{2.127}$$

$$\beta_{jk} = \frac{\mathbf{d}y_j}{\mathbf{d}x_k} \tag{2.128}$$

we have, $\forall k = 1, \ldots, m, \forall s = 1, \ldots, l,$

$$\frac{\mathbf{d}F_s}{\mathbf{d}x_k} \text{ (total impact)} = \alpha_{sk} \text{ (direct impact)} + \sum_{j=1}^{n} \gamma_{sj}\beta_{jk} \text{ (indirect impact)} \tag{2.129}$$

Thus, each such total impact $\frac{\mathbf{d}F}{\mathbf{d}x_k}$ is comparable and means that a 1 *percent point* increase in the cumulative probability of x_k is associated with a $\frac{\mathbf{d}F}{\mathbf{d}x_k}$ *percent point* increase in the cumulative probability of F. Please see Bhattacharya and Gupta (2026) for an application of this methodology to the impact of FINRA (the U.S. Financial Regulatory Authority) 2241 Rules, which constituted a major attempt by a self-regulatory body to improve market quality.

2.8 Systemic Versus Idiosyncratic

One of the most important questions in empirical work is whether a particular effect is systemic, which, however, is very little understood in the popular discourse. Consider the equation

$$Y = X\beta + \varepsilon \tag{2.130}$$

where

$$COV(X, \varepsilon) = 0 \tag{2.131}$$

then a systemic statement pertains to β whereas any statement about ε is about the idiosyncratic, the part that is not explained by the systemic component. Asserting that something is systemic does not mean that it is a large effect; all it means is that after one controls for all relevant factors such that the remainder is independent of all the controls, that the impact is statistically and actually significant. Naïve comparisons between variables, such as just comparing their averages (such as comparing American versus Norwegian average longevity as a dispositive argument in favor of socialized medicine or comparing average S&P 500 returns between Democratic and Republican administrations as a dispositive argument for a political narrative) are, at best, preliminary, because one is not controlling for all relevant variables, and it is incumbent upon us to always use proper empirical methods —

a statistical software in SAS, Stata, or R, for instance, will provide results that are only as good as the methods used.

For example, it has become popular recently to assert that the U.S. is "systemically racist." In order to test this hypothesis, one would set up the following equation,

$$\text{Positive Outcome}_{i,t} = \alpha A_i + X\gamma + \varepsilon \tag{2.132}$$

where

$$A_i = 1, \text{ if individual } i \text{ is African-American}, = 0, \text{ otherwise} \tag{2.133}$$

$$COV(A, \varepsilon) = COV(X, \varepsilon) = 0 \tag{2.134}$$

and then, test the hypothesis that α is statistically and actually significantly negative; such a test does not answer the question whether there are large differences in average outcomes between African-Americans and other Americans.

Similarly, in order to empirically test for anthropogenic climate change, one would need to set up the following equation

$$\text{Temperature}_{i,t} = \alpha F(t) + X\gamma + \varepsilon \tag{2.135}$$

where t is time, F is an increasing function, and

$$COV(F(t), \varepsilon) = COV(X, \varepsilon) = 0 \tag{2.136}$$

and then, test the hypothesis that α is statistically and actually significantly positive, which would require us to have actual data about temperatures going back centuries.

Please see Aviv (2024) for an exceptional insight into the systemic and idiosyncratic components of child deaths in a UK hospital, and the classic Gayle et al. (2012) article on whether executive compensation and job mobility outcomes are systemically biased against women.

2.9 Capital Asset Pricing Model

We use the Capital Asset Pricing Model (CAPM) — see Bhattacharya (2018) for instance — to calculate, for each security i and each day t,

$$RP_{i,t} = \beta_{M,i} RP_{M,t} + IdioR_{i,t} \tag{2.137}$$

where $R_{i,t}$ = return on day t of security i, $R_{f,t}$ = risk-free return on day t, $R_{M,t}$ = return on day t of the market index, where risk premium on day t of security i is

$$RP_{i,t} = R_{i,t} - R_{f,t} \tag{2.138}$$

and risk premium on day t of the market index is

$$RP_{M,t} = RM_t - R_{f,t} \tag{2.139}$$

and idiosyncratic return on day t of security i is $IdioR_{i,t}$.

Bodie et al. (2018) describe CAPM as a set of predictions concerning equilibrium expected return on risky assets. Shefrin (2008) and Potì and Shefrin (2014), for a study of more sophisticated versions of CAPM from a behavioral perspective. For the baseline model, we use daily returns on three-month T-bills as the risk-free rate, the daily returns, including all distributions, on the value-weighted market portfolio as the market return — VWRETD indices contain ... daily ... returns, including all distributions, on a value-weighted market portfolio (excluding American Depository Receipts) (CRSP information) — and we also check for robustness: (a) using returns on four-week, six-month, and one-year T-bill rates separately as risk-free rates, and (b) returns on the equally-weighted market portfolio — EWRETD indices contain ... daily ... returns, including all distributions, on an equally-weighted market portfolio (including ADRs) (CRSP information) — and on the S&P Composite Index as the market return.

2.10 Market Model

Separately and additionally, we also rely upon the Market Model (MM) — see Campbell et al. (1997), for instance — to run the same calculations for each security for each year and day of the year.

$$R_{i,t} = \alpha + \theta_{f,i}R_{f,t} + \theta_{M,i}R_{M,t} + \theta_{C,i}R_{C,i,t} + IdioR_{i,t} \tag{2.140}$$

where $R_{i,t}$ = return on day (or halfhour, as the case may be) t of security i, $R_{f,t}$ = risk-free return on day (or halfhour, as the case may be) t, $R_{M,t}$ = return on day (or halfhour, as the case may be) t of the market index, $R_{C,i,t}$ = return on day (or halfhour, as the case may be) t of comparables to firm i.

In this book, in the interest of full objectivity and independence, we use the value-weighted average daily (or halfhourly, as the case may be) returns of equities of all firms in the same major industrial sector as firm i — i.e., within the same two-digit Standard Industrial Classification (SIC) in Chapters 3–5 and within the same three-digit North American Industrial Classification Code (NAICS) in Chapters 6–8 — as the corresponding return for comparables.

As earlier, we denote $IdioR_{i,t}$ as the idiosyncratic return on day (or halfhour, as the case may be) t of security i. The Market Model is similar to the Arbitrage Pricing Theory (APT) and to the Capital Asset Pricing Model (CAPM) mentioned above.

In the third part, we use generalizations of these models for millisecond-level high-frequency intraday data.

2.11 Positive and Negative Proxies

Consider the standard linear model again in Equation 2.130. A random variable X is a *positive proxy* for another random variable Y if they are positively correlated; in other words, by positive proxy, all one means is that the positive proxy variable (stochastically) preserves the rank of the proxied variable. On the other hand, a random variable X is a *negative proxy* for another random variable Y if they are negatively correlated; i.e., it means that with the negative proxy variable, the ranking is (stochastically) the opposite.

2.12 Endogeneity

Consider again the standard linear model in Equation 2.130, for which Equation 2.131, that the residual variable be uncorrelated with the regressands, is essential. However, we do often find violations of Equation 2.131, in which case the residual variable is "endogenous" — i.e., determined within the system, as opposed to exogenous, which can be taken as given to the system — and so, endogeneity is arguably the most insurmountable problem in empirical work. Consider

$$Y = \alpha + \beta_1 X_1 + \beta_2 X_2 + \cdots + \eta \tag{2.141}$$

Ordinary Least Squares (OLS) is consistent if

$$Cov\,(X_1, \eta) = Cov\,(X_2, \eta) = \cdots = 0 \tag{2.142}$$

If X_1 is endogenous, this uncorrelatedness property is violated, and therefore, endogenous variables have to be instrumented; this is detailed later in Section 2.15. Otherwise, the regression above would yield inconsistent and biased estimates. For example, in this chapter, the theory shows that in the equation for market efficiency, trading volume is an endogenous variable; please see Greene (2018), for instance, that in such a situation one does not need any further justification for the use of instruments.

When an instrument W is used for an endogenous variable X, it is **not** the case that richness of information in X is lost because in the first stage of 2SLS or 3SLS, X is regressed on all exogenous variables including the instrument W and then, in the second stage, the residual of this particular regression — which captures all the information specific to X over and above what the exogenous variables including the instrument W represent — is used in the original equation instead of the endogenous variable.

2.13 Errors-in-Variables

It is common in empirical work to observe variables with error. Consider

$$Y = \alpha + \beta_1 X_1 + \beta_2 X_2 + \varepsilon \tag{2.143}$$

where instead of the actual **regressor** X_2, one observes x_2 such that

$$x_2 = X_2 + \omega \tag{2.144}$$

or more generally

$$Cov\,(x_2, X_2) \neq 0 \tag{2.145}$$

When a proxy x_2 is used for X_2, it is **not the case** that X_2 is replaced by x_2 in the regression. Instead, x_2 is treated as an endogenous variable and is suitably instrumented, as is required by the Errors-in-Variables method; please see Greene (2018), for instance. For example, in this chapter, standard deviation of analyst forecasts is used as a proxy for heterogeneity in investor valuations and is instrumented — see Section 5.5.6 — where the latter is predicted by theory to impact trading volume, but standard deviation of analyst forecasts is not a regressor. However, if the **regressand** is observed with error, the error term just gets folded into the residual in the equation without any inconsistency.

2.14 Simultaneity

In advanced empirical work, we often find ourselves having to work with systems of multiple equations. Consider, for example, the system of equations

$$Y_1 = \beta_1 X_1 + \varepsilon_1 \tag{2.146}$$

$$Y_2 = \beta_2 X_2 + \varepsilon_2 \tag{2.147}$$

If there are endogeneity (or error) issues with the regressors X_1 and/or X_2, as discussed above, one can identify instruments as above and implement 2SLS equation-by-equation. However, $Cov\,(\varepsilon_1, \varepsilon_2)$ may not be zero, in which case, equation-by-equation 2SLS is not efficient although still consistent. 3SLS makes use of the potential correlation between the residuals across equations to improve efficiency while retaining consistency.

2.15 Instrumentation

As detailed above in Section 2.12, endogeneity is a major problem in empirical work, and this is solved by using instrumental variables, as described in this section. In a system of equations $Y = X\beta + \varepsilon$, for a vector W to be an instrument, it is required (please see Greene (2018), for instance) that

- **Strong First Stage:** $Cov\,(W, X) \neq 0$

- **Exclusion Restriction:** $Cov(W, \varepsilon) = 0$. In other words, the unexplained part ("residual") ε of the regression needs to be uncorrelated with the instrument — **there is no requirement that the regressand Y itself be uncorrelated with the instrument.**

This causes the inevitable tradeoff between weakness of an instrument versus exogeneity of an instrument; see, for example, Greene (2018) and Campbell et al. (1997). In panel data econometrics, there are two popular categories of autochthonous instruments:

1. Instrument a variable $X_{i,t}$ by combination(s) of $X_{j,t}, j \neq i$. Cross-sectional variables such as corresponding variables for other geographies have been used as instruments by, for instance, Hausman et al. (1994), and the validity of such instrumentation depends on the assumption that the corresponding cross-sectional variables are correlated with the instrumented variable because of cost (or other) commonalities in the time period of interest but are not influenced by the idiosyncrasies of the geography of interest in the particular time period.
2. Instrument a variable $X_{i,t}$ by its lag(s) $X_{i,t-1}, X_{i,t-2}, \ldots$ The use of lags as instruments depends on two implicit assumptions: (a) lack of serial correlation, see, for example, Greene (2018), and (b) weak rational expectations, see, for example, Hansen and Singleton (1982).

Finally, as Wooldridge (2010) points out, most of the problems with using instrumental variables arise in small samples, which, obviously, is not the case in this book. Given these two critical qualifications, we consider in this book the following instrumentation categories, for the endogenous or proxy variables, **together and also separately** — as Wooldridge (2010) points out, "*asymptotically*, we can do no worse, and can often do better, using a larger set of *valid* instruments" [emphases added].— to ensure that our conclusions are not sensitive to particular information assumptions.

1. **Cross section:** Instrument each endogenous/proxy variable $X_{i,t}$ by the simple mean of $X_{j,t}$ over all j, i.e., across all stocks in the current year. This is based on the informational assumption that the instrument is correlated with the instrumented variable because of contemporaneous market factors, but the correlation of the instrument with the firm-year-specific residual is minimal, only to the extent of $X_{i,t}$'s contribution to the many thousands of observations over which the mean of $X_{j,t}$ across all j is calculated.
2. **Time series:** Instrument each endogenous/proxy variable by its single lag, i.e., use lagged variable $X_{i,t-1}$ as an instrument for the endogenous/proxy variable $X_{i,t}$, where i is the stock and t is the calendar year. This is based on the

informational assumption that the lagged variable is correlated with the current variable because of market and cost commonalities for a firm and its stock across time but is not correlated with the residual that is specific to the firm/stock in the calendar year of interest.

2.16 Conclusions

In this chapter, we followed up on the measure-theoretic generalization of standard probability theory under risk to a theory of generalized probability under uncertainty and the reconciliation between the two in Chapter 1 — *this result makes possible all the empirical work in this book and enables the reconciliation between traditional econometrics and statistics on one hand versus artificial intelligence and machine learning on the other.* We detailed a rigorous distinction between public information and market information, which is critical to understanding finance. We replaced each variable, except for each classification or time variable, by the standard cumulative Gaussian probability of its *Z*-score, this is a rigorization of the number of standard deviations approach to interpretation of coefficients; thus, we made the impacts systematic, objective, and comparable; this allows a systematic and objective characterization of actual significance, which is different from statistical significance — we systematically defined a full or partial association to be actually significant positive (negative) at level λ if the relevant derivative is greater than λ (less than $-\lambda$).

The next three chapters detail advanced analytics in finance using daily data. In particular, Chapter 3 uses idiosyncratic risk and arbitrage risk as negative proxies for market efficiency.

References

AFP, 2025, "Top Researcher Blasts 'Nonsense' of Superhuman AI," *Barrons*, February 06, 2025.

Akerlof, G., 1970, "The Market for 'Lemons': Quality Uncertainty and the Market Mechanism," *Quarterly Journal of Economics*, 84(3), 488–500.

Aman, H., Beekes, W., Berkman, H., Bohmann, M., Bradbury, M., Chapple, E., Chang, M., Clout, V., Faff, R., Han, J., Hillier, D., Hodgson, A., Howeison, B., Jona, J., Linnenluecke, M., Loncan, T., McCredie, B., Michayluk, D., Mroczkowski, N., Pan, Z., Patel, V., Podolski, E., Soderstrom, N., Smith, T., Tanewski, G., Walsh, K., Wee, M., and Wright, S., 2019, "Responsible Science: Celebrating the 50-Year Legacy of Ball and Brown (1968) Using a Registration-Based Framework," *Pacific-Basin Finance Journal*, 56, 129–150.

Asimov, I., 1980, "A Cult of Ignorance," *Newsweek*, January 21, 1980.

Athey, S., and Imbens, G., 2019, "Machine Learning Methods That Economists Should Know about," *Annual Review of Economics*, 11, 685–725.

Aviv, R., 2024, "A British Nurse Was Found Guilty of Killing Seven Babies. Did She Do It?," *The New Yorker*, May 13, 2024.

Bandyopadhyay, P., Brittan, G., and Taper, M., 2016, *Belief, Evidence, and Uncertainty*, Berlin, Germany: Springer Verlag.

Bauguess, S., 2016, "Has Big Data Made Us Lazy?" *U.S. Securities and Exchange Commission*, October 21, 2016.

Bhattacharya, R., 2018, "Capital Asset Pricing Model (CAPM)," In: Teece, D., and Augier, M. (Eds.), *The Palgrave Encyclopedia of Strategic Management*, pp. 98–202, London, UK: Palgrave Macmillan.

Bhattacharya, R., and Gupta, M., 2023, "Diligence, Objectivity, Quality, and Accuracy," *Journal of Accounting Literature*, 47(1), 1–30.

Bhattacharya, R., and Gupta, M., 2026, "Impact of Self-Regulation on Financial Markets," *Journal of Accounting Literature* (DOI: 10.1108/JAL-09-2024-0266).

Billingsley, P., 2012, *Probability and Measure*, New York, NY: Wiley.

Bishop, B., 2016, "Faith," In: Zalta, E. and Nodelman, U. (Eds.), *Stanford Encyclopedia of Philosophy*, Stanford, CA: Stanford University (https://plato.stanford.edu/entries/faith/).

Bodie, Z., Kane, A., and Marcus, A., 2018, *Investments*, New York, NY: McGraw-Hill/Irwin.

Bohannon, J., 2016, "Who's the Michael Jordan of Computer Science? New Tool Ranks Researchers' Influence," *Science*, April 20 2016.

Brynjolfsson, E., Chandar, B., and Chen, R., 2025, "Canaries in the Coal Mine? Six Facts about the Recent Employment Effects of Artificial Intelligence," *Stanford University Human-Centered Artificial Intelligence* (https://digitaleconomy.stanford.edu/publications/canaries-in-the-coal-mine/).

Burnistoun, 2011, "Voice Activated Elevator," *BBC Scotland* (https://www.bbc.co.uk/programmes/p00hbfjw).

Campbell, J., Lo, A., and MacKinlay, A. C., 1997, *The Econometrics of Financial Markets*, Princeton, NJ: Princeton University Press.

Cellan-Jones, R., 2014, "Stephen Hawking Warns Artificial Intelligence Could end Mankind," *BBC*.

Coacci, J., 2025, "61% of White Collar Workers Think AI Will Replace Their Current Role in 3 Years — but They're too Busy Enjoying Less Stress to Worry Right Now," *Fortune*, July 31, 2025.

Edwards, A., 1984, *Likelihood*, Cambridge, UK: Cambridge University Press.

Feynman, R., 2011, "Feynman on Scientific Method," *Seabala* (https://youtu.be/EYPapE-3FRw).

Gayle, G.-L., Golan, L., and Miller, R., 2012, "Gender Differences in Executive Compensation and Job Mobility," *Journal of Labor Economics*, 30(4), 829–872.

Goldstein, I., Spatt, C., and Ye, M., 2021, "Big Data in Finance," *Review of Financial Studies*, 34(7), 3213–3225.

Goldstein, I., Spatt, C., and Ye, M., 2025, "The Next Chapter of Big Data in Finance," *Review of Financial Studies*, 38(3), 605–622.

Greene, W., 2018, *Econometric Analysis*, Upper Saddle River, NJ: Pearson.

Ha, A., 2025, "AI Pioneer Fei-Fei Li Says AI Policy Must Be Based on 'Science, not Science Fiction,'" *TechCrunch*, February 8, 2025.

Hansen, L., and Singleton, K., 1982, "Generalized Instrumental Variables Estimation of Nonlinear Rational Expectations Models," *Econometrica*, 50(5), 1269–1286.

Hausman, J., Leonard, G., and Zona, D., 1994, "Competitive Analysis with Differenciated Products," *Annales d'Économie et de Statistique*, 34, 159–180.

Hens, T., 2022 , "Stefan Nagel: Machine Learning in Asset Pricing," *Journal of Economics*, 136, 91–92.

Jordan, J., and Luther, W., 2020, "Central Bank Independence and the Federal Reserve's New Operating Regime," *Quarterly Review of Economics and Finance*, 84, 510–515.

Kennedy, P., 2003, *A Guide to Econometrics*, Cambridge, MA: MIT Press.

Korb, K., and Nicholson, A., 2010, *Bayesian Artificial Intelligence*, Boca Raton, FL: CRC Press.

Kyburg, H., 1983, *Epistemology and Inference*, Minneapolis, MN: University of Minnesota Press.

Legal Information Institute (2025) "Chevron Deference," *Cornell Law School*, Ithaca, NY: WexLaw (https://www.law.cornell.edu/wex/chevron_deference).

Loftus, P., Lukpat, A., and O'Brien, S. A., 2025, "Inside the Crisis at Tylenol," *Wall Street Journal*, September 26, 2025.

Luper, S., 2020, "Epistemic Closure", In: Zalta, E. and Nodelman, U. (Eds.), *The Encyclopedia of Philosophy*, Stanford, CA: Stanford University (https://plato.stanford.edu/entries/closure-epistemic/).

Ma, J., 2025, "'Godfather of AI' Says the Technology Will Create Massive Unemployment and Send Profits Soaring — 'That Is the Capitalist System,"' *Fortune*, September 6, 2025.

McShane, B., and Gal, D., 2017, "Statistical Significance and the Dichotomization of Evidence," *Journal of the American Statistical Association*, 112(519), 885–895.

Nagel, S., 2021, *Machine Learning in Asset Pricing*, Princeton, NJ: Princeton University Press.

Popper, K., 1959, *The Logic of Scientific Discovery*, London, UK: Hutchinson & Co.

Potì, V., and Shefrin, H., 2014, "The Signature of Sentiment in Conditional Consumption CAPM Estimates: A Note," *Journal of Behavioral and Experimental Finance*, 2, 1–9.

Robson, D., 2020, "The Simple Maths Error That Can Lead to Bankruptcy," *BBC*, February 17, 2020.

Royall, R., 1997, *Statistical Evidence: A Likelihood Paradigm*, Boca Raton, FL: Chapman & Hall.

Shefrin, H., 2008, "Building On Kahneman's Insights in the Development of Behavioral Finance," *Loyola University Chicago Law Journal*, 44, 1401–1421.

Skyrms, B., 1984, *Pragmatism and Empiricism*, New Haven, CT: Yale University Press.

Stanford, 2021, "Gathering Strength, Gathering Storms: The One Hundred Year Study on Artificial Intelligence (AI100) 2021 Study Panel Report," *One Hundred Year Study on Artificial Intelligence* (https://ai100.stanford.edu/gathering-strength-gathering-storms-one-hundred-year-study-artificial-intelligence-ai100-2021-study).

Stryker, C., and Scapicchio, M., 2025, "What Is Generative AI?," *IBM* (https://www.ibm.com/think/topics/generative-ai).

Taper, M., and Lele, S., 2011, "Evidence, Evidence Functions, and Error Probabilities," In: Bandyopadhyay, P., and Forster, M. (Eds.), *Handbook of Philosophy of Statistics*, pp. 513–532, Amsterdam, The Netherlands: Elsevier.

Timiraos, N., 2025, "Fed Independence Reaches Its Moment of Truth as Supreme Court Weighs Cook's Fate," *Wall Street Journal*, September 25, 2025.

TipRanks, 2023, "Goldman Sachs Remains a Buy on Walmart (WMT)," *Business Insider*, April 5, 2023.

Walmart, 2023, "Walmart Outlines Growth Strategy, Unveils Next Generation Supply Chain at 2023 Investment Community Meeting," *Walmart*, April 4, 2023 (https://

corporate.walmart.com/news/2023/04/04/walmart-outlines-growth-strategy-unveils-next-generation-supply-chain-at-2023-investment-community-meeting).

WLA, 2022, "2022 WLA Prize Laureates" (https://www.thewlaprize.org/Laureates/detail/?id=490).

Wooldridge, J., 2010, *Econometric Analysis of Cross Section and Panel Data*, Cambridge, MA: MIT Press.

Wooldridge, J., 2013, *Introductory Econometrics: A Modern Approach*, Mason, OH: South-Western Cengage Learning.

Zweig, J., 2024, "The Psychologist Who Turned the Investing World on Its Head," *Wall Street Journal*, March 29, 2024.

PART II

With Daily Data

3

ARBITRAGE RISK

3.1 Introduction

Market efficiency has been widely studied in the field of finance for decades, as it provides an investor with a sense of how well the price signal works at conveying all available information, and thus informs an investor of the necessity to acquire additional information about the firm issuing the security. From finance theory, the market for a security is said to be "semistrong form efficient" if the price of the security reflects all publicly available information — please see, for instance, Fama (1970), Cornell (1977), Brennan and Schwartz (1982), Dwyer and Wallace (2002), Gilson and Kraakman (1984), Jensen (1978), Kothari (2001), Loughran and Ritter (2000), Malkiel (2003), Porta et al. (1997), Roll (1984), Samuelson (2009), and Shiller (1981). Prices of securities reflect, *albeit* to varying extents, all publicly available information; therefore, markets for securities are semistrong form efficient in varying degrees. Much research has also been done to determine the mechanisms by which the pricing signal operates, and it is widely understood that correction of mispricing of a stock primarily occurs through arbitrage activity — see, e.g., Harris (2003) and Pontiff (2006).

Since arbitrage is not a cost-free activity, and because frictions remain, whether in the form of transaction costs, idiosyncratic risk — please see, for instance Bali et al. (2005) — or other costs and risks associated with trading securities, pricing anomalies may persist — see, e.g., Pontiff (2006). As a result, everything else remaining the same, financial economics tells one that the market for a stock with a higher arbitrage cost will be less efficient — i.e., a stock's market efficiency is negatively related to its arbitrage risk. Thus, we refer to arbitrage risk as a negative proxy for market efficiency. We discuss this in detail in Section 3.2.

Consider an arbitrageur whose information suggests that a stock is underpriced. The arbitrageur will then "go long" on that stock (buy and hold the stock) in order to

DOI: 10.4324/9781003608486-5

obtain arbitrage profits by selling the stock at a later date. However, the arbitrageur will also manage the risk of holding the stock by hedging. As a result of our interviews with traders "in the trenches," we model the arbitrageur as choosing the optimal hedge stocks and the optimal hedge ratios. The risk of this optimal arbitrage portfolio is the arbitrage risk of the stock, our negative proxy for market efficiency. We discuss these calculations in detail.

We will calculate the market efficiency percentile of a stock over the relevant period based on data for a comparable measurement period. In this case "comparability" means a time interval that is proximate in location and length. For example, in *Lefkoe, et al. v. Jos. A. Bank Clothiers, Inc.*, where the class period was January 5, 2006, to June 7, 2006, we used August 1, 2005, to January 4, 2006, as the measurement period.

If it is not possible (or desirable) to use a different measurement period — e.g., if the period of interest immediately follows an initial public offering (IPO) — then we can do the calculations with the measurement period as the relevant period, and we call this the *ex post* arbitrage risk of the security for the relevant period. For example, in a recent securities class action filed against Groupon, Inc., the class period was defined as November 4, 2011, to March 30, 2012. Since the class period immediately follows the IPO, we do not have trading data from a prior period to use as the measurement period.

For this chapter, we focus on *ex ante* (baseline) arbitrage risk, but we do sensitivity analyses with *ex post* arbitrage risk as another negative proxy for market efficiency. We apply this methodology to calculate, on a yearly basis, the arbitrage risk for each U.S. exchange-listed common stock from 1988 to 2010 (subject to certain restrictions). We also perform a series of simple reduced form regressions of arbitrage risk (as a negative proxy of market efficiency) on the factors identified by courts in securities class actions. These results are summarized in Table 3.1. We detail all the variables in Sections 3.2 and 3.3. We use 5% as our level of statistical significance. If the statistical significance results are different under homoskedasticity and under heteroskedasticity-robustness (White, 1980), we refer to the statistical significance as ambiguous. Please see Chapters 5–8 for various structural regressions.

We checked the sensitivity of these results through a number of additional analyses. For one set, we replaced turnover with the logarithm of volume (or logarithm of dollar volume) but removed market capitalization from the list of factors, reflecting the fact that, *ceteris paribus*, the volume for a stock with higher market capitalization will be higher. For this set, we found that the results were the same as in Table 3.1, except that market efficiency was positively and significantly affected by the number of analysts; positively but insignificantly affected by the number of market makers (for Nasdaq stocks); positively but ambiguously affected by serial correlation; and positively and

TABLE 3.1 Impact on Market Efficiency of Various Factors

Factor	**Relation with Market Efficiency**	**Statistical Significance at 5% Level**	**Consistency with "Conventional Wisdom"**
Cammer v. Bloom			
Turnover	Negative	Significant	Inconsistent
Number of Analysts	Negative	Ambiguous	-
Number of Nasdaq Market Makers	Negative	Significant	Inconsistent
Unger v. Amidesys			
Market Capitalization	Positive	Significant	Consistent
Spread	Negative	Significant	Consistent
Public Float	Positive	Ambiguous	-
Other			
Institutional Ownership	Positive	Significant	Consistent
Serial Correlation	Positive	Significant	Inconsistent
Explanatory Power	Positive	Significant	-
Inclusion in Dow Jones Index	Negative	Significant	-

Note: If the statistical significance results are different under homoskedasticity versus under heteroskedasticity-robustness, the statistical significance is referred to as ambiguous.

significantly affected by inclusion in the Dow Jones Industrial Average (DJIA) (the latter makes sense because in this set, market capitalization is not used as an explanatory factor, whereas it was used as such for the results in Table 3.1). The second set uses only the *Cammer* Factors — please see Bhattacharya et al. (2023) for details — as explanatory variables. For this set, we found that the results were the same as in Table 3.1, except that market efficiency is positively but insignificantly affected by the logarithm of volume (or the logarithm of dollar volume); and positively and significantly affected by number of analysts.

In Section 3.2, we develop arbitrage risk as a negative proxy for market efficiency. In Section 3.3, we provide regression results that test the various factors believed to determine market efficiency — we also investigate the empirical findings that are apparently inconsistent with "conventional wisdom" and show that the empirical findings are actually consistent with the principles of financial economics. Section 3.4 concludes and provides a roadmap of future research projects.

3.2 Negative Proxy

Capital market efficiency describes how completely and accurately the pricing signal works. When all publicly available information is reflected in a security's price, the market for the security is said to be *semistrong form efficient* — see, e.g., Fama (1970) and Malkiel (2003). We interpret the concept not as an either/or, binary construct, but rather as a relative concept occurring along a continuum, and thus one often refers to a market's *relative efficiency* — see, e.g., Campbell et al. (1997). The pricing signal is thought to work through the actions of all traders who, whatever their level of knowledge and sophistication, convey their individual valuations to the market through their buy and sell decisions at various price points — see, e.g., Harris (2003). The collective actions of all traders thus push the price of a particular security toward its market equilibrium level, but do not necessarily take the market for the security all the way to perfect semistrong form efficiency.

Arbitrageurs are investors who trade on information about relative values. They trade investments that are or should be fundamentally correlated but for which they believe the market valuations are deviating from the fundamental relation. Thus arbitrageurs attempt to take advantage of the market pricing discrepancies between otherwise fundamentally correlated securities in order to earn trading profits. This activity of exploiting situations in which markets are not efficient assists the pricing signal by conveying information to the market and helping to push the market to efficiency, but does not necessarily take the market all the way to perfect semistrong form efficiency.

But as Pontiff (2006) explains, because of "costly arbitrage," arbitrageurs are unlikely to ever completely eliminate mispricing. He identifies two sources of arbitrage costs: transactions costs (e.g., commissions, brokerage fees) and holding costs (e.g., opportunity cost of capital and the idiosyncratic risk of a security), and he stresses the importance of idiosyncratic risk — please see Bali et al. (2005), for example — in making arbitrage a costly endeavor. As arbitrageurs construct their hedge portfolios of investments, supposedly correlated in returns, they cannot find perfectly positive correlations in returns and thus perfect substitutes as investments (or perfectly negative correlations in returns and perfect complements as investments), so they are always exposed to the vagaries of each individual security they hold. Even aggregated across a number of investment positions within the hedge portfolio, the legs of the arbitrage, arbitrageurs cannot eliminate the idiosyncratic risk of any security. As a result of the costs of arbitrage, including idiosyncratic risk, market inefficiencies will always remain; the better arbitrage works, the more efficient the market for a security is likely to be. As a result, the costs of arbitrage for a security provide a means to test the efficiency of the security.

Pontiff (2006) concludes that "idiosyncratic risk is the single largest cost faced by arbitrageurs," and that "idiosyncratic risk is the single largest barrier to arbitrage." Our notion of arbitrage risk is a generalization of the standard notion of idiosyncratic risk, defined as the standard deviation of residuals from the Capital Asset Pricing Model (CAPM), detailed in Section 2.9 — please also see, e.g., Bhattacharya (2018), Sharpe (1964), Markowitz (1999), and Miller (1999). If an arbitrageur is constrained to having access to only the market index and a risk-free instrument to devise an optimal zero-net-investment arbitrage portfolio, then the risk of the resulting optimal arbitrage portfolio is the standard idiosyncratic risk. For our notion of *ex ante* or *ex post* arbitrage risk, however, we model the arbitrageur as optimally choosing the components of the arbitrage portfolio from the universe of the market index and all exchange-listed U.S. common stocks, based on financial data on the returns of the stock of interest, all candidate securities, and the risk-free instrument over the measurement period. Then, given the optimal choice of the components of the arbitrage portfolio, and the risk-free instrument, we model the arbitrageur as choosing the optimal hedge ratios under a zero-net-investment constraint. The risk of this optimal arbitrage portfolio is the arbitrage risk of the stock, our negative proxy for market efficiency. Our interviews with traders "in the trenches" confirm this overall structure of hedging behavior by arbitrageurs. Wurgler and Zhuravskaya (2002) construct a similar notion of arbitrage risk, but their substitute securities are selected from similarities in product market characteristics.

We thus develop a practical and general (negative) proxy for market efficiency by quantifying the arbitrage risk associated with each individual security. This simple (negative) proxy for market efficiency then allows for an examination of a variety of factors that have been proffered by economists and lawyers as affecting market efficiency.

We calculate the arbitrage risk of a stock over a defined relevant period as follows:

- We select the relevant period, which can be a day, a week, a court-determined "class" period, or other time frame of relevance (simply for presentation in this chapter, we have chosen annual periods).
- We choose a period immediately prior to the relevant period as the measurement period, because the arbitrageur would not have had access to relevant-period data at the beginning of the relevant period (also for simplicity, we have chosen the year prior to the relevant period as the measurement period).
- On the basis of the measurement period, we determine the lowest risk portfolio that an arbitrageur would use to benefit from mispricing, as explained above. We call this portfolio the arbitrage portfolio for the stock.
- The *ex ante* (or baseline) arbitrage risk of the security for the relevant period is the risk of the arbitrage portfolio over the relevant period.

If it is not possible (or desirable) to use a different measurement period — e.g., if the period of interest immediately follows an initial public offering — then we can do the calculations where the measurement period is the same as the relevant period, and we call this the *ex post* arbitrage risk of the security for the relevant period. For this chapter, we focus on *ex ante* (baseline) arbitrage risk, but we do sensitivity analyses with *ex post* arbitrage risk as another negative proxy for market efficiency.

Consider a stock that is underpriced (overpriced) according to the information available to an arbitrageur. In order to exploit this profitable opportunity, the arbitrageur will construct the following arbitrage portfolio with zero net investment, thereby reaping arbitrage profits when closing out the investment portfolio:

- Arbitrage numerator: go long (short) on the mispriced stock; let's say by \$1 (purely a normalization).
- Other arbitrage legs:
  - Go short (long) on N other securities. We use $N = 5$ legs for the baseline model, but the results do not change qualitatively with values of $N = 10$ or 20.
  - Go short (long) on the risk-free asset.
  - The total amount on these legs has to add up to \$1 short (long).
  - How much to go short (long) on each leg is called the corresponding Hedge Ratio — we use a computational simplification provided by Wurgler and Zhuravskaya (2002).

The risk of a portfolio over a period is defined as the standard deviation of daily returns of the portfolio over that period. Since the arbitrageur does not have access to all relevant period data at the beginning of the relevant period, we choose a period immediately prior to the relevant period as the measurement period, and the arbitrage portfolio is selected to minimize the risk (i.e., the standard deviation of daily returns) of the arbitrage portfolio over the measurement period, with the requirement described above that the arbitrage portfolio requires zero investment. Arbitrageurs generally construct hedge portfolios to minimize the total risk of the portfolio, see Harris (2003), and the risk of the arbitrage portfolio over the relevant period is the arbitrage risk of the stock for the relevant period. For this chapter:

- We measure arbitrage risk for U.S. exchange-listed common stocks
- We consider only U.S. exchange-listed common stocks, and the S&P 500 index, as candidate legs of the hedge portfolio
- We use daily returns on six-month U.S. Treasury bills as the daily risk-free rate (Treasury Constant Maturities, from Federal Reserve, H15 Report)

TABLE 3.2 Examples of Market Efficiency Percentiles, 2010

Ticker	Company	Market Efficiency Percentile
ADP	AUTOMATIC DATA PROCESSING INC	100
BRK	BERKSHIRE HATHAWAY INC DEL	100
DUK	DUKE ENERGY CORP NEW	100
ED	CONSOLIDATED EDISON INC	100
HNZ	HEINZ H J CO	100
JNJ	JOHNSON & JOHNSON	100
JW	WILEY JOHN & SONS INC	100
MO	ALTRIA GROUP INC	100
NST	NSTAR	100
ADM	ARCHER DANIELS MIDLAND CO	91
CAT	CATERPILLAR INC	91
CSCO	CISCO SYSTEMS INC	91
EMC	E M C CORP MA	91
BLK	BLACKROCK INC	81
CBT	CABOT CORP	81
ENDP	ENDO PHARMACEUTICALS HLDNGS INC	81
GPS	GAP INC	81
AMZN	AMAZON COM INC	80
AXP	AMERICAN EXPRESS CO	80
ACF	AMERICREDIT CORP	51
CIEN	CIENA CORP	51
COBZ	COBIZ FINANCIAL INC	51
CPHD	CEPHEID	51
DAL	DELTA AIR LINES INC	51
ACAT	ARCTIC CAT INC	26
APKT	ACME PACKET INC	26
ARTW	ARTS WAY MANUFACTURING INC	26
ATAC	A T C TECHNOLOGY CORP	26
AVII	A V I BIOPHARMA INC	26
TEAR	OCCULOGIX INC	1
TLX	TRANS LUX CORP	1
TSTR	TERRESTAR CORP	1
VNDA	VANDA PHARMACEUTICALS INC	1
ZANE	ZANETT INC	1

Table 3.2 shows examples of exchange-listed stocks and their estimated market efficiency percentiles in 2010, on the basis of our measure of arbitrage risks of all U.S. exchange-listed common stocks. Table 3.3 demonstrates that different stocks display different patterns of market efficiency across time.

3.3 Arbitrage Risk with Standard Factors

We perform a series of simple reduced form regressions to test the empirical relation with arbitrage risk (as a negative proxy for market efficiency) of factors relied upon by courts and others as determinants of market efficiency — please see Chapters 4–8 for other measures of market efficiency. This is done for all U.S. exchange-listed common stocks from 1988 (the year of the landmark *Basic* decision, detailed in Bhattacharya et al. (2023)) to 2010, with the following restrictions.

We restricted attention to stock-year combinations consisting of stocks that had one PERMNO, one TICKER, and one CUSIP over the year in the Center for Research in Security Prices (CRSP) Daily Stock Database. We utilized each stock available from CRSP ($shrcd = 10$ or 11 in the Daily Stock Database from the Center for Research in Security Prices) for which the following data exist for at least 75% of trading days during each of the relevant and measurement periods:

- Returns
- Shares outstanding
- Trading volume
- Closing bid
- Closing ask
- Exchange membership
- Number of market makers.

To include a particular stock in our analysis, we also required data to be available for:

- The number of securities analysts (from I/B/E/S)
- Insider holdings (from Thomson Reuters)
- Institutional holdings (from Thomson Reuters)
- Inclusion in (or exclusion from) the Dow Jones Industrial Average (DJIA) index (from Phyllis Pierce, The Dow Jones Averages 1885-1995).

Table 3A.1 shows the number of stocks at the various stages after imposing the restrictions described above.

From this data, we develop measures for the various factors that courts and others have relied upon as influencing market efficiency. These measures are each defined below.

- Turnover: mean daily turnover (volume)/(shares outstanding) over the relevant period.

TABLE 3.3 Examples of Market Efficiency Percentiles Over Time

Ticker	Company Name	Year	Market Efficiency Percentile
ALG	ALAMO GROUP INC	2001	96
ALG	ALAMO GROUP INC	2002	83
ALG	ALAMO GROUP INC	2003	95
ALG	ALAMO GROUP INC	2004	68
ALG	ALAMO GROUP INC	2005	46
ALG	ALAMO GROUP INC	2006	54
ALG	ALAMO GROUP INC	2007	60
ALG	ALAMO GROUP INC	2008	68
ALG	ALAMO GROUP INC	2009	47
ALG	ALAMO GROUP INC	2010	58
CNLG	CONOLOG CORP	2001	2
CNLG	CONOLOG CORP	2002	3
CNLG	CONOLOG CORP	2003	3
CNLG	CONOLOG CORP	2004	1
CNLG	CONOLOG CORP	2005	2
CNLG	CONOLOG CORP	2006	1
CNLG	CONOLOG CORP	2007	1
CNLG	CONOLOG CORP	2008	1
CNLG	CONOLOG CORP	2009	3
CNLG	CONOLOG CORP	2010	2
ED	CONSOLIDATED EDISON INC	2001	100
ED	CONSOLIDATED EDISON INC	2002	98
ED	CONSOLIDATED EDISON INC	2003	100
ED	CONSOLIDATED EDISON INC	2004	100
ED	CONSOLIDATED EDISON INC	2005	100
ED	CONSOLIDATED EDISON INC	2006	100
ED	CONSOLIDATED EDISON INC	2007	100
ED	CONSOLIDATED EDISON INC	2008	100
ED	CONSOLIDATED EDISON INC	2009	100
ED	CONSOLIDATED EDISON INC	2010	100
FRE	FEDERAL HOME LOAN MORTGAGE CORP	2001	100
FRE	FEDERAL HOME LOAN MORTGAGE CORP	2002	100
FRE	FEDERAL HOME LOAN MORTGAGE CORP	2003	91
FRE	FEDERAL HOME LOAN MORTGAGE CORP	2004	97
FRE	FEDERAL HOME LOAN MORTGAGE CORP	2005	94
FRE	FEDERAL HOME LOAN MORTGAGE CORP	2006	95
FRE	FEDERAL HOME LOAN MORTGAGE CORP	2007	40
FRE	FEDERAL HOME LOAN MORTGAGE CORP	2008	3
FRE	FEDERAL HOME LOAN MORTGAGE CORP	2009	3
MSFT	MICROSOFT CORP	2001	55
MSFT	MICROSOFT CORP	2002	89
MSFT	MICROSOFT CORP	2003	92
MSFT	MICROSOFT CORP	2004	96
MSFT	MICROSOFT CORP	2005	98
MSFT	MICROSOFT CORP	2006	87
MSFT	MICROSOFT CORP	2007	95
MSFT	MICROSOFT CORP	2008	95
MSFT	MICROSOFT CORP	2009	89
MSFT	MICROSOFT CORP	2010	95

- Number of security analysts: number of security analysts who announced at least one projection about the security during the relevant period.
- Number of market makers for Nasdaq stocks: highest, over the relevant period, of the number of market makers on each day.
- Market capitalization: mean of daily logarithm of market capitalization over the relevant year.
- Bid-ask spread: mean of daily relative spread (closing ask – closing bid)/(closing price) over the relevant period.
- Public float ratio: mean of quarterly public float ratio (shares outstanding – insider holdings)/(shares outstanding) over the relevant period.
- Institutional ownership ratio: institutional ownership ratio (institutional holdings)/(shares outstanding) over the relevant period.
- Serial correlation in CAPM: By performing the Durbin-Watson Test on the CAPM on daily returns for a stock for a calendar year, we obtain the p-value for positive serial correlation and the p-value for negative serial correlation. The negative of the minimum of these p-values is a positive measure of serial correlation in the CAPM for the particular stock for the relevant year. Please see, for instance, Greene (2018).
- Explanatory power of CAPM: R^2 of the CAPM for the security in the relevant period.
- Inclusion in the DJIA: If a stock is on the DJIA for an entire year, the indicator variable for that stock for that year is one. If a stock is not on the DJIA for an entire year, the indicator variable for that stock for that year is zero. If a stock is on the DJIA for only part of the year, the observation for that stock for that year is deleted from the regression.

For this chapter, we perform a reduced form regression of arbitrage risk on various factors of market efficiency, controlling for year. The results of this regression — which uses 35,587 observations (stock-years) and has $R^2 = 0.463$ and adjusted $R^2 = 0.462$ (see Table 3A.2) — are shown in Table 3.4.

As with the results summarized in Table 3.1, we checked the sensitivity of these results through a number of additional analyses. For one set, we replaced turnover with the logarithm of volume (or the logarithm of dollar volume) but removed market capitalization from the list of factors, reflecting the fact that, *ceteris paribus*, the volume for a stock with higher market capitalization will be higher. For this set, we found that the results were the same as in Table 3.4, except that arbitrage risk was negatively and significantly affected by number of analysts; negatively but insignificantly affected by number of market makers (for Nasdaq stocks); negatively but ambiguously affected by serial correlation; and negatively and significantly affected by inclusion in the DJIA (the latter makes sense because in this set, market capitalization is not used as an explanatory factor, whereas it was used as such for the results in Table 3.4). The second set uses only the *Cammer*

TABLE 3.4 Detailed Regression Results

Dependent Variable: Arbitrage Risk		Under Homoskedasticity			Heteroskedasticity-Robust		
Factor	**Coefficient (%)**	**Standard Error (%)**	**t-Statistic**	**p-Value**	**Standard Error (%)**	**t-Statistic**	**p-Value**
Cammer v. Bloom							
Turnover	74.366	3.881	19.160	<0.0001	6.286	11.830	<0.0001
Number of Analysts	0.006	0.004	1.770	0.077	0.002	3.100	0.0019
Number of Nasdaq Market Makers	0.019	0.003	5.780	<0.0001	0.004	4.880	<0.0001
Unger v. Amidesys							
Market Capitalization	−0.406	0.032	−12.880	<0.0001	0.043	−9.360	<0.0001
Spread	48.975	1.750	27.980	<0.0001	9.077	5.400	<0.0001
Public Float	−0.821	0.179	−4.600	<0.0001	0.880	−0.930	0.3508
Other							
Institutional Ownership	−0.629	0.138	−4.560	<0.0001	0.142	−4.420	<0.0001
Serial Correlation	−0.423	0.195	−2.170	0.03	0.148	−2.860	0.0042
Explanatory Power	−1.411	0.280	−5.040	<0.0001	0.166	−8.520	<0.0001
Inclusion in Dow Jones Index	1.030	0.295	3.490	0.0005	0.136	7.550	<0.0001
Listed on NYSE	0.467	0.145	3.220	0.0013	0.153	3.040	0.0024

(Continued)

TABLE 3.4 (Continued)

Dependent Variable: Arbitrage Risk							
		Under Homoskedasticity			**Heteroskedasticity-Robust**		
Factor	**Coefficient (%)**	**Standard Error (%)**	**t-Statistic**	**p-Value**	**Standard Error (%)**	**t-Statistic**	**p-Value**
Listed on AMEX	−0.351	0.163	−2.150	0.0314	0.112	−3.150	0.0016
Listed on Other Exchange	0.800	2.255	0.350	0.7227	0.640	1.250	0.2113
Year 1988	6.788	0.571	11.890	<0.0001	0.878	7.730	<0.0001
Year 1989	7.640	0.550	13.900	<0.0001	0.872	8.760	<0.0001
Year 1990	12.130	0.563	21.550	<0.0001	1.267	9.570	<0.0001
Year 1991	45.566	0.568	80.230	<0.0001	4.618	9.870	<0.0001
Year 1992	11.421	0.464	24.610	<0.0001	0.976	11.700	<0.0001
Year 1993	6.968	0.457	15.240	<0.0001	0.850	8.190	<0.0001
Year 1994	6.826	0.449	15.210	<0.0001	0.852	8.010	<0.0001
Year 1995	6.743	0.447	15.070	<0.0001	0.853	7.910	<0.0001
Year 1996	7.066	0.444	15.920	<0.0001	0.856	8.260	<0.0001
Year 1997	7.381	0.439	16.830	<0.0001	0.852	8.670	<0.0001
Year 1998	7.968	0.433	18.420	<0.0001	0.848	9.400	<0.0001
Year 1999	7.966	0.437	18.210	<0.0001	0.856	9.300	<0.0001
Year 2000	8.747	0.436	20.070	<0.0001	0.859	10.180	<0.0001
Year 2001	8.742	0.424	20.610	<0.0001	0.840	10.400	<0.0001
Year 2002	8.539	0.414	20.620	<0.0001	0.830	10.290	<0.0001
Year 2003	7.963	0.412	19.330	<0.0001	0.819	9.730	<0.0001
Year 2004	7.801	0.417	18.730	<0.0001	0.823	9.480	<0.0001
Year 2005	7.694	0.416	18.480	<0.0001	0.823	9.340	<0.0001
Year 2006	7.684	0.415	18.510	<0.0001	0.824	9.320	<0.0001
Year 2007	8.080	0.411	19.650	<0.0001	0.825	9.800	<0.0001
Year 2008	9.465	0.399	23.710	<0.0001	0.828	11.430	<0.0001
Year 2009	9.677	0.393	24.630	<0.0001	0.823	11.760	<0.0001
Year 2010	7.928	0.396	20.010	<0.0001	0.820	9.670	<0.0001

Factors — see Bhattacharya et al. (2023) for details — as explanatory variables. For this set, we found that the results were the same as in Table 3.4, except that arbitrage risk is negatively but insignificantly affected by the logarithm of volume (or the logarithm of dollar volume); and negatively and significantly affected by number of analysts.

3.3.1 Trading Volume

The positive relation of trading volume or turnover with market efficiency is often considered almost axiomatic — statements such as "the more thinly traded the stock, the less efficient the market is" are common. However, this is not necessarily the case. In order to appreciate how trading volume (or turnover) is often misunderstood, one needs to appreciate that: "investors trade among themselves because they are different" Wang (1994). See also Miller (1977), Karpoff (1987), O'Hara (1997), Stickel and Verrecchia (1994), Blume et al. (1994), and Goldstein et al. (2007). As detailed in Chapter 7, one would observe higher trading volume or turnover in the market for an asset if and only if:

1. Transaction costs (including bid-ask spread, commissions, and search costs) are low relative to dispersion in investor valuations.
2. Low-valuers hold more securities than high-valuers, and short sales costs are low relative to dispersion in investor valuations.

Higher trading volume will therefore be observed with:

- Lower transaction costs,
- Lower short sales costs,
- Higher dispersion of investor valuations, and/or
- Higher likelihood that an investor holds the asset.

Clearly, market efficiency would be facilitated by lower transaction costs and lower short sales costs — and when a claim is made about higher trading volume being a factor favoring market efficiency, it is often implicitly based on this argument. However, there is no reason to conclude that, *ceteris paribus*, a higher dispersion in investor valuations, or a higher likelihood that an investor holds the asset, would lead to higher market efficiency. With high dispersion in investor valuations, one can have a high trading volume (much of which can be due to noise trading), and a higher dispersion in investor valuations does not necessarily add to the efficiency of a market.

Given these contrary dependencies, the relation of market efficiency with turnover is fundamentally an empirical question, and our empirical finding, for all U.S. exchange-listed common stocks from 1988 to 2010, is that turnover negatively and significantly affects market efficiency.

3.3.2 Number of Market Makers

From the above discussion, we can see that the demand for market making services in a Nasdaq stock is an increasing function of dispersion in investor valuations — i.e., everything else remaining the same, a firm is more likely to be a market maker in a Nasdaq stock if the investor valuation profile for that stock is more dispersed, because there would be more trades to enable more profits.

However, the higher the number of market makers, the higher the competition for trades would be, and this would reduce the transaction costs of trades. Therefore, a higher number of market makers would be observed with higher dispersion (not unambiguously facilitating market efficiency, as shown above) and/or lower transaction cost (facilitating market efficiency).

Therefore, as above, the relation between the number of Nasdaq market makers and market efficiency is fundamentally empirical, and our empirical finding, for all U.S. exchange-listed common stocks from 1988 to 2010, is that arbitrage risk for a Nasdaq stock is positively and significantly related to the number of market makers for that stock; and that market efficiency for a Nasdaq stock is negatively and significantly related to the number of market makers for that stock.

3.3.3 Serial Correlation

Serial correlation in the CAPM of a stock's daily returns, suggesting a day-to-day pattern of repeated performance, is often considered evidence of market inefficiencies. Some scholars have suggested other explanations of serial correlation that are consistent with market efficiency — see Ball and Kothari (1989), for example. In the presence of such inconsistent findings, this dependence becomes an empirical question. Our empirical findings suggest that, on the basis of all U.S. exchange-listed common stocks from 1988 to 2010, serial correlation affects market efficiency positively and significantly.

3.3.4 Other Factors

The number of securities analysts is a *Cammer* Factor, and other courts have suggested using public float as a factor favorable to a finding of market efficiency. Our empirical findings suggest that, on the basis of all U.S. exchange-listed common stocks from 1988 to 2010, the number of securities analysts and public float have an ambiguous impact on market efficiency.

Consistent with the position taken by courts and others — see Bhattacharya et al. (2023) — we find that market capitalization and institutional ownership have significant empirical support based on our analysis. The bid-ask spread of a stock, which is a measure of transaction cost of a stock, has been used by courts as a factor inhibiting market efficiency, and our results confirm this position, too.

Although we have not found a court ruling where the inclusion of the relevant stock in a major index is a factor favorable to a finding of market efficiency, expert reports and testimony commonly use such an argument. It is interesting to note, however, that because we control for market capitalization, what the indicator variable corresponding to membership in the DJIA measures is purely how much the inclusion of the stock in the DJIA adds to the efficiency of the market for the stock, over and above what the stock's market capitalization predicts. We find, for all U.S. exchange-listed common stocks from 1988 to 2010, that inclusion in the DJIA, over and above its size, significantly reduces the efficiency of the market for its stock.

It should be noted that these results are robust to alterations in the statistical model. We performed sensitivity analyses with (a) *ex post* arbitrage risk, (b) sign constraints on the correlations of returns in the determination of legs of the arbitrage portfolio, (c) sign constraints on the hedge ratios, (d) number of legs in the arbitrage portfolio, and (e) the risk-free rate. The empirical findings are qualitatively the same as for the baseline regressions.

3.4 Conclusions

In this chapter, we discussed arbitrage risk, a negative proxy for market efficiency based on financial economics, and showed how it can be applied to securities class actions. We also performed a series of simple reduced form regressions to test the dependence of arbitrage risk on various standard factors used by courts in the determination of market efficiency. Some of these empirical findings do not seem consistent with "conventional wisdom" — as Warren Buffett is famously supposed to have said, "well, it may be all right in practice, but it will never work in theory." However, we found that our empirical findings are actually consistent with economic theory.

The list of determinants of market efficiency considered in this chapter is not exhaustive. Academic research and interviews with financial practitioners have suggested additional factors such as external and internal regulations, and industrial organization (including supply and demand structures) of product markets. We intend to utilize data on industry codes, and industry properties such as pricing and concentration, to analyze these additional factors affecting market efficiency.

The next chapter, Chapter 4, proposes a systematization of purely objective measures of efficiency of the market for an equity.

TABLE 3A.1 Number of Unique Stock-Year Combinations

	Number of Unique Stock-Year Combinations			
	All	**With Unique PERMNO, TICKER, and CUSIP, in Calendar Year**	**With Calendar Year, Trading Restrictions**	**After Mergers with Other Data**
All Years	141,591	131,779	106,585	37,111
1988	5,323	4,839	4,040	538
1989	4,980	4,633	4,053	578
1990	4,772	4,454	3,923	585
1991	4,843	4,523	3,901	610
1992	6,434	5,973	4,669	652
1993	6,976	6,450	4,911	754
1994	7,367	6,871	5,160	866
1995	7,757	7,170	5,507	990
1996	8,282	7,606	5,605	1,098
1997	8,468	7,710	5,781	1,237
1998	8,254	7,544	5,869	1,415
1999	7,917	7,218	5,551	1,542
2000	7,528	6,835	5,198	1,646
2001	6,692	6,252	5,016	1,765
2002	5,955	5,562	4,850	1,917
2003	5,497	5,231	4,535	2,034
2004	5,286	5,032	4,314	2,185
2005	5,228	4,976	4,162	2,379
2006	5,179	4,893	4,085	2,619
2007	5,155	4,891	3,993	2,859
2008	4,843	4,591	3,923	2,900
2009	4,533	4,343	3,871	3,040
2010	4,322	4,182	3,668	2,902

TABLE 3A.2 Summary Regression Results

Number of Observations Read			**37,111**		
Number of Observations Used			**35,587**		
Number of Observations with Missing Values			**1,524**		
Source	**Degrees of Freedom**	**Sum of Squares (SS)**	**Mean SS**	**F-Value**	**p-Value**
Model	36	93.1478	2.58744	851.3	<0.0001
Error	35,551	108.0536	0.00304		
Uncorrected Total	35,587	201.2014			
R^2	0.463				
Adj R^2	0.462				

References

Bali, T., Cakici, N., Yan, X., and Zhang, Z., 2005, "Does Idiosyncratic Risk Really Matter?," *Journal of Finance*, 60, 905–929.

Ball, R., and Kothari, S. P., 1989, "Nonstationary Expected Returns: Implications for Tests of Market Efficiency and Serial Correlation in Returns," *Journal of Financial Economics*, 25(1), 51–74.

Bhattacharya, R., 2018, "Capital Asset Pricing Model (CAPM)," In: Teece, D., and Augier, M. (Eds.), *The Palgrave Encyclopedia of Strategic Management*, pp. 1–4, London, UK: Palgrave Macmillan.

Bhattacharya, R., Bial, J., and Evans, A., 2023, "It Is Imperative to Perform Event Studies only with High-Frequency Intraday Data for Securities Litigations and Valuations," *Journal of International Business & Law*, 23(1), 1–28.

Blume, L., Easley, D., and O'Hara, M., 1994, "Market Statistics and Technical Analysis: The Role of Volume," *Journal of Finance*, 49(1), 153–181.

Brennan, B., and Schwartz, E., 1982, "An Equilibrium Model of Bond Pricing and a Test of Market Efficiency," *Journal of Financial and Quantitative Analysis*, 17(3), 301–329.

Campbell, J., Lo, A., and MacKinlay, A. C., 1997, *The Econometrics of Financial Markets*, Princeton, NJ: Princeton University Press.

Cornell, B., 1977, "Spot Rates, Forward Rates and Exchange Market Efficiency," *Journal of Financial Economics*, 5(1), 55–65.

Dwyer, G., and Wallace, M., 2002, "Cointegration and Market Efficiency," *Journal of International Money and Finance*, 11, 318–327.

Fama, E., 1970, "Efficient Capital Markets: A Review of Theory and Empirical Work," *Journal of Finance*, 25(2), 383–417.

Gilson, R., and Kraakman, R., 1984, "The Mechanisms of Market Efficiency," *Virginia Law Review*, 70(4), 549–644.

Goldstein, M., Hotchkiss, E., and Sirri, E., 2007, "Transparency and Liquidity: A Controlled Experiment on Corporate Bonds," *Review of Financial Studies*, 20(2), 235–273.

Greene, W., 2018, *Econometric Analysis*, Upper Saddle River, NJ: Pearson.

Harris, L., 2003, *Trading & Exchanges: Market Microstructure for Practitioners*, New York, NY: Oxford University Press.

Jensen, M., 1978, "Some Anomalous Evidence Regarding Market Efficiency," *Journal of Financial Economics*, 6(2–3), 95–101.

Karpoff, J., 1987, "The Relation between Price Changes and Trading Volume: A Survey," *Journal of Financial and Quantitative Analysis*, 22(1), 109–126.

Kothari, S. P., 2001, "Capital Markets Research in Accounting," *Journal of Accounting and Economics*, 31(1–3), 105–231.

Loughran, T., and Ritter, J., 2000, "Uniformly Least Powerful Tests of Market Efficiency," *Journal of Financial Economics*, 55(3), 361–389.

Malkiel, B., 2003, "The Efficient Market Hypothesis and Its Critics," *Journal of Economic Perspectives*, 17(1), 59–82.

Markowitz, H. 1999, "The Early History of Portfolio Theory: 1600–1960," *Financial Analysts Journal*, 55, 5–16.

Miller, E., 1977, "Risk, Uncertainty, and Divergence of Opinion," *Journal of Finance*, 32(4), 1151–1168.

Miller, M., 1999, "The History of Finance," *Journal of Portfolio Management*, 95–101.

O'Hara, M., 1997, *Market Microstructure Theory*, Malden, MA: Blackwell Publishing.

Pontiff, J., 2006, "Costly Arbitrage and the Myth of Idiosyncratic Risk," *Journal of Accounting and Economics*, 42(1–2), 35–52.

Porta, R., Lakonishok, J., Shleifer, A., and Vishny, R., 1997, "Good News for Value Stocks: Further Evidence on Market Efficiency," *Journal of Finance*, 52(2), 859–874.

Roll, R., 1984, "A Simple Implicit Measure of the Effective Bid-Ask Spread in an Efficient Market," *Journal of Finance*, 39(4), 1127–1139.

Samuelson, P., 2009, "An Enjoyable Life Puzzling over Modern Finance Theory," *Annual Review of Financial Economics*, 1, 19–35.

Sharpe, W., 1964, "Capital Asset Prices: A Theory of Market Equilibrium under Conditions of Risk," *Journal of Finance*, 19(3), 425–442.

Shiller, R., 1981, "The Use of Volatility Measures in Assessing Market Efficiency," *Journal of Finance*, 36(2), 291–304.

Stickel, S., and Verrecchia, R., 1994, "Evidence That Trading Volume Sustains Stock Price Changes," *Financial Analysts Journal*, 50(6), 57–67.

Wang, J., 1994, "A Model of Competitive Stock Trading Volume," *Journal of Political Economy*, 102(1), 127–168.

White, H., 1980, "A Heteroskedasticity-Consistent Covariance Matrix Estimator and a Direct Test for Heteroskedasticity," *Econometrica*, 48(4), 817–838.

Wurgler, J., and Zhuravskaya, E., 2002, "Does Arbitrage Flatten Demand Curves for Stocks," *Journal of Business*, 75(4), 583–608.

4

OBJECTIVE MEASURES

4.1 Introduction

A market is semistrong efficient ("efficient") if prices reflect all publicly available information — please see, for example, Fama (1991, 1970), Samuelson (2009), Malkiel (2003), Harris (2003), and Shleifer (2000). A market is efficient if stock prices adjust very rapidly to new information — please see Fama et al. (1969). Finally, idiosyncratic returns, on average, are zero in an efficient market — please see, for example, Fama (1970). (1) Prices of securities reflect, *albeit* to varying extents, all publicly available information; (2) prices adjust, albeit to varying extents, to new information; and (3) idiosyncratic returns are close to zero, also albeit to various extents. Therefore, markets for securities are efficient in varying degrees, referred to as *relative efficiency* — please see, for example, Campbell et al. (1997). It is worth emphasizing that a security's being sufficiently efficient or otherwise has no *a priori* bearing on whether it is a good investment or not.

We run four different event studies for every U.S.-listed security from 2001 to 2017 to calculate four different measures of market efficiency based on the frontiers of financial and information economics — please see Section 4.2 for details. We do not ascribe any directional component to any potentially material event in this chapter, because such an ascription would require subjective judgment and/or additional information. Furthermore, it is *ad hoc* to infer from the description of an event if the event would cause, under market efficiency, the price to go up, down, or stay the same. In other words, it is impossible to objectively determine the market's perceptions immediately prior to any potentially material event and, therefore, to determine whether a particular potentially material event was better-than-expected news, worse-than-expected news, or even news at all; for example, Ferrillo et al.

DOI: 10.4324/9781003608486-6

(2004) require *ad hoc* judgment as to whether a potentially material event is news. Colloquially speaking, good news or bad news is not the relevant question here. Reaction, overreaction, correction, overcorrection, bounce-back, etc. should be out of the system within a few days after a potentially material event in an efficient market.

The measures that we use in this chapter are completely rules-based, with no judgment, subjectivity, or additional information required of any kind. The only rules are such that a reasonable person can, *a priori*, agree with: (a) for the industry index, we use all firms that are in the same major industry sector (same two-digit Standard Industrial Classification (SIC) Code) as the firm in question, and (b) idiosyncratic price reaction to an event after a few days is close to zero for an efficient market (as described earlier).

Finally, we rely upon advanced statistical techniques to estimate a relationship between market efficiency and each security for each year, providing an objective characterization of the market for a security in a year to be sufficiently efficient or otherwise.

In this chapter, we apply these methodologies to Petrobras's American Depositary Receipt (ADR), trading under the TICKER PBR on NYSE, in 2001-2017, and conclude that the Petrobras Court was in part right, but in part wrong, when it certified a 2010-2015 class period because the market for PBR was sufficiently efficient in 2010, 2011, and 2014, but not sufficiently efficient in 2012, 2013, and 2015 — please see *Petrobras Securities Litigation*, United States District Court, Southern District of New York, 1:14-cv-09662-JSR, February 2, 2016, and Bhattacharya et al. (2023) for the role of market efficiency in the class certification for securities class actions.

In this chapter, we apply these methodologies to value each U.S.-listed firm for each year in 2001-2017. Here are three examples:

Example 4.1 *The market for GS (Goldman Sachs Group, Inc., common equity) was sufficiently efficient in each year in 2001-2017, and therefore, market prices represented value for Goldman Sachs over 2001-2017.*

Example 4.2 *The market for MSFT (Microsoft Corporation, common equity) was sufficiently efficient in each of these years except 2002, and therefore, market prices represented value for Microsoft Corporation in these years except 2002. Our analyses do not address whether market prices over- or under-estimated value of Microsoft in 2002.*

Example 4.3 *The market for AAME (Atlantic American Corporation, common equity) was not sufficiently efficient in any year in 2001-2017, and therefore, market prices did not represent value for Atlantic American Corporation in 2001-2017. Our* *analyses do not address whether market prices over- or under-estimated value of Atlantic American Corporation in any of these years.*

Section 4.2 describes the four different objective measures of market efficiency and the statistical methodology we use in this chapter. Section 4.3 details the data that were relied upon for this chapter. Section 4.4 discusses the essential importance of market efficiency in valuation, and applies the four different objective measures of market efficiency to the valuation of three firms with publicly listed equity.

4.2 Methodology

In this section, we discuss the Capital Asset Pricing Model (CAPM) and the Market Model (MM) to compute idiosyncratic return for each security for each day, as outlined in Section 2.9, and in the third part, we generalize these models for millisecond-level high-frequency intraday data. We rely upon CAPM, please also see Bhattacharya (2018) for instance, to calculate, for each security i for each day t,

$$RP_{i,t} = \beta_{M,i} RP_{M,t} + IdioR_{i,t} \tag{4.1}$$

where $R_{i,t}$ = return on day t of security i, $R_{f,t}$ = risk-free return on day t, $R_{M,t}$ = return on day t of the market index, where risk premium on day t of security i is

$$RP_{i,t} = R_{i,t} - R_{f,t} \tag{4.2}$$

and risk premium on day t of the market index is

$$RP_{M,t} = RM_t - R_{f,t} R_{f,t} \tag{4.3}$$

and idiosyncratic return on day t of security i is $IdioR_{i,t}$.

Bodie et al. (2018) describe CAPM as a set of predictions concerning equilibrium expected return on risky assets. Shefrin (2008) and Potì and Shefrin (2014), for a study of more sophisticated versions of CAPM from a behavioral perspective. For the baseline model, we use daily returns on three-month T-bills as the risk-free rate, the daily returns, including all distributions, on the value-weighted market portfolio as the market return — VWRETD indices contain ... daily ... returns, including all distributions, on a value-weighted market portfolio (excluding American Depository Receipts) (CRSP information) — and we also check for robustness: (a) using returns on four-week, six-month, and one-year T-bill rates separately as risk-free rates, and (b) returns on the equally-weighted market portfolio — EWRETD indices contain ... daily ... returns, including all distributions, on an equally-weighted market portfolio (including ADRs) (CRSP information) — and on the S&P Composite Index as the market return.

Separately and additionally, we also rely upon the Market Model (MM) — as outlined in Section 2.9, please also see Campbell et al. (1977), for instance — to run the same calculations for each security i for each day t,

$$R_{i,t} = \alpha + \theta_{f,i} R_{f,t} + \theta_{M,i} R_{M,t} + \theta_{C,i} R_{C,i,t} + IdioR_{i,t} \tag{4.4}$$

where $R_{i,t}$ = return on day t of security i, $R_{f,t}$ = risk-free return on day t, $R_{M,t}$ = return on day t of the market index, $R_{C,i,t}$ = return on day t of comparables to firm i, we use the value-weighted average daily returns of equities of all firms in the same major industrial sector as firm i — i.e., with the same 2-digit Standard Industrial Classification (SIC) Code — as the corresponding return for comparables, and $IdioR_{i,t}$ = idiosyncratic return on day t of security i. The Market Model is similar to the Arbitrage Pricing Theory (APT) and to the Capital Asset Pricing Model (CAPM) mentioned above.

We use the following objective metrics, based on event studies, as separate negative measures for the efficiency of the market for a security (please see Chapters 3 and 5 for other measures of market efficiency based on daily data):

- Key Developments Idiosyncratic Response (KDIR) of the security, estimated through the Capital Asset Pricing Model (CAPM);
- KDIR of the security, estimated through the Market Model (MM);
- Earnings Announcements Idiosyncratic Response (EAIR) of the security, estimated through CAPM; and
- EAIR of the security, estimated through MM.

Over the past five decades, since Fama et al. (1969) and Ball and Brown (1968), event studies "have become a fundamental part of financial economics, valuation, and litigation. Hundreds of event studies have been conducted in the legal, financial economics, and accounting literatures. ... They test the impact, speed, and unbiasedness of the market's reaction to an event. In an efficient capital market, a security's price reaction to an event is expected to be immediate," Kothari (2001). Event studies serve an important purpose in capital market research as a way of testing market efficiency, because systematically nonzero idiosyncratic security returns that persist after a particular type of corporate event are inconsistent with market efficiency — Kothari (2001). Please see Ball (2017) for a retrospective by one of the cofounders of event studies describing the contributions of the other cofounders

We do not ascribe any directional component to any potentially material event in this chapter — if the event time is at or after 4 PM, we consider the next day as the effective day. It requires subjective judgment to infer from the description of an event if market efficiency would require the price of the security to go up, down, or stay the same. In other words, it is impossible to objectively determine the market's perceptions immediately prior to any potentially material event. To determine whether a particular potentially material event was better information than expected, worse information than expected, or just no surprise at all is not possible without additional information or *ad hoc* judgment — Ferrillo et al. (2004) is an example of work that requires such *ad hoc* judgment. Colloquially speaking, good news or bad news is not the relevant question here; and reaction, overreaction, correction, overcorrection, bounce-back, etc. should, in an efficient market, be out of the system within a few days after a potentially material event. See, for instance, Judge Jed Rakoff's discussion of directionality, and his criticisms of the subjective and *ad hoc* marking of directionality of events in the dueling expert reports, in his judgment in *Petrobras Securities Litigation* (United States District Court, Southern District of New York, 1:14-cv-09662-JSR, February 2, 2016). For instance, an "expert" used the presence or absence of the text "corrupt" in the description of an event to determine the direction of a relevant event.

How to identify a potentially material event leads to the following two paths of study:

1. For the first path of event studies research, we rely upon the marking of an event as a Key Development by Capital IQ, a service of Standard & Poor's, to tag an event as potentially material. As described earlier, we do not try to ascribe any directional component to any Key Development identified by Capital IQ — it is impossible to objectively determine whether a particular Key Development was better-than-expected news, worse-than-expected news, or simply no surprise at all. For each security and for each year, we calculate the average, for that security and that year, of the absolute value of the cumulative idiosyncratic return for the security over the last three days of a week's window following each Key Development for that security in that year — we call this the Key Developments Idiosyncratic Response (KDIR) for that security for that year and use it as a negative measure for the efficiency of the market for that security in that year.
2. For the second path of event studies research, we designate each earnings announcement as a potentially material event. Such a study of earnings announcements' impact on security prices has a long and distinguished history — please see, for instance, Ball and Brown (1968) and Collins and Kothari (1989). Any estimate of the market's consensus prediction of the EPS at the point of an EPS announcement, whether it is by using mean/medians of analyst forecasts, or by using valuation models, is sensitive to the methodology used to estimate the market's perception and the deviation from it. The actual announced EPS or its deviation from consensus does not enter into our calculations in this chapter. See, for instance, Chiang et al. (2019) for detailed descriptions of biases and robustness in the calculation of deviation from consensus. See Kothari et al. (2016) for a comprehensive survey of the literature on quality,

bias, and predictability of earnings forecasts. The impact of analyst incentives on analyst forecasts is beyond the scope of this chapter, see Bhattacharya and Gupta (2023), for a survey of recent research. For reasons explained earlier, it is impossible to objectively distill how much information about an actual earnings announcement leaked out before the actual announcement; i.e., to objectively distill the true surprise component of an earnings announcement is impossible. Therefore, we calculate the average for each security for that year, of the absolute value of the cumulative idiosyncratic return for the security over the last three days of a week's window following each earnings announcement for that security in that year — we call this the Earnings Announcements Idiosyncratic Response (EAIR) for that security for that year and use it as a negative measure for the efficiency of the market for the security in that year.

For each security, we estimate the normal (and implicitly the idiosyncratic) daily return for each year, and more specifically for each trading day in that year, by using the Capital Asset Pricing Model and Market Model separately. For each potentially material event — determined as below — we calculate the cumulative idiosyncratic return for the security over the last three days of a week's window following the potentially material event. For each security, for each potentially material event at time t, we calculate the cumulative idiosyncratic return for the

$$[(T - 1\ week) \leq t \leq (T + 1\ week)] \tag{4.5}$$

window, thus allowing for the possibility that material information could leak out about a week before the potentially material event and that it takes up to a week after the potentially material event for the unanticipated information to have its impact on security returns. From this cumulative idiosyncratic return, we subtract the cumulative idiosyncratic return for the

$$[(T - 1\ week) \leq t \leq (T + 4\ days)] \tag{4.6}$$

window in order to calculate the cumulative idiosyncratic return for the security over the last three days of a week's window following the potentially material event for that security — this, as discussed above, is closer to zero the closer a market is to efficiency.

4.2.1 Characterization as Sufficiently Efficient

As described earlier, we performed four different event studies for every U.S.-listed security available between 2001 and 2017. From these event studies, we calculated four different objective negative measures of the efficiency of the market for each of the assets for every year of the range. For each calendar year, we then transformed these negative measures of market efficiency for each stock into a positive measure of market efficiency in two ways described below. We then controlled for each measure type and the interaction of each security and each year, and therefore, the coefficient of this interaction term is the security-year-specific impact.

1. By calculating the natural exponent of the negative of the measure
2. By calculating the negative of the measure
3. We regress each market efficiency measure by using a fixed effect for each measure type and each transform, and calculate the residuals
4. We regress these residuals by using a fixed effect for each security and each year

Subsequently, for each security and each year, we test this security-year-specific impact using one-tailed hypothesis testing at a 5% level of statistical significance. This provides an objective characterization of the market for a security in a year to be *sufficiently efficient* or not.

4.3 Description of Data

Security-days that had positive closing price, positive shares outstanding, and other restrictions from CRSP:

- date
- closing price
- (discrete) return
- shares outstanding
- trading volume
- closing bid
- closing ask
- exchange membership
- number of market makers
- SIC Code
- value-weighted market return of all publicly traded U.S. securities
- equally-weighted market return of all publicly traded U.S. securities

And the issuing firms had data on the following variables:

- Earnings announcements (from I/B/E/S)
- Key Developments (from Capital IQ)
- Compustat-CRSP Merged Database

Also, the sample is further restricted to the following:

- if $ret \notin \{-44.0, -55.0, -66.0, -77.0, -88.0, -99.0\}$
- if $dlret \notin \{-55.0, -66.0, -88.0, -99.0\}$
- if $dlretx \notin \{-55.0, -66.0, -88.0, -99.0\}$
- if $dclrdt \neq 0$
- if $trtscd \neq 0$,
- if $nmsind \neq 0$
- if $vol \neq -99.0$
- if $prc > 0$
- if $bid > 0$
- if $ask > 0$
- if $vol > 0$
- if $shrout > 0$
- if $TICKER \neq ?$
- if $TICKER \neq ''$
- if $CUSIP \neq ''$
- if $substr(TICKER, 1, 4) \neq ZZZZ$;
- if $substr(CUSIP, 7, 1) \in \{0, 1, 2, 3, 4, 5, 6, 7, 8, 9\}$
- if $substr(CUSIP, 8, 1) \in \{0, 1, 2, 3, 4, 5, 6, 7, 8, 9\}$

Compustat (including Capital IQ) data sources rely upon the S&P identification of GVKEY. In this chapter, we rely upon the mapping of GVKEY to TICKER used by CRSP to match its data to Compustat. In order to maintain the integrity of the linkages between the different sources of data we rely upon, we treat a missing observation as a missing observation, not as a zero. For a small number of stock-days, we found multiple entries when sorted by TICKER, CUSIP, and date — for these stock-days, we calculate weighted averages using trading volume as weights. For a security to be in our sample for a particular calendar year, we require that the security have traded for at least half the trading days in that calendar year (for summary statistics on all U.S.-listed equities see Table 4.1; for summary statistics on all Nasdaq-listed equities, see Table 4.2; and for summary statistics for all non-Nasdaq-listed equities, see Table 4.3).

4.4 Valuation

As discussed above, if and only if the market for an asset is sufficiently efficient, and conditional on public information, the asset's market price remains a reasonable estimate of value. Whether the market price of a particular asset (or portfolio of assets) serves as a reasonable approximation of that particular asset's value depends solely on whether the market for that particular asset was sufficiently efficient. In

TABLE 4.1 Correlations between Measures of Market Efficiency, All U.S. Listed Equities, 2001-2017

Measure	KDAR (CAPM)	KDAR (MM)	EAAR (CAPM)	EAAR (MM)
KDAR (CAPM)	1.00000	0.98426	0.36738	0.37382
KDAR (MM)	0.98426	1.00000	0.37081	0.39126
EAAR (CAPM)	0.36738	0.37081	1.00000	0.97207
EAAR (MM)	0.37382	0.39126	0.97207	1.00000

TABLE 4.2 Correlations between Measures of Market Efficiency, All Nasdaq-Listed Equities, 2001-2017

Measure	KDAR (CAPM)	KDAR (MM)	EAAR (CAPM)	EAAR (MM)
KDAR (CAPM)	1.00000	0.98749	0.34723	0.35313
KDAR (MM)	0.98749	1.00000	0.35194	0.36699
EAAR (CAPM)	0.34723	0.35194	1.00000	0.97772
EAAR (MM)	0.35313	0.36699	0.97772	1.00000

TABLE 4.3 Correlations between Measures of Market Efficiency, All Non-Nasdaq-Listed Equities, 2001-2017

Measure	KDAR (CAPM)	KDAR (MM)	EAAR (CAPM)	EAAR (MM)
KDAR (CAPM)	1.00000	0.96954	0.36836	0.37160
KDAR (MM)	0.96954	1.00000	0.36472	0.40117
EAAR (CAPM)	0.36836	0.36472	1.00000	0.95194
EAAR (MM)	0.37160	0.40117	0.95194	1.00000

this chapter, we use four different objective measures of the market efficiency for an asset (detailed in Section 4.2). Relying upon advanced statistical techniques, we also estimate a relationship between market efficiency and each security for each year, which provides an objective market character for a security in a sufficiently efficient year. If a valuer proposes using market price(s) as approximation for value(s), such a proposal will need to be supported through sufficiently high measures of the market(s) efficiency for the relevant assets. Conversely, an argument against using market prices as value in a particular context will be meaningful if, and only if, objective measures of market(s) efficiency for the relevant assets show the corresponding markets to not be sufficiently efficient.

In this chapter, we apply these methodologies to each U.S.-listed firm for each year in 2001-2017; here are three examples:

1. The market for GS (Goldman Sachs Group, Inc., common equity) was sufficiently efficient in each year in 2001-2017, and therefore, the market prices represented valuc.
2. The market for MSFT (Microsoft Corporation, common equity) was sufficiently efficient in each of these years except 2002, and therefore, market prices represented value for Microsoft Corporation in these years except 2002. Our 2002 Microsoft analyses do not address whether market prices over- or under-estimated value.
3. The market for AAME (Atlantic American Corporation, common equity) was not sufficiently efficient in any year in 2001-2017, and therefore, market prices did not represent value. Our analyses do not address whether market prices over- or under-estimated value of Atlantic American Corporation in any of these years.

Mark-to-Market (MTM or M2M) accounting is based on the premise that the measured assets consist only of components that are part of, or similar to, assets that are trading in sufficiently efficient markets. Like above, an objective measure of market efficiency for the relevant assets showing the market to be sufficiently efficient must support any proposal to use MTM. Conversely, an argument against MTM in a particular context will be meaningful if and only if market efficiency's objective measures show the corresponding markets to not be sufficiently efficient. Please see Allen and Carletti (2008) for a somewhat dated summary of the pros and cons of this approach. See Ellul et al. (2014) for a post-Global Financial Crisis study.

A comparable to a firm is another firm that shares similar characteristics, "the value of most assets, from the house you buy to the stocks you invest in, are based on how similar assets are priced in the marketplace ... the value of an asset is derived from the pricing of comparable assets, standardized using a common variable such as earnings, cash flows, book value, or revenues," Damodaran (2012). This applies to all valuations that are based on comparables — real estate, for instance, strongly relies upon "comps-based" valuation methods. Given a proper choice of comparable(s) and an appropriate metric, therefore, the comparables approach to valuation is essentially a joint test of the efficiency of the market for the firm (or an asset or a portfolio). For example, by using Apple stock as a comparable to Meta and relying upon Price/Earnings (P/E) Ratio as the relevant metric, one can test the null hypothesis that Meta is correctly valued (i.e., the market for Meta common stock is semistrong form efficient). Any conclusion based on the differences between the actual price of Meta equity on one hand, and the predicted price of Meta, which equals the average P/E Ratio for Apple, multiplied by the EPS of Meta, on the other, remains grounded on the implicit assumption that Apple stock is trading on sufficiently efficient markets, provided, of course, that the P/E Ratio is an appropriate metric. It is possible for the stock market to reject this particular null

TABLE 4.4 Valuation of MSFT Equity Using AAPL as Comparable, 2023-2024

	Earnings Per Share	Price/Earnings Ratio	MSFT		
Quarter	AAPL	AAPL	EPS	Predicted Price Per Share	Actual Price Per Share
2023-Q1	$1.520	108.487	$2.450	$265.79	$288.30
2023-Q2	$1.260	153.944	$2.690	$414.11	$340.54
2023-Q3	$1.460	117.267	$2.990	$350.63	$315.75
2023-Q4	$2.180	88.317	$2.930	$258.77	$376.04
2024-Q1	$1.530	112.078	$2.940	$329.51	$420.72
2024-Q2	$1.400	150.443	$2.950	$443.81	$446.95
2024-Q3	$0.970	240.206	$3.300	$792.68	$430.30
2024-Q4	$2.400	104.342	$3.230	$337.02	$421.50

hypothesis because the stock market misprices Meta, and/or because Apple stock trades on insufficiently efficient markets, given, of course, that the P/E metric is an appropriate metric. Please see Table 4.4, with EPS = Diluted Earnings Per Share, Excluding Extraordinary Items.

Therefore, in valuation contexts, whether the comparables approach to valuation is meaningful depends on the efficiency of the market for a given asset's comparables and an appropriate metric. As stated above, objective measures of the market efficiency for the comparables must support any proposal to use the comparables valuation approach, and conversely, any argument against using the comparables' market prices will be valid if and only if objective measures of market efficiency show the corresponding markets are not sufficiently efficient.

The extent to which the market for a security is efficient informs whether an investor or analyst needs to acquire additional information about the firm issuing the security. If a security trades in a sufficiently efficient market, traded price is a good estimate of value per share, conditional on public information; otherwise, additional information will have to be acquired by the investor or analyst at additional cost. It is worth emphasizing, however, that a security being sufficiently efficient or otherwise has no *a priori* bearing on whether it is a good investment or not.

4.5 Conclusions

In this chapter, we utilized the following metrics as separate and objective negative measures, based on event studies, of the market's efficiency for a security:

- Key Developments Idiosyncratic Response (KDIR) of the security, estimated through the Capital Asset Pricing Model (CAPM)

- KDIR of the security, estimated through the Market Model (MM)
- Earnings Announcements Idiosyncratic Response (EAIR) of the security, estimated through CAPM
- EAIR of the security, estimated through MM

We did not ascribe any directional component to any potentially material event in this chapter, since it requires subjective judgment and/or additional information, and it is *ad hoc* to infer from the description of an event if the event would cause, under market efficiency, the price to go up, down, or stay the same. It is impossible to objectively determine the market's perceptions immediately prior to any potentially material event, and therefore, to determine whether a particular potentially material event was better-than-expected news, worse-than-expected news, or even news at all. Colloquially speaking, good news or bad news is not the relevant question here. Reaction, overreaction, correction, overcorrection, bounce-back, etc. should be out of the system within a few days after a potentially material event in an efficient market.

These measures are completely rules-based, with no judgment, subjectivity, or additional information required of any kind. The only rules are such that every reasonable person can, *a priori*, agree on: (a) for the industry index, we used all firms that are in the same major industry sector (same two-digit SIC Code) as the firm in question, and (b) idiosyncratic price reaction to an event after a few days is close to zero for an efficient market.

In this chapter, we applied these methodologies to value each U.S.-listed firm for each year in 2001-2017; here are three examples:

- The market for GS (Goldman Sachs Group, Inc., common equity) was sufficiently efficient in each year in 2001-2017, and therefore, market prices represented value for Goldman Sachs over 2001-2017.
- The market for MSFT (Microsoft Corporation, common equity) was sufficiently efficient in each of these years except 2002, and therefore, market prices represented value for Microsoft Corporation in these years except 2002. Our analyses do not address whether market prices over- or under-estimated value of Microsoft in 2002.
- The market for AAME (Atlantic American Corporation, common equity) was not sufficiently efficient in any year in 2001-2017, and therefore, market prices did not represent value for Atlantic American Corporation in 2001-2017. Our analyses do not address whether market prices over- or under-estimated value of Atlantic American Corporation in any of these years.

Future research projects include:

- Application of the theoretical and econometric methodologies to the three measures of market efficiency, based on securities prices following random walks in efficient markets, used by Cao et al. (2018).
- Application of the theoretical and econometric methodologies to the two measures of market efficiency, based on the asymmetry between positive and negative market returns, used by Bris et al. (2007).
- Structural model studying the relation between capital markets and industrial organization of corresponding product markets.
- The framework of an expected utility-maximizing investor, using different utility functions.

The next chapter, Chapter 5, uses deviations from Put-Call Parity of options as negative measures of the efficiency of the ecosystem consisting of equities, the risk-free bond, and options on the equities.

References

Allen, F., and Carletti, E., 2008, "Mark-to-Market Accounting and Liquidity Pricing," *Journal of Accounting and Economics*, 45(2–3), 358–378.

Ball, R., 2017, "Fama, Fisher, Jensen, and Roll (1969) — Retrospective Comments," In: Cochrane, J., and Moskowitz, T. (Eds.), *The Fama Portfolio*, pp. 203–212, Chicago, IL: University of Chicago Press.

Ball, R., and Brown, P., 1968, "An Empirical Evaluation of Accounting Income Numbers," *Journal of Accounting Research*, 6(2), 159–178.

Bhattacharya, R., 2018, "Capital Asset Pricing Model (CAPM)," In: Teece, D., and Augier, M. (Eds.), *The Palgrave Encyclopedia of Strategic Management*, pp. 1–4, London, UK: Palgrave Macmillan.

Bhattacharya, R., Bial, J., and Evans, A., 2023, "It Is Imperative to Perform Event Studies only with High-Frequency Intraday Data for Securities Litigations and Valuations," *Journal of International Business & Law*, 23(1), 1–28.

Bhattacharya, R., and Gupta, M., 2023, "Diligence, Objectivity, Quality, and Accuracy," *Journal of Accounting Literature*, 47(1), 1–30.

Bodie, Z., Kane, A., and Marcus, A., 2018, *Investments*, New York, NY: McGraw-Hill/Irwin.

Bris, A., Goetzmann, W., and Zhu, N., 2007, "Efficiency and the Bear: Short Sales and Markets Around the World," *Journal of Finance*, 62(3), 1029–1079.

Campbell, J., Lo, A., and MacKinlay, A. C., 1997, *The Econometrics of Financial Markets*, Princeton, NJ: Princeton University Press.

Cao, C., Liang, B., Lo, A., and Petrasek, L., 2018, "Hedge Fund Holdings and Stock Market Efficiency," *Review of Asset Pricing Studies*, 8(1), 77–116.

Chiang, C., Dai, W., Fan, J., Hong, H., and Tu, J., 2019, "Robust Measures of Earnings Surprises," *Journal of Finance*, 74(2), 943–983.

Collins, D., and Kothari, S. P., 1989, "An Analysis of Intertemporal and Cross-Sectional Determinants of Earnings Response Coefficients," *Journal of Accounting and Economics*, 11(2–3), 143–181.

Damodaran, A., 2012, *Investment Valuation*, Hoboken, NJ: Wiley Finance.

Ellul, A., Jotikasthira, C., Lundblad, C., and Wang, Y., 2014, "Mark-to-Market Accounting and Systemic Risk: Evidence from the Insurance Industry," *Economic Policy*, 29(78), 297–341.

Fama, E., 1970, "Efficient Capital Markets: A Review of Theory and Empirical Work," *Journal of Finance*, 25(2), 383–417.

Fama, E., 1991, "Efficient Capital Markets: II," *Journal of Finance*, 46(5), 1575–1617.

Fama, E., Fisher, L., Jensen, M., and Roll, R., 1969, "The Adjustment of Stock Prices to New Information," *International Economic Review*, 10(1), 1–21.

Ferrillo, P., Dunbar, F., and Tabak, D., 2004, "The 'Less Than' Efficient Capital Markets Hypothesis: Requiring more Proof from Plaintiffs in Fraud-on-the-Market Cases," *St. John's Law Review*, 78(1), 81–129.

Harris, L., 2003, *Trading & Exchanges: Market Microstructure for Practitioners*, New York, NY: Oxford University Press.

Kothari, S. P., 2001, "Capital Markets Research in Accounting," *Journal of Accounting and Economics*, 31(1–3), 105–231.

Kothari, S. P., So, E., and Verdi, R., 2016, "Analysts' Forecasts and Asset Pricing: A Survey," *Annual Review of Financial Economics*, 8, 197–219.

Malkiel, B., 2003, "The Efficient Market Hypothesis and Its Critics," *Journal of Economic Perspectives*, 17(1), 59–82.

Potì, V., and Shefrin, H., 2014, "The Signature of Sentiment in Conditional Consumption CAPM Estimates: A Note," *Journal of Behavioral and Experimental Finance*, 2, 1–9.

Samuelson, P., 2009, "An Enjoyable Life Puzzling over Modern Finance Theory," *Annual Review of Financial Economics*, 1, 19–35.

Shefrin, H., 2008, "Building on Kahneman's Insights in the Development of Behavioral Finance," *Loyola University Chicago Law Journal*, 44, 1401–1421.

Shleifer, A., 2000, *Inefficient Markets: An Introduction to Behavioral Finance*, New York, NY: Oxford University Press.

5

OPTIONS

5.1 Introduction

Put-Call Parity of options is necessarily and sufficiently based on the lack of arbitrage opportunities between portfolios consisting of option(s), the underlying security(ies), and risk-free investments, and since these data are available in (almost) real time, deviation from the Put-Call Parity of options implies an immediate and riskless arbitrage opportunity (a much abridged and older version of this chapter was published as Bhattacharya (2019)). Therefore, we use five separate measures of deviation from Put-Call Parity of options on a stock as separate negative measures for efficiency of the market ecosystem consisting of option(s), the underlying security(ies), and risk-free investments. We use a simple two-equation structural model that shows that the impact on market efficiency of (a) short sales and constraints and (b) trading volume are theoretically indeterminate and are, therefore, empirical questions. We use the panel nature of the data to identify appropriate instruments and use Three-Stage Least Squares to estimate this structural model. Analyzing Nasdaq stocks and non-Nasdaq stocks separately, we find, contrary to *much* previous theoretical and empirical work, based on data on U.S. stocks over 1996-2015:

1. *Ceteris paribus*, the impact of short sales costs & constraints of a stock on market efficiency is *not* significantly negative.
2. *Ceteris paribus*, the impact of normalized trading volume of a stock on market efficiency is *not* significantly positive.

DOI: 10.4324/9781003608486-7

A market is *semistrong efficient* if prices reflect all publicly available information — see, for example, Fama (1970), Malkiel (2003), Harris (2003), Shleifer (2003), and Samuelson (2009). As has been recognized, by, for example, Fama et al. (1969), a market is efficient if "stock prices adjust very rapidly to new information." Finally, as noted by, for example, Fama (1970), the notion of market efficiency is that the "total excess market value at $t + 1$ that will be generated by such a system ... which, from the 'fair game' property ... has expectation ... 0," in other words, that idiosyncratic returns, on average, are zero in an efficient market. (1) Prices of securities reflect, *albeit to varying extents*, all publicly available information, (2) prices adjust, *albeit to varying extents*, to new information, and (3) idiosyncratic returns are close to zero, also *albeit to various extents* — therefore, markets for securities are efficient in varying degrees — often referred to as *relative efficiency,* see, for example, Campbell et al. (1997). For a description of the importance of relative efficiency for securities class actions (especially class certification), please see Bhattacharya et al. (2023).

In this chapter, we use the following separate measures of *deviation from Put-Call Parity of options* on stocks without splits and dividends as separate negative measures for market efficiency, separately for Nasdaq and non-Nasdaq stocks, and explain the rationale in Section 5.2. This stochastic negative correlation between market efficiency and deviation from Put-Call Parity of options on a stock is consistent with the finding of Taylor et al. (2010) that option prices are more informative than stock returns. Please see Chapters 3 and 4 for different measures of market efficiency based on event studies and arbitrage costs. See also Cao et al. (2018) for three different measures of market efficiency based on securities prices following random walks in efficient markets. See also Bris et al. (2007) for two measures of market efficiency that depend on the asymmetry between positive and negative market returns.

1. *Relative Price Spread – Inequality (RPS-Ineq)*, defined as the simple average over the relevant time period (calendar year for this chapter) of the weighted average of the absolute value of the daily difference between prices (midpoints of closing best bids and closing best asks) of call and put options with the same strike price and expiration date relative to the **inequality** predicted by Put-Call Parity for American options, divided by the mid-point of the corresponding prices; following Ofek et al. (2004), who use a ratio instead of the difference and they also explicitly incorporate the early exercise premium of an American option over a European option — see Section 5.2 for details — and Stoll (1969), Merton (1973), and many others. We use open interest as weight, following Cremers and Weinbaum (2010). We also use open interest as weight to calculate weighted average across exchanges. For a small number of options, we found multiple entries when sorted by TICKER, CUSIP, exchange, date, expiry date,

and strike price (OptionMetrics was unable to provide a satisfactory explanation for such multiple entries) — for these options, we use weighted averages of closing price and implied volatility, using open interest as weights.

2. *Relative Price Spread – Equality (RPS-Eq)*, defined as the simple average over the relevant time period (calendar year for this chapter) of the weighted average of the absolute value of the daily difference between prices (midpoints of closing best bids and closing best asks) of call and put options with the same strike price and expiration date relative to the **equality** predicted by Put-Call Parity for European options, divided by the mid-point of the corresponding prices; following Ofek et al. (2004), Stoll (1969), Merton (1973), and many others.
3. *Implied Volatility Spread (IV-Spr)*, defined as the simple average over the relevant time period (calendar year for this chapter) of the weighted average of the absolute daily differences in implied volatility between call and put options with the same strike price and expiration date, following Cremers and Weinbaum (2010), Amin et al. (2004), and Figlewski and Webb (1993). For a small number of options, we found multiple entries when sorted by TICKER, CUSIP, exchange, date, expiry date, and strike price — OptionMetrics was unable to provide a satisfactory explanation for such multiple entries — for these options, we use weighted averages of closing price and implied volatility, using open interest as weights.
4. *Implied Volatility Standard Deviation (IV-StDev)*, defined as the simple average over the relevant time period (calendar year for this chapter) of the weighted standard deviation of implied volatilities of options on that security for that date, following Cremers and Weinbaum (2010), Amin et al. (2004), and Figlewski and Webb (1993). We use open interest as weights.
5. *Implied Volatility Dispersion (IV-Disp)*, defined as the simple average over the relevant time period (calendar year for this chapter) of the weighted standard deviation of implied volatilities of options on that security for that date, divided by the weighted mean of implied volatilities of options on that security for that date, following Cremers and Weinbaum (2010), Amin et al. (2004), and Figlewski and Webb (1993). As before, we use open interest as weights.

Measures 2–5 above are direct measures of deviation from Put-Call Parity only for European options. Since American options with low expiry periods approximate European options, so **as an additional set of sensitivity analyses**, we **also** do the analyses for American options with low enough time to expiration — expiry periods less than or equal to ten days. Also, as explained in Section 5.2, Put-Call Parity for American options approximates that for European options when interest rates are low, so **for additional robustness**, we **also** do the above analyses for 2008-2015 when interest rates were at historic lows.

Lamont and Thaler (2003) say that "short sale constraints have long been recognized as crucial to the workings of efficient markets." For the importance of short sales costs & constraints, see most importantly, Miller (1977), and, more recently, Drechsler and Drechsler (2021), Muravyev et al. (2022), Saffi and Sigurdsson (2011), Bris et al. (2007), Boehme et al. (2006), Lamont and Stein (2004), Duffie et al. (2002), Jones and Lamont (2002), Dechow et al. (2001), Easley et al. (1998), Duffie (1996), and others. However, Diamond and Verrecchia (1987) study a model where short sales constraints do not affect market efficiency. Rapach et al. (2016) "show that short interest, aggregated across securities, is arguably the strongest predictor of the equity risk premium identified to date." Boehmer et al. (2010) show that "the positive information associated with low short interest, which is publicly available, is only slowly incorporated into prices, which raises a broader market efficiency issue. Our results also cast doubt on existing theories of the impact of short sale constraints."

As detailed in Section 2.11, a random variable X is a *positive proxy* for another random variable Y if they are positively correlated; in other words, by positive proxy, all one means is that the positive proxy variable (stochastically) preserves the rank of the proxied variable. On the other hand, a random variable X is a *negative proxy* for another random variable Y if they are negatively correlated; i.e., it means that with the negative proxy variable, the ranking is (stochastically) the opposite — please see Greene (2018) for details. In this chapter, we use normalized short interest as a negative proxy for short sales costs & constraints — this is based on the *Law of Demand* hypothesis that, *ceteris paribus*, the short interest for a stock (the quantity demanded) is a decreasing function of the short sales costs & constraints (price), since, as Lamont and Thaler (2003) show, the supply is fairly constant as a function of price.

The relation of trading volume with market efficiency has been studied by, for instance, Bhattacharya and O'Brien (2015), O'Hara (1997), Stickel and Verrecchia (1994), Blume et al. (1994), Wang (1994), and Karpoff (1987) — Beaver (1968) refers to the "economist's notion that volume reflects a lack of consensus regarding the price." In particular, Bhattacharya and O'Brien (2015) estimated a reduced form, and using arbitrage risk as the negative measure for market efficiency, came to the conclusion that market efficiency was not significantly positively related to trading volume — see also the extensive discussion there on the "conventional wisdom" regarding the dependence of market efficiency on trading volume.

In this chapter, we rely upon the theoretical and econometric methodologies described in Sections 5.3 and 5.5. In the first equation, we model trading volume (and number of market makers, for Nasdaq stocks) as functions of dispersion of investor valuations, investor holding probability, transaction costs, and short sales costs. This model implies that higher trading volume will be observed with lower short sales costs, lower transaction costs, higher dispersion of investor valuations, and/or higher likelihood that an investor holds the asset. A corollary of this two-equation system is that short sales costs & constraints impact trading volume, that in turn impacts market efficiency. Given the above discussion, the impact on market efficiency of normalized trading volume, everything else remaining the same, is fundamentally an empirical question, and therefore, the impact on market efficiency of short sales costs, everything else remaining the same, is also an empirical question. In the second equation, we model, on the basis of information economics, market efficiency as a function of normalized trading volume and number of security analysts following the stock. The Fama-French (1992) Factors (market capitalization, leverage, book-to-market equity ratio, and price-to-earnings ratio) and institutional ownership are not directly in the theoretical model because there are no convincing reasons, *a priori*. However, as we explain later, we do account for these factors explicitly in our empirical analyses.

In terms of econometric methodology, we use instruments for endogenous variables as well as proxy variables — see, for instance, Greene (2018) for details. We use the natural logarithm of shares outstanding as a positive proxy for investor holding probability. We use normalized short interest as a negative proxy for short sales costs & constraints — as explained earlier, this is based on the *Law of Demand* hypothesis that, *ceteris paribus*, the short interest for a stock (the quantity demanded) is a decreasing function of the short sales costs & constraints (price), since, as Lamont and Thaler (2003) show, the supply is fairly constant as a function of price. We use the standard deviation of EPS forecasts by analysts to positively proxy for dispersion of investor valuations. We model bid-ask spread and number of market makers (the latter only for Nasdaq stocks) as determinants of transaction cost. We run each of these analyses separately for all Nasdaq and all non-Nasdaq U.S. publicly traded stocks (with the number of market makers as an additional regressor for the former), using daily data for 1996 through 2015 from OptionMetrics, CRSP, I/B/E/S, Thomson Reuters, and Compustat — see Section 5.4 for details and restrictions.

We use Errors-In-Variables methods to incorporate the proxies for the regressors when necessary — it is **not** the case that the proxies replace the proxied variables in the regressions, but the proxies have to be suitably instrumented, see Greene (2018) for details. We use the panel nature of the data to identify appropriate cross section and time series instruments; we also use combinations of instrumentation strategies to check for robustness. We use Three-Stage Least Squares to estimate this two-equation structural system; see also Greene (2018), Hainaut and Colwell (2016), Altı and Tetlock (2014), Coles et al. (2012), Wooldridge (2010), and others for details. **To check for sensitivity** — see Section 5.5 for details — we **also** estimate a reduced form of the structural model as well, and we find that the results of this chapter are robust.

We incorporate the Fama-French (1992) Factors (market capitalization, leverage, book-to-market equity ratio, and price-to-earnings ratio) and institutional ownership in the following two ways: (a) *Fixed Effects:* we run a separate 3SLS regression system for each Fama-French Factor and institutional ownership percentage point, with fixed effects for the deciles for that factor, and (b) *Separate Regressions:* we run a separate 3SLS regression system for each decile for each Fama-French Factor and institutional ownership percentage point.

For the impact on market efficiency of short sales costs & constraints, we do the following **one-tailed test:** the null hypothesis

$$H_0 : \beta_{MEff,SSCC} \left(= \frac{\partial\,(\text{Market Efficiency})}{\partial\,(\text{Short Sales Costs \& Constraints})} \right) \geq \mathbf{0} \tag{5.1}$$

versus the research hypothesis

$$H_1 : \beta_{MEff,SSCC} < \mathbf{0} \tag{5.2}$$

The parameter of interest, $\beta_{MEff,SSCC}$, is estimated by multiplying the 3SLS estimates of (1) the coefficient of volume in the market efficiency equation and (2) the coefficient of short sales costs & constraints in the volume equation — i.e., from the chain rule of differentiation, by multiplying estimates of parameters $\alpha_{SSC,i}$ and $\gamma_{Vol,i}$ (each produced by, for instance, PROC MODEL in SAS). The *p-value* of this one-tailed test above is obtained by adjusting by $1/2$ the *p-value* (reported by SAS in PROC MODEL, for instance) for the χ^2-statistic corresponding to the (two-tailed) Wald Test of the (non-linear) null hypothesis $(\alpha_{SSC,i})\left(\gamma_{Vol,i}\right) = 0$ versus the research (two-tailed) hypothesis $(\alpha_{SSC,i})\left(\gamma_{Vol,i}\right) \neq 0$.

For the impact of normalized volume on market efficiency, we do the following **one-tailed test:** the null hypothesis

$$H_0 : \gamma_{Vol} \left(= \frac{\partial\,(\text{Market Efficiency})}{\partial\,(\text{Normalized Volume})} \right) \leq \mathbf{0} \tag{5.3}$$

versus the research hypothesis

$$H_1 : \gamma_{Vol} > \mathbf{0} \tag{5.4}$$

Here, the 3SLS estimate of the parameter of interest, γ_{Vol}, is provided directly (by, for instance, PROC MODEL in SAS). The *p-value* of this one-tailed test above is obtained by adjusting by $1/2$ the *p-value* reported (by SAS, for instance, in PROC MODEL) for the *t*-statistic corresponding to the two-tailed *t* test of the (linear) null hypothesis $\gamma_{Vol} = 0$ versus the research (two-tailed, linear) hypothesis $\gamma_{Vol} \neq 0$.

The intuition behind the empirical results of this chapter can be summarized as: Separately for Nasdaq and non-Nasdaq stocks, normalized trading volume is negatively and significantly impacted by short sales costs & constraints on one hand, but does *not* positively and significantly impact market efficiency on the other; and therefore, the impact on market efficiency of short sales costs & constraints, everything else remaining the same, is *not* negatively significant.

Section 5.1 outlines deviation from Put-Call Parity of options. Section 5.2 details the determinants of market efficiency studied in this chapter. Section 5.3 describes the data. Section 5.4 describes the econometric methodology of this chapter. Section 5.5 presents the meta summaries of the thousands of regressions that were part of the main analyses. Section 5.6 concludes and provides directions for future research.

5.2 Measures of Market Efficiency

A call (put) European option provides the right, but not the obligation, to buy (sell) the security at the strike price at the time of expiration. On the other hand, a call (put) American option provides the right, but not the obligation, to buy (sell) the security at the strike price from the time of purchase up to the time of expiration. Following Hull (2017), we use the following notation:

- S_0: current stock price
- K: strike price of option
- T: time to expiration of option
- S_T: stock price at maturity
- r: continuously compounded risk-free nominal rate of interest for an investment maturing at time T
- C: value of American call option to buy one share
- P: value of American put option to sell one share
- c: value of European call option to buy one share
- p: value of European put option to sell one share

5.2.1 Inequality, for American Options

Put-Call Parity of options is necessarily and sufficiently based on the lack of immediate and riskless arbitrage opportunities between portfolios consisting of option(s), the underlying security(ies), and risk-free investment(s), and since these data are available in (almost) real time, deviation from the Put-Call Parity of options implies an immediate and riskless arbitrage opportunity under the standard assumptions underlying the derivation of the Put-Call Parity of options — see, for instance, Hull (2017). *Put-Call Parity for American options* states that for call and put American options with the same strike price and expiration date, the following **inequality** holds:

$$S_0 - K \leq C - P \leq S_0 - K\exp(-rT) \tag{5.5}$$

The daily *Relative Price Spread—Inequality* of options on a stock, as a negative measure for market efficiency, is, therefore, defined as follows, where the daily price of an option is defined as the mid-point of its daily closing best bid and its daily closing best ask:

$$0, \text{ if } S_0 - K \leq C - P \leq S_0 - K\exp(-rT) \tag{5.6}$$

$$((C - P) - (S_0 - K\exp(-rT))) \,/\, ((C + P)/2), \text{ if } (C - P) > S_0 - K\exp(-rT) \tag{5.7}$$

$$((S_0 - K) - (C - P)) \,/\, ((C + P)/2), \text{ if } (C - P) < S_0 - K \tag{5.8}$$

5.2.2 Equalities, for European Options

The following discussion applies only to European options, so we redo all the calculations under the following two conditions:

1. Since American options with low expiry periods approximate European options, so **as an additional set of sensitivity analyses**, we do the analyses for American options with low enough time to expiration — expiry periods less than or equal to ten days.
2. Put-Call Parity for American options approximates that for European options when interest rates are low, so **for additional robustness**, we also do the above analyses for 2008-2015 when interest rates were at historic lows.

5.2.3 Relative Price Spread (RPS), Equality for European Options

Put-Call Parity for European options states that for call and put European options with the same strike price and expiration date, the following **equality** holds:

$$c - p = S_0 - K\exp(-rT) \tag{5.9}$$

And so, the daily *Relative Price Spread— Equality* of options on a stock, as a negative measure for market efficiency, is, therefore, defined as follows, where the daily price of an option is defined as the mid-point of its daily closing best bid and its daily closing best ask:

$$|((S_0 - K) - (c - p)) / ((c + p) / 2)| \tag{5.10}$$

5.2.4 *Implied Volatility (IV) Spread, for European Options*

As explained in, for instance, Cremers and Weinbaum (2010), it follows from Put-Call Parity for European options on stocks without splits and dividends that the implied volatilities, as calculated by Black and Scholes (1973), of call and put European options with the same strike price and expiration dates are equal, so we use daily *Implied Volatility Spread — IV-Spr*, defined as the absolute difference in daily implied volatility between call and put options with the same strike price and expiration date, of options on a stock as a negative measure for market efficiency.

It also follows from Put-Call Parity for European options that the implied volatilities of all options, as calculated by Black and Scholes (1973), on a particular security on a particular day are equal, so we use *Implied Volatility Standard Deviation — IV-StDev*, defined as the simple average over the relevant time period (calendar year for this chapter) of the weighted (by open interest) standard deviation of implied volatilities of options on that security for that date, following Cremers and Weinbaum (2010), Amin et al. (2004), and Figlewski and Webb (1993). Implied Volatility Spread is a direct measure of deviation from Put-Call Parity only for European options. Since American options with low expiry periods approximate European options, so **as an additional set of sensitivity analyses**, we do the analyses for American options with low enough time to expiration — expiry periods less than or equal to ten days. Also, as explained in Section 5.2, Put-Call Parity for American options approximates that for European options when interest rates are low, so **for additional robustness**, we also do the above analyses for 2008-2011 when interest rates were at historic lows.

To account for different implied volatilities, we also consider *Implied Volatility Dispersion — IV-Disp*, defined as the simple average over the relevant time period (calendar year for this chapter) of the weighted (by open interest) standard deviation of implied volatilities of options on that security for that date divided by the weighted mean of implied volatilities of options on that security for that date.

5.3 Determinants of Market Efficiency

We consider a number of potential determinants of market efficiency.

5.3.1 *Trading Volume*

An investor's subjective value of an asset is the price at which the investor is indifferent between the *status quo* and a trade. Note that valuations for an asset can differ across investors for two primary reasons: private value, which could be dictated by, for instance, the investor's liquidity constraints, and private information, which could be determined by, for instance, the investor's cost of gathering information to evaluate the security. In order to appreciate how trading volume impacts market efficiency, we need to understand why a trade occurs. In particular, as Wang (1994) says, "investors trade among themselves because they are different. ... The greater the information asymmetry, the larger the abnormal trading volume when public news arrives." Beaver (1968) refers to the "economist's notion that volume reflects a lack of consensus regarding the price." Please see also Karpoff (1987), O'Hara (1997), Stickel and Verrecchia (2004), Blume et al. (1994), and Goldstein et al. (2007). For example, one would observe higher trading volume in the market for an asset if and only if transaction costs (including bid-ask spread, commissions, and search costs) are low relative to dispersion in investor valuations. With high dispersion in investor valuations, one can observe a high trading volume, much of which can be due to noise trading. A higher dispersion in investor valuations does not necessarily add to the efficiency of a market. Low-valuers hold more securities than high-valuers, and short sales costs are low relative to dispersion in investor valuations. Conversely, one would observe low volume in the market for an asset if and only if transaction costs (including bid-ask spread, commissions and search costs) are high relative to dispersion in investor valuations, high-valuers hold more assets than low-valuers, and short sales costs are high relative to dispersion in valuations. It is often the case that the holders of assets have higher valuations because of a *status quo bias* or for other private value reasons.

Consider the following example of a homeowner with a mortgage equal to $\$3,000,000$. To sell the house, the homeowner will have to pay a 6% commission, and can afford to pay at most $\$100,000$ to be clear of the mortgage; i.e., to have to pay more than $\$100,000$ out of pocket, (s)he will be better off not selling the house. Let the minimum price that the homeowner will accept be p. Then, the homeowner will get $p - 6\%\,(p)$, and so will be able to pay $p - 6\%\,(p) + \$100,000$ to clear the mortgage; i.e., $p - 6\%\,(p) + \$100,000 = \$3,000,000$ solves for $p = \$3,085,100$, which is therefore, a lower bound on the homeowner's valuation — as mentioned earlier, an investor's subjective value of an asset is the price at which the investor is indifferent between the *status quo* and a trade. This lower bound depends, for instance, positively on transaction cost and negatively on the cash or cash-equivalents available to the homeowner. Therefore, the likelihood of a trade depends negatively on transaction cost (commission in this case) and positively on the homeowner's solvency. This is an example of a situation where the lowest price at which the owner will sell is often higher than the highest price at which a potential buyer will buy, and in such a case, since short sales costs are very high, there will be no trade (short sales costs are often prohibitive for certain assets such as real estate).

Higher trading volume will therefore be observed with lower short sales costs, lower transaction costs, higher dispersion of investor valuations, and/or higher likelihood that an investor holds the asset. However, for instance, there is no reason that higher dispersion in investor valuations leads to higher market efficiency — in fact, we show an example in Section 5.3.2 where there is no dispersion in valuations and the market is perfectly semistrong form efficient but with no trades — and therefore, the impact on market efficiency of normalized trading volume, everything else remaining the same, is fundamentally an empirical question, and therefore, the impact of short sales costs & constraints on market efficiency, everything else remaining the same, is also an empirical question.

5.3.2 Simple Model of Trading Volume

Let the set of all investors (and potential investors) at time t be N_t, and let for $i \in N_t$, the valuation of investor i be $v_{i,t}$ per unit of the security and let the holding of investor i at the beginning of time t be $h_{i,t}$ (which could be positive, zero, or negative, the last for short positions). Let $\Theta_{i \longrightarrow j}$ denote the number of shares sold by investor i to investor j in period t; obviously,

$$\Theta_{j \longrightarrow i} = -\Theta_{i \longrightarrow j} \tag{5.11}$$

Let the mean transaction costs (e.g., bid-ask spread, commissions, search and matching costs) per unit of a trade at time t be τ_t, and let the mean short sales costs per unit of a trade at time t be ψ_t. Let the total cost of a trade $\Theta_{i \longrightarrow j}$ be denoted $C\left(\Theta_{i \longrightarrow j}\right)$.

Assumption 5.1 ***(Constant Average Valuation and Trading Cost Assumption)*** *Per-unit valuation $v_{i,t} \geq 0$ is constant $\forall i, t$, and per-unit transaction cost $\tau_t \geq 0$ and per-unit short sales costs $\psi_t \geq 0$ are constant, $\forall t$.*

Lemma 5.1 *Optimality will require that a trade will occur only from an investor from a lower valuation to an investor with a higher valuation. In other words,*

$$v_i > v_j \Longrightarrow \Theta_{i \longrightarrow j} \leq 0 \tag{5.12}$$

or equivalently,

$$\Theta_{i \longrightarrow j} > 0 \Longrightarrow v_i \leq v_j \tag{5.13}$$

If any of these costs is positive, these weak inequalities can be replaced by strong inequalities, which can also hold when trade is set as the default.

Lemma 5.2 *Any trade will incur the transaction costs at τ_t per unit, and if any portion of it is a short sale, the short sale portion will incur an additional ψ_t per unit. In other words, let*

$$v_i < v_j \tag{5.14}$$

then if

$$\Theta_{i \longrightarrow j} \leq h_{i,t} \tag{5.15}$$

then

$$C(\Theta_{i \longrightarrow j}) = \tau_t \Theta_{i \longrightarrow j} \tag{5.16}$$

and if

$$\Theta_{i \longrightarrow j} > h_{i,t} \tag{5.17}$$

then

$$C(\Theta_{i \longrightarrow j}) = \tau_t h_{i,t} + (\tau_t + \psi_t)(\Theta_{i \longrightarrow j} - h_{i,t}) \tag{5.18}$$

Definition 5.1 *Consider random variable sequences*

$$Z_t = (Z_{1,t}, Z_{2,t}, ...) \tag{5.19}$$

and

$$Z' = (Z'_{1,t}, Z'_{2,t}, ...) \tag{5.20}$$

such that

$$\textbf{\textit{GenProb}}(|Z_i - Z_j| > \kappa) > \textbf{\textit{GenProb}}(|Z'_i - Z'_j| > \kappa), \forall \kappa > 0, \forall i, j \in N \tag{5.21}$$

Then Z is more ***dispersed in tail-generalized probabilities of differences,*** *or simply, more* ***dispersed,*** *than Z'.*

Please see Chapter 1 for a discussion of generalized probability in the context of uncertainty.

Proposition 5.1 *If*

$$v_{i,t} = v_t^* + \varepsilon_{i,t}$$

where $(\varepsilon_{i,t})_{i \in N}$ are i.i.d. $\mathcal{N}(0, \sigma_t^2)$, and $v'_{i,t} = v_t'^* + \varepsilon'_{i,t}$ where $(\varepsilon'_{i,t})_{i \in N}$ are i.i.d. $\mathcal{N}(0, \sigma_t'^2)$, then the valuation profile

$$v_t = (v_{1,t}, v_{2,t}, ...)$$

is more dispersed than

$$v'_t = \left(v'_{1,t}, v'_{2,t}, \ldots\right)$$

if and only if $\sigma_t^2 > \sigma_t'^2$.

Assumption 5.2 ***(Independence Assumption)*** $v_{i,t}$ *is stochastically independent of* $h_{i,t} \forall i$. *In other words, an investor's valuation of the security is stochastically independent of her/his holding of the security at the beginning of the period.*

Assumption 5.3 ***(A Priori Identical Investors Assumption)***

$$\boldsymbol{GenProb}\left(h_{i,t} > 0\right) = \pi_t, \forall i \tag{5.22}$$

Lemma 5.3 *Under Assumptions 5.1, 5.2 and 5.3,* $\forall i, j$,

$$\boldsymbol{GenProb}\left(\Theta_{i \longrightarrow j} \neq 0\right) \tag{5.23}$$

is, ceteris paribus,

1. *Higher if the valuation profile is more dispersed.*
2. *Increasing in* π_t.
3. *Decreasing in* τ_t.
4. *Decreasing in* ψ_t.

In other words, under the Constant Average Cost Assumption, Independence Assumption, and *A Priori* Identical Investors Assumption, the probability of a trade between investors *i* and *j* is, *ceteris paribus,* higher,

1. If the valuation profile is more dispersed — as Wang (1994) says, "investors trade among themselves because they are different," and Beaver (1968) refers to the "economist's notion that volume reflects a lack of consensus regarding the price."
2. If the probability of an investor having a positive holding in the security is higher.
3. If transaction cost is lower.
4. If short sales costs are lower.

Proof. Case 1. $v_{i,t} > v_{j,t}$. Then $\Theta_{i \longrightarrow j} \leq 0$. In other words, there will be no trade such that the investor with the higher valuation sells to the investor with the lower valuation.

Case 1a. $v_{i,t} - v_{j,t} > \tau_t + \psi_t$. Then, $\Theta_{j \longrightarrow i} > 0$. In other words, the investor with the lower valuation will sell (could be a short sale) to the investor with the higher valuation.

Case 1b. $\tau_t \leq v_{i,t} - v_{j,t} < \tau_t + \psi_t$. Then, $\Theta_{j \longrightarrow i} > 0 \Longleftrightarrow h_{j,t} > 0$. In other words, the investor with the lower valuation will sell to the investor with the higher valuation if and only if the trade is not a short sale.

Case 1c. $v_{i,t} - v_{j,t} < \tau_t$. Then, $\Theta_{j \longrightarrow i} = 0$. In other words, there will be no trade since the difference in valuations is smaller than the transaction cost.

Case 2 $(v_{i,t} < v_{j,t})$ is a mirror image of Case 1. Therefore, the probability of a trade between investors *i* and *j*

$$\begin{aligned}
&= \textbf{\textit{GenProb}}\left(\Theta_{i \longrightarrow j} \neq 0\right) \qquad (5.24)\\
&= \textbf{\textit{GenProb}}\left(\{\Theta_{i \longrightarrow j} > 0\} \cup \{\Theta_{j \longrightarrow i} > 0\}\right)\\
&= \textbf{\textit{GenProb}}\left(v_{i,t} - v_{j,t} > \tau_t + \psi_t\right)\\
&\quad + \textbf{\textit{GenProb}}\left(v_{j,t} - v_{i,t} > \tau_t + \psi_t\right)\\
&\quad + \textbf{\textit{GenProb}}\left(\tau_t < v_{i,t} - v_{j,t} < \tau_t + \psi_t\right) \textbf{\textit{GenProb}}\left(h_j > 0\right)\\
&\quad + \textbf{\textit{GenProb}}\left(\tau_t \leq v_{j,t} - v_{i,t} < \tau_t + \psi_t\right) \textbf{\textit{GenProb}}\left(h_i > 0\right)
\end{aligned}$$

(from Assumptions 5.1 and 5.2)

$$\begin{aligned}
&= \textbf{\textit{GenProb}}\left(\left|v_{i,t} - v_{j,t}\right| > \tau_t + \psi_t\right) \qquad (5.25)\\
&\quad + \pi_t \textbf{\textit{GenProb}}\left(\tau_t \leq \left|v_{i,t} - v_{j,t}\right| < \tau_t + \psi_t\right)
\end{aligned}$$

(from Assumption 5.3)

$$\begin{aligned}
&= \pi_t \textbf{\textit{GenProb}}\left(\left|v_{i,t} - v_{j,t}\right| > \tau_t\right) \qquad (5.26)\\
&\quad + \left(1 - \pi_t\right) \textbf{\textit{GenProb}}\left(\left|v_{i,t} - v_{j,t}\right| > \tau_t + \psi_t\right)
\end{aligned}$$

is, *ceteris paribus,* higher if the valuation profile is more dispersed, increasing in π_t, and decreasing in τ_t and ψ_t. Therefore, a higher trading volume will be observed with lower short sales costs, lower transaction costs, higher dispersion of investor valuations, and/or higher likelihood that an investor holds the asset.

It is not the case that higher dispersion would unambiguously facilitate market efficiency. Consider what would happen in the limiting case where there is practically zero dispersion in investor valuations. Then, every investor would have identical valuations v_t^*, and the market would be perfectly semistrong form efficient with a notional equilibrium price $p_t = v_t^*$ that would reflect all the information available to the investors, *albeit* with no trades. In this simple model, if dispersion were to increase, the market would become less efficient. To see this more clearly, consider the special case outlined above: $v_{i,t} = v_t^* + \varepsilon_{i,t}$ where $(\varepsilon_{i,t})_{i \in N}$ are independent and identically distributed (i.i.d.) $\mathcal{N}\left(0, \sigma_t^2\right)$, and $v'_{i,t} = v_t'^* + \varepsilon'_{i,t}$ where $\left(\varepsilon'_{i,t}\right)_{i \in N}$ are i.i.d. $\mathcal{N}\left(0, \sigma_t'^2\right)$, then the valuation profile $v_t = (v_{1,t}, v_{2,t}, \ldots)$ is more dispersed than $v'_t = \left(v'_{1,t}, v'_{2,t}, \ldots\right)$ if and only if $\sigma_t^2 > \sigma_t'^2$. By the previous discussion, one can see that the limiting case of $\sigma_t'^2 = 0$ would correspond to a perfect semistrong efficient market with a notional equilibrium price $p_t = v_t^*$ that would reflect all the information available to the investors, *albeit* with no trades. In this simple model, if one observed a higher $\sigma_t^2 > \sigma_t'^2$, *ceteris paribus,* the market would become less efficient.

In conclusion, the impact on market efficiency of normalized trading volume, everything else remaining the same, is fundamentally an empirical question, and the impact of short sales costs & constraints on market efficiency, everything else remaining the same, is also an empirical question.

5.3.3 Number of Market Makers

From the above discussion, one can see that the demand for market making services is an increasing function of trading volume, for instance, through higher dispersion of the valuation profile. As a corollary, everything else remaining the same (in particular, keeping constant other incentives of investment banks, such as profits from proprietary trading) a firm is more likely to enter (or not exit) the market for market making services if there is higher trading volume (and thus, higher market making profits), for instance, through a higher dispersion of the valuation profile for that security. However, the higher the number of market makers, competition for trades would put downward pressure on the transaction costs τ_t, and economies of scale will determine the equilibrium impact on the price of market making services (τ_t) — please see Bhattacharya (2022), for instance. Therefore, the direction of the impact of the number of (Nasdaq) market makers for a security on the efficiency of the market for that security can only be determined empirically.

5.4 Description of Data

We use the following standard databases for the empirical work detailed in this chapter.

- OptionMetrics daily data for all U.S. publicly traded call and put options on all U.S. publicly traded common stocks from 1996 through 2015, restricted to option-days that have meaningful TICKERs, equity CUSIPs, positive and non-missing volume and open interest, non-missing implied volatility, and positive mid-point of closing best bid and closing best ask,

  — date
  — expiry date
  — strike price
  — highest closing bid
  — lowest closing ask
  — implied volatility

— open interest
— volume
— cumulative adjustment factor

- Stock-days that have positive closing price and positive shares outstanding and other restrictions from CRSP. We restrict attention to stocks without dividends, splits, spinoffs, or any corporate event that would require price- or share-adjustments.

— date
— closing price
— returns
— shares outstanding
— trading volume
— closing bid
— closing ask
— exchange membership
— number of market makers
— if $shrcd \in \{10, 11\}$
— if $ret \notin \{-44.0, -55.0, -66.0, -77.0, -88.0, -99.0\}$
— if $dlret \notin \{-55.0, -66.0, -88.0, -99.0\}$
— if $dlretx \notin \{-55.0, -66.0, -88.0, -99.0\}$
— if $dclrdt \neq 0$
— if $trtscd \neq 0$,
— if $nmsind \neq 0$
— if $vol \neq -99.0$
— if $prc > 0$
— if $bid > 0$
— if $ask > 0$
— if $vol > 0$
— if $shrout > 0$
— if $TICKER \neq ?$
— if $TICKER \neq ''$
— if $CUSIP \neq ''$
— if $substr(TICKER, 1, 4) \neq ZZZZ$;
— if $substr(CUSIP, 7, 1) \in \{0, 1, 2, 3, 4, 5, 6, 7, 8, 9\}$
— if $substr(CUSIP, 8, 1) \in \{0, 1, 2, 3, 4, 5, 6, 7, 8, 9\}$

- Underlying stocks had data on the following variables

— analyst projections (from I/B/E/S)

— number of securities analysts (from I/B/E/S)
— institutional holdings (from Thomson Reuters)
— short interest (from Compustat)

For a small number of stock-days, we found multiple entries when sorted by TICKER, CUSIP, and date — for these stock-days, we calculate weighted averages using trading volume as weights. Compustat (including Capital IQ) data sources rely upon the S&P identification of GVKEY. In this chapter, we rely upon the mapping of GVKEY to TICKER used by CRSP to match its data to Compustat. We do not have access to intraday data for treasury yield and foreign exchange rates from FRED; we thank B. Ravikumar for his help on this matter. For a small number of options, we found multiple entries when sorted by TICKER, CUSIP, exchange, date, expiry date, and strike price — OptionMetrics was unable to provide a satisfactory explanation for such multiple entries — for these options, we calculate weighted averages using open interest as weights; we also do not deal with the asynchronicity due to the different closing times of the options and stock markets. See Battalio and Schultz (2006) for details.

In order to maintain the integrity of the linkages between the different sources of data we rely upon, we treat a missing observation as a missing observation — in particular, with number of analysts, short interest, institutional ownership, and number of market makers — not as a zero. The Chicago Board Options Exchange started in April 1973, followed soon after by four other exchanges, but only call options were permitted to trade until June 1977 when a total of twenty-five put options were allowed to trade. The U.S. Securities and Exchange Commission ended its moratorium on new options in May 1980 and by 1983, options on over half of U.S. traded stocks were being traded. See Figlewski and Webb (1993) and Klemkosky and Resnick (1979) for more detail. As is well-known — see, for example, Cremers and Weinbaum (2010) and as confirmed by our analysis, there were no European options traded in the U.S. on U.S. equity between 1996 and 2015.

5.4.1 Summary of Measures

Tables 5.1–5.4 provide the summary statistics, including correlation coefficients, of the different negative measures for market efficiency, separately for all options and for only options with short expiry ($\leq$ 10 days, so that American options approximate European options), separately for Nasdaq and non-Nasdaq stocks. We use instruments for endogenous variables as well as proxy variables, but since the above negative measures for market efficiency are regressands, we do not need to instrument for them — see, for instance, Greene (2018) for details, and described in Section 5.5.4.

The lack of significantly positive correlation that we observe between the various *RPS* measures on one hand and the *IV* measures on the other — which changes when we restrict attention to such measures being ≤ 1 — could be because of many reasons, for instance, problems with the assumptions underlying Black-Scholes, or fundamental discontinuities between American and European options — and there is no reason to believe that these differences have anything to do with these metrics being valid measures or not of market inefficiency. It is also interesting that while the various *RPS* measures are highly correlated, we find little correlation between *IV-Spr* and *IV-StDev* and almost no correlation between *IV-Spr* and *IV-Disp*. You could investigate all these potential anomalies, especially disaggregated by year, Fama-French Factor deciles, SIC code, etc., in a future research project.

TABLE 5.1 Correlations between Measures of Market Efficiency Based on Relative Price Spread; All Nasdaq Equities, 1996-2015

Measure	RPS_Ineq	RPS_Eq	RPS_Ineq_shortexp	RPS_Eq_shortexp
RPS_Ineq	1.0000	0.0079	0.0836	−0.0047
RPS_Eq	0.0079	1.0000	0.0712	0.6538
RPS_Ineq_shortexp	0.0836	0.0712	1.0000	0.0982
RPS_Eq_shortexp	−0.0047	0.6538	0.0982	1.0000

5.5 Econometric Methodology

We consider a number of potential factors of market efficiency.

5.5.1 Factors of Market Efficiency

An investor's subjective value of an asset is the price at which the investor is indifferent between the *status quo* and a trade. Note that valuations for an asset can differ across investors for two primary reasons: private value, which could be dictated by, for instance, the investor's liquidity constraints, and private information, which could be determined by, for instance, the investor's cost of gathering information to evaluate the security. In order to appreciate how trading volume affects market efficiency, one needs to understand why a trade occurs. In particular, as Wang (1994) says, "[i]investors trade among themselves because they are different" — please also see Karpoff (1987), O'Hara (1997), Stickel and Verrecchia (2004), Blume et al. (1994), and Goldstein et al. (2007). We rely upon a simple theoretical model described in Section 5.5.1, which shows that the impact of trading volume (and number of market makers) on market efficiency, everything else remaining the same, is an empirical question, and therefore, the impact of short sales costs & constraints on market efficiency, everything else remaining the same, is also an empirical question.

TABLE 5.2 Correlations between Measures of Market Efficiency Based on Implicit Volatility Spread; All Nasdaq Equities, 1996-2015

Measure	IV_Spr	IV_ StDev	IV_ Disp	IV_Spr _shortexp	IV_StDev _shortexp	IV_Disp _shortexp
IV_Spr	1.0000	0.3822	0.1300	0.6296	0.3303	0.0632
IV_StDev	0.3822	1.0000	0.8142	0.1614	0.7659	0.6421
IV_Disp	0.1300	0.8142	1.0000	−0.0349	0.6396	0.8232
IV_Spr_shortexp	0.6296	0.1614	−0.0349	1.0000	0.3771	0.1167
IV_StDev_shortexp	0.3303	0.7659	0.6396	0.3771	1.0000	0.8131
IV_Disp_shortexp	0.0632	0.6421	0.8232	0.1167	0.8131	1.0000

TABLE 5.3 Correlations between Measures of Market Efficiency Based on Relative Price Spread; All Non-Nasdaq Equities, 1996-2015

Measure	RPS_Ineq	RPS_Eq	RPS_Ineq_shortexp	RPS_Eq_shortexp
RPS_Ineq	1.0000	0.9998	0.9892	0.9891
RPS_Eq	0.9998	1.0000	0.9891	0.9891
RPS_Ineq_shortexp	0.9892	0.9891	1.0000	0.9999
RPS_Eq_shortexp	0.9891	0.9891	0.9999	1.0000

TABLE 5.4 Correlations between Measures of Market Efficiency Based on Implicit Volatility Spread; All Non-Nasdaq Equities, 1996-2015

Measure	IV_	IV_	IV_	IV_Spr _shortexp	IV_StDev _shortexp	IV_Disp _shortexp
IV_Spr	1.0000	0.3822	0.1300	0.6296	0.3303	0.0632
IV_StDev	0.3822	1.0000	0.8142	0.1614	0.7659	0.6421
IV_Disp	0.1300	0.8142	1.0000	−0.0349	0.6396	0.8232
IV_Spr_shortexp	0.6296	0.1614	−0.0349	1.0000	0.3771	0.1167
IV_StDev_shortexp	0.3303	0.7659	0.6396	0.3771	1.0000	0.8131
IV_Disp_shortexp	0.0632	0.6421	0.8232	0.1167	0.8131	1.0000

These are the potential descriptors of interest to us.

- Annual average normalized trading volume ("turnover" = (trading volume)/(shares outstanding))
- Annual average of the logarithm of market capitalization
- Annual average of relative bid-ask spread (=absolute(closing best bid – closing best ask)/closing price))
- Annual average of normalized short interest (= (short interest)/(shares outstanding))

- Annual average of the number of analysts who made earnings forecasts about the particular firm, corresponding to each earnings announcement, in the particular year
- Annual average of the quarterly standard deviation of analyst forecasts about the particular firm, corresponding to each earnings announcement, in the particular year
- Annual average of number of market makers for the stock (Nasdaq stocks only)

Tables 5.5 and 5.6 provide summary statistics and correlation coefficients of the above descriptors of interest.

In this chapter, we incorporate the Fama-French (1992) Factors (market capitalization, book-to-market equity ratio, price-to-earnings ratio, and leverage) and institutional ownership *percent point* in the following two ways in the Three-Stage Least Squares methodology:

- *Fixed Effects:* we run a separate 3SLS regression system for each Fama-French Factor and institutional ownership percentage point, with fixed effects for the deciles for that factor.
- *Separate Regressions:* we run a separate 3SLS regression system for each decile for each Fama-French Factor and institutional ownership percentage point.

5.5.2 Testing of Hypotheses

Consider functions $f : \mathbb{R} \longrightarrow \mathbb{R}$, $g : \mathbb{R}^n \longrightarrow \mathbb{R}$, and $F : \mathbb{R}^n \longrightarrow \mathbb{R}$, such that

$$F(x_1, \ldots, x_n) = f(g(x_1, \ldots, x_n)) \tag{5.27}$$

Then, the *chain rule of differentiation* states that

$$\frac{\partial}{\partial x_i} F(x_1, \ldots, x_n) = f'(g(x_1, \ldots, x_n)) \frac{\partial}{\partial x_i} g(x_1, \ldots, x_n) \tag{5.28}$$

We rely upon the chain rule to calculate the *ceteris paribus* associations across equations, for example, of market efficiency with short sales costs & constraints from the regression coefficients of the two equations for (a) normalized trading volume and (b) market efficiency, detailed in Chapter 2.

For the impact on market efficiency of short sales costs & constraints, we do the following **one-tailed test**:

- the null hypothesis

$$H_0 : \beta_{MEff,SSCC} \left(= \frac{\partial\,(\text{Market Efficiency})}{\partial\,(\text{Short Sales Costs \& Constraints})} \right) \geq \mathbf{0} \tag{5.29}$$

TABLE 5.5 Correlations between Potential Factors of Market Efficiency; All Nasdaq Stocks, 1996-2015

Variable	Norm Volume	Log Market Cap	Rel Bid-Ask Spread	Norm Short Interest	Number Analysts	Dispersion of Analyst Valuations	Num Market Makers
Norm Volume	1.00000	0.21829	−0.19259	0.43856	0.32661	−0.00235	0.34081
Log Market Cap	0.21829	1.00000	−0.68426	0.35660	0.71989	−0.01716	0.69267
Rel Bid-Ask Spread	−0.19259	−0.68426	1.00000	−0.32742	−0.38571	0.01894	−0.54042
Norm Short Interest	0.43856	0.35660	−0.32742	1.00000	0.27012	−0.00778	0.46306
Number Analysts	0.32661	0.71989	−0.38571	0.27012	1.00000	−0.0100	0.71647
Dispersion of Analyst Valuations	−0.00235	−0.01716	0.01894	−0.00778	−0.00998	1.00000	−0.01226
Num Market Makers	0.34081	0.69267	−0.54042	0.46306	0.71647	−0.01226	1.00000

TABLE 5.6 Correlations between Potential Factors of Market Efficiency; All Non-Nasdaq Stocks, 1996-2015

Variable	Norm Volume	Log Market Cap	Rel Bid-Ask Spread	Norm Short Interest	Number Analysts	Dispersion of Analyst Valuations
Norm Volume	1.00000	0.18301	−0.23188	0.32338	0.27468	0.00272
Log Market Cap	0.18301	1.00000	−0.57445	−0.04683	0.72657	−0.01154
Rel Bid-Ask Spread	−0.23188	−0.57445	1.00000	−0.04627	−0.33291	0.02033
Norm Short Interest	0.32338	−0.04683	−0.04627	1.00000	0.02011	0.07101
Number Analysts	0.27468	0.72657	−0.33291	0.02011	1.00000	−0.01296
Dispersion of Analyst Valuations	0.00272	−0.01154	0.02033	0.07101	−0.01296	1.00000

- versus the research hypothesis

$$H_1 : \beta_{MEff,SSCC} < \mathbf{0} \tag{5.30}$$

The parameter of interest, $\beta_{MEff,SSCC}$, is estimated by multiplying the 3SLS estimates of (1) the coefficient of volume in the market efficiency equation and (2) the coefficient of short sales costs & constraints in the volume equation — i.e., by multiplying estimates of parameters $\alpha_{SSC,i}$ and $\gamma_{Vol,i}$ (each produced by, for instance, PROC MODEL in SAS). The *p-value* of this one-tailed test above is obtained by adjusting by 1/2 the *p-value* (reported by SAS in PROC MODEL, for instance) for the χ^2-statistic corresponding to the (two-tailed) Wald Test of the (non-linear) null hypothesis $(\alpha_{SSC,i})(\gamma_{Vol,i}) = 0$ versus the research (two-tailed) hypothesis $(\alpha_{SSC,i})(\gamma_{Vol,i}) \neq 0$.

For the impact of normalized volume on market efficiency, we do the following **one-tailed test**

- the null hypothesis

$$H_0 : \gamma_{Vol}\left(= \frac{\partial\,(\text{Market Efficiency})}{\partial\,(\text{Normalized Volume})}\right) \leq \mathbf{0} \tag{5.31}$$

- versus the research hypothesis

$$H_1 : \gamma_{Vol} > \mathbf{0} \tag{5.32}$$

Here, the 3SLS estimate of the parameter of interest, γ_{Vol}, is provided directly (by, for instance, PROC MODEL in SAS). The *p-value* of this one-tailed test above is obtained by adjusting by 1/2 the *p-value* reported (by SAS, for instance, in PROC MODEL) for the *t*-statistic corresponding to the two-tailed *t* test of the (linear) null hypothesis $\gamma_{Vol} = 0$ versus the research (two-tailed, linear) hypothesis $\gamma_{Vol} \neq 0$.

5.5.3 Endogeneity

As detailed in Section 2.12, consider

$$Y = \alpha + \beta_1 X_1 + \beta_1 X_1 + \cdots + \eta \tag{5.33}$$

Ordinary Least Squares (OLS) is consistent if

$$Cov\,(X_1, \eta) = Cov\,(X_2, \eta) = \cdots = 0 \tag{5.34}$$

If X_1 is endogenous — i.e., determined within the system, as opposed to exogenous, which can be taken as given to the system — this uncorrelatedness property is violated, and therefore, endogenous variables have to be instrumented;

this is detailed in Section 2.15. Otherwise, the regression above would yield inconsistent and biased estimates. For example, in this chapter, the theory shows that in the equation for market efficiency, trading volume is an endogenous variable; please see Greene (2018), for instance, that in such a situation one does not need any further justification for the use of instruments.

When an instrument W is used for an endogenous variable X, it is **not** the case that richness of information in X is lost because in the first stage of 2SLS or 3SLS, X is regressed on all exogenous variables including the instrument W and then, in the second stage, the residual of this particular regression — which captures all the information specific to X over and above what the exogenous variables including the instrument W represent — is used in the original equation instead of the endogenous variable.

5.5.4 Errors-in-Variables

As detailed in Section 2.13, consider

$$Y = \alpha + \beta_1 X_1 + \beta_2 X_2 + \varepsilon \tag{5.35}$$

where instead of the actual **regressor** X_2, one observes x_2 such that

$$x_2 = X_2 + \omega \tag{5.36}$$

or more generally

$$Cov\,(x_2, X_2) \neq 0 \tag{5.37}$$

When a proxy x_2 is used for X_2, it is **not the case** that X_2 is replaced by x_2 in the regression. Instead, x_2 is treated as an endogenous variable and is suitably instrumented, as is required by the Errors-in-Variables method; please see Greene (2018), for instance. For example, in this chapter, standard deviation of analyst forecasts is used as a proxy for heterogeneity in investor valuations and is instrumented — see Section 5.5.6 — where the latter is predicted by theory to impact trading volume, but standard deviation of analyst forecasts is not a regressor. However, if the **regressand** is observed with error, the error term just gets folded into the residual in the equation without any inconsistency.

5.5.5 Simultaneity

Consider the system of equations

$$Y_1 = \beta_1 X_1 + \varepsilon_1 \tag{5.38}$$

$$Y_2 = \beta_2 X_2 + \varepsilon_2 \tag{5.39}$$

If there are endogeneity (or error) issues with the regressors X_1 and/or X_2, as discussed above, one can identify instruments as above and implement 2SLS equation-by-equation. However, $Cov(\varepsilon_1, \varepsilon_2)$ may not be zero, in which case, equation-by-equation 2SLS is not efficient although still consistent. 3SLS makes use of the potential correlation between the residuals across equations to improve efficiency while retaining consistency.

As detailed in Section 2.15, in a system of equations $Y = X\beta + \varepsilon$, for a vector W to be an instrument, it is required (please see Greene (2018), for instance) that

- **Strong First Stage:** $Cov(W, X) \neq 0$
- **Exclusion Restriction:** $Cov(W, \varepsilon) = 0$. In other words, the unexplained part ("residual") ε of the regression needs to be uncorrelated with the instrument — **there is no requirement that the regressand Y itself be uncorrelated with the instrument.**

This causes the inevitable tradeoff between weakness of an instrument versus exogeneity of an instrument; see, for example, Greene (2018) and Campbell et al. (1997). In panel data econometrics, there are two popular categories of autochthonous instruments:

1. Instrument a variable $X_{i,t}$ by combination(s) of $X_{j,t}, j \neq i$. Cross-sectional variables such as corresponding variables for other geographies have been used as instruments by, for instance, Hausman et al. (1994) and the validity of such instrumentation depends on the assumption that the corresponding cross-sectional variables are correlated with the instrumented variable because of cost (or other) commonalities in the time period of interest but are not influenced by the idiosyncrasies of the geography of interest in the particular time period.
2. Instrument a variable $X_{i,t}$ by its lag(s) $X_{i,t-1}, X_{i,t-2}, \ldots$ The use of lags as instruments depends on two implicit assumptions: (a) lack of serial correlation, see, for example, Greene (2018), and (b) weak rational expectations, see, for example, Hansen and Singleton (1982).

We consider in this chapter the following instrumentation categories, for the endogenous or proxy variables, **together and also separately**, to ensure that our conclusions are not sensitive to particular information assumptions, as detailed in Section 2.15.

1. **Cross section:** Instrument each endogenous/proxy variable $X_{i,t}$ by the simple mean of $X_{j,t}$ over all j, i.e., across all stocks in the current year. This is based on the informational assumption that the instrument is correlated with the instrumented variable because of contemporaneous market factors, but the correlation of the

instrument with the firm-year-specific residual is minimal, only to the extent of $X_{i,t}$'s contribution to the many thousands of observations over which the mean of $X_{j,t}$ across all j is calculated.

2. **Time series:** Instrument each endogenous/proxy variable by its single lag, i.e., use lagged variable $X_{i,t-1}$ as an instrument for the endogenous/proxy variable $X_{i,t}$, where i is the stock and t is the calendar year. This is based on the informational assumption that the lagged variable is correlated with the current variable because of market and cost commonalities for a firm and its stock across time but is not correlated with the residual that is specific to the firm/stock in the calendar year of interest.

As mentioned earlier, in a system of equations $Y = X\beta + \varepsilon$, for a vector W to be an instrument, the following are required — see, for instance, Greene (2018). We explain the reasons for the instrumentation strategy for each of the endogenous/proxy variables in Section 5.5.6:

- $Cov(W, X) \neq 0$
- $Cov(W, \varepsilon) = 0$. In other words, the unexplained part ("residual") ε of the regression needs to be uncorrelated with the instrument — **there is no requirement that the regressand Y itself be uncorrelated with the instrument.**

5.5.6 Structural System

We estimate the following structural system at the stock-year level:

$$\begin{aligned} Vol_{i,t} &= \alpha_i + \alpha_{SSC,i} SSCC_{i,t} \\ &\quad + \alpha_{Disp,i} Disp_{i,t} + \alpha_{Hold,i} Hold_{i,t} \\ &\quad + \alpha_{BA,i} BASpr_{i,t} + \alpha_{MM,i} MM_{i,t} \\ &\quad + \varepsilon_{i,t} \end{aligned} \tag{5.40}$$

$$MEff_{i,t} = \gamma_i + \gamma_{Vol,i} Vol_{i,t} + \gamma_{NAn,i} NAn_{i,t} + \delta_{i,t} \tag{5.41}$$

Obviously, the number of market makers is not a regressor for non-Nasdaq stocks.

1. **Normalized trading volume** ($Vol_{i,t}$) — annual mean of (daily trading volume)/(daily shares outstanding) — of the stock for the current calendar year is a function of

   1. **Short sales costs and constraints** ($SSCC_{i,t}$)

- A random variable X is a *positive proxy* for another random variable Y if they are positively correlated; in other words, by positive proxy, all one means is that the positive proxy variable (stochastically) preserves the rank of the proxied variable. On the other hand, a random variable X is a *negative proxy* for another random variable Y if they are negatively correlated; i.e., it means that with the negative proxy variable, the ranking is (stochastically) the opposite — See Greene (2018) for details. We use the annual mean of the short interest $(SI_{i,t})$ in the stock, normalized by annual mean shares outstanding, as a negative proxy for short sales costs & constraints for the stock. This is based on the *Law of Demand* hypothesis that, *ceteris paribus*, the short interest for a stock (the quantity demanded) is a decreasing function of the short sales costs & constraints (price), since, as Lamont and Thaler (2003) show, the supply is fairly constant as a function of price. We do not have any data on short sales costs. Ofek et al. (2004) and Cremers and Weinbaum (2010), for instance, are papers that use proprietary data on rebate rates and spreads.
- We consider, as an instrument, the mean, across all stocks, of all monthly short interest $\left(\overline{SI_t}\right)$ because the short interest for the stock this year is likely to be correlated with short interest of all stocks in the current calendar year due to regulatory and/or market reasons, with minimal correlation with the disturbance term in the equation connecting normalized short interest in the stock in the current period ("quantity" of short interest) with short sales costs & constraints ("price" of short interest) of the stock in the current period.
- We also consider the once-lagged short interest $(SI_{i,t-1})$ as an instrument because the short interest for the stock during the previous calendar year is likely to be correlated with short interest of the stock in the current calendar year due to regulatory and/or market reasons without being correlated with the disturbance term in the equation connecting normalized short interest in the stock in the current period: ("quantity" of short interest) with short sales costs & constraints ("price" of short interest) of the stock in the current period.

2. **Dispersion of investor valuations** $(Disp_{i,t})$

   - As a positive proxy for the dispersion of investor valuations, we use the annual standard deviation of analyst forecasts of earnings per share for the firm with "forecast period end date" in the current calendar year $(sd(AnF_{i,t}))$. It is based on the assumption that the range of security analysts reflects the range of investor sentiment.

- As an instrument, we consider the mean across all firms of the annual mean of the quarterly standard deviation of analyst forecasts of earnings per share for the firm with "forecast period end date" in the same calendar year $\left(\overline{sd(AnF_{i,t})}\right)$. We do so since information flows are likely to be somewhat commonly affected across different stocks in the same calendar year while being only minimally correlated with the disturbance term in the equation connecting dispersion of investor valuations with dispersion of investor valuations in the same stock and same calendar year.
- As an instrument, we also consider the annual mean of the quarterly standard deviation of analyst forecasts of earnings per share for the firm with "forecast period end date" in the previous calendar year $(sd(AnF_{i,t-1}))$ since information flows are likely to be contemporaneously affected without being correlated with the disturbance term in the equation connecting dispersion of investor valuations in the stock in the current calendar year with standard deviation of analyst forecasts of the stock in the previous calendar year.

3. **Investor holding probability** $(Hold_{i,t})$

   - We use the annual mean of natural logarithm of daily shares outstanding $(\ln SO_{i,t})$ as a positive proxy of the investor holding probability.
   - Under the *A Priori* Identical Investors Assumption, this is a relatively constant multiple of the investor holding probability, so we do not need to instrument.

4. **Transaction costs**, which are functions of

   1. **Relative bid-ask spread** $(BASpr_{i,t})$

      - Measured by the annual mean of daily relative bid-ask spread where daily relative bid-ask spread = absolute(daily closing best ask – daily closing best bid)/(mid-point of daily closing best bid and best ask).
      - Endogenous.
      - We consider as instrument the mean across all stocks of the annual mean of daily relative bid-ask spread for the stock for the same calendar year $\left(\overline{BASpr_t}\right)$ because the bid-ask spread of other stocks during the current calendar year is likely to be correlated with bid-ask spread of the relevant stock during the current calendar year due to cost and/or market reasons, but with minimal correlation with the disturbance term in the trading volume equation for the stock in the current period.

- We also consider as instrument the annual mean of daily relative bid-ask spread for the stock for the previous calendar year $(BASpr_{i,t-1})$ because the bid-ask spread of the stock during the previous calendar year is likely to be correlated with bid-ask spread of the relevant stock during the current calendar year due to cost and/or market reasons, without being correlated with the disturbance term in the trading volume equation for the stock in the current period.

2. **Number of marker makers** $(MM_{i,t})$ — *for obvious reasons, we do not use this regressor when we do the regressions for non-Nasdaq stocks.*

- Measured by the mean over the calendar year of the number of market makers for the stock on each day.
- Endogenous.
- We consider as instrument the mean across all stocks of the mean of the number of market makers for the stock in the current calendar year $(\overline{MM_t})$ because the number of market makers for other stocks in a calendar year is likely to be correlated with the number of market makers for the relevant stock in the current calendar year due to cost and/or market reasons but with minimal correlation with the disturbance term in the trading volume equation for the stock in the current calendar year.
- We also consider as instrument the mean of number of market makers for the stock in the previous calendar year $(MM_{i,t-1})$, because the number of market makers for a stock in the previous calendar year is likely to be correlated with the number of market makers for the stock in the current calendar year due to cost and/or market reasons without being correlated with the disturbance term in the trading volume equation for the stock in the current calendar year.

3. **Market efficiency** $(MEff_{i,t})$ — we use the **negative** of each different metric as a separate **positive measure** for market efficiency; it is the regressand and hence, there is no need for instrumentation. It is a function of

1. **Normalized trading volume** $(Vol_{i,t})$ — annual mean of (daily trading volume)/(daily shares outstanding)

- Endogenous.
- We consider as instrument the mean across all stocks of the annual mean of (daily trading volume)/(shares outstanding) of the stock during that year $(\overline{Vol_t})$ because trading volume of other stocks during the current calendar

year is likely to be correlated with trading volume of the relevant stock in the current calendar year due to regulatory and/or market reasons but with only minimal correlation with the disturbance term in the market efficiency equation for the stock in the current calendar year.

- We also consider as instrument the annual mean of (daily trading volume)/(shares outstanding) corresponding to the stock for the previous calendar year ($Vol_{i,t-1}$) because trading volume of the stock during the previous calendar year is likely to be correlated with trading volume of the stock in the current calendar year due to regulatory and/or market reasons without being correlated with the disturbance term in the market efficiency equation for the stock in the current calendar year.

2. **Number of security analysts** ($NAn_{i,t}$)

- Measured by the annual average of the quarterly number of analysts who made EPS forecasts for the firm with "forecast period end date" in the current calendar year.
- Endogenous.
- We consider as instrument the mean across all firms of the number of analysts who made EPS forecasts for the firm with "forecast period end date" in the same calendar year ($\overline{NAn_t}$) because the numbers of analysts for other firms in the same calendar year are likely to be correlated with the number of analysts for the firm in the current calendar year due to cost and/or market reasons but with minimal correlation with the disturbance term in the market efficiency equation for the stock in the current calendar year.
- We also consider as instrument the average of the number of analysts who made EPS forecasts for the firm with "forecast period end date" in the previous calendar year ($NAn_{i,t-1}$) because the number of analysts for the firm in the previous calendar year is likely to be correlated with the number of analysts for the firm in the current calendar year due to cost and/or market reasons without being correlated with the disturbance term in the market efficiency equation for the stock in the current calendar year.

We perform each of our analyses separately for all Nasdaq stocks and all non-Nasdaq U.S. stocks, without splits or dividends for 1996 through 2015; *for obvious reasons, we do not have the number of market makers as a regressor when we do the regressions for non-Nasdaq stocks.*

5.6 Empirical Results and Their Implications

We perform each of our analyses separately for all Nasdaq stocks and all non-Nasdaq U.S. stocks, for 1996 through 2015 (for obvious reasons, we do not have the number of market makers as a regressor when we run regressions for non-Nasdaq stocks). In this chapter, we incorporate the Fama-French (1992) Factors (market capitalization, leverage, book-to-market equity ratio, and price-to-earnings ratio) and institutional ownership percentage point in the following two ways:

- *Fixed Effects:* we run a separate 3SLS regression system for each Fama-French Factor and institutional ownership percentage point, with fixed effects for the deciles for that factor.
- *Separate Regressions:* we run a separate 3SLS regression system for each decile for each Fama-French Factor and institutional ownership percentage point.

The empirical results are robust across the different measures for market efficiency, across alternate specifications and instrumentations, and across the Fama-French Factors and institutional ownership percentage point. Unless noted otherwise, all significances reported in this chapter are at 5%, and can be summarized as follows: Separately for Nasdaq and non-Nasdaq stocks,

- Normalized trading volume is negatively and significantly impacted by short sales costs & constraints on one hand, but does not positively and significantly impact market efficiency on the other — the impact on market efficiency of short sales costs & constraints, everything else remaining the same, is *not* significantly negative.
- Everything else remaining the same, market efficiency is *not* positively and significantly impacted by normalized trading volume.
- The theory predicts that short sales costs & constraints negatively impact trading volume, and that is overwhelmingly supported by our empirical results.

That market efficiency is not positively related with trading volume is also the conclusion of Chapter 3 using a reduced form on arbitrage risk as a negative measure for market efficiency. **We also do the following checks for robustness:** (a) restricting attention to options with short expiry periods and (b) restricting attention to years with low interest rates (the reason being that Put-Call Parity for American options approximates that for European options in these scenarios). **As an additional set of analyses**, we also took the naïve approach and estimated the corresponding one-equation reduced form, but as with this chapter, correcting for endogeneity and errors-in-variables, and incorporating the Fama-French (1992)

TABLE 5.7 Regression Results: Do Short Sales Costs & Constraints Negatively Affect Market Efficiency? Using Fama-French Factors and Institutional Ownership Deciles as Fixed Effects

	Nasdaq Stocks		Non-Nasdaq Stocks	
Factor	**Number of Regressions**	**Number of Rejections**	**Number of Regressions**	**Number of Rejections**
Overall	30	8	30	1
Book to Market Ratio	6	2	6	0
Leverage	6	1	6	0
Market Cap	6	1	6	0
Price/Earnings Ratio	6	1	6	1
Institutional Ownership	6	2	6	0

Factors and institutional ownership (by using fixed effects)

$$\begin{aligned} MEff_{i,t} &= \gamma_i + \lambda_{SSC,i}SSC_{i,t} + \lambda_{Vol,i}Vol_{i,t} + \lambda_{Disp,i}Disp_{i,t} \\ &\quad +\lambda_{Hold,i}Hold_{i,t} + \lambda_{BA,i}BA_{i,t} + \lambda_{MM,i}MM_{i,t} \\ &\quad +\lambda_{MCap,i}MCap_{i,t} + \lambda_{NAn,i}NAn_{i,t} \\ &\quad +\eta_{i,t} \end{aligned} \tag{5.42}$$

This set of Two-Stage Least Squares regressions yields similar conclusions about the *association* of market efficiency with (a) short sales costs & constraints and (b) normalized trading volume — note that we use *association* rather than *impact* in the context of interpreting one equation that is not directly based upon theory; because there is no reason based on financial economics or information economics for market efficiency to be a *direct function* of short sales costs & constraints. We present in this chapter only the meta summaries of the thousands of regressions that were part of the main analyses.

5.6.1 Do Short Sales Costs & Constraints Negatively Affect Market Efficiency?

The null and research hypotheses relevant for this section are, therefore,

$$\mathbf{H}_0: \beta_{MEff,SSCC} \geq \mathbf{0} \text{ vs. } \mathbf{H}_1: \beta_{MEff,SSCC} < \mathbf{0} \tag{5.43}$$

Table 5.7 provides the meta summaries of the results, using Fama-French Factor and institutional ownership deciles as fixed effects. Table 5.8 provides the meta summaries of the results, doing separate regressions for each Fama-French Factor and institutional ownership decile.

TABLE 5.8 Regression Results: Do Short Sales Costs & Constraints Negatively Affect Market Efficiency? Doing Separate Regressions for Each Fama-French Factors and Institutional Ownership Decile

	Nasdaq Stocks		Non-Nasdaq Stocks	
Factor	**Number of Regressions**	**Number of Rejections**	**Number of Regressions**	**Number of Rejections**
Overall	274	39	270	16
Book to Market Ratio	60	9	60	3
Leverage	40	5	40	0
Market Cap	60	9	60	2
Price/Earnings Ratio	54	8	50	6
Institutional Ownership	60	8	60	5

TABLE 5.9 Regression Results: Does Relative Trading Volume Positively Affect Market Efficiency? Using Fama-French Factors and Institutional Ownership Deciles as Fixed Effects

	Nasdaq Stocks		Non-Nasdaq Stocks	
Factor	**Number of Regressions**	**Number of Rejections**	**Number of Regressions**	**Number of Rejections**
Overall	30	16	30	3
Book to Market Ratio	6	4	6	0
Leverage	6	4	6	0
Market Cap	6	3	6	0
Price/Earnings Ratio	6	3	6	3
Institutional Ownership	6	4	6	0

5.6.2 Does Relative Trading Volume Positively Affect Market Efficiency?

The null and research hypotheses relevant for this section are, therefore,

$$\mathbf{H}_0: \beta_{MEff,Vol} \leq \mathbf{0} \text{ vs. } \mathbf{H}_1: \beta_{MEff,Vol} > \mathbf{0} \tag{5.44}$$

Table 5.9 provides the meta summaries of the results, using Fama-French Factor and institutional ownership deciles as fixed effects. Table 5.10 provides the meta summaries of the results, doing separate regressions for each Fama-French Factor and institutional ownership decile.

5.7 Conclusions

In this chapter, we utilized deviation from Put-Call Parity of options measured by different versions of *Implied Volatility Spread* and *Relative Price Spread* on a stock

TABLE 5.10 Regression Results: Does Relative Trading Volume Positively Affect Market Efficiency? Doing Separate Regressions for Each Fama-French Factors and Institutional Ownership Decile

	Nasdaq Stocks		Non-Nasdaq Stocks	
Factor	**Number of Regressions**	**Number of Rejections**	**Number of Regressions**	**Number of Rejections**
Overall	274	84	270	21
Book to Market Ratio	60	21	60	4
Leverage	40	10	40	0
Market Cap	60	17	60	3
Price/Earnings Ratio	54	15	50	6
Institutional Ownership	60	21	60	8

without splits or dividends as separate negative measures for market efficiency. We analyzed all U.S. traded options on all U.S. publicly traded common stocks from 1996 through 2015, and we did the analyses separately for Nasdaq stocks and non-Nasdaq stocks.

We used a simple two-equation structural model that shows that the relationships between market efficiency and (a) short sales and constraints and (b) trading volume are theoretically indeterminate and are, therefore, empirical questions. We used the panel nature of the data to identify appropriate instruments and used Three-Stage Least Squares to estimate this structural model. We performed each of these analyses separately for all Nasdaq and all non-Nasdaq U.S. stocks without splits or dividends (with the number of market makers an additional regressor for the former), using daily data on all U.S. traded options and their underlying stocks (and firms) for 1996 through 2015 from OptionMetrics, CRSP, I/B/E/S, Thomson Reuters, and Compustat. We incorporated the Fama-French (1992) Factors (market capitalization, leverage, book-to-market equity ratio, and price-to-earnings ratio) and institutional ownership percentage point in the following two ways: (a) *Fixed Effects:* we ran a separate 3SLS regression system for each Fama-French Factor and institutional ownership percentage point, with fixed effects for the deciles for that factor and (b) *Separate Regressions:* we ran a separate 3SLS regression system for each decile for each Fama-French Factor and institutional ownership percentage point. We found, separately for Nasdaq stocks and non-Nasdaq stocks, that between 1996 and 2015, contrary to *much* previous theoretical and empirical work:

- Everything else remaining the same, the impact on market efficiency of short sales costs & constraints of the stock is *not* significantly negative.
- Everything else remaining the same, the impact on market efficiency of normalized trading volume of the stock is *not* significantly positive.

Future research projects include:

1. The lack of significantly positive correlation that we observed in this chapter between the various *RPS* measures on one hand and the *IV* measures on the other — which changes when we restrict attention to such measures being ≤ 1 — could be because of many reasons, for instance, problems with the assumptions underlying Black-Scholes, or fundamental differences between American and European options. It is also interesting that we find little correlation between *IV-Spr* and *IV-StDev* and almost no correlation between *IV-Spr* and *IV-Disp*. You should investigate all these differences, especially disaggregated by year, Fama-French Factor deciles, SIC code, etc., in a future research project.
2. You should investigate the measures discussed in this chapter for stocks with somewhat reliable dividend profiles.
3. You should apply the theoretical and econometric methodologies of this chapter to the three measures of market efficiency, based on securities prices following random walks in efficient markets, used by Cao et al. (2018).
4. You should apply the theoretical and econometric methodologies of this chapter to the two measures of market efficiency, based on the asymmetry between positive and negative market returns, used by Bris et al. (2007).

The next three chapters detail advanced analytics in finance using millisecond-level high-frequency intraday data. In particular, Chapter 6 details intraday event studies in the measurement of market efficiency.

References

Altı, A., and Tetlock, P., 2014, "Biased Beliefs, Asset Prices, and Investment: A Structural Approach," *Journal of Finance*, 69(1), 325–361.

Amin, K., Coval, J., and Seyhun, N., 2004, "Index Option Prices and Stock Market Momentum," *The Journal of Business*, 77(4), 835–874.

Battalio, R., and Schultz, P., 2006, "Options and the Bubble," *Journal of Finance*, 61(5), 2071–2102.

Beaver, W., 1968, "The Information Content of Annual Earnings Announcements," *Journal of Accounting Research*, 6, 67–92.

Bhattacharya, R., 2019, "An Option Theoretic Approach to Market Efficiency," *Annals of Financial Economics*, 14(4), 1–21.

Bhattacharya, R., 2022, "Strong Non-Monotonicity of Equilibrium Price: Static and Dynamic Models," *SSRN* (https://ssrn.com/abstract=2980215).

Bhattacharya, R., Bial, J., and Evans, A., 2023, "It Is Imperative to Perform Event Studies Only with High-Frequency Intraday Data for Securities Litigations and Valuations," *Journal of International Business & Law*, 23(1), 1–28.

Bhattacharya, R., and O'Brien, S., 2015, "Arbitrage Risk and Market Efficiency: Applications to Securities Class Actions," *Santa Clara Law Review*, 55(3), 643–672.

Black, F., and Scholes, M., 1973, "The Pricing of Options and Corporate Liabilities," *Journal of Political Economy*, 81(3), 637–654.

Blume, L., Easley, D., and O'Hara, M., 1994, "Market Statistics and Technical Analysis: The Role of Volume," *Journal of Finance*, 49(1), 153–181.

Boehme, R., Danielsen, B., and Sorescu, S., 2006, "Short-Sale Constraints, Differences of Opinion, and Overvaluation," *Journal of Financial and Quantitative Analysis*, 41(2), 455–487.

Boehmer, E., Huszar, Z., and Jordan, B., 2010, "The Good News in Short Interest," *Journal of Financial Economics*, 96(1), 80–97.

Bris, A., Goetzmann, W., and Zhu, N., 2007, "Efficiency and the Bear: Short Sales and Markets Around the World," *Journal of Finance*, 62(3), 1029–1079.

Campbell, J., Lo, A., and MacKinlay, A. C., 1997, *The Econometrics of Financial Markets*, Princeton, NJ: Princeton University Press.

Cao, C., Liang, B., Lo, A., and Petrasek, L., 2018, "Hedge Fund Holdings and Stock Market Efficiency," *Review of Asset Pricing Studies*, 8(1), 77–116.

Coles, J., Lemmon, M., and Meschke, F., 2012, "Structural Models and Endogeneity in Corporate Finance: The Link between Managerial Ownership and Corporate Performance," *Journal of Financial Economics*, 103(1), 149–168.

Cremers, M., and Weinbaum, D., 2010, "Deviations from Put-Call Parity and Stock Return Predictability," *Journal of Financial and Quantitative Analysis*, 45(2), 335–367.

Dechow, P., Hutton, A., Meulbroek, L., and Sloan, R., 2001, "Short-Sellers, Fundamental Analysis, and Stock Returns," *Journal of Financial Economics*, 61(1), 77–106.

Diamond, D., and Verrecchia, R., 1987, "Constraints on Short-Selling and Asset Price Adjustment to Private Information," *Journal of Financial Economics*, 18(2), 277–311.

Drechsler, I., and Drechsler, Q., 2021, "The Shorting Premium and Asset Pricing Anomalies," *SSRN* (https://ssrn.com/abstract=2387099).

Duffie, D., 1996, "Special Repo Rates," *Journal of Finance*, 51(2), 493–526.

Duffie, D., Garleanu, N., and Pedersen, L., 2002, "Securities Lending, Shorting, and Pricing," *Journal of Financial Economics*, 66, 307–339.

Easley, D., O'Hara, M., and Srinivas, P.S., 1998, "Option Volume and Stock Prices: Evidence on Where Informed Traders Trade," *Journal of Finance*, 53(2), 431–465.

Fama, E., 1970, "Efficient Capital Markets: A Review of Theory and Empirical Work," *Journal of Finance*, 25(2), 383–417.

Fama, E., Fisher, L., Jensen, M., and Roll, R., 1969, "The Adjustment of Stock Prices to New Information," *International Economic Review*, 10(1), 1–21.

Fama, E., and French, K., 1992, "The Cross-Section of Expected Stock Returns," *Journal of Finance*, 47(2), 427–465.

Figlewski, S., and Webb, G., 1993, "Options, Short Sales, and Market Completeness," *Journal of Finance*, 48(2), 761–777.

Goldstein, M., Hotchkiss, E., and Sirri, E., 2007, "Transparency and Liquidity: A Controlled Experiment on Corporate Bonds," *Review of Financial Studies*, 20(2), 235–273.

Greene, W., 2018, *Econometric Analysis*, Upper Saddle River, NJ: Pearson.

Hainaut, D., and Colwell, D., 2016, "A Structural Model for Credit Risk with Switching Processes and Synchronous Jumps," *European Journal of Finance*, 22(11), 1040–1062.

Hansen, L., and Singleton, K., 1982, "Generalized Instrumental Variables Estimation of Nonlinear Rational Expectations Models," *Econometrica*, 50(5), 1269–1286.

Harris, L., 2003, *Trading & Exchanges: Market Microstructure for Practitioners*, New York, NY: Oxford University Press.

Hausman, J., Leonard, G., and Zona, D., 1994, "Competitive Analysis with Differenciated Products," *Annales d'Économie et de Statistique*, 34, 159–180.

Hull, J., 2017, *Options, Futures, and Other Derivatives*, Upper Saddle River, NJ: Pearson.

Jones, C., and Lamont, O., 2002, "Short-Sale Constraints and Stock Returns," *Journal of Financial Economics*, 66(2–3), 207–239.

Karpoff, J., 1987, "The Relation between Price Changes and Trading Volume: A Survey," *Journal of Financial and Quantitative Analysis*, 22(1), 109–126.

Klemkosky, R., and Resnick, B., 1979, "Put-Call Parity and Market Efficiency," *Journal of Finance*, 34(5), 1141–1155.

Lamont, O., and Stein, J., 2004, "Aggregate Short Interest and Market Valuations," *American Economic Review*, 94(2), 29–32.

Lamont, O., and Thaler, R., 2003, "Can the Market Add and Subtract? Mispricing in Tech Stock Carve-Outs," *Journal of Political Economy*, 111(2), 227–268.

Malkiel, B., 2003, "The Efficient Market Hypothesis and its Critics," *Journal of Economic Perspectives*, 17(1), 59–82.

Merton, R., 1973, "The Relationship between Put and Call Option Prices: Comment," *Journal of Finance*, 28(1), 183–184.

Miller, E., 1977, "Risk, Uncertainty, and Divergence of Opinion," *Journal of Finance*, 32(4), 1151–1168.

Muravyev, D., Pearson, N., and Pollet, J., 2022, "Is There a Risk Premium in the Stock Lending Market? Evidence from Equity Options," *Journal of Finance*, 77(3), 1787–1828.

Ofek, E., Richardson, M., and Whitelaw, R., 2004, "Limited Arbitrage and Short Sales Restrictions: Evidence from the Options Markets," *Journal of Financial Economics*, 74(2), 305–342.

O'Hara, M., 1997, *Market Microstructure Theory*, Malden, MA: Blackwell Publishing.

Rapach, D., Ringgenberg, M., and Zhou, Z., 2016, "Short Interest and Aggregate Stock Returns," *Journal of Financial Economics*, 121(1), 46–65.

Saffi, P., and Sigurdsson, K., 2011, "Price Efficiency and Short Selling," *Review of Financial Studies*, 24(3), 821–852.

Samuelson, P., 2009, "An Enjoyable Life Puzzling over Modern Finance Theory," *Annual Review of Financial Economics*, 1, 19–35.

Shleifer, A., 2000, *Inefficient Markets: An Introduction to Behavioral Finance*, New York, NY: Oxford University Press.

Stickel, S., and Verrecchia, R., 1994, "Evidence That Trading Volume Sustains Stock Price Changes," *Financial Analysts Journal*, 50(6), 57–67.

Stoll, H., 1969, "The Relationship between Put and Call Option Prices," *Journal of Finance*, 24(5), 801–824.

Taylor, S., Yadav, P., and Zhang, Y., 2010, "The Information Content of Implied Volatilities and Model-Free Volatility Expectations: Evidence from Options Written on Individual Stocks," *Journal of Banking & Finance*, 34(4), 871–881.

Wang, J., 1994, "A Model of Competitive Stock Trading Volume," *Journal of Political Economy*, 102(1), 127–168.

Wooldridge, J., 2010, *Econometric Analysis of Cross Section and Panel Data*, Cambridge, MA: MIT Press.

PART III

With Intraday Data

6
EVENT STUDIES

6.1 Introduction

Since Fama et al. (1969) and Ball and Brown (1968), "hundreds of event studies have been conducted in the legal, financial economics, and accounting literatures... They test the impact, speed, and unbiasedness of the market's reaction to an event," as pointed out by Kothari (2001). Ball (2017) provides a retrospective by one of the cofounders of event studies describing the contributions of the other cofounders, and please see Brown and Warner (1985) for a summary of event studies using daily data. Please see Section 6.4 for a review of event studies using millisecond-level high-frequency intraday data; this current chapter substantially extends, systematizes, and generalizes these small- and medium-sample studies to the robust new finding that for all publicly traded U.S. stocks from January 2014 to September 2021 (these date limits are set purely by constraints on availability and storage), idiosyncratic reactions are systemically all out of the system within two hours after a potentially material event, and that, therefore, it is imperative to use intraday data for event studies work: (1) two hours are systemically sufficient to measure the impact of a potentially material event in question, and (2) if one were to use daily data, one would miss the impact of an event that reverts quickly, and/or worse yet, one could erroneously attribute the impact of entirely unrelated events to the potentially material event in question, and thus, all previous event studies and market efficiency work using daily data, while of enormous and ground-breaking significance in the past, have only historical value now, with the important *caveat* that any empirical study has, of course, to work within its data and computational constraints. We also compile a dataset of systematic, independent, and objective characterizations of each TICKER-year, TICKER-halfyear, TICKER-quarter, and

DOI: 10.4324/9781003608486-9

TICKER-month, as statistically and actually significant efficient, statistically and actually significant inefficient, or otherwise. Finally, we find that capital markets during the first two to three months of the COVID-19 lockdown were statistically and actually significantly less efficient (please see Bhattacharya (2024) for details). Of course, some events have longer horizons, but that is the nature of idiosyncrasies versus a strongly persuasive systemic result; we also do comparative statics for 1.5 hours and 2.5 hours, and the results are qualitatively the same.

6.2 Motivating Example

To motivate this chapter, consider the following example: On September 18, 2018, at 11:42 AM U.S. Eastern, Bloomberg posted that "Tesla Inc. is under investigation by the Justice Department over public statements made by the company and Chief Executive Officer Elon Musk, according to two people familiar with the matter," Schoenberg and Robinson (2018). We divide each trading day into 15 "halfhours" as follows: halfhour 0 for prior to 9:30 AM U.S. Eastern, halfhours 1–13 for each halfhour of the trading hours 9:30 AM – 4 PM U.S. Eastern, and halfhour 14 for after 4 PM U.S. Eastern. For this motivating example, we use the actual absolute returns, not the absolute idiosyncratic returns that we describe later. For TSLA, over June 30, 2010 to May 12, 2023, the mean and standard deviation of daily returns were 0.144% and 3.599%, and therefore, the mean and standard deviation of halfhourly returns were 0.010% and 0.929%. **For this particular example**, we consider a halfhourly return to be substantial in absolute terms if

$$\begin{aligned} \textit{Half Hourly Return} &\notin (\textit{Mean Half Hourly Return} \\ &\mp 1\ \textit{St Dev Half Hourly Return}) \\ &= (-0.920\%, +0.939\%) \end{aligned} \tag{6.1}$$

In Table 6.1, the "halfhours" with substantial positive (negative) halfhourly returns are filled in light (dark) gray, and the halfhours that saw no substantial absolute returns are without filling, and as one can see from Table 6.1, all reaction, overreaction, correction, overcorrection, bounceback, etc., were almost all out of the system within two hours after the potentially material event.

6.3 Potentially Material Events

In this chapter we systematically and objectively identify a potentially material event separately as (1) a "key development" (marked by S&P Global CapitalIQ, event types include earnings, dividends, mergers and acquisitions, buybacks, public offerings, management changes, debt defaults, dividend cancellations, and regulatory agency inquiries, sourced from regulatory filings and news vendors, see S&P (2024)), and (2) an earnings announcement or revision, or analyst forecast

TABLE 6.1 TSLA Intraday Returns on September 18–19, 2018

Date	Beginning Time	End Time	Adjusted VWAP	"Halfhourly" Return (%)
09-18-2018	11.00 AM	11.30 AM	$300.80	0.803
09-18-2018	**11.30 AM**	**12.00 PM**	**$285.55**	**−5.202**
09-18-2018	12.00 PM	12.30 PM	$282.40	−1.107
09-18-2018	12.30 PM	1.00 PM	$279.34	−1.093
09-18-2018	1.00 PM	1.30 PM	$284.66	1.887
09-18-2018	1.30 PM	2.00 PM	$284.27	−0.137
09-18-2018	2.00 PM	2.30 PM	$284.56	0.102
09-18-2018	2.30 PM	3.00 PM	$283.04	−0.534
09-18-2018	3.00 PM	3.30 PM	$284.55	0.532
09-18-2018	3.30 PM	4.00 PM	$284.37	−0.062
09-19-2018	9.30 AM	10.00 AM	$284.90	1.263
09-19-2018	10.00 AM	10.30 AM	$286.03	0.397
09-19-2018	10.30 AM	11.00 AM	$288.83	0.973
09-19-2018	11.00 AM	11.30 AM	$290.37	0.533
09-19-2018	11.30 AM	12.00 PM	$289.52	−0.294
09-19-2018	12.00 PM	12.30 PM	$292.12	0.896
09-19-2018	12.30 PM	1.00 PM	$293.88	0.600
09-19-2018	1.00 PM	1.30 PM	$293.90	0.006
09-19-2018	1.30 PM	2.00 PM	$292.78	-0.381
09-19-2018	2.00 PM	2.30 PM	$294.37	0.542
09-19-2018	2.30 PM	3.00 PM	$296.35	0.671
09-19-2018	3.00 PM	3.30 PM	$298.39	0.683
09-19-2018	3.30 PM	4.00 PM	$298.74	0.117

Note: Positive (negative) returns of 1%, 5%, 10%, indicated by light (dark) gray filling, with normal font, bold font, and bold & italic font.

or revision. We use event studies controlling for intraday market equity returns, Nasdaq listing equity returns, industry (3-digit NAICS Code) equity returns, market capitalization decile equity returns, intraday volatility decile equity returns, dividend decile equity returns, Fama-French Factor (Fama and French, 1992, 1993, 2015), decile equity returns, fixed income yield, and daily risk-free and foreign exchange rates, and rely upon controlled contrasts between halfhour-level absolute idiosyncratic returns in post-window halfhours on one hand versus control halfhours (non-announcement and non-relevant halfhours) on the other, measured by the negative of the coefficient of the one-, two-, and three-way fixed effects regressions of halfhour-level absolute idiosyncratic returns on TICKERs, time periods, and interactions — please see Greene (2018), Wooldridge (2010), and Campbell et al. (1997), for details. As described in Section 2.6, this chapter normalizes each variable (except for a classification or time variable) by the Gaussian cumulative probability of its $Z\text{-}Score\,(x) = (x\ minus\ Mean\,(x)) \,/\, (Standard\ Deviation\,(x))$, this is a rigorization of the number of standard deviations approach to interpretation of coefficients, which also implicitly assumes Gaussian distributions. This makes the coefficients comparable and thus, allows a systematic and objective computation of actual significance, which is different from statistical significance. As detailed in Chapter 2, statistical significance is well understood; it is a measure of the precision of the estimate of the association of two variables; please see, for instance, McShane and Gal (2017). Also, "almost any parameter can be found to be significantly different from zero if the sample size is large enough," (Kennedy, 2003) and "with large sample sizes, parameters can be estimated very precisely ... which usually results in statistical significance," (Wooldridge, 2013) — in other words, pretty much everything is statistically significant when one is working with massive datasets, as we do in this chapter.

We find, as suggested by the motivating example of TSLA in Table 6.1, that for all publicly traded U.S. stocks for January 2014 – September 2021, halfhour-level absolute idiosyncratic returns for the six trading halfhours following each relevant window following each potentially material event (detailed below), are not actually significantly higher than all control halfhours (all non-announcement and all non-relevant window trading halfhours); i.e., reaction, overreaction, correction, overcorrection, bounceback, etc., are systemically all out of the system within two hours after a potentially material event; please note that, otherwise, the coefficients of the post-event indicator variables in the fixed effects regressions of halfhour-level absolute idiosyncratic returns on TICKERs, time periods, and interactions, would have to be statistically and actually significant positive; please see the regression results in Table 6.5. This chapter uses high-frequency millisecond-level intraday data from TAQ, TRACE, I/B/E/S, and Capital IQ, and daily data from CRSP, Thomson Reuters, Compustat, CRSP-Compustat Merged Database, and FRED (tens of trillions of observations), please see summary statistics in Table 6.4.

In this chapter, we use two different measures of market efficiency, based on idiosyncratic responses to (a) "key developments" (identified by S&P Global CapitalIQ), and (b) earnings announcements and revisions, and analyst forecasts and revisions, as separate objective, systematic, and ordinal actual measures of the efficiency of the market for a stock. Based on event studies relying, as before, upon a market model controlling for intraday market equity returns, Nasdaq listing equity returns, industry (3-digit NAICS Code) equity returns, market capitalization decile equity returns, intraday volatility decile equity returns, dividend decile equity returns, Fama-French Factor decile equity returns, fixed income yield, and daily risk-free and foreign exchange rates, we calculate the absolute idiosyncratic return for each stock and for each halfhour. A systematic controlled contrast between absolute values of idiosyncratic returns for relevant halfhours on one hand versus control halfhours (non-announcement and non-relevant halfhours) on the other, measured by the negative of the coefficient of the fixed effect of the interaction between the indicator variable for a relevant halfhour, and as the case maybe, TICKER and/or time period of interest, in the regression of halfhour-level absolute idiosyncratic returns on TICKERs, time periods, and interactions, allows us to compile a database (available upon request) of systematic, independent, and objective characterizations of markets in each TICKER-year, TICKER-halfyear, TICKER-quarter, and TICKER-month, and each year, halfyear, quarter, and month, as statistically and actually significant efficient, statistically and actually significant inefficient, or otherwise. These metrics are systematic, objective, ordinal, and **actual** measures of the efficiency of the market for a stock, which eliminates the need for the correlation-based market efficiency measures that have previously been used. Finally, we find that capital markets during the first two to three months of the COVID-19 lockdown (March and April, 2020) were statistically and actually significantly less efficient (please see Bhattacharya (2024) for details).

Please note that this does not imply that greater volatility clustering, which can occur as a result of news clustering, implies less efficiency, because this chapter relies upon a controlled contrast between relevant halfhours and control halfhours. Please see Bhattacharya et al. (2023) for implications for valuation and securities litigation.

6.4 Literature Review

The study of how quickly prices react to new information has a distinguished history, and more recently, insightful research has been done using millisecond-level high-frequency intraday data; here is a brief review. Martineau (2022) concludes that "in modern financial markets, stock prices fully reflect earnings surprises on the announcement date, leading to the disappearance of post-earnings announcement drifts." Grégoire and Martineau (2022) find that "the best quote instantly adjusts to earning surprises." Saggu (2022) finds that "Bitcoin responds positively to ... minting events over 5- to 30-minute event windows, but this response begins declining after 60 minutes." Rogers et al. (2017) find that "prices, volumes, and spreads respond to the news contained in filings beginning around 30 seconds before public posting." Budish et al. (2015) "use millisecond-level direct-feed data from exchanges to document a series of stylized facts about how the continuous market works at high-frequency time horizons: (i) correlations completely break down; which (ii) leads to obvious mechanical arbitrage opportunities; and (iii) competition has not affected the size or frequency of the arbitrage opportunities." Li et al. (2015) state that their "analysis of the regular-hour recommendation revisions shows large preannouncement returns and trading volume in the [−1 day, −21 minute] window although [they] also find statistically and economically significant returns and trading volume in the announcement window [−20 minute, +20 minute] and in the postannouncement window [+21 minute, +1 day]. In contrast, [their] analysis of the after-hours revisions shows that most of the price and volume reactions occur in the postannouncement window." Jiang et al. (2012) find that "a significant portion of the price change and price discovery occurs immediately after the earnings releases." Matsumoto et al. (2011) use "intraday trading data to calculate absolute returns during each segment. ... [They] first examine the incremental information content of each segment of the call and find that both the presentation and discussion have incremental information content over the accompanying press release. However, [they] find statistically greater abnormal absolute returns during the discussion portion of the call relative to the presentation." Altınkılıç and Hansen (2009) "measure revision returns using narrow return intervals around daytime revision announcements ... for identifying daytime dividend announcement returns from other event returns. [They] find the mean 40 minutes revision announcement returns are economically unimportant ... These results are robust to wider windows of one hour and two hours." Chordia et al. (2005) find that for actively traded NYSE stocks, in "thirty minutes, they are well along on their daily quest." Busse and Green (2002) "analyze 322 stocks featured on the Morning Call and Midday Call segments. [They] find that stocks discussed positively experience a statistically and economically significant price impact beginning seconds after the stock is first mentioned and lasting approximately one minute. The response to negative reports is more gradual, lasting up to 15 minutes, perhaps due to the higher costs of short selling. They conclude that prices adjust to stock mentions within 15 seconds." Kim et al. (1997) find that "on average, it takes five minutes of trading for NYSE/AMEX stocks and 15 minutes for NASDAQ stocks to reflect the private information contained in ... buy recommendations that are pre-released to important clients before the stock market opens." For other recent event studies using intraday data, please see, for instance, Kaourma et al. (2021), and Marshall et al. (2019); please also see, Graham et al. (2006), Barclay and Litzenberger (1988), Jennings and Starks (1986), Patell and Wolfson (1984), Keown and Pinkerton (1981), Davies and Canes (1978), and Dann et al. (1977).

A market is *semistrong efficient* if prices reflect all publicly available information; please see, for example, Fama (1970), Jensen (1978), Grossman and Stiglitz (1980), Porta et al. (1997), Harris (2003), Loughran and Ritter (2000), Shleifer (2000), Samuelson (2009), and Rosch et al. (2017). As has been recognized, by, for example, Fama et al. (1969), a market is efficient if "stock prices adjust very rapidly to new information," and therefore, calendar-time is relevant to a discussion of market efficiency whereas transaction-time is not, *per se*, relevant, please see Kyle and Obizhaeva (2016) for further details. Prices of securities adjust, *albeit* to varying extents, to new information; therefore, markets for securities are efficient in varying degrees, often referred to as *relative efficiency*; see, for example, Campbell et al. (1997) — please also see, for instance, Bhattacharya et al. (2023), Cornell and Rutten (2006), and Bhattacharya and O'Brien (2015) for the role of market efficiency in securities litigation. For a description of the importance of relative efficiency for valuations (especially Mark-to-Market) and securities class actions (especially class certification), see Bhattacharya (2019). Other measures of market efficiency, (1) based on securities prices following random walks in efficient markets used by Cao et al. (2018) and Boehmer and Kelley (2009), (2) the two purely empirical measures of market efficiency based on the asymmetry between positive and negative market returns used by Bris et al. (2007), (3) the variance ratio measures of random walk (the last two methods were also used by Saffi and Sigurdsson (2011)) — see Campbell et al. (1997) for details, (4) the friction measures of market efficiency — see Hou and Moskowitz (2005) and Boehmer and Wu (2013) — and (5) the mispricing score based on eleven return anomalies used by Stambaugh et al. (2015), are all **indirect measures** of market efficiency based on a posited positive correlation between each of these indirect measures and the actual efficiency of the market for a security, which are relevant only in the absence of an actual measure of market efficiency.

These discussions yield the following research question and hypotheses that are tested in this chapter:

Research Hypothesis 1: Absolute idiosyncratic reactions in six halfhours following two hours including a potentially material event are higher than in halfhours that are not in the two hours including any potentially material event. The data reject this hypothesis, as detailed in Table 6.6.

Research Question 1: How can one develop systematic, objective, and **actual** measures of the efficiency of the market for a stock? The answers are detailed in Section 6.7.3.

Research Hypothesis 2: The COVID-19 lockdowns had a negative impact on market efficiency.

6.5 Description of Data

We use data on all publicly traded U.S. stocks for January 2014 to September 2021. We use high-frequency millisecond-level intraday equity trading data from TAQ and high-frequency millisecond-level intraday fixed income security trading data from TRACE. We restrict attention to stocks corresponding to publicly traded firms that did not have more than one PERMNO or TICKER or 3-digit NAICS code during January 2014 to September 2021. We further restrict attention to stock-days that did not have splits, reverse splits, or dividends, and to stock-days that have positive closing price and positive shares outstanding and other restrictions, that had the following fields in CRSP: date, closing price, return, shares outstanding, trading volume, closing bid and ask, exchange membership, NAICS code, and had data on the following variables: high-frequency millisecond-level intraday analyst forecasts and revisions (from I/B/E/S), high-frequency millisecond-level intraday earnings announcements and revisions (from I/B/E/S), high-frequency millisecond-level intraday key developments (from S&P Global Capital IQ, (Marketplace, 2024), daily data from Compustat-CRSP Merged Database, and daily data for T-Bill yields and Nominal Broad U.S. Dollar Index from Federal Reserve of St. Louis (FRED). The sample is further restricted to the following:

- if $|yield| \leq 100\%$ (purely an attempt to eliminate potential errors)
- if $|EPS| \leq \$100$ (purely an attempt to eliminate potential errors)
- if $shrcd \in \{10, 11\}$
- if $ret \notin \{-44.0, -55.0, -66.0, -77.0, -88.0, -99.0\}$
- if $dlret \notin \{-55.0, -66.0, -88.0, -99.0\}$
- if $dlretx \notin \{-55.0, -66.0, -88.0, -99.0\}$
- if $dclrdt \neq 0$
- if $trtscd \neq 0$,
- if $nmsind \neq 0$
- if $vol \neq -99.0$
- if $prc > 0$
- if $bid > 0$
- if $ask > 0$
- if $vol > 0$
- if $shrout > 0$
- if $TICKER \neq ?$
- if $TICKER \neq ''''$
- if $CUSIP \neq ''''$
- if $substr(TICKER, 1, 4) \neq ZZZZ$;
- if $substr(CUSIP, 7, 1) \in \{0, 1, 2, 3, 4, 5, 6, 7, 8, 9\}$
- if $substr(CUSIP, 8, 1) \in \{0, 1, 2, 3, 4, 5, 6, 7, 8, 9\}$

For a small number of stock-days, there were multiple entries when sorted by TICKER, CUSIP, and date — for these stock-days, weighted averages were calculated using trading volume as weights. Compustat (including Capital IQ) data sources rely upon the S&P identification of GVKEY. The mapping of GVKEY to TICKER used by CRSP to match its data to Compustat was relied upon. We do not have access to intraday data for treasury yield and foreign exchange rates from FRED (we thank B. Ravikumar for his help on this matter). Please see Table 6.2 for a comparison of high-frequency millisecond-level intraday and daily data.

TABLE 6.2 Comparison of Intraday Data and Daily Data, January 2014 to September 2021

	Intraday Data				Daily Data		
Year-Quarter	Number of Equity Trades	Dollar Value of Equity Trades	Number Fixed Income Trades	Dollar Value of Fixed Income Trades	Number of Observations	Number of Equity Trades	Dollar Value of Equity Trades
2014-1	1,926,239,343	$17,325,394,026,361	4,020,360	$3,175,662,358,003	406,135	610,688,409	$16,561,835,009,089
2014-2	1,819,263,091	$16,870,778,971,035	3,894,265	$3,345,962,083,196	423,927	608,695,640	$15,101,700,758,067
2014-3	1,707,216,092	$15,653,454,170,425	3,598,767	$2,814,186,446,991	436,861	551,627,996	$14,784,073,442,796
2014-4	2,130,705,576	$18,881,074,072,187	3,717,768	$2,761,439,273,092	439,750	620,399,242	$18,072,918,510,342
2015-1	1,962,515,129	$17,945,195,452,977	4,051,157	$3,515,582,919,475	419,932	573,169,320	$17,159,703,006,802
2015-2	1,819,257,164	$16,923,993,048,630	3,933,485	$3,217,949,348,199	435,121	571,228,779	$16,149,517,762,112
2015-3	2,246,183,807	$19,442,171,278,550	3,764,267	$2,846,661,200,411	446,279	682,920,742	$18,473,574,210,343
2015-4	2,190,577,282	$18,038,112,447,226	4,041,987	$2,491,898,904,323	445,217	650,250,048	$17,221,476,055,313
2016-1	2,573,524,217	$19,557,899,479,956	4,797,632	$3,167,909,880,109	422,681	719,933,406	$18,330,922,510,727
2016-2	2,182,293,644	$1,7,648,220,098,305	4,840,824	$2,983,717,736,637	442,125	634,565,530	$16,572,525,778,322
2016-3	1,960,121,791	$16,497,805,893,703	4,741,883	$3,399,978,725,728	441,043	581,883,805	$15,661,244,171,624
2016-4	2,095,576,792	$1,8,451,657,041,161	4,642,104	$2,840,805,528,573	434,923	611,300,335	$16,983,988,660,102
2017-1	1,985,023,203	$18,330,144,176,777	5,547,976	$3,808,230,612,062	430,830	599,386,840	$16,484,927,265,961
2017-2	1,996,798,376	$1,9,096,466,633,198	5,080,229	$2,807,783,242,248	438,367	636,673,058	$17,100,088,311,885
2017-3	1,834,993,857	$17,942,809,260,986	4,837,590	$2,983,970,309,925	439,735	609,004,162	$16,005,584,543,889
2017-4	1,927,015,182	$19,563,715,121,913	5,071,931	$3,465,996,879,419	443,069	655,140,250	$17,459,055,144,045
2018-1	2,304,180,434	$25,586,514,195,804	5,815,831	$3,655,777,849,862	433,696	754,355,501	$22,988,132,556,037
2018-2	2,177,514,051	$2,3,416,749,216,858	5,753,988	$3,370,717,409,037	454,271	736,971,155	$20,957,921,093,798
2018-3	2,013,157,733	$21,536,136,794,314	5,495,425	$3,727,590,043,464	450,465	712,470,057	$19,337,285,812,799
2018-4	2,701,465,727	$2,8,112,617,971,647	5,934,010	$3,212,327,539,018	457,096	898,983,275	$25,364,396,813,419

(Continued)

TABLE 6.2 (Continued)

	Intraday Data				Daily Data		
Year-Quarter	Number of Equity Trades	Dollar Value of Equity Trades	Number Fixed Income Trades	Dollar Value of Fixed Income Trades	Number of Observations	Number of Equity Trades	Dollar Value of Equity Trades
2019-1	2,212,168,304	$2,3,111,156,936,584	6,503,878	$3,605,987,852,834	444,984	763,001,652	$20,669,373,385,765
2019-2	2,271,740,093	$22,578,787,230,748	6044,307	$3,336,416,204,852	461,168	79,6,301,541	$20,206,977,932,884
2019-3	2,416,943,077	$23,517,503,011,696	5,903,773	$3,104,341,630,452	471,874	822,578,085	$20,005,572,861,668
2019-4	2,324,607,671	$2,44,26,64,70,56,441	57,49,135	$2,804,876,287,796	473,664	813,980,031	$19,332,691,236,845
2020-1	3,677,867,162	$3,6,816,084,177,934	6,617,358	$4,513,126,813,699	461,706	1,278,523,131	$30,981,985,774,839
2020-2	4,003,414,165	$34,717,522,262,877	6,536,712	$4,300,699,316,331	468,303	1,465,416,736	$29,508,606,104,973
2020-3	3,531,389,334	$3,4,721,783,580,982	5,470,990	$3,276,410,577,952	481,823	1,517,808,342	$29,223,224,882,992
2020-4	3,650,186,844	$3,6,971,749,242,935	5,424,712	$2,950,194,339,277	493,679	1,561,035,312	$30,510,486,861,305
2021-1	4,303,573,977	$40,573,491,653,630	6,378,585	$4,012,258,125,333	490,660	2,203,796,372	$3,7,891,833,934,853
2021-2	3,247,963,604	$3,2,508,643,000,085	5,943,040	$3,600,868,839,454	527,913	1,800,262,049	$33,347,651,060,651
2021-3	3,978,095,420	$3,9,199,715,706,215	5,323,463	$2,995,045,350,079	554,454	1,756,773,810	$32,523,026,167,471

6.6 Event Studies

In this chapter, we do *not* ascribe any directional component to any potentially material event, because it is impossible, without additional information or *ad hoc* judgment, to objectively determine the market's perception prior to any potentially material event and to determine whether a particular potentially material event was better-than-expected news, worse-than-expected news, or even a surprise at all. Colloquially speaking: Good news or bad news is not the relevant question here, and it requires subjective judgment to infer from the description of an event if market efficiency would require the price of the security to go up, down, or stay the same. For instance,

- Facebook (FB) closed on Thursday, July 11, 2019 at $201.23
- FB opened on Friday, July 12, 2019 at $199.68
- At 3:52 PM, Friday, July 12, 2019, news emerged that the U.S. Federal Trade Commission (FTC) planned to fine FB a record $5 billion for the Cambridge Analytica data scandal (Price, 2019)
- FB closed on Friday, July 12, 2019 at $204.87
    - Increase of 1.8% over previous day's closing price
    - Increase of 2.6% over current day's open price
- Even though the reported settlement amount was $2 billion more than the company had reserved for the settlement

In his judgment in *Petrobras Securities Litigation* (United States District Court, Southern District of New York, 1:14-cv-09662-JSR, February 2, 2016), Judge Jed Rakoff discussed the issue of directionality and stringently criticized the subjective and *ad hoc* marking of directionality of events in the dueling "expert" reports — for example, one of the "experts" in the litigation used the presence or absence of the text "corrupt" in the description of an event to determine the relevant directionality of a potentially material event.

6.6.1 HalfHour-Level Averages

We use high-frequency millisecond-level intraday equity trading data from TAQ and high-frequency millisecond-level intraday fixed income security trading data from TRACE. As discussed earlier, calendar-time, rather than transaction-time, is relevant for market efficiency discussions — see Kyle and Obizhaeva (2016) for further details. Therefore, we divide each trading day into 15 halfhours as follows: halfhour 0 for prior to 9:30 AM U.S. Eastern, halfhours 1-13 for each halfhour of the trading hours 9:30 AM – 4 PM U.S. Eastern, and halfhour 14 for after

TABLE 6.3 HalfHour-Level Summary Statistics, January 2014 to September 2021

"HalfHour"	Description	Number of Equity Trades	Dollar Value of Equity Trades	Number of Fixed Income Trades	Dollar Value of Fixed Income Trades
0	Before 9:30 AM U.S. Eastern	640,483,038	$6,777,863,422,227	11,305,416	$11,206,970,976,201
1	9:30 AM - 10 AM U.S. Eastern	8,765,560,268	$88,342,871,897,940	6,734,369	$4,372,031,645,262
2	10 AM - 10:30 AM U.S. Eastern	7,186,315,118	$57,282,665,647,677	8,691,571	$4,860,415,458,364
3	10:30 AM - 11 AM U.S. Eastern	6,289,105,358	$48,329,343,516,871	9,759,649	$5,614,909,986,256
4	11 AM - 11:30 AM U.S. Eastern	5,706,463,977	$43,620,109,464,877	10,553,069	$5,794,441,646,635
5	11:30 AM - 12 PM U.S. Eastern	5,049,692,932	$38,297,562,040,105	10,058,513	$5,099,021,334,234
6	12 PM - 12:30 PM U.S. Eastern	4,534,691,961	$33,924,575,217,106	9,866,459	$5,107,833,767,588
7	12:30 PM - 1 PM U.S. Eastern	4,278,316,329	$31,571,903,696,950	8,850,021	$4,336,087,866,003
8	1 PM - 1:30 PM U.S. Eastern	4,160,932,285	$31,092,087,818,446	8,883,699	$4,498,974,933,412
9	1:30 PM - 2 PM U.S. Eastern	4,278,402,702	$31,160,890,672,212	11,018,262	$5,783,461,072,224
10	2 PM - 2:30 PM U.S. Eastern	4,792,257,411	$3,5,486,737,961,208	9,883,277	$5,392,447,019,295
11	2:30 PM - 3 PM U.S. Eastern	5,010,038,857	$36,504,042,353,304	10,307,489	$5,775,356,612,305
12	3 PM - 3:30 PM U.S. Eastern	6,106,685,431	$43,987,366,210,054	12,052,614	$7,383,178,562,403
13	3:30 PM - 4 PM U.S. Eastern	14,313,900,845	$103,332,011,862,963	16,454,641	$9,619,493,708,915
14	After 4 PM U.S. Eastern	490,529,064	$151,474,382,823,856	15,058,383	$1,7,249,749,038,735

4 PM U.S. Eastern — this aggregation of millisecond-level high-frequency data onto halfhours is a simplification; in particular, you should consider aggregating these millisecond-level high-frequency data into, say, every ten minutes, fifteen minutes, or hour. For each stock *i*, for each trading day, for each halfhour $\tau = \{0, 1, ..., 14\}$ with positive volume, we calculate the volume-weighted average price (VWAP) of trading prices, and then calculate the relevant continuously compounded return for halfhour τ. We calculate the various weighted averages for equity returns. For each fixed income security TICKER-CUSIP, we calculate the volume-weighted average yield (VWAY), and for each TICKER, we calculate the simple average of VWAY over all CUSIPs corresponding to that TICKER. Since we are using yield-to-maturity (YTM) with traded prices for the FI securities, one has comparability across different coupons, maturities, and periodicities; thus, average yield is meaningful, and we use a simple average to avoid the volatility of TICKER-halfhour-yield because of substantially differing trading volumes, and we calculate the various weighted averages for FI returns. These calculations are detailed in Appendix 6A— one is still left with other complexities such as seniority and convertibility, but we do not have these data. Please see Table 6.3 for halfhour-level summary statistics for all U.S.-listed equities and fixed income securities.

6.6.2 Market Model

The market model below controls for intraday market equity returns, Nasdaq listing equity returns, industry (3-digit NAICS Code) equity returns, market capitalization decile equity returns, intraday volatility decile equity returns, dividend decile equity returns, Fama-French Factor decile equity returns, fixed income yield, and daily risk-free and foreign exchange rates. Having the risk-free rate as a regressor in the market model is a generalization of using excess return (yield) of security = return (yield) of security minus risk-free rate, in all equity (fixed income) security calculations. We do not have access to intraday data for foreign exchange rates or T-bill yields.

The return of equity *i* in halfhour τ,

$$
\begin{aligned}
& EqRet_{i,\tau} \qquad (6.2) \\
= \; & \pi \\
& + \left(\pi_{EqRet\_All\ Half\ Hour}\right)\left(EqRet\_All\ Half Hour_{\tau}\right) \\
& + \left(\pi_{EqRet\_Nasdaq\ Half\ Hour}\right)\left(EqRet\_Nasdaq\ Half Hour_{i,\tau}\right)
\end{aligned}
$$

$$
\begin{aligned}
&+ \left(\pi_{EqRet\_NAICS3Dig\ Half\ Hour}\right)\left(EqRet\_NAICS3Dig\ Half\ Hour_{i,\tau}\right)\\
&+ \left(\pi_{EqRet\_MCapDecileHalfHour}\right)\left(EqRet\_MCapDecile\ Half\ Hour_{i,\tau}\right)\\
&+ \left(\pi_{EqRet\_IntraVtyDecile\ Half\ Hour}\right)\left(EqRet\_IntraVtyDecile\ Half\ Hour_{i,\tau}\right)\\
&+ \left(\pi_{EqRet\_DivYieldDecileHalfHour}\right)\left(EqRet\_DivYieldDecile\ Half\ Hour_{i,\tau}\right)\\
&+ \left(\pi_{EqRet\_BMRatioDecile\ Half\ Hour}\right)\left(EqRet\_BMRatioDecile\ Half\ Hour_{i,\tau}\right)\\
&+ \left(\pi_{EqRet\_PERatioDecile\ Half\ Hour}\right)\left(EqRet\_PERatioDecile\ Half\ Hour_{i,\tau}\right)\\
&+ \left(\pi_{EqRet\_DERatioDecile\ Half\ Hour}\right)\left(EqRet\_DERatioDecile\ Half\ Hour_{i,\tau}\right)\\
&+ \left(\pi_{FIYld\_All\ Half\ Hour}\right)\left(FIYld\_All\ Half\ Hour_{\tau}\right)\\
&+ \left(\pi_{RiskFree}\right)\left(RiskFree_{\tau}\right)\\
&+ \left(\pi_{NomBroadUSDIndex}\right)\left(NomBroadUSDIndex_{\tau}\right)\\
&+ IdioEqRet_{i,\tau}
\end{aligned}
$$

This enables one to predict or benchmark the equity return for that firm i and that halfhour τ — the "normal return" or expected return $\widehat{EqRet_{i,\tau}}$, and therefore, to measure the **idiosyncratic return**

$$\widehat{IdioEqRet_{i,\tau}} = EqRet_{i,\tau} - \widehat{EqRet_{i,\tau}} \tag{6.3}$$

Table 6.3 provides summary statistics of the market model variables referred to above.

6.6.3 *Controlled Contrasts*

Fix universe of analysis $\mathfrak{T}$ as set of halfhours. Fix announcement window length $n \geq 1$, relevant window length $m \geq 1$, and post-relevant window length $l \geq 1$. Consider a fixed time period t (e.g., quarter, month) as set of halfhours. Consider event identification method $\mathfrak{I} \subseteq \mathfrak{T}$ as potentially material events; in this chapter, we use two separate identification methods for potentially material events: (a) key developments (KD), identified by S&P Global CapitalIQ, and (b) earnings announcements and revisions, and analyst forecasts and revisions (EA). For potentially material event at halfhour $T \in t \cap \mathfrak{T}$,

$$\boldsymbol{AnnouncementHalfHours}\,(T, n) = \{T, ..., T + n - 1\} \tag{6.4}$$

(n halfhours),

$$\boldsymbol{RelevantHalfHours}\,(T, n, m) = \{T + n, ..., T + n + m - 1\} \tag{6.5}$$

(m halfhours), and, therefore,

$$
\begin{aligned}
\boldsymbol{TreatmentHalfHours}\,(T, n, m) &= \boldsymbol{Announcement\ Half\ Hours}\,(T, n)\\
&\quad \cup \boldsymbol{Relevant\ Half\ Hours}\,(T, n, m)\\
&= \{T, ..., T + n + m - 1\}
\end{aligned} \tag{6.6}
$$

TABLE 6.4 Summary Statistics of Market Model Variables; 2014 to September 2021

Regressor	Mean	Standard Deviation	Upper Quartile	Median	Lower Quartile
EqRet_Ticker Half Hour	−0.0000010	0.0886823	0.0025405	0.0000000	−0.0025618
EqRet_All Half Hour	0.0019833	0.0280379	0.0026144	0.0002849	−0.0019915
EqRet_Nasdaq Half Hour	0.0016141	0.0304606	0.0026501	0.0002452	−0.0021699
EqRet_NAICS3Dig Half Hour	−0.0001584	0.0397222	0.0021762	0.0000352	−0.0020869
EqRet_MCapDecile Half Hour	0.0008127	0.0401322	0.0034137	0.0001037	−0.0032963
EqRet_IntraVtyDecile Half Hour	−0.0009897	0.0975003	0.0078628	0.0001303	−0.0071964
EqRet_DivYieldDecile Half Hour	−0.0001597	0.0307727	0.0021047	0.0001144	−0.0018948
EqRet_BMRatioDecile Half Hour	0.0005654	0.0408437	0.0030663	0.0001485	-0.0028001
EqRet_PERatioDecile Half Hour	0.0006007	0.0325037	0.0024571	0.0001316	-0.0022033
EqRet_DERatioDecile Half Hour	0.0002127	0.0336754	0.0028886	0.0000606	-0.0027801
NomBroadUSDIndex	110.92702	6.97292	115.31330	112.65630	109.04920
TBill_4Wk	0.0070353	0.0082358	0.0150000	0.0023000	0.0004000
FIYld_All Half Hour	0.0385361	0.0168060	0.0425658	0.0371158	0.0318501

($n + m$ half hours), and therefore,

$$\boldsymbol{ControlHalfHours}(t, n, m, \mathfrak{T}) \tag{6.7}$$

consists of each halfhour in t that is not a treatment halfhour for any potentially material event at halfhour $T \in t \cap \mathfrak{T}$, and, therefore, equals

$$\{\tau \in t : \tau \notin \{T, ..., T + n + m - 1\}, \forall T \in t \cap \mathfrak{T}\} \tag{6.8}$$

And, finally, the list of post-relevant halfhours for event at time halfhour $T \in t$ is

$$\boldsymbol{PostRelevantHalfHours}\,(T, n, m, l) = \{T + n + m, ..., T + n + m + l - 1\} \tag{6.9}$$

(l halfhours immediately following the relevant halfhours).

For fixed n, m, l, a systematic and controlled comparison between

$$\left|\widehat{IdioEqRet_{i,\tau}}\right| \tag{6.10}$$

for

$$\boldsymbol{PostRelevantHalfHours}\,(T, n, m, l) \tag{6.11}$$

versus

$$\left|\widehat{IdioEqRet_{i,\tau}}\right| \tag{6.12}$$

for

$$\boldsymbol{ControlHalfHours}(t, n, m, \mathfrak{T}) \tag{6.13}$$

is a measure of whether there is any systemic impact of the potentially material event T beyond the announcement and relevant halfhours — the rational expectations models say that the speed of impact probably depends on whether there is further information that has not been disclosed; please see Foster and Viswanathan (1996) and O'Hara (1997), for example. If this contrast is not statistically and actually significant positive, it would demonstrate that (1) $(n + m)$ halfhours are systemically sufficient to measure the impact over l halfhours of a potentially material event in question, and (2) if one were to use daily data, one would miss the impact of an event that reverts quickly, and/or worse yet, one could erroneously attribute the impact of entirely unrelated events to the potentially material event in question, and, therefore, although of enormous historical significance, event studies using daily data would be entirely unreliable today.

For fixed n, m, a systematic and controlled contrast between

$$\left|\widehat{IdioEqRet_{i,\tau}}\right| \tag{6.14}$$

for

$$\textbf{\textit{RelevantHalfHours}}\,(T, n, m) \tag{6.15}$$

versus

$$\left|\widehat{IdioEqRet_{i,\tau}}\right| \tag{6.16}$$

for

$$\textbf{\textit{ControlHalfHours}}(t, n, m, \mathfrak{T}) \tag{6.17}$$

would be necessary for an objective, systematic, and ordinal direct measure of market efficiency with n announcement halfhours and m relevant halfhours. From the theory, it follows that

$$\left|\widehat{IdioEqRet_{i,\tau}}\right| \tag{6.18}$$

should be weakly higher for relevant halfhours than for control halfhours, and therefore, in this chapter, for each of the identification systems for potentially material events (KD and EA), for each n, m, for each security i, for each quarter t, we provide an ordinal direct **measure of market efficiency** for that security for that quarter as the negative of the coefficient of the interaction between the indicator variable for relevant halfhours versus control halfhours, and as the case maybe, TICKER and/or time period of interest, in a fixed effects regression of halfhour-level absolute idiosyncratic returns on TICKERs, time periods, and interactions. In Chapter 7, an objective, systematic, and ordinal direct measure of market efficiency is provided by the negative of the positive part of the difference in quarterly means between absolute idiosyncratic returns for relevant halfhours and absolute idiosyncratic returns for control halfhours.

6.6.4 Announcement Windows, Relevant Windows, and Post-Event Windows

Depending on how one determines a potentially material event, we have two separate paths of research on event studies. For the first path, we rely upon the marking of an event as a "key development" (identified by S&P Global CapitalIQ, event types include earnings, dividends, mergers and acquisitions, buybacks, public offerings, management changes, debt defaults, dividend cancellations, and regulatory agency inquiries, sourced from regulatory filings and news vendors, see S&P (2024)) to study as a potentially material event for the issuing firm. For each such key development for the firm, for each relevant window halfhour following the key development, we calculate the absolute idiosyncratic return

— we call this the *Key Developments Idiosyncratic Response (KDIR) for that window halfhour following that Key Development.* As mentioned earlier, we do not try to ascribe any directional component to any key development, because it is impossible to objectively and systematically determine from publicly available data the market's perceptions immediately prior to the relevant key development and, therefore, it is impossible to objectively and systematically determine whether a particular key development was better-than-expected news, worse-than-expected news, or just expected (even if one were to make an *ad hoc* inference about the directionality of the surprise information in a key development, with errors about market information at the time of a key development, from its description, one would compound error upon error, each of which would be non-identifiable).

The second path studies the impact of earnings announcements and forecasts on security prices and has a long and distinguished history; see, for instance, Ball and Brown (1968), Collins and Kothari (1989), and Kothari and Warner (2007). For each earnings announcement, earnings announcement revision, analyst forecast, and analyst forecast revision, we calculate the absolute idiosyncratic return for each relevant window halfhour following the earnings announcement, earnings announcement revision, analyst forecast, and analyst forecast revision — we call this the *Earnings Announcements Idiosyncratic Response (EAIR) for that* earnings announcement, earnings announcement revision, analyst forecast, and analyst forecast revision. Please note that the actual announced EPS or its deviation from "consensus" forecasts do not enter into our calculations; for a number of reasons. Any estimate of the market's "consensus" prediction of the EPS at the point of an EPS announcement, whether it is by using means or medians of analyst forecasts, or by using valuation models, is sensitive to the methodology used to estimate the market's perception and the deviation from it — see, for instance, Chiang et al. (2019) for detailed descriptions of biases in the calculation of deviation from consensus; also see Kothari et al. (2016) for a comprehensive survey of the literature on quality, bias, and predictability of earnings forecasts, treating these analyst forecasts as representing market information at the time of a potentially material event, with forecast errors, would need compounding error upon error, each of which would be non-identifiable. The impact of analyst incentives on analyst forecasts is beyond the scope of this chapter — please see Bhattacharya and Gupta (2023), for instance. It is impossible to objectively and systematically measure how much information about an actual earnings announcement or forecast leaked out before the actual announcement or forecast, and, therefore, it is impossible to objectively and systematically measure, from publicly available data, the "surprise" component of the earnings announcement or forecast.

For each stock, for each potentially material event at halfhour T, we consider the announcement window halfhours to be

$$\tau \in \{T, ..., T+2-1\} = \{T, T+1\} \tag{6.19}$$

($n = 2$ halfhours), the relevant window halfhours to be

$$\tau \in \{T+1+1, ..., T+2+2-1\} = \{T+2, T+3\} \tag{6.20}$$

($m = 2$ halfhours), and the post-relevant windows to be

$$\tau \in \{T+2+2, ..., T+2+2+6-1\} = \{T+4, ..., T+9\} \tag{6.21}$$

($l = 6$ halfhours). We calculate the absolute idiosyncratic return

$$\left|\widehat{IdioEqRet}_{i,\tau}\right| \tag{6.22}$$

for each stock i and for each halfhour τ. Please see Bhattacharya and Gupta (2026) for different sensitivities.

6.7 Methodology and Empirical Results

Please see Aman et al. (2019) for a robust defense of "responsible science," that science needs to have integrity and relevance.

6.7.1 *Actual Significance*

As described in Section 2.5, when dealing with large numbers of observations, we replace each variable x, except for each classification or time variable, by its normalization

$$\Phi\left(Z\text{-}Score\left(x\right)\right) = \Phi\left(\frac{x - Mean\left(x\right)}{StDev\left(x\right)}\right)$$

where Φ is the cumulative probability function of a standard Gaussian random variable. Actually significant positive (negative) association is indicated by light (dark) grey shading. Actual significance at level 1 is indicated by regular font, actual significance at level 5 by bold font, and actual significance at level 10 by bold and italic font.

6.7.2 *Post-Relevant Halfhours Versus Control Halfhours*

Using the fixed effects coefficients in the regressions of halfhour-level absolute idiosyncratic returns on fixed effects for TICKERs, time periods, and interactions — please see Greene (2018), Wooldridge (2010), and Campbell et al., for details

— we find, as suggested by the motivating example of TSLA in Table 6.1, that for all publicly traded U.S. stocks for January 2014 to September 2021, halfhour-level absolute idiosyncratic returns for the six trading halfhours following each relevant window following each potentially material event (identified in Section 6.6.4), are not actually significantly higher than all control halfhours (all non-announcement and all non-relevant window trading halfhours); i.e., reaction, overreaction, correction, overcorrection, bounceback, etc., are systemically all out of the system within two hours after a potentially material event; please note that, otherwise, the coefficients of the post-event indicator variables in the fixed effects regressions of halfhour-level absolute idiosyncratic returns on TICKERs, time periods, and interactions, would have to be statistically and actually significant positive — please note the interpretation of regression coefficients in Section 2.6 and please see the regression results in Table 6.4. Therefore, it is imperative to use intraday data for event studies work: (1) two hours are systemically sufficient to measure the impact of a potentially material event in question, and (2) if one were to use daily data, one would miss the impact of an event that reverts quickly, and/or worse yet, one could erroneously attribute the impact of entirely unrelated events to the potentially material event in question. Thus, all previous event studies and market efficiency work using daily data, while of enormous and ground-breaking significance in the past, have only historical value now.

6.7.3 Measures of Market Efficiency

For each stock, for each potentially material event at halfhour T, we consider the announcement window halfhours to be

$$\tau \in \{T, ..., T + 2 - 1\} = \{T, T + 1\} \tag{6.23}$$

($n = 2$ halfhours), the relevant window halfhours to be

$$\tau \in \{T + 1 + 1, ..., T + 2 + 2 - 1\} = \{T + 2, T + 3\} \tag{6.24}$$

($m = 2$ halfhours), and the control halfhours are all the halfhours that are neither announcement window halfhours nor relevant window halfhours. We calculate the absolute idiosyncratic return

$$\left| \widehat{IdioEqRet_{i,\tau}} \right| \tag{6.25}$$

for each stock i, for each halfhour τ. A systematic and controlled contrast between

$$\left| \widehat{IdioEqRet_{i,\tau}} \right| \tag{6.26}$$

for relevant window halfhours versus control (non-announcement and non-relevant) window halfhours — measured by the negative of the coefficient of the fixed

TABLE 6.5 Fixed Effects on Market Efficiency; Post-Relevant Halfhours Versus Control Halfhours, 2014 to September 2021

Control Variable	Fixed Effect	Measure of Market Efficiency: Based on Key Developments Abnormal Returns	Measure of Market Efficiency: Based on Earnings Announcements Abnormal Returns
Ticker	**Intercept**	***44.756******	***44.818******
		(1,021.073)	***(1,004.707)***
	Post-Relevant HalfHours	0.006	−0.272***
		(1.160)	(−69.235)
Ticker * Year	**Intercept**	***44.791******	***44.864******
		(371.198)	***(376.214)***
	Post-Relevant HalfHours	−0.013***	−0.301***
		(−2.654)	(−80.512)
Ticker * Half-Year	**Intercept**	***44.584******	***44.688******
		(249.479)	***(270.393)***
	Post-Relevant HalfHours	−0.013***	−0.313***
		(−2.607)	(−85.104)
Ticker * Quarter	**Intercept**	***44.726******	***44.826******
		(181.610)	***(189.107)***
	Post-Relevant HalfHours	−0.011**	−0.333***
		(−2.378)	(−91.710)
Ticker * Month	**Intercept**	***44.537******	***44.721******
		(114.610)	***(113.223)***
	Post-Relevant HalfHours	−0.038***	−0.399***
		=(−7.988)	(−109.804)
Ticker and Year	**Intercept**	***44.623******	***44.687******
		(1,019.048)	***(1,002.605)***
	Post-Relevant HalfHours	−0.016***	−0.320***
		(−3.036)	(−81.579)
Ticker and Half-Year	**Intercept**	***45.184******	***45.242******
		(1,031.151)	***(1,014.331)***
	Post-Relevant HalfHours	−0.018***	−0.333***
		(−3.458)	(−84.956)
Ticker and Quarter	**Intercept**	***46.555******	***46.627******
		(1,059.023)	***(1,041.791)***
	Post-Relevant HalfHours	−0.012**	−0.349***
		(−2.352)	(−89.224)
Ticker and Month	**Intercept**	***46.867******	***46.957******
		(1,052.597)	***(1,034.992)***
	Post-Relevant HalfHours	−0.003	−0.372***
		(−0.489)	(−95.395)

t-statistics are reported in parentheses. ***, **, and * denote two-tailed statistical significance at 1%, 5%, and 10% levels.
Positive (negative) actual associations at level 1, 5, and 10, indicated by light (dark) gray filling, with normal font, bold font, and bold & italic font.

effect of the interaction between the indicator variable, and as the case maybe, TICKER and/or time period of interest, in the regression of halfhour-level absolute idiosyncratic returns on TICKERs, time periods, and interactions — provides an **objective, systematic, and ordinal actual measure of market efficiency** for the relevant TICKER, time period, or TICKER-time period. Please note that this does not imply that greater volatility clustering, which can occur as a result of news clustering, implies less efficiency, because this chapter relies upon a controlled contrast between relevant window bins and control bins. In Chapter 7, we provide an ordinal direct measure of market efficiency for that security for that quarter as the negative of the positive part of the difference in quarterly means between absolute idiosyncratic returns for relevant halfhours and absolute idiosyncratic returns for control halfhours.

A database of systematic, independent, and objective characterizations of each TICKER-year, TICKER-halfyear, TICKER-quarter, and TICKER-month, and each year, halfyear, quarter, and month, January 2014 to September 2021, as statistically and actually significant efficient, statistically and actually significant inefficient, or otherwise, is available upon request from the author.

6.7.4 Impact of COVID-19

We find, as shown in Table 6.6, that capital markets during the first two to three months of the COVID-19 lockdowns (March and April, 2020) were statistically and actually significantly less efficient.

6.8 Conclusions

Analyzing all publicly traded U.S. stocks for January 2014 to September 2021, using high-frequency millisecond-level intraday data from TAQ, TRACE, I/B/E/S, and Capital IQ, using daily data from CRSP, Compustat, CRSP-Compustat Merged Database, and FRED, we found that all reaction, overreaction, correction, overcorrection, bounceback, etc., were systemically all out of the system within two hours after a potentially material event for all equities over January 2014 to September 2021. Therefore, it is imperative to use intraday data for event studies work for two reasons: (1) two hours are systemically sufficient to measure the impact of a potentially material event in question, and (2) if one were to use daily data, one would miss the impact of an event that reverts quickly, and/or worse yet, one could erroneously attribute the impact of entirely unrelated events to the potentially material event in question — please see, for instance, Li et al. (2015) and Altınkılıç and Hansen (2009). Thus, all previous event studies and market efficiency work using daily data, while of enormous and ground-breaking significance in the past, have only historical value now. Systematic, independent, and objective characterizations of each TICKER-year, TICKER-halfyear, TICKER-quarter, and TICKER-month, and each year, halfyear, quarter, and month, January 2014 to September 2021, as statistically and actually significant efficient, statistically and

TABLE 6.6 Fixed Effects on Objective, Systematic, and Ordinal Actual Measures of Market Efficiency, 2020

Control Variables	Fixed Effect	Measure of Market Efficiency: Based on Key Developments Abnormal Returns	Measure of Market Efficiency: Based on Earnings Announcements Abnormal Returns
Window * Month	2020-01	0.178** (2.369)	0.705*** (15.733)
Window * Month	2020-02	−0.751*** (−10.446)	−0.057 (−1.172)
Window * Month	2020-03	**−5.726*** (−72.115)**	−4.635*** (−110.695)
Window * Month	2020-04	−2.636*** (−38.034)	−1.658*** (−40.661)
Window * Month	2020-05	−1.864*** (−27.717)	−0.993*** (−21.968)
Window * Month	2020-06	−0.962*** (−13.323)	−0.400*** (−8.230)
Window * Month	2020-07	(−10.206) (−10.206)	(−5.959) (−5.959)
Window * Month	2020-08	−0.905*** (−12.376)	−0.043 (−0.922)
Window * Month	2020-09	−0.379*** (−4.621)	0.197*** (−3.658)
Window * Month	2020-10	−0.217*** (−3.127)	0.153*** (−3.504)
Window * Month	2020-11	−1.435*** (−18.736)	−0.534*** (−11.264)
Window * Month	2020-12	−1.062*** (−11.793)	0.290*** (−5.746)

t-statistics are reported in parentheses. ***, **, and * denote two-tailed statistical significance at 1%, 5%, and 10% levels.

Positive (negative) actual association at levels 1, 5, and 10, indicated by light (dark) gray filling, with normal font, bold font, and bold & italic font.

actually significant inefficient, or otherwise, are available upon request from the author. We found that capital markets during the first two to three months of the COVID-19 lockdown were statistically and actually significantly less efficient.

The next chapter, Chapter 7, uses excess returns in the two hours after the one hour including a potentially material event as a negative measure of efficiency of the market for the equity.

Appendix 6A

We use high-frequency millisecond-level intraday equity trading data from TAQ and high-frequency millisecond-level intraday fixed income security trading data from TRACE. We divide each trading day into 15 halfhours as follows: halfhour 0 for prior to 9:30 AM, halfhour 14 for after 4 PM, and halfhours 1-13 for each halfhour of the trading hours.

For each stock i, for each trading day, for each halfhour $\tau = \{0,1,...,14\}$ with positive volume, we calculate the Volume-Weighted Average Price

$$VWAP_{i,\tau} = \frac{\sum_{l \in \tau} \left[\begin{array}{c} (Trading\_Price_{i,l}) \\ \times (Equity\_Volume_{i,l}) \end{array} \right]}{\sum_{l \in \tau} (Equity\_Volume_{i,l})} \tag{6.27}$$

of trading prices, and then calculate the relevant continuously compounded return for halfhour τ

$$EqRet_{i,\tau} = \ln(VWAP_{i,\tau}) - \ln(VWAP_{i,\tau-1}) \tag{6.28}$$

where

$$Equity\_Volume_{i,\tau} \tag{6.29}$$

and

$$Fixed\_Income\_Volume_{i,\tau} \tag{6.30}$$

denote the equity volume and fixed income volume for TICKER i in halfhour τ.

We calculate the various weighted averages for equity returns as follows.

$$EqRet\_All\ Half\ Hour_{\tau} = \frac{\sum_{j} \left[\begin{array}{c} (EqRet\_TICKER\ Half\ Hour_{j,\tau}) \\ \times (Equity\_Volume_{j,\tau}) \end{array} \right]}{\sum_{j} (Equity\_Volume_{j,\tau})} \tag{6.31}$$

$$EqRet\_Nasdaq\ Half\ Hour_{i,\tau} = \frac{\sum_{j \in Nasdaq} \left[\begin{array}{c} (EqRet\_TICKER\ Half\ Hour_{j,\tau}) \\ \times (Equity\_Volume_{j,\tau}) \end{array} \right]}{\sum_{j \in Nasdaq} (Equity\_Volume_{j,\tau})} \tag{6.32}$$

$$EqRet\_NAICS3Dig\ Half\ Hour_{i,\tau} = \frac{\sum_{j \in NAICS\_3Digit} \left[\begin{array}{c} (EqRet\_TICKER\ Half\ Hour_{j,\tau}) \\ \times (Equity\_Volume_{j,\tau}) \end{array} \right]}{\sum_{j \in NAICS\_3Digit} (Equity\_Volume_{j,\tau})}$$

(6.33)

$$EqRet\_MCapDecile\,HalfHour_{i,\tau} = \frac{\sum_{j \in Market\_Cap\_Decile} \left[\begin{array}{c} (EqRet\_TICKER\,HalfHour_{j,\tau}) \\ \times (Equity\_Volume_{j,\tau}) \end{array} \right]}{\sum_{j \in Market\_Cap\_Decile} (Equity\_Volume_{j,\tau})} \tag{6.34}$$

$$EqRet\_IntraVtyDecile\,HalfHour_{i,\tau} = \frac{\sum_{j \in IntraDay\_Volatility\_Decile} \left[\begin{array}{c} (EqRet\_TICKER\,HalfHour_{j,\tau}) \\ \times (Equity\_Volume_{j,\tau}) \end{array} \right]}{\sum_{j \in IntraDay\_Volatility\_Decile} Equity\_Volume_{j,\tau}} \tag{6.35}$$

$$EqRet\_DivYieldDecile\,HalfHour_{i,\tau} = \frac{\sum_{j \in Dividend\_Yield\_Decile} \left[\begin{array}{c} (EqRet\_TICKER\,HalfHour_{j,\tau}) \\ \times (Equity\_Volume_{j,\tau}) \end{array} \right]}{\sum_{j \in Dividend\_Yield\_Decile} (Equity\_Volume_{j,\tau})} \tag{6.36}$$

$$EqRet\_BMRatioDecile\,HalfHour_{i,\tau} = \frac{\sum_{j \in Book\_to\_Market\_Ratio\_Decile} \left[\begin{array}{c} (EqRet\_TICKER\,HalfHour_{j,\tau}) \\ \times (Equity\_Volume_{j,\tau}) \end{array} \right]}{\sum_{j \in Book\_to\_Market\_Ratio\_Decile} (Equity\_Volume_{j,\tau})} \tag{6.37}$$

$$EqRet\_PERatioDecile\,HalfHour_{i,\tau} = \frac{\sum_{j \in Price\_to\_Earnings\_Ratio\_Decile} \left[\begin{array}{c} (EqRet\_TICKER\,HalfHour_{j,\tau}) \\ \times (Equity\_Volume_{j,\tau}) \end{array} \right]}{\sum_{j \in Price\_to\_Earnings\_Ratio\_Decile} (Equity\_Volume_{j,\tau})} \tag{6.38}$$

$$EqRet\_DERatioDecile\ HalfHour_{i,\tau} = \frac{\sum_{j \in Debt\_to\_Equity\_Ratio\_Decile} \begin{bmatrix} (EqRet\_TICKER\ HalfHour_{j,\tau}) \\ \times (Equity\_Volume_{j,\tau}) \end{bmatrix}}{\sum_{j \in Debt\_to\_Equity\_Ratio\_Decile} (Equity\_Volume_{j,\tau})} \tag{6.39}$$

For each fixed income security TICKER-CUSIP, we calculate the Volume-Weighted Average Yield (VWAY)

$$VWAY_{i,\tau} = FIYld\_TICKER\_CUSIP\_HalfHour_{i,\tau} = \frac{\sum_{l \in \tau} \begin{bmatrix} (Fixed\_Income\_Yield_{i,l}) \\ \times (Fixed\_Income\_Volume_{i,l}) \end{bmatrix}}{\sum_{l \in \tau} (Fixed\_Income\_Volume_{i,l})} \tag{6.40}$$

and for each TICKER, we calculate the simple average of VWAY over all CUSIPs corresponding to that TICKER. Since we are using yield-to-maturity (YTM) with traded prices for the FI securities, one has comparability across different coupons, maturities, and periodicities, thus, the following average is meaningful, and we use a simple average to avoid the volatility of TICKER-halfhour-yield because of substantially differing trading volumes. We are still left with other complexities such as seniority and convertibility, but we do not have these data.

$$FIYld\_TICKER\ HalfHour_{i,\tau} = \frac{\sum_{CUSIP \in TICKER} (FIYld\_TICKER\_CUSIP\_HalfHour_{i,\tau})}{\sum_{CUSIP \in TICKER} (1)} \tag{6.41}$$

$$FIYld\_All\ HalfHour_{\tau} = \frac{\sum_{j} \begin{bmatrix} (FIYld\_TICKER\ HalfHour_{j,\tau}) \\ \times (Fixed\_Income\_Volume_{j,\tau}) \end{bmatrix}}{\sum_{j} (Fixed\_Income\_Volume_{j,\tau})} \tag{6.42}$$

And

$$RiskFree_{\tau} = \text{Yield of T-Bill, 4-Week Maturity, for Date including HalfHour } \tau \tag{6.43}$$

$$NomBroadUSDIndex_{\tau} = \text{Nominal Broad U.S. Dollar Index for Date including HalfHour } \tau \tag{6.44}$$

References

Altınkılıç, O., and Hansen, R., 2009, "On the Information Role of Stock Recommendation Revisions," *Journal of Accounting and Economics*, 48, 17–36.

Aman, H., Beekes, W., Berkman, H., Bohmann, M., Bradbury, M., Chapple, E., Chang, M., Clout, V., Faff, R., Han, J., Hillier, D., Hodgson, A., Howeison, B., Jona, J., Linnenluecke, M., Loncan, T., McCredie, B., Michayluk, D., Mroczkowski, N., Pan, Z., Patel, V., Podolski, E., Soderstrom, N., Smith, T., Tanewski, G., Walsh, K., Wee, M., and Wright, S., 2019, "Responsible Science: Celebrating the 50-Year Legacy of Ball and Brown (1968) Using a Registration-Based Framework," *Pacific-Basin Finance Journal*, 56, 129–150.

Ball, R., 2017, "Fama, Fisher, Jensen, and Roll (1969): Retrospective Comments," In: Cochrane, J., and Moskowitz, T. (Eds.), *The Fama Portfolio*, pp. 203–212, Chicago, IL: University of Chicago Press.

Ball, R., and Brown, P., 1968, "An Empirical Evaluation of Accounting Income Numbers," *Journal of Accounting Research*, 6(2), 159–178.

Barclay, M., and Litzenberger, R., 1988, "Announcement Effects of New Equity Issues and the Use of Intraday Price Data," *Journal of Financial Economics*, 21, 71–99.

Bhattacharya, R., 2019, "Objective Measures of Market Efficiency; Applications to Securities Class Actions and Valuations," *Berkeley Business Law Journal*, 16, 249–266.

Bhattacharya, R., 2024, "Impact of COVID-19 on Market Efficiency," *Journal of Accounting Literature*, 48(1), 332–358.

Bhattacharya, R., Bial, J., and Evans, A., 2023, "It Is Imperative to Perform Event Studies Only with High-Frequency Intraday Data for Securities Litigations and Valuations," *Journal of International Business & Law*, 23(1), 1–28.

Bhattacharya, R., and Gupta, M., 2023, "Diligence, Objectivity, Quality, and Accuracy," *Journal of Accounting Literature*, 47(1), 1–30.

Bhattacharya, R., and Gupta, M., 2026, "Impact of Self-Regulation on Financial Markets," *Journal of Accounting Literature*. (https://doi.org/10.1108/JAL-09-2024-0266).

Bhattacharya, R., and O'Brien, S., 2015, "Arbitrage Risk and Market Efficiency: Applications to Securities Class Actions," *Santa Clara Law Review*, 55(3), 643–672.

Boehmer, E., and Kelley, E., 2009, "Institutional Investors and the Informational Efficiency of Prices," *Review of Financial Studies*, 22(9), 3563–3594.

Boehmer, E., and Wu, J., 2013, "Short Selling and the Price Discovery Process," *Review of Financial Studies*, 26(2), 287–322.

Bris, A., Goetzmann, W., and Zhu, N., 2007, "Efficiency and the Bear: Short Sales and Markets Around the World," *Journal of Finance*, 62(3), 1029–1079.

Brown, S., and Warner, J., 1985, "Using Daily Stock Returns: The Case of Event Studies," *Journal of Financial Economics*, 14(1), 3–31.

Budish, E., Cramton, P., and Shim, J., 2015, "The High-Frequency Trading Arms Race: Frequent Batch Auctions as a Market Design Response," *Quarterly Journal of Economics*, 130(4), 1547–1621.

Busse, J., and Green, T. C., 2002, "Market Efficiency in Real Time," *Journal of Financial Economics*, 65(3), 415–437.

Campbell, J., Lo, A., and MacKinlay, A. C., 1997, *The Econometrics of Financial Markets*, Princeton, NJ: Princeton University Press.

Cao, C., Liang, B., Lo, A., and Petrasek, L., 2018, "Hedge Fund Holdings and Stock Market Efficiency," *Review of Asset Pricing Studies*, 8(1), 77–116.

Chiang, C., Dai, W., Fan, J., Hong, H., and Tu, J., 2019, "Robust Measures of Earnings Surprises," *Journal of Finance*, 74(2), 943–983.

Chordia, T., Roll, R., and Subrahmanyam, A., 2005, "Evidence on the Speed of Convergence to Market Efficiency," *Journal of Financial Economics*, 76(2), 271–292.

Collins, D., and Kothari, S. P., 1989, "An Analysis of Intertemporal and Cross-Sectional Determinants of Earnings Response Coefficients," *Journal of Accounting and Economics*, 11(2–3), 143–181.

Cornell, B., and Rutten, J., 2006, "Market Efficiency, Crashes, and Securities Litigation," *Tulane Law Review*, 81(2), 443–472.

Dann, L., Mayers, D., and Raab, R., 1977, "Trading Rules, Large Blocks and the Speed of Adjustment," *Journal of Financial Economics*, 4, 3–22.

Davies, P. L., and Canes, M., 1978, "Stock Prices and the Publication of Second-Hand Information," *Journal of Business*, 51, 43–56.

Fama, E., 1970, "Efficient Capital Markets: A Review of Theory and Empirical Work," *Journal of Finance*, 25(2), 383–417.

Fama, E., Fisher, L., Jensen, M., and Roll, R., 1969, "The Adjustment of Stock Prices to New Information," *International Economic Review*, 10(1), 1–21.

Fama, E., and French, K., 1992, "The Cross-Section of Expected Stock Returns," *Journal of Finance*, 47(2), 427–465.

Fama, E., and French, K., 1993, "Common Risk Factors in the Returns on Stocks and Bonds," *Journal of Financial Economics*, 33(1), 3–56.

Fama, E., and French, K., 2015, "A Five-Factor Asset Pricing Model," *Journal of Financial Economics*, 116, 1–22.

Foster, F., and Viswanathan, S., 1996, "Strategic Trading When Agents Forecast the Forecasts of Others," *Journal of Finance*, 51(4), 1437–1478.

Graham, J. R., Koski, J., and Loewenstein, U., 2006, "Information Flow and Liquidity around Anticipated and Unanticipated Dividend Announcements," *Journal of Business*, 79, 2301–2336.

Greene, W., 2018, *Econometric Analysis*, Upper Saddle River, NJ: Pearson.

Grégoire, V., and Martineau, C., 2022, "How Is Earnings News Transmitted to Stock Prices?" *Journal of Accounting Research*, 60(1), 261–297.

Grossman, S., and Stiglitz, J., 1980, "On the Impossibility of Informationally Efficient Markets," *American Economic Review*, 70(3), 393–408.

Harris, L., 2003, *Trading & Exchanges: Market Microstructure for Practitioners*, New York, NY: Oxford University Press.

Hou, K., and Moskowitz, T., 2005, "Market Frictions, Price Delay, and the Cross-Section of Expected Returns," *Review of Financial Studies*, 18(3), 981–1020.

Jennings, R., and Starks, L., 1986, "Earnings Announcements, Stock Price Adjustment, and the Existence of Option Markets," *Journal of Finance*, 41(1), 107–125.

Jensen, M., 1978, "Some Anomalous Evidence Regarding Market Efficiency," *Journal of Financial Economics*, 6(2–3), 95–101.

Jiang, C., Likitapiwat, T., and McInish, T., 2012, "Information Content of Earnings Announcements: Evidence from After-Hours Trading," *Journal of Financial and Quantitative Analysis*, 47(6), 1303–1330.

Kaourma, T., Milidonis, A., Nishiotis, G., and Panayides, M. A., 2021, "News and Intraday Retail Investor Order Flow in Foreign Exchange Markets," *SSRN* (https://ssrn.com/abstract=3796753).

Kennedy, P., 2003, *A Guide to Econometrics*, Cambridge, MA: MIT Press.

Keown, A., and Pinkerton, J., 1981, "Merger Announcements and Insider Trading Activity: An Empirical Investigation," *Journal of Finance*, 36(4), 855–869.

Kim, S., Lin, J., and Slovin, M., 1997, "Market Structure, Informed Trading, and Analysts' Recommendations," *Journal of Financial and Quantitative Analysis*, 32, 507–524.

Kothari, S. P., 2001, "Capital Markets Research in Accounting," *Journal of Accounting and Economics*, 31(1–3), 105–231.

Kothari, S. P., So, E., and Verdi, R., 2016, "Analysts' Forecasts and Asset Pricing: A Survey," *Annual Review of Financial Economics*, 8, 197–219.

Kothari, S. P., and Warner, J., 2007, "Econometrics of Event Studies," In: Eckbo, E. (Ed.), *Handbook of Empirical Corporate Finance*, vol. 1, pp. 3–36, Amsterdam, The Netherlands: Elsevier/North-Holland.

Kyle, A., and Obizhaeva, A., 2016, "Market Microstructure Invariance: Empirical Hypotheses," *Econometrica*, 84(4), 1345–1404.

Li, E. X., Ramesh, K., Shen, M., and Wu, J. S., 2015, "Do Analyst Stock Recommendations Piggyback on Recent Corporate News? An Analysis of Regular-Hour and After-Hours Revisions," *Journal of Accounting Research*, 53, 821–861.

Loughran, T., and Ritter, J., 2000, "Uniformly Least Powerful Tests of Market Efficiency," *Journal of Financial Economics*, 55(3), 361–389.

Malkiel, B., 2003, "The Efficient Market Hypothesis and Its Critics, " *Journal of Economic Perspectives*, 17(1), 59–82.

Marshall, B., Nguyen, N., and Visaltanachoti, N., 2019, "A Note on Intraday Event Studies," *European Accounting Review*, 28(3), 605–619.

Martineau, C., 2022, "Rest in Peace Post-Earnings Announcement Drift," *Critical Finance Review*, 11(3–4), 613–646.

Matsumoto, D., Pronk, M., and Roelofsen, E., 2011, "What Makes Conference Calls Useful? The Information Content of Managers' Presentations and Analysts' Discussion Sessions," *The Accounting Review*, 86, 1383–1414.

McShane, B., and Gal, D., 2017, "Statistical Significance and the Dichotomization of Evidence," *Journal of the American Statistical Association*, 112(519), 885–895.

O'Hara, M., 1997, *Market Microstructure Theory*, Malden, MA: Blackwell Publishing.

Patell, J., and Wolfson, M., 1984, "The Intraday Speed of Adjustment of Stock Prices to Earnings and Dividend Announcements," *Journal of Financial Economics*, 13, 223–252.

Porta, R., Lakonishok, J., Shleifer, A., and Vishny, R., 1997, "Good News for Value Stocks: Further Evidence on Market Efficiency," *Journal of Finance*, 52(2), 859–874.

Rogers, J. L., Skinner, D. J., and Zechman, S. L., 2017, "Run EDGAR Run: SEC Dissemination in a High-Frequency World," *Journal of Accounting Research*, 55, 459–505.

Rosch, D., Subrahmanyam, A., and Dijk, M., 2017, "The Dynamics of Market Efficiency," *Review of Financial Studies*, 30(4), 1151–1187.

Saffi, P., and Sigurdsson, K., 2011, "Price Efficiency and Short Selling," *Review of Financial Studies*, 24(3), 821–852.

Saggu, A., 2022, "The Intraday Bitcoin Response to Tether Minting and Burning Events: Asymmetry, Investor Sentiment, and 'Whale Alerts' on Twitter," *Finance Research Letters*, 49, 103096.

Samuelson, P., 2009, "An Enjoyable Life Puzzling over Modern Finance Theory," *Annual Review of Financial Economics*, 1, 19–35.

Shleifer, A., 2000, *Inefficient Markets: An Introduction to Behavioral Finance*, New York, NY: Oxford University Press.

S&P, 2024, "Key Developments," *Global Market Intelligence* (https://www.marketplace.spglobal.com/en/datasets/key-developments-(15)).

Stambaugh, R., Yu, J., and Yuan, Y., 2015, "Arbitrage Asymmetry and the Idiosyncratic Volatility Puzzle," *Journal of Finance*, 70(5), 1903–1948.

Wooldridge, J., 2010, *Econometric Analysis of Cross Section and Panel Data*, Cambridge, MA: MIT Press.

Wooldridge, J., 2013, *Introductory Econometrics: A Modern Approach*, Mason, OH: South-Western Cengage Learning.

7
EQUITIES

7.1 Introduction

We use two different metrics — based on idiosyncratic responses to (a) "key developments" (as indicated by Standard & Poor's) and (b) earnings announcements and revisions, and analyst forecasts and revisions — with three separate 60-minute, 90-minute, and 120-minute announcement windows for each, based on event studies, controlling for intraday market equity returns, Nasdaq listing (indicator variable for Nasdaq listing = 1, for a Nasdaq-listed firm, and = 0, otherwise) equity returns, industry (3-digit NAICS Code) equity returns, market capitalization decile equity returns, intraday volatility decile equity returns, dividend decile equity returns, Fama-French Factors (Fama and French, 1992, 1993, 2015), decile equity returns, fixed income yield, and daily risk-free and foreign exchange rates, with high-frequency millisecond-level intraday data for equity, fixed income securities, earnings announcements and revisions, and analyst forecasts and revisions, on all publicly traded U.S. companies over January 2014 to September 2021, tens of trillions of observations (for perspective, the total number of stars in the Milky Way is estimated to be 100 billion, less than a hundredth of the number of observations analyzed in this book), about 25 TB of data (analyzing Big Data is not a scalable version of the programming that is done for smaller datasets), as separate objective, systematic, and ordinal actual measures of the efficiency of the market for a stock. The definition of "Big Data" has two schools of thought. The economist's perspective was probably best articulated by Scott Bauguess, then deputy chief economist at the U.S. Securities and Exchange Commission, in 2016: "data that takes more time to process than it took to create it" (Bauguess, 2016), please also see Goldstein et al. (2021, 2025) — we use about 25 TB

DOI: 10.4324/9781003608486-10

of data for this book — whereas the computer scientist's vision is more about techniques.

Kyle and Obizhaeva (2016) and Bhattacharya (2019) show that the questions raised in this chapter have ambiguous theoretical predictions, and we use the market microstructure models in these papers, detailed in the Appendix — please see the comprehensive literature surveys therein — to develop an eight-equation structural model that has (a) market efficiency as a function of exogenous factors, namely, year and quarter, dispersion in investor valuations (proxied by the quarterly standard deviation of analyst forecasts of earnings per share for the firm with "forecast period end date" in the current calendar quarter), short sales costs & constraints (proxied by the cost of a synthetic short sale, which is short one call option and long one put option, at the money, with the same expiration), and transaction costs & constraints (proxied by bid-ask spread), and endogenous market activities, namely, Kyle-Obizhaeva liquidity measure (Kyle and Obizhaeva, 2016), normalized short interest, analyst coverage, institutional ownership of equity, log of market capitalization, and log of shares outstanding, and (b) each endogenous market activity as a function of the exogenous factors and all other endogenous market activities. Analyzing all publicly traded U.S. stocks for January 2014 to September 2021, using high-frequency millisecond-level intraday data from TAQ, TRACE, I/B/E/S, and Capital IQ, using daily data from CRSP, Thomson Reuters, Compustat, CRSP-Compustat Merged Database, OptionMetrics, and FRED, we find that time have a statistically and actually insignificant impact on market efficiency, that investor valuation dispersion has a statistically significant but actually insignificant positive impact on market efficiency, that short sales costs & constraints have a statistically ambiguous and actually insignificant impact on market efficiency, and that transaction costs & constraints have a statistically and actually significant negative impact on market efficiency.

We use the panel nature of the data to identify appropriate instruments for the endogenous variables and for the variables that are measured with error, and we use Three Stage Least Squares and Errors in Variables to estimate this eight-equation structural model and test the hypotheses provided by the theory. We develop the methodology to calculate the total impact of a factor, which is the sum of the direct impact and the indirect impacts, and by using the Gaussian cumulative probability of the $Z\text{-}Score\,(x) = (x \; minus \; Mean\,(x)) \, / \, (Standard\; Deviation\,(x))$ of each variable (except for a classification or time variable), this is a rigorization of the number of standard deviations approach to interpretation of coefficients, which also implicitly assumes Gaussian distributions; thus, we make the impacts comparable, allowing a systematic and objective definition of actual significance, which is different from statistical significance — as detailed in Chapter 2, pretty much everything is statistically significant when working with huge datasets.

To motivate this chapter, consider the following example, described in Section 6.2: On September 18, 2018, at 11:42 AM U.S. Eastern, Bloomberg announced that "Tesla Inc. is under investigation by the Justice Department over public statements made by the company and Chief Executive Officer Elon Musk, according to two people familiar with the matter. The criminal probe is running alongside a previously reported civil inquiry by securities regulators," Schoenberg and Robinson (2018). Table 6.1 shows that the halfhour where the announcement took place and the following halfhour had substantial absolute returns, the following hour had substantial absolute returns, and an overwhelming majority of the following few hours had negligible absolute returns, and as shown in Chapter 6, all reaction, overreaction, correction, overcorrection, bounceback, etc., are almost all out of the system within two hours after a potentially material event. Therefore, it is imperative to use intraday data for event studies and market efficiency work; otherwise, one is capturing only noise that is irrelevant to a potentially material event in question, and worse yet, one can otherwise erroneously attribute the impact of events entirely unrelated to the potentially material event in question — please see, for instance, Li et al. (2105). Thus, all previous event studies and market efficiency work using daily data, while of enormous and ground-breaking significance in the past, have only historical value now — with the *caveat* that any empirical work has, of course, to be done within its data and computational constraints — for recent event studies using intraday data, please see, for instance, Saggu (2022), Kaourma et al. (2021), and Marshall et al. (2019), in reverse chronological order.

7.2 Literature Review and Hypothesis Development

A market is *semistrong efficient* if prices reflect all publicly available information — see, for example, Fama (1970), Jensen (1978), Grossman and Stiglitz (1980), Malkiel (2003), Porta et al. (1997), Harris (2003), Loughran and Ritter (2000), Shleifer (2000), Samuelson (2009), and Rosch et al. (2017). As has been recognized, by, for example, Fama et al. (1969), a market is efficient if "stock prices adjust very rapidly to new information" — this makes clear that calendar-time is relevant to a discussion of market efficiency whereas transaction-time is not, *per se*, relevant; please see Kyle and Obizhaeva (2016) for further details. Prices of securities adjust, *albeit* to varying extents, to new information; therefore, markets for securities are efficient in varying degrees — often referred to as *relative efficiency*; see, for example, Campbell et al. (1997) — please see, for instance, Cornell and Rutten (2006) and Bhattacharya and O'Brien (2015) for the role of market efficiency in securities litigation. For a description of the importance of relative efficiency for valuations (especially Mark-to-Market) and securities class actions (especially class certification), see Bhattacharya (2019). Other measures of market efficiency based on securities prices following random walks in efficient markets used by Cao et al. (2018) and Boehmer and Kelley (2009), the two purely empirical measures of market efficiency based on the asymmetry between positive and negative market returns used by Bris et al. (2007); the variance ratio measures of random walk (the last two methods were also used by Saffi and Sigurdsson (2011), please also see Campbell et al. (1997) for details); the friction measures of market efficiency (Hou and Moskowitz, 2005; Boehmer and Wu, 2013); and the mispricing score based on eleven return anomalies used by Stambaugh et al. (2015), are all **indirect measures** of market efficiency based on a posited positive correlation between each of these indirect measures and the actual efficiency of the market for a security, which is not *per se* relevant but relevant only in the absence of an actual measure of market efficiency. In this chapter, we use two metrics, with three variations on each, as separate, objective, ordinal, and **actual** measures of the efficiency of the market for a stock, which eliminates the need for the correlation-based measures referred to above — see Section 7.5.

According to the market microstructure literature, the questions raised in this chapter do not admit unambiguous theoretical answers and are, therefore, empirical questions. The impact of listing exchange on market quality has a distinguished history; see, for example, Dang et al. (2018), Hendershott and Moulton (2011), Diether et al. (2009), and Bennet and Wei (2006), where the theoretical and empirical results are indeterminate.

Lamont and Thaler (2003) say that "short sale constraints have long been recognized as crucial to the workings of efficient markets." For the importance of short sales costs & constraints, see most importantly, Miller (1977), and, more recently, Boehmer et al. (2019, 2020), Diamond and Verrecchia (1987), Drechsler and Drechsler (2021), Muravyev et al. (2022), Massa et al. (2015), Boehmer and Wu (2013), Saffi and Sigurdsson (2011), Boehmer et al. (2010), Goldstein and Guembel (2008), Bris et al. (2007), Boehme et al. (2006), Lamont and Stein (2004), Duffie et al. (2002), Jones and Lamont (2002), Dechow et al. (2001), Easley et al. (1998), Duffie (1996), and others. The overwhelming conclusion of the extant literature is that the impact of short sales costs & constraints is theoretically indeterminate and empirically ambiguous.

In order to appreciate how trading volume impacts market efficiency, one needs to understand why a trade occurs. In particular, as Wang (1994) points out, "investors trade among themselves because they are different," and, as Beaver (1968) points out, "volume reflects a lack of consensus regarding the price" — see, also, Miller (1977). As shown in Bhattacharya (2019), the dispersion in investor valuations and transaction costs & constraints determine trading volume, and therefore, trading volume is not a measure of liquidity, and has nothing whatsoever to do with market efficiency. In particular, Bhattacharya and O'Brien (2015) estimated a reduced form, and using arbitrage risk as the measure of market efficiency, came to the conclusion that market efficiency was not significantly positively related to trading volume — see also the extensive discussion there on the "conventional wisdom" and erroneous case law (especially *Cammer* Factor 1) regarding the dependence of market efficiency on trading volume.The relation of dispersions of investor valuations and transaction costs & constraints with market efficiency has been studied by, for instance, Bhattacharya (2019), Bhattacharya and O'Brien (2015), Loh (2010), O'Hara (1997), Stickel and Verrecchia (1994), Blume et al. (1994), Wang (1994), and Karpoff (1987). The conclusion of the extant literature is that the impacts on market efficiency of investor valuations and transaction costs & constraints are theoretically indeterminate and the empirical conclusions are not conclusive.

This chapter is firmly situated in these intellectual traditions and this discussion yields the following research hypotheses that are tested in this chapter:

Research Hypothesis 1: Market efficiency of equities improved over the time period under study.

Research Hypothesis 2: Market efficiency of equities is related to dispersions in investor valuations, short sales costs & constraints, and transaction costs & constraints of the equity of the issuing firm.

7.3 Description of Data

As in Section 6.5, we use data on all publicly traded U.S. stocks for January 2014 – September 2021. We use high-frequency millisecond-level intraday equity trading data from TAQ and high-frequency millisecond-level intraday fixed income security trading data from TRACE. We restrict attention to stocks corresponding to publicly traded firms that did not have more than one PERMNO or TICKER or 3-digit NAICS code during January 2014 to September 2021. We further restrict attention to stock-days that did not have splits, reverse splits, or dividends, and to stock-days that have positive closing price and positive shares outstanding and other restrictions, that had the following fields in CRSP: date, closing price, return, shares outstanding, trading volume, closing bid and ask, exchange membership, NAICS code, and had data on the following variables: high-frequency millisecond-level intraday analyst forecasts and revisions (from I/B/E/S), high-frequency millisecond-level intraday earnings announcements and revisions (from I/B/E/S), high-frequency millisecond-level intraday key developments (from S&P Global Capital IQ, Marketplace (2024)), daily data from Compustat-CRSP Merged Database, and daily data for T-Bill yields and Nominal Broad U.S. Dollar Index from Federal Reserve of St. Louis (FRED); in addition, we use institutional holdings (from Thomson Reuters), short interest (from Compustat), and daily options data from OptionMetrics. The sample is further restricted to the following:

- if $|yield| \leq 100\%$
- if $|EPS| \leq \$100$
- if $shrcd \in \{10, 11\}$
- if $ret \notin \{-44.0, -55.0, -66.0, -77.0, -88.0, -99.0\}$
- if $dlret \notin \{-55.0, -66.0, -88.0, -99.0\}$
- if $dlretx \notin \{-55.0, -66.0, -88.0, -99.0\}$
- if $dclrdt \neq 0$
- if $trtscd \neq 0$,
- if $nmsind \neq 0$
- if $vol \neq -99.0$
- if $prc > 0$
- if $bid > 0$
- if $ask > 0$
- if $vol > 0$
- if $shrout > 0$
- if $TICKER \neq ?$
- if $TICKER \neq ''$
- if $CUSIP \neq ''$
- if $substr(TICKER, 1, 4) \neq ZZZZ$;
- if $substr(CUSIP, 7, 1) \in \{0, 1, 2, 3, 4, 5, 6, 7, 8, 9\}$
- if $substr(CUSIP, 8, 1) \in \{0, 1, 2, 3, 4, 5, 6, 7, 8, 9\}$

For a small number of stock-days, there were multiple entries when sorted by TICKER, CUSIP, and date — for these stock-days, weighted averages were calculated using trading volume as weights. Compustat (including Capital IQ) data sources rely upon the S&P identification of GVKEY. The mapping of GVKEY to TICKER used by CRSP to match its data to Compustat was relied upon. We do not have access to intraday data for treasury yield and foreign exchange rates from FRED (we thank B. Ravikumar for his help on this matter).

In order to maintain the integrity of the linkages between the different sources of data we rely upon, we treat a missing observation as a missing observation — in particular, with number of analysts, short interest, and institutional ownership — not as a zero. For a small number of stock-days, we found multiple entries when sorted by TICKER, CUSIP, and date — for these stock-days, we calculate weighted averages using trading volume as weights. We do not have access to actual short sales costs & constraints data — dealing with missing data is one of the biggest challenges in empirical work, and appropriately proxying for the unavailable data is one of the innovations of this chapter, where we use the cost of a synthetic short sale (short one call option and long one put option, at the money, with the same expiration) as a measure of short sales costs & constraints for the underlying stock. Compustat (including Capital IQ) data sources rely upon the S&P identification of GVKEY. In this chapter, we rely upon the mapping of GVKEY to TICKER used by CRSP to match its data to Compustat. We do not have access to intraday data for treasury yield and foreign exchange rates from FRED. Table 6.1 provides comparisons of high-frequency millisecond-level intraday and daily data.

7.4 Event Studies

Since Fama et al. (1969) and Ball and Brown (1968), "hundreds of event studies have been conducted in the legal, financial economics, and accounting literatures... They test the impact, speed, and unbiasedness of the market's reaction to an event. In an efficient capital market, a security's price reaction to an event is expected to be immediate and subsequent price movement is expected to be unrelated to the event-period reaction," as pointed out by Kothari (2001).

In this chapter, we do *not* ascribe any directional component to any potentially material event, because it is impossible, without additional information or *ad hoc* judgment, to objectively determine the market's perception prior to any potentially material event and to determine whether a particular potentially material event was better-than-expected news, worse-than-expected news, or even a surprise at all. Colloquially speaking: Good news or bad news is not the relevant question here; and it requires subjective judgment to infer from the description of an event if market efficiency would require the price of the security to go up, down, or stay the same. To repeat the example from Chapter 6,

- FB closed on Thursday, July 11, 2019 at $201.23
- FB opened on Friday, July 12, 2019 at $199.68
- At 3:52 PM, Friday, July 12, 2019, news emerged that the U.S. Federal Trade Commission (FTC) planned to fine FB a record $5 billion for the Cambridge Analytica data scandal (Price, 2019)
- FB closed on Friday, July 12, 2019 at $204.87

- Increase of 1.8% over previous day's closing price
- Increase of 2.6% over current day's open price

- Even though the reported settlement amount was $2 billion more than the company had reserved for the settlement

In his judgment in *Petrobras Securities Litigation,* (United States District Court, Southern District of New York, 1:14-cv-09662-JSR, February 2, 2016), Judge Jed Rakoff discussed the issue of directionality and stringently criticized the subjective and *ad hoc* marking of directionality of events in the dueling "expert" reports — for example, one of the "experts" in the litigation used the presence or absence of the text "corrupt" in the description of an event to determine the relevant directionality of a potentially material event.

7.4.1 HalfHour-Level Averages

We use high-frequency millisecond-level intraday equity trading data from TAQ and high-frequency millisecond-level intraday fixed income security trading data from TRACE. As discussed earlier, calendar-time, rather than transaction-time, is relevant for market efficiency discussions — see Kyle and Obizhaeva (2016) for further details. Therefore, we divide each trading day into 15 "halfhours" as follows: halfhour 0 for prior to 9:30 AM U.S. Eastern, halfhours 1–13 for each halfhour of the trading hours 9:30 AM–4 PM U.S. Eastern, and halfhour 14 for after 4 PM U.S. Eastern — this aggregation of millisecond-level high-frequency data onto halfhours is a simplification; in particular, you should consider aggregating millisecond-level high-frequency data into, say, every ten minutes, fifteen minutes, or hour. For each stock i, for each trading day, for each halfhour $\tau = \{0, 1, ..., 14\}$ with positive volume, we calculate the Volume-Weighted Average Price of trading prices, and then calculate the relevant continuously compounded return for halfhour τ. We calculate the various weighted averages for equity returns. For each fixed income security TICKER-CUSIP, we calculate the volume-weighted average yield (VWAY) and for each TICKER, we calculate the simple average of VWAY over all CUSIPs corresponding to that TICKER. Since we are using yield-to-maturity (YTM) with traded prices for the FI securities, one has comparability across different coupons, maturities, and periodicities, thus, the following average is meaningful, and we use a simple average to avoid the volatility of TICKER-halfhour-yield because of substantially differing trading volumes, and we calculate the various weighted averages for FI returns. These calculations are detailed in Appendix 7B and Table 6.2 provides halfhour-level summary statistics. One is still left with other complexities such as seniority and convertibility, but we do not have these data.

7.4.2 Market Model

The return of equity i in halfhour τ,

$$
\begin{aligned}
& EqRet_{i,\tau} \\
= \; & \pi \\
& + (\pi_{EqRet\_AllHalfHour}) (EqRet\_AllHalfHour_{\tau}) \\
& + (\pi_{EqRet\_NasdaqHalfHour}) (EqRet\_NasdaqHalfHour_{i,\tau}) \\
& + (\pi_{EqRet\_NAICS3DigHalfHour}) (EqRet\_NAICS3DigHalfHour_{i,\tau}) \\
& + (\pi_{EqRet\_MCapDecileHalfHour}) (EqRet\_MCapDecileHalfHour_{i,\tau}) \\
& + (\pi_{EqRet\_IntraVtyDecileHalfHour}) (EqRet\_IntraVtyDecileHalfHour_{i,\tau}) \\
& + (\pi_{EqRet\_DivYieldDecileHalfHour}) (EqRet\_DivYieldDecileHalfHour_{i,\tau}) \\
& + (\pi_{EqRet\_BMRatioDecileHalfHour}) (EqRet\_BMRatioDecileHalfHour_{i,\tau}) \\
& + (\pi_{EqRet\_PERatioDecileHalfHour}) (EqRet\_PERatioDecileHalfHour_{i,\tau}) \\
& + (\pi_{EqRet\_DERatioDecileHalfHour}) (EqRet\_DERatioDecileHalfHour_{i,\tau}) \\
& + (\pi_{FIYld\_AllHalfHour}) (FIYld\_AllHalfHour_{\tau}) \\
& + (\pi_{RiskFree}) (RiskFree_{\tau}) \\
& + (\pi_{NomBroadUSDIndex}) (NomBroadUSDIndex_{\tau}) \\
& + IdioEqRet_{i,\tau} \qquad (7.1)
\end{aligned}
$$

The market model above controls for intraday market equity returns, Nasdaq listing (indicator variable for Nasdaq listing $=$ 1 for a Nasdaq-listed firm, and $=$ 0 otherwise) equity returns, industry (3-digit NAICS Code) equity returns, market capitalization decile equity returns, intraday volatility decile equity returns, dividend decile equity returns, Fama-French Factor decile equity returns, fixed income yield, and daily risk-free and foreign exchange rates. Having the risk-free rate as a regressor in the market model is a generalization of using excess return of equity = return of equity minus risk-free rate, in all calculations. We do not have access to intraday data for foreign exchange rates or T-bill yields. Table 6.3 provides summary statistics of the market model variables.

7.4.3 Controlled Contrasts

Fix universe of analysis $\mathfrak{T}$ as set of halfhours. Fix announcement window length $n \geq 1$, relevant window length $m \geq 1$, and post-relevant window length $l \geq 1$. Consider a fixed time period t (e.g., quarter, month) as set of halfhours.

Consider event identification method $\mathfrak{I} \subseteq \mathfrak{T}$ as potentially material events; in this chapter, we use two separate identification methods for potentially material events: (a) key developments (KD), identified by S&P Global CapitalIQ, and (b) earnings announcements and revisions, and analyst forecasts and revisions (EA). For potentially material event at halfhour $T \in t \cap \mathfrak{T}$,

$$\boldsymbol{AnnouncementHalfHours}\,(T, n) = \{T, \ldots, T+n-1\} \tag{7.2}$$

(n halfhours),

$$\boldsymbol{RelevantHalfHours}\,(T, n, m) = \{T+n, \ldots, T+n+m-1\} \tag{7.3}$$

(m halfhours), and, therefore,

$$\begin{aligned} \boldsymbol{TreatmentHalfHours}\,(T, n, m) &= \boldsymbol{AnnouncementHalfHours}\,(T, n) \\ &\quad \cup \boldsymbol{RelevantHalfHours}\,(T, n, m) \\ &= \{T, \ldots, T+n+m-1\} \end{aligned} \tag{7.4}$$

($n + m$ halfhours), and therefore, $\boldsymbol{ControlHalfHours}(t, n, m, \mathfrak{T})$ consists of each halfhour in t that is not a treatment halfhour for any potentially material event at halfhour $T \in t \cap \mathfrak{T}$, and, therefore, equals

$$\{\tau \in t : \tau \notin \{T, \ldots, T+n+m-1\}\,, \forall T \in t \cap \mathfrak{T}\} \tag{7.5}$$

And, finally, the list of post-relevant halfhours for event at time halfhour $T \in t$ is

$$\boldsymbol{PostRelevantHalfHours}\,(T, n, m, l) = \{T+n+m, \ldots, T+n+m+l-1\} \tag{7.6}$$

(l halfhours immediately following the relevant halfhours).

For fixed n, m, l, a systematic and controlled comparison between

$$\left|\widehat{IdioEqRet_{i,\tau}}\right| \tag{7.7}$$

for

$$\boldsymbol{PostRelevantHalfHours}\,(T, n, m, l) \tag{7.8}$$

versus

$$\left|\widehat{IdioEqRet_{i,\tau}}\right| \tag{7.9}$$

for

$$\boldsymbol{ControlHalfHours}(t, n, m, \mathfrak{T}) \tag{7.10}$$

is a measure of whether there is any systemic impact of the potentially material event T beyond the announcement and relevant halfhours — the rational expectations models say that the speed of impact probably depends on whether there is further information that has not been disclosed; please see Foster and Viswanathan (1996) and O'Hara (1997), for example. If this contrast is not statistically and actually significant positive, it would demonstrate that (1) $(n + m)$ halfhours are systemically sufficient to measure the impact over l halfhours of a potentially material event in question, and (2) if one were to use daily data, one would miss the impact of an event that reverts quickly, and/or worse yet, one could erroneously attribute the impact of entirely unrelated events to the potentially material event in question, and, therefore, although of enormous historical significance, events studies using daily data would be entirely unreliable today. Chapter 6 shows that for all publicly traded U.S. stocks for January 2014 to September 2021 (the date limits are set purely by constraints on availability and storage), idiosyncratic reactions are systemically all out of the system within two hours after a potentially material event. Of course, some events have longer horizons, but that is the nature of idiosyncrasies versus a strongly persuasive systemic result.

For fixed n, m, a systematic and controlled contrast between

$$\left|Idio\widehat{EqRet}_{i,T}\right| \tag{7.11}$$

for

$$\boldsymbol{RelevantHalfHours}\,(T, n, m) \tag{7.12}$$

versus

$$\left|Idio\widehat{EqRet}_{i,T}\right| \tag{7.13}$$

for

$$\boldsymbol{ControlHalfHours}(t, n, m, \mathfrak{T}) \tag{7.14}$$

would be necessary for an objective, systematic and ordinal direct measure of market efficiency with n announcement halfhours and m relevant halfhours. From the theory, it follows that

$$\left|Idio\widehat{EqRet}_{i,T}\right| \tag{7.15}$$

should be weakly higher for relevant halfhours than for control halfhours, and therefore, in this chapter, for each of the identification systems for potentially material events (KD and EA), for each n, m, for each security i, for each quarter t, we provide an ordinal direct **measure of market efficiency** for that security for that quarter as the negative of the positive chapter of the difference in quarterly means between absolute idiosyncratic returns for relevant halfhours and absolute idiosyncratic returns for control halfhours. In Chapter 6, an objective, systematic and ordinal direct measure of market efficiency for that security for that quarter is provided as the negative of the coefficient of the interaction between the indicator variable for relevant halfhours versus control halfhours, and as the case maybe, TICKER and/or time period of interest, in a fixed effects regression of halfhour-level absolute idiosyncratic returns on TICKERs, time periods, and interactions.

7.4.4 Windows

Depending on how one determines a potentially material event, we have two separate paths of research on event studies. For the first path, we rely upon the marking of an event as a "Key Development" by Capital IQ, a service of Standard & Poor's, to study as a potentially material event for the issuing firm. For each such Key Development for the firm, for each relevant window halfhour following the Key Development, we calculate the absolute idiosyncratic return — we call this the *Key Developments Idiosyncratic Response (KDIR) for that Key Development.* As mentioned earlier, we do not try to ascribe any directional component to any Key Development, because it is impossible to objectively and systematically determine from publicly available data the market's perceptions immediately prior to the relevant Key Development and, therefore, it is impossible to objectively and systematically determine whether a particular Key Development was better-than-expected news, worse-than-expected news, or just expected — even if one were to make an *ad hoc* inference about the directionality of the surprise information in a key development, with errors about market information at the time of a key development, from its description, one would compound error upon error, each of which would be non-identifiable.

The second path studies the impact of earnings announcements and forecasts on security prices and has a long and distinguished history; see, for instance, Ball and Brown (1968), Collins and Kothari (1989), and Kothari and Warner (2007). For each earnings announcement, earnings announcement revision, analyst forecast, and analyst forecast revision, we calculate the absolute idiosyncratic return for each relevant window halfhour following the earnings announcement, earnings announcement revision, analyst forecast, and analyst forecast revision — we call this the *Earnings Announcements Idiosyncratic Response (EAIR) for that* earnings announcement, earnings announcement revision, analyst forecast, or analyst forecast revision. Please note that the actual announced earnings or forecast or its deviation from "consensus" forecasts does not enter into our calculations; for a number of reasons. Any estimate of the market's "consensus" prediction of the EPS at the point of an EPS announcement, whether it is by using mean/medians of analyst forecasts, or by using valuation models, is sensitive to the methodology used to estimate the market's perception and the deviation from it — see, for instance, Chiang et al. (2019) for detailed descriptions of biases in the calculation of deviation from consensus; also see Kothari et al. (2016) for a comprehensive survey of the literature on quality, bias, and predictability of earnings forecasts — treating these analyst forecasts as representing market information at the time of a potentially material event, with forecast errors, would need compounding error upon error, each of which would be non-identifiable. The impact of analyst incentives on analyst forecasts is beyond the scope of this chapter — please see Bhattacharya and Gupta (2023), for instance — it is impossible to objectively and systematically measure how much information about an actual earnings announcement or forecast leaked out before the actual announcement or forecast, and, therefore, it is impossible to objectively and systematically measure, from publicly available data, the "surprise" component of the earnings announcement or forecast.

7.5 Measures of Market Efficiency

As exemplified in Table 6.1, and as convincingly demonstrated in Chapter 6, absolute idiosyncratic returns for the six trading halfhours following each relevant window following each potentially material event are not actually significantly higher than all non-announcement and all non-relevant window trading halfhours; i.e., all reaction, overreaction, correction, overcorrection, bounceback, etc., are all systemically out of the system within a few hours after a potentially material event. Therefore, it is imperative to use intraday data for event studies and market efficiency work; otherwise, one is capturing only noise that is irrelevant to a potentially material event in question, and worse yet, one can otherwise erroneously attribute the impact of events entirely unrelated to the potentially material event in question — please see, for instance, Li et al. (2015). Thus, all previous event studies and market efficiency work using daily data, while of enormous and ground-breaking significance in the past, have only historical value now.

Given the *a priori* analytical framework of the market model and the announcement window length $n \geq 1$ and relevant window length $m \geq 1$, for an event T, a systematic and controlled comparison of

$$|IdioEqRet_{i,\tau}| \tag{7.16}$$

for

$$\begin{aligned} &\boldsymbol{RelevantHalfHours}\,(T, n, m) \\ &\quad = \{T + n, T + n + m - 1\} \end{aligned} \tag{7.17}$$

versus

$$|IdioEqRet_{i,\tau}| \tag{7.18}$$

for

$$\textbf{\textit{ControlHalfHours}}(t, n, m, \mathfrak{T}) = \{\tau \in t : \tau \notin \{T, T+1, \ldots, T+n+m-1\}, \forall T \in t \cap \mathfrak{T}\} \tag{7.19}$$

in time period t (halfhours that are not announcement or relevant halfhours), would be a measure of noise impact of the potentially material event, the negative of which is a systematic, objective, and ordinal measure of market efficiency.

Given an announcement window of

$$n \in \{2, 3, 4\} \tag{7.20}$$

halfhours, in a given quarter t, for each stock i, for each potentially material event at halfhour T in quarter t, we consider the announcement halfhours to be

$$\tau \in \{T, \ldots, T+n-1\} \tag{7.21}$$

and the relevant halfhours to be

$$\tau \in \{T+n, T+n+1\} \tag{7.22}$$

We calculate the absolute idiosyncratic return

$$|IdioEqRet_{i,\tau}| \tag{7.23}$$

for each halfhour τ, and for each stock i. A systematic and controlled comparison between

$$|IdioEqRet_{i,\tau}| \tag{7.24}$$

for relevant halfhours versus control halfhours (non-announcement and non-relevant halfhours) would be necessary for an objective, systematic and ordinal actual measure of market efficiency. From the theory, it follows that

$$|IdioEqRet_{i,\tau}| \tag{7.25}$$

should be weakly higher for relevant halfhours than for control halfhours, and therefore, for each of KDIR and EAIR, for each announcement window length, for each security i, for each quarter t, the ordinal actual **measure of market efficiency** for that security for that quarter is:

$$-\max\left\{0, \begin{array}{c} Mean_{\tau \in \text{Quarter } t, \tau \in \text{Relevant Window}} |IdioEqRet_{i,\tau}| \\ minus \\ Mean_{\tau \in \text{Quarter } t, \tau \in \text{Control Window}} |IdioEqRet_{i,\tau}| \end{array}\right\} \tag{7.26}$$

The above aggregations of our halfhourly idiosyncratic returns computations onto quarters is intended purely as a simplification and to test our hypotheses; in particular, you should consider aggregating halfhourly computations onto, say, daily, weekly, monthly (as we have done in Chapter 6), halfyearly, or annually, or for that matter, any test period. In this chapter, we use these two different and objective metrics (based on KDIR or EAIR) with three variations in length of announcement period (30 minutes, 60 minutes, or 90 minutes), as separate, ordinal, systematic, and objective actual measures of the efficiency of the market for a stock in a quarter — summarized in Table 7.1.

In Chapter 6, an objective, systematic and ordinal *per se* measure of market efficiency is provided by the negative of the coefficient of the interaction between the indicator variable for relevant windows versus non-announcement and non-relevant window bins, and as the case maybe, TICKER and/or time period of interest, in a fixed effects regression of bin-level absolute idiosyncratic returns.

7.6 Structural Empirical System

We estimate the following structural system at the stock-quarter level, where i represents the stock and t represents the quarter. The characterization of a variable as exogenous or endogenous is based on its role in the particular financial market of a security. Market efficiency is modeled as a function of exogenous factors, namely, year and quarter, dispersion in investor valuations (proxied by the quarterly standard deviation of analyst forecasts of earnings and earnings revisions per share for the firm with "forecast period end date" in the current calendar quarter), short sales costs & constraints (proxied by the cost of a synthetic short sale, which is short one call option and long one put option, at the money, with the same expiration), and transaction costs & constraints (proxied by bid-ask spread), and endogenous market activities, namely, Kyle-Obizhaeva liquidity measure (Kyle and Obizhaeva, 2016) normalized short interest, analyst coverage, institutional ownership of equity, log of market capitalization, and log of shares outstanding. Each endogenous market activity is a function of the exogenous factors and all other endogenous market activities.

7.6.1 Notations

- $MEff_{i,t}$ = each separate ordinal measure of market efficiency for stock i in quarter t, described in Section 6.7.3

Exogenous factors:

- YQ_t = number corresponding to quarter t
- $Disp_{i,t}$ = dispersion in investor valuations for stock i in quarter t

TABLE 7.1 Correlations between Quarterly Ordinal Measures of Market Efficiency, January 2014 to September 2021

			Quarterly Ordinal Measure of Market Efficiency Based On					
			Key Developments Idiosyncratic Response			Earnings Announcements Idiosyncratic Response		
			60-Minute Announcement Window	90-Minute Announcement Window	120-Minute Announcement Window	60-Minute Announcement Window	90-Minute Announcement Window	120-Minute Announcement Window
Quarterly Ordinal Measure of Market Efficiency Based On	Key Developments Idiosyncratic Response	60-Minute Announcement Window	1.000	0.921	0.793	0.176	0.171	0.173
	Earnings Announcements Idiosyncratic Response	90-Minute Announcement Window	0.921	1.000	0.892	0.186	0.183	0.193
		120-Minute Announcement Window	0.793	0.891	1.000	0.158	0.168	0.169
		60-Minute Announcement Window	0.176	0.186	0.158	1.000	0.938	0.821
		90-Minute Announcement Window	0.171	0.183	0.168	0.937	1.000	0.924
		120-Minute Announcement Window	0.173	0.193	0.169	0.821	0.924	1.000

- $SSCC_{i,t}$ = short sales costs & constraints of stock i in quarter t
- $TrCC_{i,t}$ = transaction costs & constraints of stock i in quarter t

Endogenous market activities:

- $Nasdaq_{i,t}$ = Indicator variable for Nasdaq listing of firm i at time t, = 1, for a Nasdaq-listed firm, and = 0, otherwise
- $KOLiq_{i,t}$ = Kyle-Obizhaeva liquidity of stock i in quarter t = cube root [(quarterly mean of halfhour dollar volume)/(square of quarterly standard deviation of halfhour returns)]
- $NormSI_{i,t}$ = quarterly mean of (monthly short interest)/(daily shares outstanding) of stock i in quarter t
- $AnCov_{i,t}$ = number of EPS forecasts and revisions by analysts for firm i with "forecast period end date" in quarter t
- $NormInst_{i,t}$ = quarterly mean of institutional ownership percentage point in stock i in quarter t
- $logMCap_{i,t}$ = quarterly mean of natural logarithm of daily market capitalization for stock i in quarter t
- $logShrsOut_{i,t}$ = quarterly mean of natural logarithm of daily shares outstanding for stock i in quarter t

7.6.2 Market Efficiency

Market efficiency is modeled as a linear function of the exogenous factors, namely, year and quarter, dispersion in investor valuations, short sales costs & constraints, and transaction costs & constraints, and endogenous market activities, namely, Kyle-Obizhaeva liquidity measure (Kyle and Obizhaeva, 2016), normalized short interest, analyst coverage, institutional ownership of equity, log of market capitalization, and log of shares outstanding, as follows.

$$
\begin{aligned}
MEff_{i,t} = \; & \varrho + \gamma_{YQ} YQ_t \\
& + \gamma_{Disp} Disp_{i,t} + \gamma_{SSCC} SSCC_{i,t} \\
& + \gamma_{TrCC} TrCC_{i,t} + \gamma_{Nasdaq} Nasdaq_{i,t} \\
& + \gamma_{KOLiq} KOLiq_{i,t} + \gamma_{NormSI} NormSI_{i,t} \\
& + \gamma_{AnCov} AnCov_{i,t} + \gamma_{NormInst} NormInst_{i,t} \\
& + \gamma_{LogMCap} logMCap_{i,t} + \gamma_{logShrsOut} logShrsOut_{i,t} \\
& + \delta_{i,t}
\end{aligned}
\tag{7.27}
$$

7.6.3 Endogenous Market Activities

Each endogenous market activity, namely, Kyle-Obizhaeva liquidity measure, normalized short interest, analyst coverage, institutional ownership of equity, log of market capitalization, and log of shares outstanding, is modeled as a function of the exogenous factors and all other endogenous market activities, based on the market microstructure models in Kyle and Obizhaeva (2016) and Bhattacharya (2019), leading to seven equations, of which one is presented below, and the rest are detailed in Appendix 7C.

$$\begin{aligned} Nasdaq_{i,t} = {} & \beta + \beta_{YQ}YQ_t \\ & + \beta_{Disp}Disp_{i,t} + \beta_{SSCC}SSCC_{i,t} \\ & + \beta_{TrCC}TrCC_{i,t} + \beta_{KOLiq}KOLiq_{i,t} \\ & + \beta_{NormSI}NormSI_{i,t} + \beta_{AnCov}AnCov_{i,t} \\ & + \beta_{NormInst}NormInst_{i,t} + \beta_{logMCap}logMCap_{i,t} \\ & + \beta_{logShrsOut}logShrsOut_{i,t} \\ & + \varkappa_{i,t} \end{aligned} \tag{7.28}$$

7.7 Methodology

Because some of the exogenous factors are measured with error, they are instrumented (detailed in Section 2.15) in accordance with the Errors-In-Variables method, see Section 5.5.4, Greene (2018), Griliches and Hausman (1986) and Hausman and Taylor (1981) for details.

7.7.1 Transaction Costs & Constraints

We use normalized bid-ask spread, the quarterly mean of daily relative bid-ask spread where daily relative bid-ask spread = (daily closing best ask – daily closing best bid)/(mid-point of daily closing best bid and best ask), as a proxy for transaction costs — see, for instance, Hasbrouck (2009).

7.7.2 Short Sales Costs & Constraints

We do not have access to actual data on short sales costs & constraints — we have tried many times, with very influential deans of business schools, as well as C.E.O.s of investment banks, but since the Global Financial Crisis, such data have become essentially unavailable to a researcher. Ofek et al. (2004) and Cremers and Weinbaum (2010) are examples of papers that use proprietary data on rebate rates and spreads. Dealing with missing or unavailable data is one of the biggest challenges in empirical work, and appropriately proxying for the unavailable data is one of the innovations of this chapter. In particular, we use the cost of a synthetic short sale (short one call option and long one put option, at the money, with the same expiration) as a measure of short sales costs & constraints for the underlying stock — please note that this implies that the analyses in this chapter are restricted to firms that have traded options written on their equities, and one can see the significant resulting reduction in the number of observations in the summary statistics in Table 7.2; please see, Evans et al. (2009), Lamont and Thaler (2003), and Geczy et al. (2002) — as follows:

- Consider all options with strike prices within $\mp 2.5\%$ of underlying price — we do sensitivity analyses for $\mp 0.5\%$ and $\mp 5\%$, and the results stay qualitatively the same
- Calculate best ask for put minus best bid for call
- Restrict to positive
- Calculate weighted (by volume) average
- Normalize by underlying price

7.7.3 Dispersions of Investor Valuations

The dispersion of investor valuations, which is also a function of the level of uncertainty within the market about the particular firm i in quarter t, is proxied by calculating the quarterly standard deviation of analyst forecasts and analyst forecast revisions of earnings per share (EPS) for firm i, restricted to forecasts and revisions between $-\$100$ per share and $+\$100$ per share, for the firm i with each "forecast period end date" in the current calendar quarter t.

Table 7.2 provides summary statistics for all exogenous factors and endogenous market activities referred to above.

We use Three Stage Least Squares (3SLS) and Errors in Variables (EiV) to account for the endogeneities and simultaneities in our model. Please see Liu and Saraiva (2019), Kahouli (2018), and Lee et al. (2016), in reverse chronological order, for robustness of this methodology. In particular, "under conditional homoskedasticity, GMM reduces to 3SLS if the set of instrumental variables is common to all equations." Kahouli (2018).

7.7.4 Instruments

In a system of equations $Y = X\beta + \varepsilon$, for a vector W to be an instrument, it is required that **Strong First Stage:** $Cov(W, X) \neq 0$, and **Exclusion Restriction:** $Cov(W, \varepsilon) = 0$ — in other words, the unexplained part ("residual") ε of the regression needs to be uncorrelated with the instrument — this *does not* require that the regressand Y itself be uncorrelated with the instrument. As Wooldridge (2010) points out, most of the problems with using instrumental variables arise in small samples, which, obviously, is not the case in this chapter. Wooldridge

TABLE 7.2 All Exogenous Factors and Endogenous Market Activities, at Year-Quarter Level, January 2014 to September 2021

Regressor	Mean	Standard Deviation	Upper Quartile	Median	Lower Quartile
Year-Quarter	16.000	9.092	24.000	16.000	8.000
Nasdaq Listing	0.621	0.485	1.000	1.000	0.000
Short Sales Costs & Constraints	0.025	0.036	0.024	0.016	0.013
Investor Valuation Dispersions	20.466	9.598	27.639	20.788	13.187
Transaction Costs & Constraints	0.005	0.009	0.004	0.001	0.000
Kyle-Obizhaeva Liquidity Measure	3,773.516	4,334.302	4,938.349	2,440.097	1,108.995
Normalized Short Interest	0.045	0.055	0.057	0.025	0.012
Analyst Coverage	354.044	476.418	405.000	198.000	88.000
Institutional Ownership of Equity	0.668	0.349	0.893	0.745	0.446
Log of Market Capitalization	20.768	2.138	22.199	20.771	19.246
Log of Shares Outstanding	17.709	1.384	18.530	17.609	16.803
T-Bill Daily Yield, 4-Week Maturity	0.698%	0.827%	1.414%	0.234%	0.038%
Nominal Broad USD Index, Daily	110.904	6.943	115.701	112.373	109.627

(2010) points out that "asymptotically, we can do no worse, and can often do better, using a larger set of valid instruments." Given these two critical qualifications, we consider in this chapter the following instrumentation categories together to ensure that our conclusions are not sensitive to particular information assumptions. In panel data econometrics, there are two popular categories of autochthonous instruments.

1. **Cross-Sectional Instruments**: Instrument a variable $X_{i,t}$ by combination(s) of $X_{j,t}, j \neq i$. Cross-sectional variables (such as corresponding variables for other geographies) have been used as instruments by, for instance, Hausman et al. (1994) and the validity of such instrumentation depends on the assumption that

the corresponding cross-sectional variables are correlated with the instrumented variable because of cost (or other) commonalities in the time period of interest but are not influenced by the idiosyncrasies of the stock (or geography) of interest in the particular time period. In particular, we use, as cross-sectional instrument, the average across the cross section excluding the particular variable, i.e., for variable $X_{(i,j),t}$ such that $\#\{k \neq (i,j)\} > 0$, we use $average_{k \neq (i,j)}(X_{k,t})$ as instrument.

2. **Time Series Instruments.** Instrument a variable $X_{i,t}$ by its lag(s) $X_{i,t-1}, X_{i,t-2}, \ldots$ The use of lags as instruments depends on two implicit assumptions: (a) lack of serial correlation, see, for example, Greene (2018), and (b) weak rational expectations, see, for example, Hansen and Singleton (1982); Wintoki et al. (2012) and Roberts and Whited (2011) show that the traditional statistical tests for the use of lagged variables in panel estimation are not particularly useful, so we do not use them in this chapter. In particular, we use as time series instrument the first lag of the relevant variable, i.e., for variable $X_{i,t}$, we use $X_{i,t-1}$ as instrument.

7.7.5 *Actual Significance*

As described in Section 2.5, when dealing with large numbers of observations, we replace each variable x, except for each classification or time variable, by its normalization

$$\Phi\left(Z\text{-}Score\left(x\right)\right) = \Phi\left(\frac{x - Mean\left(x\right)}{StDev\left(x\right)}\right) \tag{7.29}$$

where Φ is the cumulative probability of a standard Gaussian random variable. Actual significance at positive (negative) level is denoted by light (dark) shading. Actual significance at level 1 is indicated by regular font, actual significance at level 5 by bold font, and actual significance at level 10 by bold and italic font. Please see Aman et al. (2019) for a robust defense of "responsible science," that science needs to have integrity and relevance.

7.8 Total Impact of Each Exogenous Factor

As detailed in Section 2.7, the total impact of each exogenous factor ($ExogFactor$) on market efficiency ($MEff$) is given by the corresponding (cross-equation) total derivative as follows (please see Appendix 7D for details).

$$\begin{aligned}\frac{\mathbf{d}MEff}{\mathbf{d}ExogFactor} = & \frac{\partial MEff}{\partial ExogFactor} \\ & + \frac{\partial MEff}{\partial Nasdaq}\frac{\mathbf{d}Nasdaq}{\mathbf{d}ExogFactor} + \frac{\partial MEff}{\partial KOLiq}\frac{\mathbf{d}KOLiq}{\mathbf{d}ExogFactor} \\ & + \frac{\partial MEff}{\partial NormSI}\frac{\mathbf{d}NormSI}{\mathbf{d}ExogFactor} + \frac{\partial MEff}{\partial AnCov}\frac{\mathbf{d}AnCov}{\mathbf{d}ExogFactor} \\ & + \frac{\partial MEff}{\partial NormInst}\frac{\mathbf{d}NormInst}{\mathbf{d}ExogFactor} + \frac{\partial MEff}{\partial logMCap}\frac{\mathbf{d}logMCap}{\mathbf{d}ExogFactor} \\ & + \frac{\partial MEff}{\partial logShrsOut}\frac{\mathbf{d}logShrsOut}{\mathbf{d}ExogFactor} \end{aligned} \tag{7.30}$$

We perform each of our analyses for January 2014 to September 2021 and testing separately for each factor, we find, as shown in Table 7.3, that year-quarter has a statistically and actually insignificant impact on market efficiency, that investor valuation dispersion has a statistically significant but actually insignificant positive impact on market efficiency, that short sales costs & constraints have a statistically ambiguous and actually insignificant impact on market efficiency, and that transaction costs & constraints have a statistically and actually significant negative impact on market efficiency.

7.9 Conclusions

In this chapter, we used two different metrics, with three separate 60-minute, 90-minute, and 120-minute announcement windows for each, based on event studies, controlling for intraday market equity returns, Nasdaq listing equity returns, industry (3-digit NAICS Code) equity returns, market capitalization decile equity returns, intraday volatility decile equity returns, dividend decile equity returns, Fama-French Factor decile equity returns, fixed income yield, and daily risk-free and foreign exchange rates, with high-frequency millisecond-level intraday data for equity, fixed income securities, earnings announcements and revisions, and analyst forecasts and revisions, on all publicly traded U.S. companies over January 2014 to September 2021, tens of trillions of observations (for perspective, the total number of stars in the Milky Way is estimated to be 100 billion, less than a hundredth of the number of observations analyzed in this book), about 25 TB of data), as separate objective, systematic, and actual ordinal measures of the efficiency of the market for a stock, clearly demonstrating the irrelevance of other non-actual measures that are based on posited correlations with actual market efficiency. Chapter 6 showed that it is imperative to use intraday data for event studies and market efficiency work. Kyle and Obizhaeva (2016) and Bhattacharya (2019) showed that the questions raised here have indeterminate theoretical predictions, and we used the

TABLE 7.3 Total Impact of Exogenous Factors on Market Efficiency of Equities, January 2014 to September 2021

	Measure of Market Efficiency Based On					
	Key Developments Abnormal Returns			**Earnings Announcements Abnormal Returns**		
	60-Minute Announcement Window	**90-Minute Announcement Window**	**120-Minute Announcement Window**	**60-Minute Announcement Window**	**90-Minute Announcement Window**	**120-Minute Announcement Window**
Total Derivative of Market Efficiency with respect to						
Year and Quarter	−0.009**	−0.005	−0.005	−0.013***	0.000	0.000
	(5.25797)	(1.74360)	(1.71215)	(9.94765)	(0.00156)	(0.00016)
Investor Valuation	0.402**	0.326**	0.386**	0.638***	0.637***	0.488***
Dispersions	(5.91617)	(4.03368)	(5.45424)	(14.70271)	(19.64527)	(9.76243)
Short Sales Costs	4.469***	2.597***	1.863**	−0.947	−0.669	−0.790
& Constraints	(31.94526)	(11.22648)	(5.56389)	(1.40808)	(0.94063)	(1.11248)
Transaction Costs	−3.049**	−4.095***	**−5.352*****	(1.37435)	(7.81964)	(8.77787)
& Constraints	(5.65592)	(10.99511)	**(18.80001)**	(1.37435)	(7.81964)	(8.77787)

χ^2-statistics are reported in parentheses. ***, ** and * denote two-tailed statistical significance at 1%, 5% and 10% levels.
Positive (negative) actual association at levels 1, 5, and 10, indicated by light (dark) gray filling, with normal font, bold font, and bold & italic font.

market microstructure models in these papers to develop an eight-equation structural model that has (a) market efficiency as a function of exogenous factors, namely, year and quarter, dispersion in investor valuations, short sales costs & constraints, and transaction costs & constraints, and endogenous market activities, namely, Kyle-Obizhaeva liquidity measure, normalized short interest, analyst coverage, institutional ownership of equity, log of market capitalization, and log of shares outstanding; and (b) each endogenous market activity as a function of the exogenous factors and all other endogenous market activities. Analyzing Big Data is not a scalable version of the programming that is done for smaller datasets. The definition of "Big Data" has two schools of thought. The economist's perspective was probably best articulated by Scott Bauguess, then deputy chief economist at the U.S. Securities and Exchange Commission, in 2016: "data that takes more time to process than it took to create it" (Bauguess, 2016), please also see Goldstein et al. (2025, 2021) — we use about 25 TB of data for this book — whereas the computer scientist's vision is more about techniques.

We used the panel nature of the data to identify appropriate instruments for the endogenous variables and for the variables that are measured with error, and we used Three Stage Least Squares (3SLS) and Errors in Variables (EiV) to estimate this eight-equation structural model and test the hypotheses provided by the theory. We developed the methodology to calculate the total impact of a factor which is the sum of the direct impact and the indirect impacts, and by using the Gaussian cumulative distribution of the $Z\text{-}Score\,(x) = (x\ minus\ Mean\,(x))\,/\,(Standard\ Deviation\,(x))$ of each variable (except for a classification or time variable), we made the impacts comparable, thus allowing a systematic and objective definition of actual significance. Using high-frequency millisecond-level intraday data from TAQ, TRACE, I/B/E/S, and Capital IQ, using daily data from CRSP, Thomson Reuters, Compustat, CRSP-Compustat Merged Database, OptionMetrics, and FRED, we found that, for all publicly traded U.S. stocks for January 2014 to September 2021, time has a statistically and actually insignificant impact on market efficiency, that investor valuation dispersion has a statistically significant but actually insignificant positive impact on market efficiency, that short sales costs & constraints have a statistically ambiguous and actually insignificant impact on market efficiency, and that transaction costs & constraints has a statistically and actually significant negative impact on market efficiency.

Chapter 8 uses excess returns in the two hours after the one hour including a potentially material event as a negative measure of efficiency of the market for the fixed income security.

Appendix

Appendix 7A: Summary Statistics

To motivate this chapter, consider the following example: On September 18, 2018, at 11:42 AM U.S. Eastern, Bloomberg announced that "Tesla Inc. is under investigation by the Justice Department over public statements made by the company and Chief Executive Officer Elon Musk, according to two people familiar with the matter. The criminal probe is running alongside a previously reported civil inquiry by securities regulators," Schoenberg and Robinson (2018). We divide each trading day into 15 "halfhours" as follows: halfhour 0 for prior to 9:30 AM U.S. Eastern, halfhours 1–13 for each halfhour of the trading hours 9:30 AM to 4 PM U.S. Eastern, and halfhour 14 for after 4 PM U.S. Eastern. For this motivating example, we use the actual absolute returns, not the absolute idiosyncratic returns that we describe later. For TSLA, over June 30, 2010 to May 12, 2023, the mean and standard deviation of daily returns were 0.144% and 3.599%, and therefore, the mean and standard deviation of halfhourly returns were 0.010% and 0.929%. **For this particular example**, we consider a halfhourly return to be substantial in absolute terms if

$$\begin{aligned} HalfHourlyReturn &\notin (MeanHalfHourlyReturn \\ &\mp 1\ StDevHalfHourlyReturn) \\ &= (-0.920\%, +0.939\%) \end{aligned} \tag{7.31}$$

In Table 6.1, the "halfhours" with substantial positive (negative) halfhourly returns are filled in light (dark) gray, and the halfhours that saw no substantial absolute returns are without filling, and as one can see from Table 6.1, all reaction, overreaction, correction, overcorrection, bounceback, etc., were almost all out of the system within two hours after the potentially material event.

Appendix 7B: HalfHour-Level Averages

We use high-frequency millisecond-level intraday equity trading data from TAQ and high-frequency millisecond-level intraday fixed income security trading data from TRACE. We divide each trading day into 15 halfhours as follows: halfhour 0 for prior to 9:30 AM, halfhour 14 for after 4 PM, and halfhours 1–13 for each halfhour of the trading hours.

For each stock i, for each trading day, for each halfhour $\tau = \{0,1,...,14\}$ with positive volume, we calculate the Volume-Weighted Average Price

$$VWAP_{i,\tau} = \frac{\sum_{l \in \tau} \left[\begin{array}{c} (Trading\_Price_{i,l}) \\ \times (Equity\_Volume_{i,l}) \end{array} \right]}{\sum_{l \in \tau} (Equity\_Volume_{i,l})} \tag{7.32}$$

of trading prices, and then calculate the relevant continuously compounded return for halfhour τ

$$EqRet_{i,\tau} = \ln\left(VWAP_{i,\tau}\right) - \ln\left(VWAP_{i,\tau-1}\right) \tag{7.33}$$

where

$$Equity\_Volume_{i,\tau} \tag{7.34}$$

and

$$Fixed\_Income\_Volume_{i,\tau} \tag{7.35}$$

denote the equity volume and fixed income volume for TICKER i in halfhour τ.

We calculate the various weighted averages for equity returns as follows.

$$EqRet\_AllDateHalfhour_{\tau} = \frac{\sum_{j}\left[\begin{array}{c}(EqRet\_TICKERDateHalfhour_{j,\tau})\\ \times (Equity\_Volume_{j,\tau})\end{array}\right]}{\sum_{j}(Equity\_Volume_{j,\tau})} \tag{7.36}$$

$$EqRet\_NasdaqDateHalfhour_{i,\tau} = \frac{\sum_{j\in Nasdaq}\left[\begin{array}{c}(EqRet\_TICKERDateHalfhour_{j,\tau})\\ \times (Equity\_Volume_{j,\tau})\end{array}\right]}{\sum_{j\in Nasdaq}(Equity\_Volume_{j,\tau})} \tag{7.37}$$

$$\begin{aligned} &EqRet\_NAICS3DigDateHalfhour_{i,\tau} \\ &= \frac{\sum_{j\in NAICS\text{-}3Digit}\left[\begin{array}{c}(EqRet\_TICKERDateHalfhour_{j,\tau})\\ \times (Equity\_Volume_{j,\tau})\end{array}\right]}{\sum_{j\in NAICS\text{-}3Digit}(Equity\_Volume_{j,\tau})} \end{aligned} \tag{7.38}$$

$$\begin{aligned} &EqRet\_MCapDecileDateHalfhour_{i,\tau} \\ &= \frac{\sum_{j\in Market\text{-}Cap\text{-}Decile}\left[\begin{array}{c}(EqRet\_TICKERDateHalfhour_{j,\tau})\\ \times (Equity\_Volume_{j,\tau})\end{array}\right]}{\sum_{j\in Market\text{-}Cap\text{-}Decile}(Equity\_Volume_{j,\tau})} \end{aligned} \tag{7.39}$$

$$EqRet\_IntraVtyDecileDateHalfhour_{i,\tau} = \frac{\sum_{j \in IntraDay\text{-}Volatility\text{-}Decile} \begin{bmatrix} (EqRet\_TICKERDateHalfhour_{j,\tau}) \\ \times (Equity\_Volume_{j,\tau}) \end{bmatrix}}{\sum_{j \in IntraDay\text{-}Volatility\text{-}Decile} Equity\_Volume_{j,\tau}} \tag{7.40}$$

$$EqRet\_DivYieldDecileDateHalfhour_{i,\tau} = \frac{\sum_{j \in Dividend\text{-}Yield\text{-}Decile} \begin{bmatrix} (EqRet\_TICKERDateHalfhour_{j,\tau}) \\ \times (Equity\_Volume_{j,\tau}) \end{bmatrix}}{\sum_{j \in Dividend\text{-}Yield\text{-}Decile} (Equity\_Volume_{j,\tau})} \tag{7.41}$$

$$EqRet\_BMRatioDecileDateHalfhour_{i,\tau} = \frac{\sum_{j \in Book\text{-}to\text{-}Market\text{-}Ratio\text{-}Decile} \begin{bmatrix} (EqRet\_TICKERDateHalfhour_{j,\tau}) \\ \times (Equity\_Volume_{j,\tau}) \end{bmatrix}}{\sum_{j \in Book\text{-}to\text{-}Market\text{-}Ratio\text{-}Decile} (Equity\_Volume_{j,\tau})} \tag{7.42}$$

$$EqRet\_PERatioDecileDateHalfhour_{i,\tau} = \frac{\sum_{j \in Price\text{-}to\text{-}Earnings\text{-}Ratio\text{-}Decile} \begin{bmatrix} (EqRet\_TICKERDateHalfhour_{j,\tau}) \\ \times (Equity\_Volume_{j,\tau}) \end{bmatrix}}{\sum_{j \in Price\text{-}to\text{-}Earnings\text{-}Ratio\text{-}Decile} (Equity\_Volume_{j,\tau})} \tag{7.43}$$

$$EqRet\_DERatioDecileDateHalfhour_{i,\tau} = \frac{\sum_{j \in Debt\text{-}to\text{-}Equity\text{-}Ratio\text{-}Decile} \begin{bmatrix} (EqRet\_TICKERDateHalfhour_{j,\tau}) \\ \times (Equity\_Volume_{j,\tau}) \end{bmatrix}}{\sum_{j \in Debt\text{-}to\text{-}Equity\text{-}Ratio\text{-}Decile} (Equity\_Volume_{j,\tau})} \tag{7.44}$$

For each fixed income security TICKER-CUSIP, we calculate the volume-weighted average yield (VWAY)

$$VWAY_{i,\tau} = FIYld\_TICKER\_CUSIP\_Date\_HalfHour_{i,\tau} = \frac{\sum_{l\in\tau}\left[\begin{array}{c}(Fixed\_Income\_Yield_{i,l}) \\ \times (Fixed\_Income\_Volume_{i,l})\end{array}\right]}{\sum_{l\in\tau}(Fixed\_Income\_Volume_{i,l})} \tag{7.45}$$

and for each TICKER, we calculate the simple average of VWAY over all CUSIPs corresponding to that TICKER. Since we are using yield-to-maturity (YTM) with traded prices for the FI securities, one has comparability across different coupons, maturities, and periodicities, thus, the following average is meaningful, and we use a simple average to avoid the volatility of TICKER-halfhour-yield because of substantially differing trading volumes. We are still left with other complexities such as seniority and convertibility, but we do not have these data.

$$FIYld_{i,\tau} = \frac{\sum_{CUSIP\in TICKER}(FIYld\_TICKER\_CUSIP\_Date\_HalfHour_{i,\tau})}{\sum_{CUSIP\in TICKER}(1)} \tag{7.46}$$

$$FIYld\_AllDateHalfhour_{\tau} = \frac{\sum_{j}\left[\begin{array}{c}(FIYld\_TICKERDateHalfhour_{j,\tau}) \\ \times (Fixed\_Income\_Volume_{j,\tau})\end{array}\right]}{\sum_{j}(Fixed\_Income\_Volume_{j,\tau})} \tag{7.47}$$

And

$$RiskFree_{\tau} = \text{Yield of T-Bill, 4-Weeks Maturity, for Date including HalfHour } \tau \tag{7.48}$$

$$NomBroadUSDIndex_{\tau} = \text{Nominal Broad U.S. Dollar Index for Date including HalfHour } \tau \tag{7.49}$$

Appendix 7C: Structural System

Market efficiency is modeled as a linear function of the exogenous factors and endogenous market activities as follows.

$$
\begin{aligned}
MEff_{i,t} = \; & \varrho + \gamma_{YQ} YQ_t \\
& + \gamma_{Disp} Disp_{i,t} + \gamma_{SSCC} SSCC_{i,t} + \gamma_{TrCC} TrCC_{i,t} \\
& + \gamma_{Nasdaq} Nasdaq_{i,t} + \gamma_{KOLiq} KOLiq_{i,t} + \gamma_{NormSI} NormSI_{i,t} \\
& + \gamma_{AnCov} AnCov_{i,t} + \gamma_{NormInst} NormInst_{i,t} \\
& + \gamma_{LogMCap} logMCap_{i,t} + \gamma_{logShrsOut} logShrsOut_{i,t} \\
& + \delta_{i,t} \qquad (7.50)
\end{aligned}
$$

Each endogenous market activity is modeled as a linear function of exogenous factors and other endogenous market activities, based on the market microstructure models in Kyle and Obizhaeva (2016) and Bhattacharya (2019), leading to the following seven equations.

$$
\begin{aligned}
Nasdaq_{i,t} = \; & \beta + \beta_{YQ} YQ_t \\
& + \beta_{Disp} Disp_{i,t} + \beta_{SSCC} SSCC_{i,t} \\
& + \beta_{TrCC} TrCC_{i,t} + \beta_{KOLiq} KOLiq_{i,t} \\
& + \beta_{NormSI} NormSI_{i,t} + \beta_{AnCov} AnCov_{i,t} \\
& + \beta_{NormInst} NormInst_{i,t} + \beta_{logMCap} logMCap_{i,t} \\
& + \beta_{logShrsOut} logShrsOut_{i,t} \\
& + \varkappa_{i,t} \qquad (7.51)
\end{aligned}
$$

$$
\begin{aligned}
KOLiq_{i,t} = \; & \alpha + \alpha_{YQ} YQ_t \\
& + \alpha_{Disp} Disp_{i,t} + \alpha_{SSCC} SSCC_{i,t} \\
& + \alpha_{TrCC} TrCC_{i,t} + \alpha_{Nasdaq} Nasdaq_{i,t} \\
& + \alpha_{NormSI} NormSI_{i,t} + \alpha_{AnCov} AnCov_{i,t} \\
& + \alpha_{NormInst} NormInst_{i,t} + \alpha_{logMCap} logMCap_{i,t} \\
& + \alpha_{logShrsOut} logShrsOut_{i,t} \\
& + \varepsilon_{i,t} \qquad (7.52)
\end{aligned}
$$

$$
\begin{aligned}
NormSI_{i,t} = \; & \theta + \theta_{YQ} YQ_t \\
& + \theta_{Disp} Disp_{i,t} + \theta_{SSCC} SSCC_{i,t} \\
& + \theta_{TrCC} TrCC_{i,t} + \theta_{Nasdaq} Nasdaq_{i,t} \\
& + \theta_{KOLiq} KOLiq_{i,t} + \theta_{NormInst} NormInst_{i,t} \\
& + \theta_{AnCov} AnCov_{i,t} + \theta_{logMCap} logMCap_{i,t} \\
& + \theta_{logShrsOut} logShrsOut_{i,t} \\
& + \eta_{i,t} \qquad (7.53)
\end{aligned}
$$

$$
\begin{aligned}
AnCov_{i,t} \quad = \quad & \zeta + \zeta_{YQ} YQ_{i.t} \\
& + \zeta_{Disp} Disp_{i,t} + \zeta_{SSCC} SSCC_{i,t} \\
& + \zeta_{TrCC} TrCC_{i,t} + \zeta_{Nasdaq} Nasdaq_{i,t} \\
& + \zeta_{KOLiq} KOLiq_{i,t} + \zeta_{NormSI} NormSI_{i,t} \\
& + \zeta_{NormInst} NormInst_{i,t} + \zeta_{logMCap_{i,t}} logMCap_{i,t} \\
& + \zeta_{logShrsOut} logShrsOut_{i,t} \\
& + \vartheta_{i,t}
\end{aligned} \tag{7.54}
$$

$$
\begin{aligned}
NormInst_{i,t} \quad = \quad & \psi + \psi_{YQ} YQ_{t} \\
& + \psi_{Disp} Disp_{i,t} + \psi_{SSCC} SSCC_{i,t} \\
& + \psi_{TrCC} TrCC_{i,t} + \psi_{Nasdaq} Nasdaq_{i,t} \\
& + \psi_{KOLiq} KOLiq_{i,t} + \psi_{NormSI} NormSI_{i,t} \\
& + \psi_{AnCov} AnCov_{i,t} + \psi_{logMCap_{i,t}} logMCap_{i,t} \\
& + \psi_{logShrsOut} logShrsOut_{i,t} \\
& + \nu_{i,t}
\end{aligned} \tag{7.55}
$$

$$
\begin{aligned}
logMCap_{i,t} \quad = \quad & \xi + \xi_{YQ} YQ_{t} \\
& + \xi_{TrCC} TrCC_{i,t} + \xi_{SSCC} SSCC_{i,t} \\
& + \xi_{Disp} Disp_{i,t} + \xi_{Nasdaq} Nasdaq_{i,t} \\
& + \xi_{KOLiq} KOLiq_{i,t} + \xi_{NormSI} NormSI_{i,t} \\
& + \xi_{AnCov} AnCov_{i,t} + \xi_{NormInst} NormInst_{i,t} \\
& + \xi_{logShrsOut} logShrsOut_{i,t} \\
& + \upsilon_{i,t}
\end{aligned} \tag{7.56}
$$

$$
\begin{aligned}
logShrsOut_{i,t} \quad = \quad & \omega + \omega_{YQ} YQ_{t} \\
& + \omega_{Disp} Disp_{i,t} + \omega_{SSCC} SSCC_{i,t} \\
& + \omega_{TrCC} TrCC_{i,t} + \omega_{Nasdaq} Nasdaq_{i,t} \\
& + \omega_{KOLiq} KOLiq_{i,t} + \omega_{NormSI} NormSI_{i,t} \\
& + \omega_{AnCov} AnCov_{i,t} + \omega_{NormInst} NormInst_{i,t} \\
& + \omega_{logMCap} logMCap_{i,t} \\
& + \varsigma_{i,t}
\end{aligned} \tag{7.57}
$$

Appendix 7D: Total Impact of Each Exogenous Factor

Following Section 2.7, the total impact of each exogenous factor on market efficiency is given by the corresponding (cross-equation) total derivative as follows.

$$
\begin{aligned}
\frac{\mathbf{d}MEff}{\mathbf{d}YQ} &= \frac{\partial MEff}{\partial YQ} \\
&+ \frac{\partial MEff}{\partial Nasdaq}\frac{\mathbf{d}Nasdaq}{\mathbf{d}YQ} + \frac{\partial MEff}{\partial KOLiq}\frac{\mathbf{d}KOLiq}{\mathbf{d}YQ} \\
&+ \frac{\partial MEff}{\partial NormSI}\frac{\mathbf{d}NormSI}{\mathbf{d}YQ} + \frac{\partial MEff}{\partial AnCov}\frac{\mathbf{d}AnCov}{\mathbf{d}YQ} \\
&+ \frac{\partial MEff}{\partial NormInst}\frac{\mathbf{d}NormInst}{\mathbf{d}YQ} + \frac{\partial MEff}{\partial logMCap}\frac{\mathbf{d}logMCap}{\mathbf{d}YQ} \\
&+ \frac{\partial MEff}{\partial logShrsOut}\frac{\mathbf{d}logShrsOut}{\mathbf{d}YQ} \\
&= \gamma_{YQ} \\
&+ \gamma_{Nasdaq}\beta_{YQ} + \gamma_{KOLiq}\alpha_{YQ} \\
&+ \gamma_{NormSI}\theta_{YQ} + \gamma_{AnCov}\zeta_{YQ} \\
&+ \gamma_{NormInst}\psi_{YQ} + \gamma_{logMCap}\xi_{YQ} \\
&+ \gamma_{logShrsOut}\omega_{YQ}
\end{aligned} \tag{7.58}
$$

$$
\begin{aligned}
\frac{\mathbf{d}MEff}{\mathbf{d}Disp} &= \frac{\partial MEff}{\partial Disp} \\
&+ \frac{\partial MEff}{\partial Nasdaq}\frac{\mathbf{d}Nasdaq}{\mathbf{d}Disp} + \frac{\partial MEff}{\partial KOLiq}\frac{\mathbf{d}KOLiq}{\mathbf{d}Disp} \\
&+ \frac{\partial MEff}{\partial NormSI}\frac{\mathbf{d}NormSI}{\mathbf{d}Disp} + \frac{\partial MEff}{\partial AnCov}\frac{\mathbf{d}AnCov}{\mathbf{d}Disp} \\
&+ \frac{\partial MEff}{\partial NormInst}\frac{\mathbf{d}NormInst}{\mathbf{d}Disp} + \frac{\partial MEff}{\partial logMCap}\frac{\mathbf{d}logMCap}{\mathbf{d}Disp} \\
&+ \frac{\partial MEff}{\partial logShrsOut}\frac{\mathbf{d}logShrsOut}{\mathbf{d}Disp} \\
&= \gamma_{Disp} \\
&+ \gamma_{Nasdaq}\beta_{Disp} + \gamma_{KOLiq}\alpha_{Disp} \\
&+ \gamma_{NormSI}\theta_{Disp} + \gamma_{AnCov}\zeta_{Disp} \\
&+ \gamma_{NormInst}\psi_{Disp} + \gamma_{logMCap}\xi_{Disp} \\
&+ \gamma_{logShrsOut}\omega_{Disp}
\end{aligned} \tag{7.59}
$$

$$\begin{aligned}\frac{\mathbf{d}MEff}{\mathbf{d}SSCC} &= \frac{\partial MEff}{\partial SSCC} \\ &+\frac{\partial MEff}{\partial Nasdaq}\frac{\mathbf{d}Nasdaq}{\mathbf{d}SSCC}+\frac{\partial MEff}{\partial KOLiq}\frac{\mathbf{d}KOLiq}{\mathbf{d}SSCC} \\ &+\frac{\partial MEff}{\partial NormSI}\frac{\mathbf{d}NormSI}{\mathbf{d}SSCC}+\frac{\partial MEff}{\partial AnCov}\frac{\mathbf{d}AnCov}{\mathbf{d}SSCC} \\ &+\frac{\partial MEff}{\partial NormInst}\frac{\mathbf{d}NormInst}{\mathbf{d}SSCC}+\frac{\partial MEff}{\partial logMCap}\frac{\mathbf{d}logMCap}{\mathbf{d}SSCC} \\ &+\frac{\partial MEff}{\partial logShrsOut}\frac{\mathbf{d}logShrsOut}{\mathbf{d}SSCC} \\ &= \gamma_{SSCC} \\ &+\gamma_{Nasdaq}\beta_{SSCC}+\gamma_{KOLiq}\alpha_{SSCC} \\ &+\gamma_{NormSI}\theta_{SSCC}+\gamma_{AnCov}\zeta_{SSCC} \\ &+\gamma_{NormInst}\psi_{SSCC}+\gamma_{logMCap}\xi_{SSCC} \\ &+\gamma_{logShrsOut}\omega_{SSCC}\end{aligned} \tag{7.60}$$

$$\begin{aligned}\frac{\mathbf{d}MEff}{\mathbf{d}TrCC} &= \frac{\partial MEff}{\partial TrCC} \\ &+\frac{\partial MEff}{\partial Nasdaq}\frac{\mathbf{d}Nasdaq}{\mathbf{d}TrCC}+\frac{\partial MEff}{\partial KOLiq}\frac{\mathbf{d}KOLiq}{\mathbf{d}TrCC} \\ &+\frac{\partial MEff}{\partial NormSI}\frac{\mathbf{d}NormSI}{\mathbf{d}TrCC}+\frac{\partial MEff}{\partial AnCov}\frac{\mathbf{d}AnCov}{\mathbf{d}TrCC} \\ &+\frac{\partial MEff}{\partial NormInst}\frac{\mathbf{d}NormInst}{\mathbf{d}TrCC}+\frac{\partial MEff}{\partial logMCap}\frac{\mathbf{d}logMCap}{\mathbf{d}TrCC} \\ &+\frac{\partial MEff}{\partial logShrsOut}\frac{\mathbf{d}logShrsOut}{\mathbf{d}TrCC} \\ &= \gamma_{TrCC} \\ &+\gamma_{Nasdaq}\beta_{TrCC}+\gamma_{KOLiq}\alpha_{TrCC} \\ &+\gamma_{NormSI}\theta_{TrCC}+\gamma_{AnCov}\zeta_{TrCC} \\ &+\gamma_{NormInst}\psi_{TrCC}+\gamma_{logMCap}\xi_{TrCC} \\ &+\gamma_{logShrsOut}\omega_{TrCC}\end{aligned} \tag{7.61}$$

References

Aman, H., Beekes, W., Berkman, H., Bohmann, M., Bradbury, M., Chapple, E., Chang, M., Clout, V., Faff, R., Han, J., Hillier, D., Hodgson, A., Howeison, B., Jona, J., Linnenluecke, M., Loncan, T., McCredie, B., Michayluk, D., Mroczkowski, N., Pan, Z., Patel, V., Podolski, E., Soderstrom, N., Smith, T., Tanewski, G., Walsh, K., Wee, M., and Wright, S., 2019, "Responsible Science: Celebrating the 50-Year Legacy of Ball and Brown (1968) Using a Registration-Based Framework," *Pacific-Basin Finance Journal*, 56, 129–150.

Ball, R., and Brown, P., 1968, "An Empirical Evaluation of Accounting Income Numbers," *Journal of Accounting Research*, 6(2), 159–178.

Bauguess, S., 2016, "Has Big Data Made Us Lazy?" *U.S. Securities and Exchange Commission*, October 21, 2016 (https://www.sec.gov/newsroom/speeches-statements/bauguess-american-accounting-association-102116).

Beaver, W., 1968, "The Information Content of Annual Earnings Announcements," *Journal of Accounting Research*, 6, 67–92.

Bennett, P., and Wei, L., 2006, "Market Structure, Fragmentation, and Market Quality," *Journal of Financial Markets*, 9(1), 49–78.

Bhattacharya, R., 2019, "An Option Theoretic Approach to Market Efficiency," *Annals of Financial Economics*, 14(4), 1–21.

Bhattacharya, R., and Gupta, M., 2023, "Diligence, Objectivity, Quality, and Accuracy," *Journal of Accounting Literature*, 47(1), 1–30.

Bhattacharya, R., and O'Brien, S., 2015, "Arbitrage Risk and Market Efficiency: Applications to Securities Class Actions," *Santa Clara Law Review*, 55(3), 643–672.

Blume, L., Easley, D., and O'Hara, M., 1994, "Market Statistics and Technical Analysis: The Role of Volume," *Journal of Finance*, 49(1), 153–181.

Boehme, R., Danielsen, B., and Sorescu, S., 2006, "Short-Sale Constraints, Differences of Opinion, and Overvaluation," *Journal of Financial and Quantitative Analysis*, 41(2), 455–487.

Boehmer, E., Huszar, Z., and Jordan, B., 2010, "The Good News in Short Interest," *Journal of Financial Economics*, 96(1), 80–97.

Boehmer, E., Jones, C., Wu, J., and Zhang, X., 2020, "What Do Short Sellers Know?" *Review of Finance*, 24(6), 1203–1235.

Boehmer, E., Jones, C., and Zhang, X., 2019, "Potential Pilot Problems: Treatment Spillovers in Financial Regulatory Experiments," *Journal of Financial Economics*, 135(1), 68–87.

Boehmer, E., and Kelley, E., 2009, "Institutional Investors and the Informational Efficiency of Prices," *Review of Financial Studies*, 22(9), 3563–3594.

Boehmer, E., and Wu, J., 2013, "Short Selling and the Price Discovery Process," *Review of Financial Studies*, 26(2), 287–322.

Bris, A., Goetzmann, W., and Zhu, N., 2007, "Efficiency and the Bear: Short Sales and Markets Around the World," *Journal of Finance*, 62(3), 1029–1079.

Campbell, J., Lo, A., and MacKinlay, A. C., 1997, *The Econometrics of Financial Markets*, Princeton, NJ: Princeton University Press.

Cao, C., Liang, B., Lo, A., and Petrasek, L., 2018, "Hedge Fund Holdings and Stock Market Efficiency," *Review of Asset Pricing Studies*, 8(1), 77–116.

Chiang, C., Dai, W., Fan, J., Hong, H., and Tu, J., 2019, "Robust Measures of Earnings Surprises," *Journal of Finance*, 74(2), 943–983.

Collins, D., and Kothari, S. P., 1989, "An Analysis of Intertemporal and Cross-Sectional Determinants of Earnings Response Coefficients," *Journal of Accounting and Economics*, 11(2–3), 143–181.

Cornell, B., and Rutten, J., 2006, "Market Efficiency, Crashes, and Securities Litigation," *Tulane Law Review*, 81(2), 443–472.

Cremers, M., and Weinbaum, D., 2010, "Deviations from Put-Call Parity and Stock Return Predictability," *Journal of Financial and Quantitative Analysis*, 45(2), 335–367.

Dang, V., Michayluk, D., and Pham, T., 2018, "The Curious Case of Changes in Trading Dynamics: When Firms Switch from NYSE to NASDAQ," *Journal of Financial Markets*, 41, 17–35.

Dechow, P., Hutton, A., Meulbroek, L., and Sloan, R., 2001, "Short-Sellers, Fundamental Analysis, and Stock Returns," *Journal of Financial Economics*, 61(1), 77–106.

Diamond, D., and Verrecchia, R., 1987, "Constraints on Short-Selling and Asset Price Adjustment to Private Information," *Journal of Financial Economics*, 18(2), 277–311.

Diether, K., Lee, K., and Werner, I., 2009, "It's SHO Time! Short-Sale Price Tests and Market Quality," *Journal of Finance*, 64(1), 37–73.

Drechsler, I., and Drechsler, Q., 2021, "The Shorting Premium and Asset Pricing Anomalies," *SSRN* (https://ssrn.com/abstract=2387099).

Duffie, D., 1996, "Special Repo Rates," *Journal of Finance*, 51(2), 493–526.

Duffie, D., Garleanu, N., and Pedersen, L., 2002, "Securities Lending, Shorting, and Pricing," *Journal of Financial Economics*, 66, 307–339.

Easley, D., O'Hara, M., and Srinivas, P. S., 1998, "Option Volume and Stock Prices: Evidence on Where Informed Traders Trade," *Journal of Finance*, 53(2), 431–465.

Evans, R., Geczy, C., Musto, D., and Reed, A., 2009, "Failure Is an Option: Impediments to Short Selling and Options Prices," *Review of Financial Studies*, 22(5), 1955–1980.

Fama, E., 1970, "Efficient Capital Markets: A Review of Theory and Empirical Work," *Journal of Finance*, 25(2), 383–417.

Fama, E., Fisher, L., Jensen, M., and Roll, R., 1969, "The Adjustment of Stock Prices to New Information," *International Economic Review*, 10(1), 1–21.

Fama, E., and French, K., 1992, "The Cross-Section of Expected Stock Returns," *Journal of Finance*, 47(2), 427–465.

Fama, E., and French, K., 1993, "Common Risk Factors in the Returns on Stocks and Bonds," *Journal of Financial Economics*, 33(1), 3–56.

Fama, E., and French, K., 2015, "A Five-Factor Asset Pricing Model," *Journal of Financial Economics*, 116, 1–22.

Foster, F., and Viswanathan, S., 1996, "Strategic Trading When Agents Forecast the Forecasts of Others," *Journal of Finance*, 51(4), 1437–1478.

Geczy, C., Musto, D., and Reed, A., 2002, "Stocks Are Special Too: An Analysis of the Equity Lending Markets," *Journal of Financial Economics*, 66(2–3), 241–269.

Goldstein, I., and Guembel, A., 2008, "Manipulation and the Allocational Role of Prices," *Review of Economic Studies*, 75, 133–164.

Goldstein, I., Spatt, C., and Ye, M., 2021, "Big Data in Finance," *Review of Financial Studies*, 34(7), 3213–3225.

Goldstein, I., Spatt, C., and Ye, M., 2025, "The Next Chapter of Big Data in Finance," *Review of Financial Studies*, 38(3), 605–622.

Greene, W., 2018, *Econometric Analysis*, Upper Saddle River, NJ: Pearson.

Griliches, Z., and Hausman, J., 1986, "Errors in Variables in Panel Data," *Journal of Econometrics*, 31, 93–118.
Grossman, S., and Stiglitz, J., 1980, "On the Impossibility of Informationally Efficient Markets," *American Economic Review*, 70(3), 393–408.
Hansen, L., and Singleton, K., 1982, "Generalized Instrumental Variables Estimation of Nonlinear Rational Expectations Models," *Econometrica*, 50(5), 1269–1286.
Harris, L., 2003, *Trading & Exchanges: Market Microstructure for Practitioners*, New York, NY: Oxford University Press.
Hasbrouck, J., 2009, "Trading Costs and Returns for U.S. Equities: Estimating Effective Costs from Daily Data," *Journal of Finance*, LXIV(3), 1445–1477.
Hausman, J., Leonard, G., and Zona, D., 1994, "Competitive Analysis with Differenciated Products," *Annales d'Économie et de Statistique*, 34, 159–180.
Hausman, J., and Taylor, W., 1981, "Panel Data and Unobservable Individual Effects," *Econometrica*, 49(6), 1377–1398.
Hendershott, T., and Moulton, M., 2011, "Automation, Speed, and Stock Market Quality: The NYSE's Hybrid," *Journal of Financial Markets*, 14(4), 568–604.
Hou, K., and Moskowitz, T., 2005, "Market Frictions, Price Delay, and the Cross-Section of Expected Returns," *Review of Financial Studies*, 18(3), 981–1020.
Jensen, M., 1978, "Some Anomalous Evidence Regarding Market Efficiency," *Journal of Financial Economics*, 6(2–3), 95–101.
Jones, C., and Lamont, O., 2002, "Short-Sale Constraints and Stock Returns," *Journal of Financial Economics*, 66(2–3), 207–239.
Kaourma, T., Milidonis, A., Nishiotis, G., and Panayides, M. A., 2021, "News and Intraday Retail Investor Order Flow in Foreign Exchange Markets," *SSRN* (https://ssrn.com/abstract=3796753).
Karpoff, J., 1987, "The Relation between Price Changes and Trading Volume: A Survey," *Journal of Financial and Quantitative Analysis*, 22(1), 109–126.
Kothari, S. P., 2001, "Capital Markets Research in Accounting," *Journal of Accounting and Economics*, 31(1–3), 105–231.
Kothari, S. P., So, E., and Verdi, R., 2016, "Analysts' Forecasts and Asset Pricing: A Survey," *Annual Review of Financial Economics*, 8, 197–219.
Kothari, S. P., and Warner, J., 2007, "Econometrics of Event Studies," In: Eckbo, E. (Ed.), *Handbook of Empirical Corporate Finance*, vol. 1, pp. 3–36, Amsterdam, The Netherlands: Elsevier/North-Holland.
Kyle, A., and Obizhaeva, A., 2016, "Market Microstructure Invariance: Empirical Hypotheses," *Econometrica*, 84(4), 1345–1404.
Lamont, O., and Stein, J., 2004, "Aggregate Short Interest and Market Valuations," *American Economic Review*, 94(2), 29–32.
Lamont, O., and Thaler, R., 2003, "Can the Market Add and Subtract? Mispricing in Tech Stock Carve-Outs," *Journal of Political Economy*, 111(2), 227–268.
Li, E. X., Ramesh, K., Shen, M., and Wu, J. S., 2015, "Do Analyst Stock Recommendations Piggyback on Recent Corporate News? An Analysis of Regular-Hour and After-Hours Revisions," *Journal of Accounting Research*, 53, 821–861.
Loh, R., 2010, "Investor Inattention and the Under-Reaction to Stock Recommendations," *Financial Management*, 39(3), 1223–1252.
Loughran, T., and Ritter, J., 2000, "Uniformly Least Powerful Tests of Market Efficiency," *Journal of Financial Economics*, 55(3), 361–389.

Malkiel, B., 2003, "The Efficient Market Hypothesis and Its Critics," *Journal of Economic Perspectives*, 17(1), 59–82.

Marshall, B., Nguyen, N., and Visaltanachoti, N., 2019, "A Note on Intraday Event Studies," *European Accounting Review*, 28(3), 605–619.

Massa, M., Qian, W., Xu, W., and Zhang, H., 2015, "Competition of the Informed: Does the Presence of Short Sellers Affect Insider Selling?" *Journal of Financial Economics*, 118(2), 268–288.

Miller, E., 1977, "Risk, Uncertainty, and Divergence of Opinion," *Journal of Finance*, 32(4), 1151–1168.

Muravyev, D., Pearson, N., and Pollet, J., 2022, "Is There a Risk Premium in the Stock Lending Market? Evidence from Equity Options," *Journal of Finance*, 77(3), 1787–1828.

Ofek, E., Richardson, M., and Whitelaw, R., 2004, "Limited Arbitrage and Short Sales Restrictions: Evidence from the Options Markets," *Journal of Financial Economics*, 74(2), 305–342.

O'Hara, M., 1997, *Market Microstructure Theory*, Malden, MA: Blackwell Publishing.

Porta, R., Lakonishok, J., Shleifer, A., and Vishny, R., 1997, "Good News for Value Stocks: Further Evidence on Market Efficiency," *Journal of Finance*, 52(2), 859–874.

Roberts, M., and Whited, T., 2011, "Endogeneity in Empirical Corporate Finance," In: Constantinides, G., Harris, M., and Stulz, R. (Eds.), *Handbook of the Economics of Finance*, 493–572. Amsterdam, The Netherlands: Elsevier.

Rosch, D., Subrahmanyam, A., and Dijk, M., 2017, "The Dynamics of Market Efficiency," *Review of Financial Studies*, 30(4), 1151–1187.

Saffi, P., and Sigurdsson, K., 2011, "Price Efficiency and Short Selling," *Review of Financial Studies*, 24(3), 821–852.

Saggu, A., 2022, "The Intraday Bitcoin Response to Tether Minting and Burning Events: Asymmetry, Investor Sentiment, and 'Whale Alerts' on Twitter," *Finance Research Letters*, 49, 103096.

Samuelson, P., 2009, "An Enjoyable Life Puzzling Over Modern Finance Theory," *Annual Review of Financial Economics*, 1, 19–35.

Schoenberg, T., and Robinson, R., 2018, "Tesla Is Facing U.S. Criminal Probe Over Elon Musk Statements," *Bloomberg*, September 18, 2018.

Shleifer, A., 2000, *Inefficient Markets: An Introduction to Behavioral Finance*, New York, NY: Oxford University Press.

Stambaugh, R., Yu, J., and Yuan, Y., 2015, "Arbitrage Asymmetry and the Idiosyncratic Volatility Puzzle," *Journal of Finance*, 70(5), 1903–1948.

Stickel, S., and Verrecchia, R., 1994, "Evidence That Trading Volume Sustains Stock Price Changes," *Financial Analysts Journal*, 50(6), 57–67.

Wang, J., 1994, "A Model of Competitive Stock Trading Volume," *Journal of Political Economy*, 102(1), 127–168.

Wintoki, B., Linck, J., and Netter, J., 2012, "Endogeneity and the Dynamics of Internal Corporate Governance," *Journal of Financial Economics*, 105(3), 581–606.

Wooldridge, J., 2010, *Econometric Analysis of Cross Section and Panel Data*, Cambridge, MA: MIT Press.

8

FI SECURITIES

8.1 Introduction

In this chapter, we use two different metrics, depending on how a potential material event is determined (detailed in Section 6.7.3), as actual, objective, independent, and systematic ordinal measures of the efficiency of the market for a fixed income (FI) security, with three separate 60-minute, 90-minute, and 120-minute announcement windows for each, based on event studies controlling for intraday market FI yields, Nasdaq listing FI yields, industry (3-digit NAICS Code) FI yields, market capitalization decile FI yields, intraday volatility decile FI yields, dividend decile FI yields, Fama-French Factor (Fama and French, 2015, 1993, 1992), decile FI yields, market equity returns, and daily risk-free and foreign exchange rates, with intraday FI and equity trading data on all publicly traded U.S. companies over January 2014 to September 2021 (about 25 TB of data). We find that the data reject the first research hypothesis of this chapter that the market efficiency of FI securities improves with time. We find that the tests of the second research hypothesis that market efficiency of FI securities is associated with characteristics of the issuing firm has varying results: the associations of investor valuation dispersion and short sales costs & constraints of the equity of the issuing firm are significant whereas the association of transaction costs & constraints is ambiguous.

Kyle and Obizhaeva (2016) and Bhattacharya (2019) show that all the questions raised here have indeterminate theoretical predictions, and we use the market microstructure models in these papers to use an eight-equation structural model that has (a) market efficiency as a function of exogenous factors, namely, year-quarter, dispersion in investor valuations (proxied by the quarterly standard deviation of analyst forecasts of earnings per share for the firm with "forecast period end date"

DOI: 10.4324/9781003608486-11

in the current calendar quarter) of issuing firm, short sales costs & constraints (proxied by the cost of a synthetic short sale, which is short one call option and long one put option, at the money, with the same expiration), and transaction costs & constraints (proxied by bid-ask spread) of equity of listing firm, and endogenous market activities, namely, Nasdaq listing of issuing firm, Kyle-Obizhaeva liquidity measure, normalized short interest of equity, analyst coverage of the issuing firm, institutional ownership of equity, log of market capitalization, and log of equity shares outstanding; and (b) each endogenous market activity as a function of the exogenous factors and all other endogenous market activities. We use the panel nature of the data to identify appropriate instruments for the endogenous and for the variables that are measured with error, and we use Three Stage Least Squares (3SLS) and Errors in Variables (EiV) to estimate this eight-equation structural model and test the hypotheses provided by the theory; see Appendix D for details. We calculate the total association of a factor which is the sum of the direct association and the indirect associations. As in Section 2.6, we use the standard Gaussian cumulative probability of the $\textit{Z-Score}\,(x) = (x \textit{ minus Mean}\,(x)) \,/\, (\textit{Standard Deviation}\,(x))$ of each variable (except for a classification or time variable), this is a rigorization of the number of standard deviations approach to interpretation of coefficients, which also implicitly assumes Gaussian distributions; this makes the associations comparable and thus, allows a systematic and objective definition of actual significance, which is different from statistical significance — as detailed in Chapter 2, pretty much everything is statistically significant when working with huge datasets.

8.2 Literature Review and Hypothesis Development

Fixed income (FI) securities are substantially more complex than equities and have, as a result, received far less attention in financial econometrics than equities — see, for instance, Sundaresan (2009) — especially in event studies — see, for instance, van Binsbergen et al. (2022), Bauer et al. (2022), Schrimpf et al. (2021), Sever et al. (2021), Gürkaynak et al. (2020), Henisz and McGlinch (2019), and Gürkaynak and Wright (2012). A market for an FI security is *semistrong efficient* if yields reflect all publicly available information — see, for example, Fama (1970), Jensen (1978), Grossman and Stiglitz (1980), Malkiel (2003), Harris (2003), Shleifer (2000), and Samuelson (2009). As has been recognized, by, for example, Fama et al. (1969), a market is efficient if yields "adjust very rapidly to new information" — this makes clear that calendar-time is relevant to a discussion of market efficiency whereas transaction-time is not, *per se*, relevant; please see Kyle and Obizhaeva (2016) for further details. Prices of securities adjust, *albeit* to varying extents, to new information, therefore, markets for securities are efficient in varying degrees — often referred to as *relative efficiency*; see, for example, Campbell et al. (1997). Please see, for instance, Cornell and Rutten (2006) and Bhattacharya and O'Brien

(2015) for the role of market efficiency in securities litigation. See also Jiang et al. (2012), Chordia et al. (2005), Woodruff and Senchack (1998), and Jennings and Starks (1986), in reverse chronological order; for a description of the importance of relative efficiency for valuations (especially Mark-to-Market) and securities class actions (especially class certification), see Bhattacharya (2019b). Other measures of market efficiency based on securities prices following random walks in efficient markets used by Cao et al. (2018) and Boehmer and Kelley (2009); the two purely empirical measures of market efficiency based on the asymmetry between positive and negative market returns used by Bris et al. (2007); the variance ratio measures of random walk (the last two methods were also used by Saffi and Sigurdsson (2011), also please see Campbell et al. (1997)); the friction measures of market efficiency (Hou and Moskowitz, 2005; Boehmer and Wu, 2013); and the mispricing score based on eleven return anomalies used by Stambaugh et al. (2015), are all **indirect measures** of market efficiency based on a posited positive correlation between each of these indirect measures and the actual efficiency of the market for a security, which is not *per se* relevant but relevant only in the absence of an actual measure of market efficiency. In this chapter, we use two metrics, with three variations on each, as separate, objective, ordinal, and **actual** measures of the efficiency of the market for a stock, which eliminates the need for the correlation-based measures referred to above — see Section 6.7.3.

The impact of listing exchange of issuing firm on market quality has a distinguished history; see, for example, Dang et al. (2018), Hendershott and Moulton (2011), Diether et al. (2009), and Bennett and Wei (2006). Lamont and Thaler (2003) say that "short sale constraints have long been recognized as crucial to the workings of efficient markets." For the importance of short sales costs & constraints, see most importantly, Miller (1977), and, more recently, Boehmer et al. (2019), Boehmer et al. (2020), Diamond and Verrecchia (1987), Drechsler and Drechsler (2021), Muravyev et al. (2022), Massa et al. (2015), Boehmer and Wu (2013), Saffi and Sigurdsson (2011), Boehmer et al. (2010), Goldstein and Guembel (2008), Bris et al. (2006, 2007), Boehme et al. (2006), Lamont and Stein (2004), Duffie et al. (2002), Jones and Lamont (2002), Dechow et al. (2001), Easley et al. (1998), Duffie (1996), and others. The overwhelming conclusion of the extant literature is that the impact of short sales costs & constraints is theoretically indeterminate and empirically ambiguous. The relation of dispersions of investor valuations and transaction costs & constraints with market efficiency has been studied by, for instance, Bhattacharya (2019b), Bhattacharya and O'Brien (2015), Loh (2010), O'Hara (1997), Stickel and Verrecchia (1994), Blume et al. (1994), Wang (1994), and Karpoff (1987). Beaver (1968) refers to the "economist's notion that volume reflects a lack of consensus regarding the price." In particular, Bhattacharya and O'Brien (2015) estimated a reduced form, and using arbitrage risk as the measure of market efficiency, came to the conclusion that market efficiency was not significantly positively related to trading volume — see also the extensive discussion there on the "conventional wisdom" regarding the dependence of market efficiency on trading volume. The conclusion of the extant literature is that the impacts of investor valuations and transaction costs & constraints are theoretically indeterminate and the empirical conclusions are not conclusive.

This chapter is firmly situated in these intellectual traditions and this discussion yields the following research hypotheses that are tested in this chapter:

Research Hypothesis 1. Market efficiency of FI securities improved over the time period under study.

Research Hypothesis 2. Market efficiency of FI securities is related to dispersions in investor valuations, short sales costs & constraints, and transaction costs & constraints of the equity of the issuing firm.

8.3 Measures of Market Efficiency

In this chapter, we use two different and objective metrics, with three variations of each, as systematic, independent, and actual ordinal quarterly measures of the efficiency of the market for an FI security, and Table 8A.1 provides summary statistics of these different ordinal measures of market efficiency. Since Fama et al. (1969) and Ball and Brown (1968), "hundreds of event studies have been conducted in the legal, financial economics, and accounting literatures... Event studies are tests of market efficiency. They test the impact, speed, and unbiasedness of the market's reaction to an event. In an efficient capital market, a security's [yield] reaction to an event is expected to be immediate," as pointed out by Kothari (2001).

As in Chapter 6, we do *not* ascribe any directional component to any potentially material event, because it is impossible, without additional information or *ad hoc* judgment, to objectively determine the market's perception prior to any potentially material event and to determine whether a particular potentially material event was better-than-expected news, worse-than-expected news, or even a surprise at all. Colloquially speaking: Good news or bad news is not the relevant question here, and it requires subjective judgment to infer from the description of an event if market efficiency would require the yield of the security to go up, down, or stay the same. We look, in this chapter, at the same example we looked at in Chapter 6, (a) FB equity closed on Thursday, July 11, 2019 at $201.23; (b) FB equity opened on Friday, July 12, 2019 at $199.68; (c) at 3:52 PM, Friday, July 12, 2019, news emerged that the U.S. Federal Trade Commission (FTC) planned to fine FB a record $5 billion for the Cambridge Analytica data scandal (Price, 2019); (d) FB equity closed on Friday, July 12, 2019 at $204.87; (e) increase of 1.8% over previous day's closing price; (f) increase of 2.6% over current day's open price; (g) even though the reported settlement amount was $2 billion more than the company had reserved for the settlement. In his judgment in *Petrobras Securities Litigation,* Judge Jed

Rakoff discussed the issue of directionality and stringently criticized the subjective and *ad hoc* marking of directionality of events in the dueling "expert" reports; for example, one of the "experts" in the litigation used the presence or absence of the text "corrupt" in the description of an event to determine the relevant directionality of a potentially material event.

8.3.1 HalfHour-Level Averages

We use high-frequency millisecond-level intraday FI security trading data from TRACE and high-frequency millisecond-level intraday equity trading data from TAQ. Calendar-time, rather than transaction-time, is relevant for market efficiency discussions — see Kyle and Obizhaeva (2016) for further details. Therefore, we divide each trading day into 15 "halfhours" as follows: halfhour 0 for prior to 9:30 AM, halfhour 14 for after 4 PM, and halfhours 1–13 for each halfhour of the trading hours — this aggregation of millisecond-level high-frequency data onto halfhours is a simplification; in particular, you should consider aggregating millisecond-level high-frequency data into, say, every ten minutes, fifteen minutes, or hour. For each TICKER, for each FI security CUSIP, for each halfhour 0-14 with positive FI security trading volume, we calculate the volume-weighted average yield (VWAY), then for each TICKER, we calculate the simple average of VWAY over all CUSIPs corresponding to that TICKER. For each FI security *i*, for each halfhour τ with positive volume, we calculate the Volume-Weighted Average Price of equity of issuing firm and then calculate the relevant continuously compounded return and weighted averages. Please see details in Appendix Table 8.A1, Table 8.A2, and Table 8.A3.

8.3.2 Market Model

The market model below controls for intraday market FI yields, Nasdaq listing FI yields, industry (3-digit NAICS Code) FI yields, market capitalization decile FI yields, millisecond-level intraday volatility decile FI yields, dividend decile FI yields, Fama-French Factor decile FI yields, market equity returns, and daily risk-free and foreign exchange rates. Having the risk-free rate as a regressor in the market model is a generalization of using excess return (yield) of security = return (yield) of security minus risk-free rate, in all equity (fixed income) security calculations. We do not have access to intraday data for foreign exchange rates or T-bill yields.

The yield for fixed income security (CUSIP) *i* in halfhour τ,

$$
\begin{aligned}
&FIYld_{i,\tau} \\
&\qquad = \pi \\
&\qquad\quad + (\pi_{FIYld\_All})\,(FIYld\_All_{\tau})
\end{aligned}
$$

$$
\begin{aligned}
&+ (\pi_{FIYld\_Nasdaq}) (FIYld\_Nasdaq_{i,\tau}) \\
&+ (\pi_{FIYld\_NAICS3Dig}) (FIYld\_NAICS3Dig_{i,\tau}) \\
&+ (\pi_{FIYld\_MCapDecile}) (FIYld\_MCapDecile_{i,\tau}) \\
&+ (\pi_{FIYld\_IntraVtyDecile}) (FIYld\_IntraVtyDecile_{i,\tau}) \\
&+ (\pi_{FIYld\_DivYieldDecile}) (FIYld\_DivYieldDecile_{i,\tau}) \\
&+ (\pi_{FIYld\_BMRatioDecile}) (FIYld\_BMRatioDecile_{i,\tau}) \\
&+ (\pi_{FIYld\_PERatioDecile}) (FIYld\_PERatioDecile_{i,\tau}) \\
&+ (\pi_{FIYld\_DERatioDecile}) (FIYld\_DERatioDecile_{i,\tau}) \\
&+ (\pi_{EqRet\_All}) (EqRet\_All_{\tau}) \\
&+ (\pi_{Risk\_Free}) (Risk\_Free_{\tau}) \\
&+ (\pi_{Nom\_Broad\_USD\_Index}) (Nom\_Broad\_USD\_Index_{\tau}) \\
&+ IdioFIYld_{i,\tau}
\end{aligned}
\tag{8.1}
$$

This enables one to predict or benchmark the FI yield for that firm i and that halfhour τ — the "normal yield" or expected yield $\widehat{FIYld}_{i,\tau}$, and therefore, to measure the **idiosyncratic yield** $Idio\widehat{FIYld}_{i,\tau} = FIYld_{i,\tau} - \widehat{FIYld}_{i,\tau}$.

8.3.3 Controlled Contrasts

Fix universe of analysis $\mathfrak{T}$ as set of halfhours. Fix announcement window length $n \geq 1$, relevant window length $m \geq 1$, and post-relevant window length $l \geq 1$. Consider a fixed time period t (e.g., quarter, month) as set of halfhours. Consider event identification method $\mathfrak{I} \subseteq \mathfrak{T}$ as potentially material events; in this chapter, we use two separate identification methods for potentially material events: (a) key developments (KD), identified by S&P Global CapitalIQ, and (b) earnings announcements and revisions, and analyst forecasts and revisions (EA); see Appendix Table 8.A1, Table 8.A2, and Table 8.A3 for details. For potentially material event at halfhour $T \in t \cap \mathfrak{T}$,

$$\boldsymbol{AnnouncementHalfHours}\,(T, n) = \{T, ..., T + n - 1\} \tag{8.2}$$

(n halfhours),

$$\boldsymbol{RelevantHalfHours}\,(T, n, m) = \{T + n, ..., T + n + m - 1\} \tag{8.3}$$

(m halfhours), and, therefore,

$$
\begin{aligned}
&\boldsymbol{TreatmentHalfHours}\,(T, n, m) \\
= \;&\boldsymbol{AnnouncementHalfHours}\,(T, n) \\
&\cup \boldsymbol{RelevantHalfHours}\,(T, n, m) \\
= \;&\{T, ..., T + n + m - 1\}
\end{aligned}
\tag{8.4}
$$

($n + m$ halfhours), and therefore,

$$\boldsymbol{ControlHalfHours}(t, n, m, \mathfrak{T}) \tag{8.5}$$

consists of each halfhour in t that is not a treatment halfhour for any potentially material event at halfhour $T \in t \cap \mathfrak{T}$, and, therefore, equals

$$\{\tau \in t : \tau \notin \{T, ..., T + n + m - 1\}, \forall T \in t \cap \mathfrak{T}\} \tag{8.6}$$

For fixed n, m, a systematic and controlled contrast between

$$\left|\widehat{IdioFIYld}_{i,\tau}\right| \tag{8.7}$$

for

$$\boldsymbol{RelevantHalfHours}\,(T, n, m) \tag{8.8}$$

versus

$$\left|\widehat{IdioFIYld}_{i,\tau}\right| \tag{8.9}$$

for

$$\boldsymbol{ControlHalfHours}(t, n, m, \mathfrak{T}) \tag{8.10}$$

would be necessary for an objective, systematic and ordinal direct measure of market efficiency with n announcement halfhours and m relevant halfhours. From the theory, it follows that

$$\left|\widehat{IdioFIYld}_{i,\tau}\right| \tag{8.11}$$

should be weakly higher for relevant halfhours than for control halfhours, and therefore, for each of the identification systems for potentially material events (KD and EA), for each announcement window length $n \in \{2, 3, 4\}$, for each security i, for each quarter t, an ordinal direct **measure of market efficiency** for that FI security for that quarter is:

$$-\max\left\{0, \begin{array}{c} Mean_{\tau \in \text{Quarter } t, \tau \in \text{Relevant HalfHour}} \left|\widehat{IdioFIYld}_{i,\tau}\right| \\ minus \\ Mean_{\tau \in \text{Quarter } t, \tau \in \text{Control HalfHour}} \left|\widehat{IdioFIYld}_{i,\tau}\right| \end{array}\right\} \tag{8.12}$$

The above aggregation of our halfhourly idiosyncratic yield computations onto quarters is intended purely as a simplification and to test our hypotheses; in particular, you should consider aggregating halfhourly computations into, say, daily (although we will run into missing results because FI securities are often not traded frequently enough), weekly, monthly (as we have done in Chapter 6), halfyearly, or annually, or for that matter, any test period. In Chapter 6, an objective, systematic and ordinal direct measure of market efficiency is provided by the negative of the coefficient of the interaction between the indicator variable for relevant halfhours versus control halfhours, and as the case may be, TICKER and/or time period of interest, in a fixed effects regression of halfhour-level absolute idiosyncratic equity returns on the relevant interaction terms.

8.3.4 Announcement Windows and Relevant Windows

Given an announcement window of $n \in \{2,3,4\}$ halfhours, for each FI security, for each potentially material event at halfhour T, we consider the announcement window halfhours to be $\{T+1, ..., T+n\}$ and the relevant window halfhours to be $\{T+n+1, ..., T+30\}$. We calculate the absolute idiosyncratic yield for each relevant window halfhour, and for each FI security and each quarter, we calculate the average of all absolute idiosyncratic yields for all relevant window halfhours in that quarter. Reaction, overreaction, correction, overcorrection, bounceback, etc., should, in an efficient market, be out of the system within a few hours after a potentially material event, so the closer a market is to efficiency, the closer this average will be to zero.

Depending on how one determines a potentially material event, we have two separate paths of research on event studies. For the first path, we rely upon the marking of an event as a "Key Development" (identified by S&P Global CapitalIQ, event types include earnings, dividends, mergers and acquisitions, buybacks, public offerings, management changes, debt defaults, dividend cancellations, and regulatory agency inquiries, sourced from regulatory filings and news vendors, (Marketplace, 2024), to study as a potentially material event for the issuing firm. For each FI security-quarter, we calculate the average, for that FI security-quarter, of all absolute idiosyncratic yields for all relevant halfhours in that quarter following each such Key Development for that FI security in that quarter, minus the average of all absolute idiosyncratic yields for all control halfhours in that quarter— we call this the *Key Developments Idiosyncratic Response (KDIR) for that FI security-quarter and use it as a measure of the efficiency of the market for the FI security in that quarter.* The second path studies the impact of earnings announcements and analyst forecasts on security yields, and has a long and distinguished history; see, for instance, Ball and Brown (1968), Collins and Kothari (1989), and Kothari and Warner (2007). For each FI security-quarter, we calculate the average, for that FI security-quarter, of all absolute idiosyncratic yields for all relevant halfhours in that quarter following each such earnings announcement, announcement revision, analyst forecast, and analyst forecast revision, for that

FI security-quarter, minus the average of all absolute idiosyncratic yields for all control halfhours in that quarter — we call this the *Earnings Announcements Idiosyncratic Response (EAIR) for that FI security-quarter and use it as a measure of the efficiency of the market for the FI security in that quarter*. Please note that the actual announced EPS or its deviation from "consensus" forecasts do not enter into our calculations; for a number of reasons. Any estimate of the market's "consensus" prediction of the EPS at the point of an EPS announcement, whether it is by using mean/medians of analyst forecasts, or by using valuation models, is sensitive to the methodology used to estimate the market's perception and the deviation from it — see, for instance, Chiang et al. (2019) for detailed descriptions of biases in the calculation of deviation from consensus. See Kothari et al. (2016) for a comprehensive survey of the literature on quality, bias, and predictability of earnings forecasts. The impact of analyst incentives on analyst forecasts is beyond the scope of this book — see Bhattacharya and Gupta (2023), for instance.

8.4 Description of Data

Similar to the databases described in Section 7.3, in this chapter, we use data on all publicly traded U.S. firms for January 2014 to September 2021. We use millisecond-level intraday FI trading data from TRACE and high-frequency millisecond-level intraday equity trading data from TAQ. As discussed earlier, we divide each trading day into 15 "halfhours" as follows: halfhour 0 for prior to 9:30 AM, halfhour 14 for after 4 PM, and halfhours 1–13 for each halfhour of the trading hours. For each FI security CUSIP, for each halfhour, we calculate the volume-weighted average yield (VWAY) of all FI trades, then for each TICKER, we calculate the simple average of VWAY over all CUSIPs corresponding to that TICKER (because of sparse data, a weighted average would be too responsive to the number of trades for each different CUSIP). For each FI security, for each halfhour 0–14 with positive volume, we calculate the volume-weighted average price (VWAP) of trading prices of the equity of the issuing firm of FI security, and then calculate the relevant halfhour-to-halfhour continuously compounded return for the equity of the issuing firm of the FI security. We restrict attention to stocks corresponding to publicly traded firms that did not change PERMNO or TICKER or 3-digit NAICS code during January 2014 to September 2021. We further restrict attention to stock-days that did not have splits, reverse splits, or dividends, and to stock-days that have positive closing price and positive shares outstanding and other restrictions from CRSP: date, closing price, return, shares outstanding, trading volume, closing bid and ask, exchange membership, NAICS code, and had data on the following variables: analyst forecasts and revisions (from I/B/E/S), earnings announcements and revisions (from I/B/E/S), institutional holdings (from Thomson Reuters), short interest (from Compustat), Key Developments (from

Capital IQ), Compustat-CRSP Merged Database, OptionMetrics, and daily data for T-Bill yields and Nominal Broad U.S. Dollar Index (from FRED).

In order to maintain the integrity of the linkages between the different sources of data we rely upon, we treat a missing observation as a missing observation — in particular, with number of analysts, short interest, and institutional ownership — not as a zero. For a small number of stock-days, we found multiple entries when sorted by TICKER, CUSIP, and date — for these stock-days, we calculate weighted averages using trading volume as weights. We do not have access to actual short sales costs & constraints data — dealing with missing data is one of the biggest challenges in empirical work, and appropriately proxying for the unavailable data is one of the innovations of this chapter, where we use the cost of a synthetic short sale (short one call option and long one put option, at the money, with the same expiration) as a measure of short sales costs & constraints for the underlying stock. Compustat (including Capital IQ) data sources rely upon the S&P identification of GVKEY. In this chapter, we rely upon the mapping of GVKEY to TICKER used by CRSP to match its data to Compustat. We do not have access to intraday data for treasury yield and foreign exchange rates from FRED. The sample is further restricted to the following:

- if $|yield| \leq 100\%$
- if $|EPS| \leq \$100$
- if $shrcd \in \{10, 11\}$
- if $ret \notin \{-44.0, -55.0, -66.0, -77.0, -88.0, -99.0\}$
- if $dlret \notin \{-55.0, -66.0, -88.0, -99.0\}$
- if $dlretx \notin \{-55.0, -66.0, -88.0, -99.0\}$
- if $dclrdt \neq 0$
- if $trtscd \neq 0$,
- if $nmsind \neq 0$
- if $vol \neq -99.0$
- if $prc > 0$
- if $bid > 0$
- if $ask > 0$
- if $vol > 0$
- if $shrout > 0$
- if $TICKER \neq ?$
- if $TICKER \neq ''$
- if $CUSIP \neq ''$
- if $substr(TICKER, 1, 4) \neq ZZZZ;$
- if $substr(CUSIP, 7, 1) \in \{0, 1, 2, 3, 4, 5, 6, 7, 8, 9\}$
- if $substr(CUSIP, 8, 1) \in \{0, 1, 2, 3, 4, 5, 6, 7, 8, 9\}$

8.5 Structural Empirical System

Similarly to Section 7.6, in this chapter, we estimate the following structural system at the TICKER-CUSIP-year-quarter level. Market efficiency is modeled as a linear function of the exogenous factors, namely year-quarter, dispersion in investor valuations, short sales costs & constraints, and transaction costs & constraints of equity of issuing firm, and endogenous market activities, namely, Nasdaq listing of equity of issuing firm of FI security, Kyle-Obizhaeva liquidity measure (Kyle and Obizhaeva, 2016), normalized short interest, analyst coverage, institutional ownership of equity, log of market capitalization, and log of shares outstanding, as follows.

$$\begin{aligned} MEff_{i,t} = {} & \varrho + \gamma_{YQ} YQ_t \\ & + \gamma_{Disp} Disp_{i,t} + \gamma_{SSCC} SSCC_{i,t} \\ & + \gamma_{TrCC} TrCC_{i,t} + \gamma_{Nasdaq} Nasdaq_{i,t} \\ & + \gamma_{KOLiq} KOLiq_{i,t} + \gamma_{NormSI} NormSI_{i,t} \\ & + \gamma_{AnCov} AnCov_{i,t} + \gamma_{NormInst} NormInst_{i,t} \\ & + \gamma_{LogMCap} logMCap_{i,t} + \gamma_{logShrsOut} logShrsOut_{i,t} \\ & + \delta_{i,t} \end{aligned} \tag{8.13}$$

Each endogenous market activity, namely, Nasdaq listing of equity of issuing firm of FI security, Kyle-Obizhaeva liquidity measure, normalized short interest, analyst coverage, institutional ownership of equity, log of market capitalization, and log of shares outstanding, is modeled as a function of the exogenous factors and all other endogenous market activities, based on the market microstructure models in Kyle and Obizhaeva (2016) and Bhattacharya (2019a), leading to seven equations, of which one is presented below, and the rest are detailed in Table 8.A1, Table 8.A2, and Table 8.A3.

$$\begin{aligned} Nasdaq_{i,t} = {} & \beta + \beta_{YQ} YQ_t \\ & + \beta_{Disp} Disp_{i,t} + \beta_{SSCC} SSCC_{i,t} \\ & + \beta_{TrCC} TrCC_{i,t} + \beta_{KOLiq} KOLiq_{i,t} \\ & + \beta_{NormSI} NormSI_{i,t} + \beta_{AnCov} AnCov_{i,t} \\ & + \beta_{NormInst} NormInst_{i,t} + \beta_{logMCap} logMCap_{i,t} \\ & + \beta_{logShrsOut} logShrsOut_{i,t} \\ & + \varkappa_{i,t} \end{aligned} \tag{8.14}$$

Where

- $MEff_{i,t}$ = each separate ordinal measure of market efficiency for FI security i in quarter t, described in Section 6.7.3

- YQ_t = number corresponding to quarter t
- $Disp_{i,t}$ = dispersion in investor valuations for issuing firm of FI security i in quarter t
- $SSCC_{i,t}$ = short sales costs & constraints for issuing firm of FI security i in quarter t
- $TrCC_{i,t}$ = transaction costs & constraints for equity of issuing firm of FI security i in quarter t
- $Nasdaq_{i,t}$ = indicator variable for Nasdaq listing of issuing firm of FI security i in quarter t
- $KOLiq_{i,t}$ = Kyle-Obizhaeva liquidity of FI security i in quarter t = cube root [(quarterly mean of halfhour dollar volume)/(square of quarterly standard deviation of halfhour yields)] (Kyle and Obizhaeva, 2016)
- $NormSI_{i,t}$ = quarterly mean of (monthly short interest)/(daily shares outstanding) for equity of issuing firm of FI security i in quarter t
- $AnCov_{i,t}$ = number of EPS forecasts and adjustments by analysts for the issuing firm of FI security i with "forecast period end date" in quarter t
- $NormInst_{i,t}$ = quarterly mean of institutional ownership percentage point in equity of issuing firm of FI security i in quarter t
- $logMCap_{i,t}$ = quarterly mean of natural logarithm of market capitalization of issuing firm of FI security i in quarter t
- $logShrsOut_{i,t}$ = quarterly mean of natural logarithm of daily equity shares outstanding for issuing firm of FI security i in quarter t

8.6 Total Association of each Exogenous Factor

As detailed in Section 2.5, when dealing with large numbers of observations, we replace each variable x, except for each classification or time variable, by its normalization

$$\Phi\left(Z\text{-}Score\left(x\right)\right) = \Phi\left(\frac{x - Mean\left(x\right)}{StDev\left(x\right)}\right) \tag{8.15}$$

where Φ is the cumulative probability of a standard Gaussian random variable. Actual significance at level 1 is indicated by regular font, actual significance at level 5 by bold font, and actual significance at level 10 by bold and italic font. Please see Aman et al. (2019) for a robust defense of "responsible science," that science needs to have integrity and relevance. Following Section 2.7, the total association of each exogenous factor (*ExogFactor*) with market efficiency (*MEff*) is given by the corresponding (cross-equation) total derivative as follows.

$$\begin{aligned}\frac{\mathbf{d}MEff}{\mathbf{d}ExogFactor} = & \frac{\partial MEff}{\partial ExogFactor} \\ & + \frac{\partial MEff}{\partial Nasdaq}\frac{\mathbf{d}Nasdaq}{\mathbf{d}ExogFactor} + \frac{\partial MEff}{\partial KOLiq}\frac{\mathbf{d}KOLiq}{\mathbf{d}ExogFactor} \\ & + \frac{\partial MEff}{\partial NormSI}\frac{\mathbf{d}NormSI}{\mathbf{d}ExogFactor} + \frac{\partial MEff}{\partial AnCov}\frac{\mathbf{d}AnCov}{\mathbf{d}ExogFactor} \\ & + \frac{\partial MEff}{\partial NormInst}\frac{\mathbf{d}NormInst}{\mathbf{d}ExogFactor} + \frac{\partial MEff}{\partial logMCap}\frac{\mathbf{d}logMCap}{\mathbf{d}ExogFactor} \\ & + \frac{\partial MEff}{\partial logShrsOut}\frac{\mathbf{d}logShrsOut}{\mathbf{d}ExogFactor} \end{aligned} \quad (8.16)$$

As explained in Appendix Table 8.A1, Table 8.A2, and Table 8.A3, a 1 *percent point* increase in the cumulative generalized probability of x is associated with a $\frac{dy}{dx}$ *percent point* increase in the cumulative generalized probability of y, and similarly, $\frac{dy}{d\mathbf{1}}$ where **1** is an indicator variable means that there is a $\frac{dy}{d\mathbf{1}}$ higher cumulative generalized probability of y for membership in **1**, and $\frac{dy}{d\mathbf{t}}$ for time period **t** means that there is a $\frac{dy}{d\mathbf{t}}$ increase in cumulative generalized probability of y from one time period to the next. Actually significant positive (negative) association is indicated by light (dark) grey shading. Actual significance at level 1 is indicated by regular font, actual significance at level 5 by bold font, and actual significance at level 10 by bold and italic font. We perform each of our analyses for January 2014 to September 2021 and find, as shown in Table 8.1 that year-quarter has a statistically significant but actually insignificant negative association with market efficiency of FI securities, that short sales costs & constraints of equity of issuing firm have a statistically and actually significant negative association with market efficiency of FI securities, and that transaction costs & constraints of equity of issuing firm have a statistically and actually ambiguous association with market efficiency of FI securities.

8.7 Conclusions

Fixed income securities are substantially more complex than equities and have, as a result, received far less attention in financial econometrics than equities. In this chapter, we used two different metrics, with three separate 60-minute, 90-minute, and 120-minute announcement windows for each, based on event studies, controlling for market FI yields, Nasdaq listing FI yields, industry (3-digit NAICS Code) FI yields, market capitalization decile FI yields, intraday volatility decile FI yields, dividend decile FI yields, Fama-French Factor decile FI yields, daily risk-free and foreign exchange rates, with high-frequency millisecond-level intraday equity and FI securities data on all publicly traded U.S. companies over

TABLE 8.1 Total Association of Market Efficiency of Fixed Income Securities With Exogenous Factors, January 2014 to September 2021

	Quarterly Ordinal Measure of FI Market Efficiency Based On					
	Key Developments Idiosyncratic Response			**Earnings Announcements Idiosyncratic Response**		
	60-Minute Announcement Window	**90-Minute Announcement Window**	**120-Minute Announcement Window**	**60-Minute Announcement Window**	**90-Minute Announcement Window**	**120-Minute Announcement Window**
Total Derivative of Market Efficiency with respect to						
Year-Quarter	−0.065*** (189.77220)	−0.057*** (137.17852)	−0.036*** (55.68593)	−0.217*** (930.23346)	−0.215*** (771.22012)	−0.00.151*** (532.21894)
Investor Valuation Dispersions for Issuing Firm	**−6.404*** (1,917.47157)**	**−6.094*** (1,677.51265)**	**−5.250*** (1,287.11791)**	***−12.684*** (3,188.49392)***	***−13.296*** (3,001.74846)***	***−10.824*** (2,729.98380)***
Short Sales Costs & Constraints of Equity of Issuing Firm	***−11.027*** (532.46882)***	***−12.765*** (653.57827)***	***−14.326*** (796.22495)***	**−9.382*** (218.92494)**	***−11.115*** (256.81753)***	***−10.629*** (317.19443)***
Transaction Costs & Constraints for Equity of Issuing Firm	**−6.246*** (147.00509)**	−4.932*** (87.16625)	**−8.325*** (243.08526)**	**9.391*** (152.83592)**	**6.290*** (57.80707)**	0.110 (0.02426)

χ^2–statistics are reported in parentheses. ***, **, and * denote two-tailed statistical significance at 1%, 5% and 10% levels. Positive (negative) actual associations at levels 1, 5, and 10, indicated by light (dark) gray filling, with normal font, bold font, and bold & italic font.

January 2014 to September 2021 (tens of trillions of observations), as separate objective and systematic ordinal measures of the efficiency of the market for an FI security. Kyle and Obizhaeva (2016) and Bhattacharya (2019b) showed that the questions raised here have ambiguous theoretical predictions and, as in Bhattacharya and Gupta (2026), we use the market microstructure models in these papers to develop an eight-equation structural model that has (a) market efficiency as a function of exogenous factors, namely, year-quarter, dispersion in investor valuations (proxied by the quarterly standard deviation of analyst forecasts and revisions of earnings per share for the firm with "forecast period end date" in the current calendar quarter) of issuing firm, short sales costs & constraints (proxied by the cost of a synthetic short sale, which is short one call option and long one put option, at the money, with the same expiration), and transaction costs & constraints (proxied by bid-ask spread) of equity of issuing firm, and endogenous market activities, namely, Nasdaq listing of issuing firm. Kyle-Obizhaeva liquidity measure, normalized short interest on equity of issuing firm, analyst coverage of issuing firm, institutional ownership of equity, log of market capitalization of issuing firm, and log of equity shares outstanding, and (b) each endogenous market activity as a function of the exogenous factors and all other endogenous market activities. It is important for us to keep in mind that analyzing Big Data is not a scalable version of the programming that is done for smaller datasets.

We used the panel nature of the data to identify appropriate instruments for the endogenous variables and for the variables that are measured with error, and we used Three Stage Least Squares (3SLS) and Errors in Variables (EiV) to estimate this eight-equation structural model and test the hypotheses provided by the theory. We calculated the total association of a factor, and by using the Gaussian cumulative probability of the $Z\text{-}Score\,(x) = (x\ minus\ Mean\,(x))\,/\,(Standard\ Deviation\,(x))$ of each variable (except for a classification or time variable), we made the impacts comparable; this allowed a systematic and objective definition of actual significance. Analyzing all publicly traded U.S. FI securities over January 2014 to September 2021, using high-frequency millisecond-level intraday FI trading data from TRACE and high-frequency millisecond-level intraday equity trading data from TAQ, using daily U.S. data from CRSP, I/B/E/S, Thomson Reuters, Compustat, Capital IQ, CRSP-Compustat Merged Database, OptionMetrics, and FRED, we found that market efficiency of FI securities did not improve with time, that investor valuation dispersion and short sales costs & constraints of equity of the issuing firm had significant negative associations with market efficiency of FI securities, and that transaction costs & constraints of equity of issuing firm had an ambiguous association with market efficiency of FI securities.

You should consider applying the AI/ML approach and applying the models estimated in this chapter for U.S. FI securities to Australian and other FI securities.

The next chapter summarizes the conclusions of the book and lists future research projects.

Appendix

8A.1 HalfHour-Level Averages

We use high-frequency millisecond-level intraday FI security trading data from TRACE and high-frequency millisecond-level intraday equity trading data from TAQ. We divide each trading day into 15 "halfhours" as follows: halfhour 0 for prior to 9:30 AM, halfhour 14 for after 4 PM, and halfhours 1–13 for each halfhour of the trading hours (Table 8.A1, Table 8.A2, and Table 8.A3).

For each TICKER, for each FI security CUSIP, for each halfhour 0–14 with positive FI security trading volume, we calculate the volume-weighted average yield (VWAY), then for each TICKER, we calculate the simple average of VWAY over all CUSIPs corresponding to that TICKER, where

$$FIVol_{i,\tau} \tag{8.17}$$

and

$$EqVol_{i,\tau} \tag{8.18}$$

denote the FI volume for FI security i in halfhour τ and equity volume for firm issuing FI security i in halfhour τ.

$$\begin{aligned} VWAY_{i,\tau} &= FIYld\_CUSIP_{i,\tau} \\ &= \frac{\sum_{l\in\tau}\left[\begin{array}{c}(FIYld_{i,l}) \\ \times (FIVol_{i,l})\end{array}\right]}{\sum_{l\in\tau}(FIVol_{i,l})} \end{aligned} \tag{8.19}$$

$$FIYld\_TICKER_{i,\tau} = \frac{\sum_{CUSIP\in TICKER}(FIYld\_CUSIP_{i,\tau})}{\sum_{CUSIP\in TICKER}(1)}$$

$$FIYld\_All_{\tau} = \frac{\sum_{j}\left[\begin{array}{c}(FIYld\_TICKER_{j,\tau}) \\ \times (FIVol_{j,\tau})\end{array}\right]}{\sum_{j}(FIVol_{j,\tau})} \tag{8.20}$$

TABLE 8.A1 Correlations between Quarterly Ordinal Measures of Fixed Income Market Efficiency Based On

			Key Developments Idiosyncratic Response			Earnings Announcements Idiosyncratic Response		
			60-Minute Announcement Window	90-Minute Announcement Window	120-Minute Announcement Window	60-Minute Announcement Window	90-Minute Announcement Window	120-Minute Announcement Window
Quarterly Ordinal Measures of FI Market Efficiency Based On	Key Developments Idiosyncratic Response	60-Minute Announcement Window	1.000	0.962	0.923	0.631	0.612	0.535
	Earnings Announcements Idiosyncratic Response	90-Minute Announcement Window	0.962	1.000	0.966	0.610	0.602	0.520
		120-Minute Announcement Window	0.923	0.966	1.000	0.587	0.579	0.503
		60-Minute Announcement Window	0.631	0.610	0.587	1.000	0.986	0.908
		90-Minute Announcement Window	0.612	0.602	0.579	0.986	1.000	0.938
		120-Minute Announcement Window	0.535	0.520	0.503	0.908	0.938	1.000

TABLE 8.A2 Comparison of Intraday Data and Daily Data, January 2014 to September 2021

		Intraday Data				Daily Data		
Year	**Quarter**	**Number of Fixed Income Trades**	**Dollar Value of Fixed Income Trades**	**Number of Equity Trades**	**Dollar Value of Equity Trades**	**Number of Observations**	**Number of Equity Trades**	**Dollar Value of Equity Trades**
2014	1	4,020,360	$3,175,662,358,003	1,926,239,343	$17,325,394,026,361	406,135	610,688,409	$16,561,835,009,089
2014	2	3,894,265	$3,345,962,083,196	181,9,263,091	$16,870,778,971,035	423,927	608,695,640	$15,101,700,758,067
2014	3	3,598,767	$281,418,6,446,991	170,7,216,092	$15,653,454,170,425	436,861	551,627,996	$14,784,073,442,796
2014	4	3,717,768	$2,761,439,273,092	2,130,705,576	$18,881,074,072,187	439,750	620,399,242	$18,072,918,510,342
2015	1	4,051,157	$35,1,558,2,919,475	1,962,515,129	$17,945,195,452,977	419,932	573,169,320	$17,159,703,006,802
2015	2	3,933,485	$3,217,949,348,199	1,819,257,164	$16,923,993,048,630	435,121	571,228,779	$16,149,517,762,112
2015	3	37,64,267	$2,846,661,200,411	2,246,183,807	$19,442,171,278,550	446,279	682,920,742	$18,473,574,210,343
2015	4	4,041,987	$2,491,898,904,323	2,190,577,282	$18,038,112,447,226	445,217	650,250,048	$17,221,476,055,313
2016	1	4,797,632	$3,167,909,880,109	2,573,524,217	$19,557,899,479,956	422,681	719,933,406	$18,330,922,510,727
2016	2	4,840,824	$2,983,717,736,637	2,182,293,644	$17,648,220,098,305	442,125	634,565,530	$16,572,525,778,322
2016	3	4,741,883	$3,399,978,725,728	1,960,121,791	$16,497,805,893,703	441,043	581,883,805	$15,661,244,171,624
2016	4	4,642,104	$2,840,805,528,573	2,095,576,792	$18,451,657,041,161	434,923	611,300,335	$16,983,988,660,102
2017	1	5,547,976	$3,808,230,612,062	1,985,023,203	$18,330,144,176,777	430,830	599,386,840	$16,484,927,265,961
2017	2	5,080,229	$2,807,783,242,248	1,996,798,376	$19,096,466,633,198	438,367	636,673,058	$17,100,088,311,885
2017	3	4,837,590	$2,983,970,309,925	1,834,993,857	$17,942,809,260,986	439,735	609,004,162	$16,005,584,543,889
2017	4	5,071,931	$3,465,996,879,419	1,927,015,182	$19,563,715,121,913	443,069	655,140,250	$17,459,055,144,045
2018	1	5,815,831	$3,655,777,849,862	2,304,180,434	$25,586,514,195,804	433,696	754,355,501	$22,988,132,556,037
2018	2	5,753,988	$3,370,717,409,037	2,177,514,051	$23,416,749,216,858	454,271	736,971,155	$20,957,921,093,798
2018	3	5,495,425	$3,727,590,043,464	2,013,157,733	$21,536,136,794,314	450,465	712,470,057	$19,337,285,812,799
2018	4	5,934,010	$3,212,327,539,018	2,701,465,727	$28,112,617,971,647	457,096	898,983,275	$25,364,396,813,419

(continued)

TABLE 8.A2 (Continued)

		Intraday Data				Daily Data		
Year	Quarter	Number of Fixed Income Trades	Dollar Value of Fixed Income Trades	Number of Equity Trades	Dollar Value of Equity Trades	Number of Observations	Number of Equity Trades	Dollar Value of Equity Trades
2019	1	6,503,878	$3,605,987,852,834	2,212,168,304	$23,111,156,936,584	444,984	763,001,652	$20,669,373,385,765
2019	2	6,044,307	$3,336,416,204,852	2,271,740,093	$22,578,787,230,748	461,168	796,301,541	$20,206,977,932,884
2019	3	5,903,773	$3,104,341,630,452	2,416,943,077	$23,517,503,011,696	471,874	822,578,085	$20,005,572,861,668
2019	4	5,749,135	$2,804,876,287,796	2,324,607,671	$24,426,647,056,441	473,664	813,980,031	$19,332,691,236,845
2020	1	6,617,358	$4,513,126,813,699	3,677,867,162	$36,816,084,177,934	461,706	1,278,523,131	$30,981,985,774,839
2020	2	6,536,712	$4,300,699,316,331	4,003,414,165	$34,717,522,262,877	468,303	1,465,416,736	$29,508,606,104,973
2020	3	5,470,990	$3,276,410,577,952	3,531,389,334	$34,721,783,580,982	481,823	1,517,808,342	$29,223,224,882,992
2020	4	5,424,712	$2,950,194,339,277	3,650,186,844	$36,971,749,242,935	493,679	1,561,035,312	$30,510,486,861,305
2021	1	6,378,585	$4,012,258,125,333	4,303,573,977	$40,573,491,653,630	490,660	2,203,796,372	$37,891,833,934,853
2021	2	5,943,040	$3,600,868,839,454	3,247,963,604	$32,508,643,000,085	527,913	1,800,262,049	$33,347,651,060,651
2021	3	5,323,463	$2,995,045,350,079	3,978,095,420	$39,199,715,706,215	554,454	1,756,773,810	$32,523,026,167,471

TABLE 8.A3 HalfHour-Level Summary Statistics, January 2014 to September 2021

"HalfHour"	Description	Number of Fixed Income Trades	Dollar Value of Fixed Income	Number of Equity Trades	Dollar Value of Equity Trades
0	Before 9:30 AM U.S. Eastern	11,305,416	$11,206,970,976,201	640,483,038	$6,777,863,422,227
1	9:30 AM - 10 AM U.S. Eastern	6,734,369	$4,372,031,645,262	8,765,560,268	$88,342,871,897,940
2	10 AM - 10:30 AM U.S. Eastern	8,691,571	$4,860,415,458,364	7,186,315,118	$57,282,665,647,677
3	10:30 AM - 11 AM U.S. Eastern	9,759,649	$5,614,909,986,256	6,289,105,358	$48,329,343,516,871
4	11 AM - 11:30 AM U.S. Eastern	10,553,069	$5,794,441,646,635	5,706,463,977	$43,620,109,464,877
5	11:30 AM - 12 PM U.S. Eastern	10,058,513	$5,099,021,334,234	5,049,692,932	$38,297,562,040,105
6	12 PM - 12:30 PM U.S. Eastern	9,866,459	$5,107,833,767,588	4,534,691,961	$33,924,575,217,106
7	12:30 PM - 1 PM U.S. Eastern	8,850,021	$4,336,087,866,003	4,278,316,329	$31,571,903,696,950
8	1 PM - 1:30 PM U.S. Eastern	8,883,699	$4,498,974,933,412	4,160,932,285	$31,092,087,818,446
9	1:30 PM - 2 PM U.S. Eastern	11,018,262	$5,783,461,072,224	4,278,402,702	$31,160,890,672,212
10	2 PM - 2:30 PM U.S. Eastern	9,883,277	$5,392,447,019,295	4,792,257,411	$35,486,737,961,208
11	2:30 PM - 3 PM U.S. Eastern	10,307,489	$5,775,356,612,305	5,010,038,857	$36,504,042,353,304
12	3 PM - 3:30 PM U.S. Eastern	12,052,614	$7,383,178,562,403	6,106,685,431	$43,987,366,210,054
13	3:30 PM - 4 PM U.S. Eastern	16,454,641	$9,619,493,708,915	14,313,900,845	$103,332,011,862,963
14	After 4 PM U.S. Eastern	15,058,383	$17,249,749,038,735	490,529,064	$151,474,382,823,856

We calculate the various weighted averages for FI yields as follows.

$$FIYld\_All_{i,\tau} = \frac{\sum_{j} \begin{bmatrix} (FIYld\_TICKER_{j,\tau}) \\ \times (FIVol_{j,\tau}) \end{bmatrix}}{\sum_{j} (FIVol_{j,\tau})} \tag{8.21}$$

$$FIYld\_Nasdaq_{i,\tau} = \frac{\sum_{j \in Nasdaq} \begin{bmatrix} (FIYld\_TICKER_{j,\tau}) \\ \times (FIVol_{j,\tau}) \end{bmatrix}}{\sum_{j \in Nasdaq} (FIVol_{j,\tau})} \tag{8.22}$$

$$FIYld\_NAICS3Dig_{i,\tau} = \frac{\sum_{j \in NAICS\text{-}3Digit} \begin{bmatrix} (FIYld\_TICKER_{j,\tau}) \\ \times (FIVol_{j,\tau}) \end{bmatrix}}{\sum_{j \in NAICS\text{-}3Digit} (FIVol_{j,\tau})} \tag{8.23}$$

$$FIYld\_MCapDecile_{i,\tau} = \frac{\sum_{j \in Market\text{-}Cap\text{-}Decile} \begin{bmatrix} (FIYld\_TICKER_{j,\tau}) \\ \times (FIVol_{j,\tau}) \end{bmatrix}}{\sum_{j \in Market\text{-}Cap\text{-}Decile} (FIVol_{j,\tau})} \tag{8.24}$$

$$FIYld\_IntraVtyDecile_{i,\tau} = \frac{\sum_{j \in IntraDay\text{-}Volatility\text{-}Decile} \begin{bmatrix} (FIYld\_TICKER_{j,\tau}) \\ \times (FIVol_{j,\tau}) \end{bmatrix}}{\sum_{j \in IntraDay\text{-}Volatility\text{-}Decile} (FIVol_{j,\tau})} \tag{8.25}$$

$$FIYld\_DivYieldDecile_{i,\tau} = \frac{\sum_{j \in Dividend\text{-}Yield\text{-}Decile} \begin{bmatrix} (FIYld\_TICKER_{j,\tau}) \\ \times (FIVol_{j,\tau}) \end{bmatrix}}{\sum_{j \in Dividend\text{-}Yield\text{-}Decile} (FIVol_{j,\tau})} \tag{8.26}$$

$$FIYld\_BMRatioDecile_{i,\tau} = \frac{\sum_{j \in Book\text{-}to\text{-}Market\text{-}Ratio\text{-}Decile} \begin{bmatrix} (FIYld\_TICKER_{j,\tau}) \\ \times (FIVol_{j,\tau}) \end{bmatrix}}{\sum_{j \in Book\text{-}to\text{-}Market\text{-}Ratio\text{-}Decile} (FIVol_{j,\tau})} \tag{8.27}$$

$$FIYld\_PERatioDecile_{i,\tau} = \frac{\sum_{j \in Price\text{-}to\text{-}Earnings\text{-}Ratio\text{-}Decile} \begin{bmatrix} (FIYld\_TICKER_{j,\tau}) \\ \times (FIVol_{j,\tau}) \end{bmatrix}}{\sum_{j \in Price\text{-}to\text{-}Earnings\text{-}Ratio\text{-}Decile} (FIVol_{j,\tau})} \quad (8.28)$$

$$FIYld\_DERatioDecile_{i,\tau} = \frac{\sum_{j \in Debt\text{-}to\text{-}Equity\text{-}Ratio\text{-}Decile} \begin{bmatrix} (FIYld\_TICKER_{j,\tau}) \\ \times (FIVol_{j,\tau}) \end{bmatrix}}{\sum_{j \in Debt\text{-}to\text{-}Equity\text{-}Ratio\text{-}Decile} (FIVol_{j,\tau})} \quad (8.29)$$

For each FI security i, for each halfhour τ with positive volume, we calculate the Volume-Weighted Average Price of equity of issuing firm

$$VWAP_{i,\tau} = \frac{\sum_{l \in \tau} \begin{bmatrix} (Trading\_Price_{i,l}) \\ \times (EqVol_{i,l}) \end{bmatrix}}{\sum_{l \in \tau} (EqVol_{i,l})} \quad (8.30)$$

and then calculate the relevant continuously compounded return

$$EqRet\_TICKER_{i,\tau} = \ln (VWAP_{i,\tau}) - \ln (VWAP_{i,\tau-1}) \quad (8.31)$$

and

$$EqRet\_All_{\tau} = \frac{\sum_{j} \begin{bmatrix} (EqRet\_TICKER_{j,\tau}) \\ \times (EqVol_{j,\tau}) \end{bmatrix}}{\sum_{j} (EqVol_{j,\tau})} \quad (8.32)$$

Finally,

$$Risk\_Free_{\tau} = \text{Yield of T-Bill, 4-Weeks Maturity, for Date including HalfHour } \tau \quad (8.33)$$

$$
\begin{aligned}
&Nom\_Broad\_USD\_Index_{\tau} \\
&\quad = \text{Nominal Broad U.S. Dollar Index for Date including} \\
&\quad\quad \text{HalfHour } \tau
\end{aligned}
\tag{8.34}
$$

Similarly to Section 7.6, market efficiency is modeled in this chapter as a linear function of the exogenous factors and endogenous market activities as follows.

$$
\begin{aligned}
MEff_{i,t} &= \varrho + \gamma_{YQ} YQ_t \\
&+ \gamma_{Disp} Disp_{i,t} + \gamma_{SSCC} SSCC_{i,t} \\
&+ \gamma_{TrCC} TrCC_{i,t} + \gamma_{Nasdaq} Nasdaq_{i,t} \\
&+ \gamma_{KOLiq} KOLiq_{i,t} + \gamma_{NormSI} NormSI_{i,t} \\
&+ \gamma_{AnCov} AnCov_{i,t} + \gamma_{NormInst} NormInst_{i,t} \\
&+ \gamma_{LogMCap} logMCap_{i,t} + \gamma_{logShrsOut} logShrsOut_{i,t} \\
&+ \delta_{i,t}
\end{aligned}
\tag{8.35}
$$

Each endogenous market activity is modeled as a linear function of exogenous factors and other endogenous market activities, based on the market microstructure models in Kyle and Obizhaeva (2016) and Bhattacharya (2019), leading to the following seven equations.

$$
\begin{aligned}
Nasdaq_{i,t} &= \beta + \beta_{YQ} YQ_t \\
&+ \beta_{Disp} Disp_{i,t} + \beta_{SSCC} SSCC_{i,t} \\
&+ \beta_{TrCC} TrCC_{i,t} + \beta_{KOLiq} KOLiq_{i,t} \\
&+ \beta_{NormSI} NormSI_{i,t} + \beta_{AnCov} AnCov_{i,t} \\
&+ \beta_{NormInst} NormInst_{i,t} + \beta_{logMCap} logMCap_{i,t} \\
&+ \beta_{logShrsOut} logShrsOut_{i,t} \\
&+ \varkappa_{i,t}
\end{aligned}
\tag{8.36}
$$

$$
\begin{aligned}
KOLiq_{i,t} &= \alpha + \alpha_{YQ} YQ_t \\
&+ \alpha_{Disp} Disp_{i,t} + \alpha_{SSCC} SSCC_{i,t} \\
&+ \alpha_{TrCC} TrCC_{i,t} + \alpha_{Nasdaq} Nasdaq_{i,t} \\
&+ \alpha_{NormSI} NormSI_{i,t} + \alpha_{AnCov} AnCov_{i,t} \\
&+ \alpha_{NormInst} NormInst_{i,t} + \alpha_{logMCap} logMCap_{i,t} \\
&+ \alpha_{logShrsOut} logShrsOut_{i,t} \\
&+ \varepsilon_{i,t}
\end{aligned}
\tag{8.37}
$$

$$
\begin{aligned}
NormSI_{i,t} \quad = \quad & \theta + \theta_{YQ}YQ_t \\
& + \theta_{Disp}Disp_{i,t} + \theta_{SSCC}SSCC_{i,t} \\
& + \theta_{TrCC}TrCC_{i,t} + \theta_{Nasdaq}Nasdaq_{i,t} \\
& + \theta_{KOLiq}KOLiq_{i,t} + \theta_{NormInst}NormInst_{i,t} \\
& + \theta_{AnCov}AnCov_{i,t} + \theta_{logMCap}logMCap_{i,t} \\
& + \theta_{logShrsOut}logShrsOut_{i,t} \\
& + \eta_{i,t} \qquad (8.38)
\end{aligned}
$$

$$
\begin{aligned}
AnCov_{i,t} \quad = \quad & \zeta + \zeta_{YQ}YQ_{i.t} \\
& + \zeta_{Disp}Disp_{i,t} + \zeta_{SSCC}SSCC_{i,t} \\
& + \zeta_{TrCC}TrCC_{i,t} + \zeta_{Nasdaq}Nasdaq_{i,t} \\
& + \zeta_{KOLiq}KOLiq_{i,t} + \zeta_{NormSI}NormSI_{i,t} \\
& + \zeta_{NormInst}NormInst_{i,t} + \zeta_{logMCap_{i,t}}logMCap_{i,t} \\
& + \zeta_{logShrsOut}logShrsOut_{i,t} \\
& + \vartheta_{i,t} \qquad (8.39)
\end{aligned}
$$

$$
\begin{aligned}
NormInst_{i,t} \quad = \quad & \psi + \psi_{YQ}YQ_t \\
& + \psi_{Disp}Disp_{i,t} + \psi_{SSCC}SSCC_{i,t} \\
& + \psi_{TrCC}TrCC_{i,t} + \psi_{Nasdaq}Nasdaq_{i,t} \\
& + \psi_{KOLiq}KOLiq_{i,t} + \psi_{NormSI}NormSI_{i,t} \\
& + \psi_{AnCov}AnCov_{i,t} + \psi_{logMCap_{i,t}}logMCap_{i,t} \\
& + \psi_{logShrsOut}logShrsOut_{i,t} \\
& + \nu_{i,t} \qquad (8.40)
\end{aligned}
$$

$$
\begin{aligned}
logMCap_{i,t} \quad = \quad & \xi + \xi_{YQ}YQ_t \\
& + \xi_{TrCC}TrCC_{i,t} + \xi_{SSCC}SSCC_{i,t} \\
& + \xi_{Disp}Disp_{i,t} + \xi_{Nasdaq}Nasdaq_{i,t} \\
& + \xi_{KOLiq}KOLiq_{i,t} + \xi_{NormSI}NormSI_{i,t} \\
& + \xi_{AnCov}AnCov_{i,t} + \xi_{NormInst}NormInst_{i,t} \\
& + \xi_{logShrsOut}logShrsOut_{i,t} \\
& + \upsilon_{i,t} \qquad (8.41)
\end{aligned}
$$

$$
\begin{aligned}
logShrsOut_{i,t} \quad = \quad & \omega + \omega_{YQ} YQ_t \\
& + \omega_{Disp} Disp_{i,t} + \omega_{SSCC} SSCC_{i,t} \\
& + \omega_{TrCC} TrCC_{i,t} + \omega_{Nasdaq} Nasdaq_{i,t} \\
& + \omega_{KOLiq} KOLiq_{i,t} + \omega_{NormSI} NormSI_{i,t} \\
& + \omega_{AnCov} AnCov_{i,t} + \omega_{NormInst} NormInst_{i,t} \\
& + \omega_{logMCap} logMCap_{i,t} \\
& + \varsigma_{i,t}
\end{aligned} \tag{8.42}
$$

Because some of the exogenous factors are measured with error, they are instrumented (detailed in Appendix Section 8A.1.4) in accordance with the Errors-In-Variables method; see Greene (2018), Griliches and Hausman (1986) and Hausman and Taylor (1981) for details.

8A.1.1 Transaction Costs & Constraints of Equity of Issuing Firm

We use normalized bid-ask spread, the quarterly mean of daily relative bid-ask spread where daily relative bid-ask spread = (daily closing best ask – daily closing best bid)/(mid-point of daily closing best bid and best ask), as a proxy for transaction costs — see, for instance, Hasbrouck (2009).

8A.1.2 Short Sales Costs & Constraints of Equity of Issuing Firm

We do not have access to actual data on short sales costs & constraints. In particular, we use the cost of a synthetic short sale (short one call option and long one put option, at the money, with the same expiration) as a measure of short sales costs & constraints for the underlying stock — please note that this implies that the analyses in this chapter are restricted to FI securities issued by firms that have traded options written on their equities; please also see Evans et al. (2009), Lamont and Thaler (2003), and Geczy et al. (2002) — as follows:

- Consider all options with strike prices within $\mp 2.5\%$ of underlying price — we do sensitivity analyses for $\mp 0.5\%$ and $\mp 5\%$, and the results stay qualitatively the same
- Calculate best ask for put minus best bid for call
- Restrict to positive
- Calculate weighted (by volume) average
- Normalize by underlying price

8A.1.3 Dispersions of Investor Valuations for Issuing Firm

The dispersion of investor valuations, which is also a function of the level of uncertainty within the market about the particular stock, is proxied by calculating the standard deviation of analyst forecasts and analyst forecast revisions of earnings per share (EPS), restricted to forecasts and revisions between $-\$100$ per share and

+\$100 per share, for the firm with each "forecast period end date" in the current calendar quarter.

As detailed in Sections 2.12–2.14, in this chapter, we use Three Stage Least Squares (3SLS) and Errors in Variables (EiV) to account for the endogeneities and simultaneities in our model.

8A.1.4 Instruments

As detailed in Section 2.15, in a system of equations $Y = X\beta + \varepsilon$, for a vector W to be an instrument, it is required that **Strong First Stage:** $Cov(W, X) \neq 0$, and **Exclusion Restriction:** $Cov(W, \varepsilon) = 0$. As Wooldridge (2010) points out, most of the problems with using instrumental variables arise in small samples, which, obviously, is not the case in this chapter. Wooldridge (2010) points out that "asymptotically, we can do no worse, and can often do better, using a larger set of valid instruments." Given these two critical qualifications, we consider in this chapter the following instrumentation categories together to ensure that our conclusions are not sensitive to particular information assumptions. In panel data econometrics, there are two popular categories of autochthonous instruments.

1. **Cross-Sectional Instruments**: Instrument a variable $X_{i,t}$ by combination(s) of $X_{j,t}, j \neq i$. Cross sectional variables (such as corresponding variables for other geographies) have been used as instruments by, for instance, Hausman et al. (1994) and the validity of such instrumentation depends on the assumption that the corresponding cross-sectional variables are correlated with the instrumented variable because of cost (or other) commonalities in the time period of interest but are not influenced by the idiosyncrasies of the stock (or geography) of interest in the particular time period. In particular, we use, as cross-sectional instrument the average across the cross section excluding the particular variable, i.e., for variable $X_{(i,j),t}$ such that $\#\{k \neq (i,j)\} > 0$, we use $average_{k \neq (i,j)}(X_{k,t})$ as instrument.
2. **Time Series Instruments**: Instrument a variable $X_{i,t}$ by its lag(s) $X_{i,t-1}, X_{i,t-2}, \ldots$ The use of lags as instruments depends on two implicit assumptions: (a) lack of serial correlation, see, for example, Greene (2018), and (b) weak rational expectations, see, for example, Hansen and Singleton (1982). In particular, we use as time series instrument the first lag of the relevant variable, i.e., for variable $X_{i,t}$, we use $X_{i,t-1}$ as instrument.

As detailed in Section 2.7. the total association of each exogenous factor with market efficiency is given by the corresponding (cross-equation) total derivative as follows.

$$\begin{aligned}
\frac{\mathbf{d}MEff}{\mathbf{d}YQ} &= \frac{\partial MEff}{\partial YQ} \\
&+ \frac{\partial MEff}{\partial Nasdaq}\frac{\mathbf{d}Nasdaq}{\mathbf{d}YQ} + \frac{\partial MEff}{\partial KOLiq}\frac{\mathbf{d}KOLiq}{\mathbf{d}YQ} \\
&+ \frac{\partial MEff}{\partial NormSI}\frac{\mathbf{d}NormSI}{\mathbf{d}YQ} + \frac{\partial MEff}{\partial AnCov}\frac{\mathbf{d}AnCov}{\mathbf{d}YQ} \\
&+ \frac{\partial MEff}{\partial NormInst}\frac{\mathbf{d}NormInst}{\mathbf{d}YQ} + \frac{\partial MEff}{\partial logMCap}\frac{\mathbf{d}logMCap}{\mathbf{d}YQ} \\
&+ \frac{\partial MEff}{\partial logShrsOut}\frac{\mathbf{d}logShrsOut}{\mathbf{d}YQ} \\
&= \gamma_{YQ} \\
&+ \gamma_{Nasdaq}\beta_{YQ} + \gamma_{KOLiq}\alpha_{YQ} \\
&+ \gamma_{NormSI}\theta_{YQ} + \gamma_{AnCov}\zeta_{YQ} \\
&+ \gamma_{NormInst}\psi_{YQ} + \gamma_{logMCap}\xi_{YQ} \\
&+ \gamma_{logShrsOut}\omega_{YQ}
\end{aligned} \tag{8.43}$$

$$\begin{aligned}
\frac{\mathbf{d}MEff}{\mathbf{d}Disp} &= \frac{\partial MEff}{\partial Disp} \\
&+ \frac{\partial MEff}{\partial Nasdaq}\frac{\mathbf{d}Nasdaq}{\mathbf{d}Disp} + \frac{\partial MEff}{\partial KOLiq}\frac{\mathbf{d}KOLiq}{\mathbf{d}Disp} \\
&+ \frac{\partial MEff}{\partial NormSI}\frac{\mathbf{d}NormSI}{\mathbf{d}Disp} + \frac{\partial MEff}{\partial AnCov}\frac{\mathbf{d}AnCov}{\mathbf{d}Disp} \\
&+ \frac{\partial MEff}{\partial NormInst}\frac{\mathbf{d}NormInst}{\mathbf{d}Disp} + \frac{\partial MEff}{\partial logMCap}\frac{\mathbf{d}logMCap}{\mathbf{d}Disp} \\
&+ \frac{\partial MEff}{\partial logShrsOut}\frac{\mathbf{d}logShrsOut}{\mathbf{d}Disp} \\
&= \gamma_{Disp} \\
&+ \gamma_{Nasdaq}\beta_{Disp} + \gamma_{KOLiq}\alpha_{Disp} \\
&+ \gamma_{NormSI}\theta_{Disp} + \gamma_{AnCov}\zeta_{Disp} \\
&+ \gamma_{NormInst}\psi_{Disp} + \gamma_{logMCap}\xi_{Disp} \\
&+ \gamma_{logShrsOut}\omega_{Disp}
\end{aligned} \tag{8.44}$$

$$\begin{aligned}
\frac{\mathbf{d}MEff}{\mathbf{d}SSCC} &= \frac{\partial MEff}{\partial SSCC} \\
&+\frac{\partial MEff}{\partial Nasdaq}\frac{\mathbf{d}Nasdaq}{\mathbf{d}SSCC}+\frac{\partial MEff}{\partial KOLiq}\frac{\mathbf{d}KOLiq}{\mathbf{d}SSCC} \\
&+\frac{\partial MEff}{\partial NormSI}\frac{\mathbf{d}NormSI}{\mathbf{d}SSCC}+\frac{\partial MEff}{\partial AnCov}\frac{\mathbf{d}AnCov}{\mathbf{d}SSCC} \\
&+\frac{\partial MEff}{\partial NormInst}\frac{\mathbf{d}NormInst}{\mathbf{d}SSCC}+\frac{\partial MEff}{\partial logMCap}\frac{\mathbf{d}logMCap}{\mathbf{d}SSCC} \\
&+\frac{\partial MEff}{\partial logShrsOut}\frac{\mathbf{d}logShrsOut}{\mathbf{d}SSCC} \\
&= \gamma_{SSCC} \\
&+\gamma_{Nasdaq}\beta_{SSCC}+\gamma_{KOLiq}\alpha_{SSCC} \\
&+\gamma_{NormSI}\theta_{SSCC}+\gamma_{AnCov}\zeta_{SSCC} \\
&+\gamma_{NormInst}\psi_{SSCC}+\gamma_{logMCap}\xi_{SSCC} \\
&+\gamma_{logShrsOut}\omega_{SSCC}
\end{aligned} \tag{8.45}$$

$$\begin{aligned}
\frac{\mathbf{d}MEff}{\mathbf{d}TrCC} &= \frac{\partial MEff}{\partial TrCC} \\
&+\frac{\partial MEff}{\partial Nasdaq}\frac{\mathbf{d}Nasdaq}{\mathbf{d}TrCC}+\frac{\partial MEff}{\partial KOLiq}\frac{\mathbf{d}KOLiq}{\mathbf{d}TrCC} \\
&+\frac{\partial MEff}{\partial NormSI}\frac{\mathbf{d}NormSI}{\mathbf{d}TrCC}+\frac{\partial MEff}{\partial AnCov}\frac{\mathbf{d}AnCov}{\mathbf{d}TrCC} \\
&+\frac{\partial MEff}{\partial NormInst}\frac{\mathbf{d}NormInst}{\mathbf{d}TrCC}+\frac{\partial MEff}{\partial logMCap}\frac{\mathbf{d}logMCap}{\mathbf{d}TrCC} \\
&+\frac{\partial MEff}{\partial logShrsOut}\frac{\mathbf{d}logShrsOut}{\mathbf{d}TrCC} \\
&= \gamma_{TrCC} \\
&+\gamma_{Nasdaq}\beta_{TrCC}+\gamma_{KOLiq}\alpha_{TrCC} \\
&+\gamma_{NormSI}\theta_{TrCC}+\gamma_{AnCov}\zeta_{TrCC} \\
&+\gamma_{NormInst}\psi_{TrCC}+\gamma_{logMCap}\xi_{TrCC} \\
&+\gamma_{logShrsOut}\omega_{TrCC}
\end{aligned} \tag{8.46}$$

References

Aman, H., Beekes, W., Berkman, H., Bohmann, M., Bradbury, M., Chapple, E., Chang, M., Clout, V., Faff, R., Han, J., Hillier, D., Hodgson, A., Howeison, B., Jona, J., Linnenluecke,

M., Loncan, T., McCredie, B., Michayluk, D., Mroczkowski, N., Pan, Z., Patel, V., Podolski, E., Soderstrom, N., Smith, T., Tanewski, G., Walsh, K., Wee, M., and Wright, S., 2019, "Responsible Science: Celebrating the 50-Year Legacy of Ball and Brown (1968) Using a Registration-Based Framework," *Pacific-Basin Finance Journal*, 56, 129–150.

Ball, R., and Brown, P., 1968, "An Empirical Evaluation of Accounting Income Numbers," *Journal of Accounting Research*, 6(2), 159–178.

Bauer, M., Lakdawala, A., and Mueller, P., 2022, "Market-Based Monetary Policy Uncertainty," *Economic Journal*, 132(644), 1290–1308.

Beaver, W., 1968, "The Information Content of Annual Earnings Announcements," *Journal of Accounting Research*, 6, 67–92.

Bennett, P., and Wei, L., 2006, "Market Structure, Fragmentation, and Market Quality," *Journal of Financial Markets*, 9(1), 49–78.

Bhattacharya, R., 2019a, "An Option Theoretic Approach to Market Efficiency," *Annals of Financial Economics*, 14(4), 1–21.

Bhattacharya, R., 2019b, "Objective Measures of Market Efficiency; Applications to Securities Class Actions and Valuations," *Berkeley Business Law Journal*, 16, 249–266.

Bhattacharya, R., and Gupta, M., 2023, "Diligence, Objectivity, Quality, and Accuracy," *Journal of Accounting Literature*, 47(1), 1–30.

Bhattacharya, R., and Gupta, M., 2026, "Impact of Self-Regulation on Financial Markets," *Journal of Accounting Literature* (DOI: 10.1108/JAL-09-2024-0266).

Bhattacharya, R., and O'Brien, S., 2015, "Arbitrage Risk and Market Efficiency: Applications to Securities Class Actions," *Santa Clara Law Review*, 55(3), 643–672.

Blume, L., Easley, D., and O'Hara, M., 1994, "Market Statistics and Technical Analysis: The Role of Volume," *Journal of Finance*, 49(1), 153–181.

Boehme, R., Danielsen, B., and Sorescu, S., 2006, "Short-Sale Constraints, Differences of Opinion, and Overvaluation," *Journal of Financial and Quantitative Analysis*, 41(2), 455–487.

Boehmer, E., Huszar, Z., and Jordan, B., 2010, "The Good News in Short Interest," *Journal of Financial Economics*, 96(1), 80–97.

Boehmer, E., Jones, C., Wu, J., and Zhang, X., 2020, "What Do Short Sellers Know?" *Review of Finance*, 24(6), 1203–1235.

Boehmer, E., Jones, C., and Zhang, X., 2019, "Potential Pilot Problems: Treatment Spillovers in Financial Regulatory Experiments," *Journal of Financial Economics*, 135(1), 68–87.

Boehmer, E., and Kelley, E., 2009, "Institutional Investors and the Informational Efficiency of Prices," *Review of Financial Studies*, 22(9), 3563–3594.

Boehmer, E., and Wu, J., 2013, "Short Selling and the Price Discovery Process," *Review of Financial Studies*, 26(2), 287–322.

Bris, A., Goetzmann, W., and Zhu, N., 2007, "Efficiency and the Bear: Short Sales and Markets Around the World," *Journal of Finance*, 62(3), 1029–1079.

Campbell, J., Lo, A., and MacKinlay, A. C., 1997, *The Econometrics of Financial Markets*, Princeton, NJ: Princeton University Press.

Cao, C., Liang, B., Lo, A., and Petrasek, L., 2018, "Hedge Fund Holdings and Stock Market Efficiency," *Review of Asset Pricing Studies*, 8(1), 77–116.

Chiang, C., Dai, W., Fan, J., Hong, H., and Tu, J., 2019, "Robust Measures of Earnings Surprises," *Journal of Finance*, 74(2), 943–983.

Chordia, T., Roll, R., and Subrahmanyam, A., 2005, "Evidence on the Speed of Convergence to Market Efficiency," *Journal of Financial Economics*, 76(2), 271–292.

Collins, D., and Kothari, S. P., 1989, "An Analysis of Intertemporal and Cross-Sectional Determinants of Earnings Response Coefficients," *Journal of Accounting and Economics*, 11(2–3), 143–181.

Cornell, B., and Rutten, J., 2006, "Market Efficiency, Crashes, and Securities Litigation," *Tulane Law Review*, 81(2), 443–472.

Dang, V., Michayluk, D., and Pham, T., 2018, "The Curious Case of Changes in Trading Dynamics: When Firms Switch from NYSE to NASDAQ," *Journal of Financial Markets*, 41, 17–35.

Dechow, P., Hutton, A., Meulbroek, L., and Sloan, R., 2001, "Short-Sellers, Fundamental Analysis, and Stock Returns," *Journal of Financial Economics*, 61(1), 77–106.

Diamond, D., and Verrecchia, R., 1987, "Constraints on Short-Selling and Asset Price Adjustment to Private Information," *Journal of Financial Economics*, 18(2), 277–311.

Diether, K., Lee, K., and Werner, I., 2009, "It's SHO Time! Short-Sale Price Tests and Market Quality," *Journal of Finance*, 64(1), 37–73.

Drechsler, I., and Drechsler, Q., 2021, "The Shorting Premium and Asset Pricing Anomalies," *SSRN* (https://ssrn.com/abstract=2387099).

Duffie, D., 1996, "Special Repo Rates," *Journal of Finance*, 51(2), 493–526.

Duffie, D., Garleanu, N., and Pedersen, L., 2002, "Securities Lending, Shorting, and Pricing," *Journal of Financial Economics*, 66, 307–339.

Easley, D., O'Hara, M., and Srinivas, P. S., 1998, "Option Volume and Stock Prices: Evidence on Where Informed Traders Trade," *Journal of Finance*, 53(2), 431–465.

Evans, R., Geczy, C., Musto, D., and Reed, A., 2009, "Failure Is an Option: Impediments to Short Selling and Options Prices," *Review of Financial Studies*, 22(5), 1955–1980.

Fama, E., 1970, "Efficient Capital Markets: A Review of Theory and Empirical Work," *Journal of Finance*, 25(2), 383–417.

Fama, E., Fisher, L., Jensen, M., and Roll, R., 1969, "The Adjustment of Stock Prices to New Information," *International Economic Review*, 10(1), 1–21.

Fama, E., and French, K., 1992, "The Cross-Section of Expected Stock Returns," *Journal of Finance*, 47(2), 427–465.

Fama, E., and French, K., 1993, "Common Risk Factors in the Returns on Stocks and Bonds," *Journal of Financial Economics*, 33(1), 3–56.

Fama, E., and French, K., 2015, "A Five-Factor Asset Pricing Model," *Journal of Financial Economics*, 116, 1–22.

Geczy, C., Musto, D., and Reed, A., 2002, "Stocks Are Special Too: An Analysis of the Equity Lending Markets," *Journal of Financial Economics*, 66(2–3), 241–269.

Goldstein, I., and Guembel, A., 2008, "Manipulation and the Allocational Role of Prices," *Review of Economic Studies*, 75, 133–164.

Greene, W., 2018, *Econometric Analysis*, Upper Saddle River, NJ: Pearson.

Griliches, Z., and Hausman, J., 1986, "Errors in Variables in Panel Data," *Journal of Econometrics*, 31, 93–118.

Grossman, S., and Stiglitz, J., 1980, "On the Impossibility of Informationally Efficient Markets," *American Economic Review*, 70(3), 393–408.

Gürkaynak, R., Kisacikoğlu, B., and Wright, J., 2020, "Missing Events in Event Studies: Identifying the Effects of Partially Measured News Surprises," *American Economic Review*, 110(12), 3871–3912.

Gürkaynak, R., and Wright, J., 2012, "Identification and Inference Using Event Studies," *Special Issue: Proceedings of the Money, Macroeconomics and Finance Research Group*, 2013, 48–65.

Hansen, L., and Singleton, K., 1982, "Generalized Instrumental Variables Estimation of Nonlinear Rational Expectations Models," *Econometrica*, 50(5), 1269–1286.

Harris, L., 2003, *Trading & Exchanges: Market Microstructure for Practitioners*, New York, NY: Oxford University Press.

Hasbrouck, J., 2009, "Trading Costs and Returns for U.S. Equities: Estimating Effective Costs from Daily Data," *Journal of Finance*, LXIV(3), 1445–1477.

Hausman, J., Leonard, G., and Zona, D., 1994, "Competitive Analysis with Differenciated Products," *Annales d'Économie et de Statistique*, 34, 159–180.

Hausman, J., and Taylor, W., 1981, "Panel Data and Unobservable Individual Effects," *Econometrica*, 49(6), 1377–1398.

Hendershott, T., and Moulton, M., 2011, "Automation, Speed, and Stock Market Quality: The NYSE's Hybrid," *Journal of Financial Markets*, 14(4), 568–604.

Henisz, W., and McGlinch, J., 2019, "ESG, Material Credit Events, and Credit Risk," *Journal of Applied Corporate Finance*, 31(2), 105–117.

Hou, K., and Moskowitz, T., 2005, "Market Frictions, Price Delay, and the Cross-Section of Expected Returns," *Review of Financial Studies*, 18(3), 981–1020.

Jennings, R., and Starks, L., 1986, "Earnings Announcements, Stock Price Adjustment, and the Existence of Option Markets," *Journal of Finance*, 41(1), 107–125.

Jensen, M., 1978, "Some Anomalous Evidence Regarding Market Efficiency," *Journal of Financial Economics*, 6(2–3), 95–101.

Jiang, C., Likitapiwat, T., and McInish, T., 2012, "Information Content of Earnings Announcements: Evidence from After-Hours Trading," *Journal of Financial and Quantitative Analysis*, 47(6), 1303–1330.

Jones, C., and Lamont, O., 2002, "Short-Sale Constraints and Stock Returns," *Journal of Financial Economics*, 66(2–3), 207–239.

Karpoff, J., 1987, "The Relation between Price Changes and Trading Volume: A Survey," *Journal of Financial and Quantitative Analysis*, 22(1), 109–126.

Kothari, S. P., 2001, "Capital Markets Research in Accounting," *Journal of Accounting and Economics*, 31(1–3), 105–231.

Kothari, S. P., So, E., and Verdi, R., 2016, "Analysts' Forecasts and Asset Pricing: A Survey," *Annual Review of Financial Economics*, 8, 197–219.

Kothari, S. P., and Warner, J., 2007, "Econometrics of Event Studies," In: Eckbo, E. (Ed.), *Handbook of Empirical Corporate Finance*, vol. 1, pp. 3–36, Amsterdam, The Netherlands: Elsevier/North-Holland.

Kyle, A., and Obizhaeva, A., 2016, "Market Microstructure Invariance: Empirical Hypotheses," *Econometrica*, 84(4), 1345–1404.

Lamont, O., and Stein, J., 2004, "Aggregate Short Interest and Market Valuations," *American Economic Review*, 94(2), 29–32.

Lamont, O., and Thaler, R., 2003, "Can the Market Add and Subtract? Mispricing in Tech Stock Carve-Outs," *Journal of Political Economy*, 111(2), 227–268.

Loh, R., 2010, "Investor Inattention and the Under-Reaction to Stock Recommendations," *Financial Management*, 39(3), 1223–1252.

Malkiel, B., 2003, "The Efficient Market Hypothesis and Its Critics," *Journal of Economic Perspectives*, 17(1), 59–82.

Marketplace, 2024, "Key Developments," *Marketplace, S&P Global, 2024* (https://www.marketplace.spglobal.com/en/datasets/key-developments-(15)).

Massa, M., Qian, W., Xu, W., and Zhang, H., 2015, "Competition of the Informed: Does the Presence of Short Sellers Affect Insider Selling?" *Journal of Financial Economics*, 118(2), 268–288.

Miller, E., 1977, "Risk, Uncertainty, and Divergence of Opinion," *Journal of Finance*, 32(4), 1151–1168.

Muravyev, D., Pearson, N., and Pollet, J., 2022, "Is There a Risk Premium in the Stock Lending Market? Evidence from Equity Options," *Journal of Finance*, 77(3), 1787–1828.

O'Hara, M., 1997, *Market Microstructure Theory*, Malden, MA: Blackwell Publishing.

Price, R., 2019, "The FTC Has Approved a Roughly $5 Billion Settlement with Facebook," *Business Insider*, July 12, 2019.

Saffi, P., and Sigurdsson, K., 2011, "Price Efficiency and Short Selling," *Review of Financial Studies*, 24(3), 821–852.

Samuelson, P., 2009, "An Enjoyable Life Puzzling over Modern Finance Theory," *Annual Review of Financial Economics*, 1, 19–35.

Schrimpf, A., Shin, H., and Sushko, V., 2021, "Leverage and Margin Spirals in Fixed Income Markets during the COVID-19 Crisis," *SSRN* (https://ssrn.com/abstract=3761873).

Sever, C., Goel, R., Drakopoulos, D., and Papageorgiou, E., 2021, "Effects of Emerging Market Asset Purchase Program Announcements on Financial Markets during the COVID-19 Pandemic," *SSRN* (https://ssrn.com/abstract=3772498).

Shleifer, A., 2000, *Inefficient Markets: An Introduction to Behavioral Finance*, New York, NY: Oxford University Press.

Stambaugh, R., Yu, J., and Yuan, Y., 2015, "Arbitrage Asymmetry and the Idiosyncratic Volatility Puzzle," *Journal of Finance*, 70(5), 1903–1948.

Stickel, S., and Verrecchia, R., 1994, "Evidence That Trading Volume Sustains Stock Price Changes," *Financial Analysts Journal*, 50(6), 57–67.

Sundaresan, S., 2009, *Fixed Income Markets and Their Derivatives*, Amsterdam, The Netherlands: Elsevier.

van Binsbergen, J., Diamond, W., and Grotteria, M., 2022, "Risk-Free Interest Rates," *Journal of Financial Economics*, 143(1), 1–29.

Wang, J., 1994, "A Model of Competitive Stock Trading Volume," *Journal of Political Economy*, 102(1), 127–168.

Wooldridge, J., 2010, *Econometric Analysis of Cross Section and Panel Data*, Cambridge, MA: MIT Press.

Woodruff, C., and Senchack, A., 1988, "Intradaily Price-Volume Adjustments of NYSE Stocks to Unexpected Earnings," *Journal of Finance*, 43(6), 467–491.

PART IV

Conclusions

9

RESEARCH PROJECTS

In Chapter 1, we provided a measure-theoretic generalization of standard probability theory under risk to a theory of generalized probability under uncertainty, and we provided the reconciliation between the two — this result makes possible all the empirical work in this book and enables the reconciliation between traditional econometrics and statistics on one hand versus artificial intelligence and machine learning on the other. The world of finance is full of unknown unknowns, such as (a) self-regulatory bodies such as FINRA, (b) federal regulators such as the SEC, CFTC, and CFPB, (c) international organizations such as WB, IMF, FSB, and BIS, (d) state regulators, (e) central banks such as the U.S. Fed, ECB, RBA, RBI, (f) financial engineering by investment banks, hedge funds, and other financial players, (g) technological developments such as FinTech, artificial intelligence, and machine learning, (h) transformations of attitude to risk by investors and proprietary traders, and (i) pandemics and wars. It is, therefore, essential that we use the methods of uncertainty, generalized events, and generalized probability that we have developed in this book for any serious work in finance. In Chapter 2, we replaced each variable, except for each classification or time variable, by the standard cumulative Gaussian probability of its *Z*-score, thus, we made the impacts systematic, objective, and comparable; this allows a systematic and objective characterization of actual significance.

In Chapter 3, we discussed arbitrage risk, a negative proxy for market efficiency based on financial economics, and showed how it can be applied to securities class actions. We also performed a series of simple reduced form regressions to test the dependence of arbitrage risk on various standard factors used by courts in the determination of market efficiency. Some of these empirical findings do not seem

DOI: 10.4324/9781003608486-13

consistent with "conventional wisdom," however, we found that our empirical findings are actually consistent with economic theory. The list of determinants of market efficiency considered in this chapter is not exhaustive, and academic research and interviews with financial practitioners have suggested additional factors such as external and internal regulations, and industrial organization (including supply and demand structures) of product markets; we recommended that you utilize data on industry codes, and industry properties such as pricing and concentration, to analyze these additional factors affecting market efficiency.

In Chapter 4, we utilized the following metrics as separate and objective negative measures, based on event studies, of the market's efficiency for a security:

- Key Developments Idiosyncratic Response (KDIR) of the security, estimated through the Capital Asset Pricing Model (CAPM)
- KDIR of the security, estimated through the Market Model (MM)
- Earnings Announcements Idiosyncratic Response (EAIR) of the security, estimated through CAPM
- EAIR of the security, estimated through MM

These measures are completely rules-based, with no judgment, subjectivity, or additional information required of any kind. The only rules are such that every reasonable person can, *a priori*, agree on: (a) for the industry index, we used all firms that are in the same major industry sector (same two-digit SIC Code) as the firm in question, and (b) idiosyncratic price reaction to an event after a few days is close to zero for an efficient market. In this chapter, we applied these methodologies to value each U.S.-listed firm for each year in 2001-2017. Future research projects include:

- Application of the theoretical and econometric methodologies to the three measures of market efficiency, based on securities prices following random walks in efficient markets, used by Cao et al. (2018).
- Application of the theoretical and econometric methodologies to the two measures of market efficiency, based on the asymmetry between positive and negative market returns, used by Bris et al. (2007).
- Structural model studying the relation between capital markets and industrial organization of corresponding product markets.
- The framework of an expected utility-maximizing investor, using different utility functions.

In Chapter 5, we utilized deviation from Put-Call Parity of options measured by different versions of *Implied Volatility Spread (IV)* and *Relative Price Spread (RPS)* on a stock without splits or dividends as separate negative measures for market efficiency. We analyzed all U.S. traded options on all U.S. publicly traded common stocks from 1996 through 2015, and we did the analyses separately for Nasdaq stocks and non-Nasdaq stocks. We used a simple two-equation structural model that shows that the relationships between market efficiency and (a) short sales and constraints and (b) trading volume are theoretically indeterminate, and we found that:

- Everything else remaining the same, the impact on market efficiency of short sales costs & constraints of the stock is *not* significantly negative.
- Everything else remaining the same, the impact on market efficiency of normalized trading volume of the stock is *not* significantly positive.

You should consider the following future research projects:

- The lack of significantly positive correlation that we observed in this chapter between the various *RPS* measures on one hand and the *IV* measures on the other — which changes when we restrict attention to such measures being ≤ 1 — could be because of many reasons, for instance, problems with the assumptions underlying Black-Scholes, or fundamental differences between American and European options. It is also interesting that we find little correlation between *IV-Spr* and *IV-StDev* and almost no correlation between *IV-Spr* and *IV-Disp*. You should investigate all these differences, especially disaggregated by year, Fama-French Factor deciles, SIC code, etc., in a future research project.
- You could investigate the measures discussed in this chapter for stocks with somewhat reliable dividend profiles
- Application of the theoretical and econometric methodologies of this chapter to the three measures of market efficiency, based on securities prices following random walks in efficient markets
- Application of the theoretical and econometric methodologies of this chapter to the two measures of market efficiency, based on the asymmetry between positive and negative market returns
- Structural model studying the relation between capital markets and industrial organization of corresponding product markets

As detailed in Section 2.6, the focus of traditional statistics and econometrics is explanation of the real world, whereas the focus of machine learning and artificial intelligence is prediction. In Chapters 6–8, all variables are stripped of cardinality, therefore, every data point is an approximate percentile and hence, ordinal, and such comparability enables non-parametric work. Because our statements are modest and use ordinal variables and instrumental variables, applying the training model to make predictions about unknown unknowns makes perfect sense — for example, the results in this book are based on training data of the U.S., and one can apply these estimated coefficients to make predictions about Australian or other data.

In Chapter 6, analyzing all publicly traded U.S. stocks for January 2014 to September 2021, using high-frequency millisecond-level intraday data from TAQ, TRACE, I/B/E/S, and Capital IQ, using daily data from CRSP, Compustat, CRSP-Compustat Merged Database, and FRED, we found that all reaction, overreaction, correction, overcorrection, bounceback, etc., were systemically all out of the system within two hours after a potentially material event for all equities over January 2014 to September 2021. Therefore, it is imperative to use high-frequency millisecond-level intraday data for event studies work for two reasons: (1) two hours are systemically sufficient to measure the impact of a potentially material event in question, and (2) if one were to use daily data, one would miss the impact of an event that reverts quickly, and/or worse yet, one could erroneously attribute the impact of entirely unrelated events to the potentially material event in question. Thus, all previous event studies and market efficiency work using daily data, while of enormous and ground-breaking significance in the past, have only historical value now. Systematic, independent, and objective characterizations of each TICKER-year, TICKER-halfyear, TICKER-quarter, and TICKER-month, and each year, halfyear, quarter, and month, January 2014 to September 2021, as statistically and actually significant efficient, statistically and actually significant inefficient, or otherwise, are available upon request from the author. We found that capital markets during the first two-three months of the COVID-19 lockdown were statistically and actually significantly less efficient. You should consider using artificial intelligence logic and apply the estimates from these training data of U.S. equity markets to other equity markets, for instance, in Australia, New Zealand, and Sweden, which had substantially different responses to the COVID-19 pandemic.

In Chapter 7, we used two different metrics, with three separate 60-minute, 90-minute, and 120-minute announcement windows for each, based on event studies, controlling for intraday market equity returns, Nasdaq listing equity returns, industry (3-digit NAICS Code) equity returns, market capitalization decile equity returns, intraday volatility decile equity returns, dividend decile equity returns, Fama-French Factor decile equity returns, fixed income yield, and daily risk-free and foreign exchange rates, with intraday data for equity, fixed income securities, earnings announcements and revisions, and analyst forecasts and revisions, on all publicly traded U.S. companies over January 2014 to September 2021, as separate objective, systematic, and actual ordinal measures of the efficiency of the market for a stock, we showed that it is imperative to use high-frequency millisecond-level intraday data for event studies and market efficiency work. We found that, for all publicly traded U.S. stocks for January 2014 to September 2021, time has a statistically and actually insignificant impact on market efficiency, that investor valuation dispersion has a statistically significant but actually insignificant positive impact on market efficiency, that short sales costs & constraints have a statistically ambiguous and actually insignificant impact on market efficiency, and that transaction costs & constraints has a statistically and actually significant negative impact on market efficiency. As with Chapter 8, you should consider using artificial intelligence logic and apply the estimates from these training data of U.S. equities markets to other major equities markets, for instance, in the UK and Japan.

In Chapter 8, we used two different metrics for market efficiency of fixed income (FI) securities, with three separate 60-minute, 90-minute, and 120-minute announcement windows for each, based on event studies, controlling for market FI yields, Nasdaq listing FI yields, industry (3-digit NAICS Code) FI yields, market capitalization decile FI yields, intraday volatility decile FI yields, dividend decile FI yields, Fama-French Factor decile FI yields, daily risk-free and foreign exchange rates, with high-frequency millisecond-level intraday equity and FI securities data on all publicly traded U.S. companies over January 2014 to September 2021, as separate objective and systematic ordinal measures of the efficiency of the market for an FI security. We found that market efficiency of FI securities did not improve with time, that investor valuation dispersion and short sales costs & constraints of equity of issuing firm had significant negative associations with market efficiency of FI securities, and that transaction costs & constraints of equity of issuing firm had an ambiguous association with market efficiency of FI securities. You should consider using artificial intelligence logic and apply the estimates from these training data of U.S. FI markets to other major FI markets, for instance, in Germany and France.

Examples of questions that one can use the methods and databases of this book to answer include (a) Was the Global Financial Crisis a structural change? (b) How different are bonds or options from stocks in terms of risk? (c) How can an investor make extraordinary returns? (d) What are the impacts of events such as a merger or acquisition? (e) What are the fundamental differences between different market systems such as in the U.S., Australia, Sweden, China, and India? and (f) How can a society use financial policies to achieve its socioeconomic objectives?

Finally, we hope that all readers of this book will understand that our criticisms, even when strident, are all intended in good faith and as honest descriptions of the stringent requirements of the scientific method, especially when applied to Big Data in finance.

INDEX

Note: **Bold** page numbers refer to tables and *italic* page numbers refer to figures.

For Product Safety Concerns and Information please contact our EU representative GPSR@taylorandfrancis.com Taylor & Francis Verlag GmbH, Kaufingerstraße 24, 80331 München, Germany